Teaching Design and Technology in Secondary Schools

The Open University *Flexible* Postgraduate Certificate of Education

The readers and the companion volumes in the *flexible* PGCE series are:

Aspects of Teaching and Learning in Secondary Schools: Perspectives on practice

Teaching, Learning and the Curriculum in Secondary Schools: A reader

Aspects of Teaching Secondary Mathematics: Perspectives on practice

Teaching Mathematics in Secondary Schools: A reader

Aspects of Teaching Secondary Science: Perspectives on practice

Teaching Science in Secondary Schools: A reader

Aspects of Teaching Secondary Modern Foreign Languages: Perspectives on practice

Teaching Modern Foreign Languages in Secondary Schools: A reader

Aspects of Teaching Secondary Geography: Perspectives on practice

Teaching Geography in Secondary Schools: A reader

Aspects of Teaching Secondary Design and Technology: Perspectives on practice

Teaching Design and Technology in Secondary Schools: A reader

Aspects of Teaching Secondary Music: Perspectives on practice

Teaching Music in Secondary Schools: A reader

All of these subjects are part of the Open University's initial teacher education course, the *flexible* PGCE, and constitute part of an integrated course designed to develop critical understanding. The set books, reflecting a wide range of perspectives, and discussing the complex issues that surround teaching and learning in the twenty-first century, will appeal to both beginning and experienced teachers, to mentors, tutors, advisers and other teacher educators.

If you would like to receive a *flexible* PGCE prospectus please write to the Course Reservations Centre at The Call Centre, The Open University, Milton Keynes MK7 6ZS. Other information about programmes of professional development in education is available from the same address.

Teaching Design and Technology in Secondary Schools
A reader

Teaching Design and Technology in Secondary Schools: A reader introduces and explores a broad range of contemporary issues and key ideas and will provide a useful background for those teaching and training to teach this exciting subject.

The book is concerned with exploring the bigger picture of design and technology education. Divided into sections to help structure reading, it covers:

- Links between the different components that make up design and technology
- Aspects of capability: problem solving; design ability; creativity; modelling
- The difficulty of assessing capability
- Pupils' attitudes to the subject
- The relationship between design and technology and science
- International trends
- The role of research
- The influence of gender and vocational issues

The *Teaching in Secondary Schools* series brings together collections of articles by highly experienced educators that focus on the issues surrounding the teaching of National Curriculum subjects. They are invaluable resources for those studying to become teachers, and for newly qualified teachers and more experienced practitioners, particularly those mentoring students and NQTs. The companion volume to this book is *Aspects of Teaching Secondary Design and Technology: Perspectives on practice*.

Gwyneth Owen-Jackson is a Lecturer at The Open University and has responsibility for the Open University *flexible* PGCE Design and Technology course.

Set book for the Open University *flexible* PGCE Course, Design and Technology, code EXT880.

Teaching
Design and Technology
in Secondary Schools
A reader

Edited by Gwyneth Owen-Jackson

The Open
University

London and New York

First published 2002
by RoutledgeFalmer
11 New Fetter Lane, London EC4P 4EE

Simultaneously published in the USA and Canada
by RoutledgeFalmer
29 West 35th Street, New York, NY 10001

RoutledgeFalmer is an imprint of the Taylor & Francis Group

© 2002 Compilation, original and editorial matter,
The Open University

Typeset in Goudy by Bookcraft Ltd, Stroud, Gloucestershire
Printed and bound in Great Britain by Bell & Bain Ltd, Glasgow

British Library Cataloguing in Publication Data
A catalogue record for this book is available from the British Library

Library of Congress Cataloging in Publication Data
A catalog record has been requested

ISBN 0–415–26072–8 (hbk)

ISBN 0–415–26073–6 (pbk)

Contents

Figures

Tables

Abbreviations

ACCAC   Qualifications Curriculum and Assessment Authority for Wales
AQA   Assessment and Qualifications Alliance
AVCE   Advanced Vocational Certificate in Education
BTEC   Business and Technology Education Council
CGLI   City of Guilds of London Institute
DENI   Department of Education Northern Ireland
DfEE   Department for Education and Employment (now Department for Education and Skills, DfE)
GCE   General Certificate of Education
GCSE   General Certificate of Secondary Education
GNVQ   General National Vocational Qualification
NCVQ   National Council for Vocational Qualifications
NVQ   National Vocational Qualification
OCR   Oxford, Cambridge and RSA Examinations
QCA   Qualifications and Curriculum Authority
RSA   Royal Society of Arts
VET   Vocational Education and Training

Note
In the chapters which have previously been published elsewhere an ellipsis denotes omitted material, while an ellipsis in square brackets [...] indicates that a paragraph or more has been omitted.

Sources

Where a chapter in this book is based on or is a reprint or revision of material previously published elsewhere, details are given below, with grateful acknowledgements to the original publishers. In some cases chapter titles are different to the original title of publication; in such cases the original title is given below.

Chapter 1 This is an edited version of an article originally published as 'The immensity of technology … and the role of the individual' in the *International Journal of Technology and Design Education* 9, Kluwer Academic Publishers, Dordrecht (1999).

Chapter 2 This is an edited version of a chapter originally published in Kimbell, R., Stables, K. and Green, R. (1996) *Understanding Practice in Design and Technology*, Open University Press, Buckingham.

Chapter 3 This is an edited version of a chapter originally published in Banks, F. (1994) (ed.) *Teaching Technology*, Routledge, London.

Chapter 6 This is an edited version of a paper originally published as 'Recent research in learning technological concepts and processes' in the *International Journal of Technology and Design Education* 7, Kluwer Academic Publishers, Dordrecht (1997).

Chapter 7 This is an edited version of an article originally published as 'Capability lost and found?' The Maurice Brown Memorial Lecture in the *Journal of Design and Technology Education* 4(1), Design and Technology Association, Wellesbourne (1999).

Chapter 8 This is an edited version of a chapter originally published in Banks, F. (1994) (ed.) *Teaching Technology*, Routledge, London.

Chapter 10 This is an edited version of an article originally published in the *Journal of Design and Technology Education* 4(3), Design and Technology Association, Wellesbourne (1999).

Chapter 11 Based on Murray, J. 'The relationship between modelling and designing and making with food as a material in design and technology', in Banks, F. (ed.) (1994) *Teaching Technology*, London: Routledge/The Open University, pp. 82–8.

Chapter 12   This is an edited version of an article originally published in the *International Journal of Technology and Design Education* 10, Kluwer Academic Publishers, Dordrecht (2000).

Chapter 13   This is an edited version of a booklet originally published as *Interaction: The relationship between science and design and technology in the Secondary School Curriculum*, commissioned by the Engineering Council and the Engineering Employers' Federation, 2000.

Chapter 14   This is an edited version of a chapter originally published in Kimbell, R., Stables, K. and Green, R. (1996) *Understanding Practice in Design and Technology*, Open University Press, Buckingham.

Chapter 15   This is an edited version of a chapter originally published in Banks, F. (ed.) *Teaching Technology*, Routledge, London and now includes material from Kimbell, R. (1997) *Assessing Technology*, Open University Press, Buckingham.

Chapter 16   This is an edited version of an article originally published in the *Journal of Design and Technology Education* 2(1), Design and Technology Association, Wellesbourne (1997). It is one of a set of papers from the Royal College of Art Schools Technology Project. The full set of papers is available at nominal cost from the Project on 020 7590 4246.

Chapter 17   This is an edited version of a paper presented at the Design and Technology International Millennium Conference 2000.

Chapter 18   This is an edited version of a chapter originally published as 'Learning in and for community', in Conway, R. (2000) *Choices at the Heart of Technology*, Trinity Press International, Harrisburg, PA.

Chapter 20   This is an edited version of a paper presented at IDATER 98, published in a final report, *Learning Through Making – Executive Summary*, The Crafts Council (1998).

Chapter 21   This is an edited version of a chapter originally published as 'Technology education: Towards a new school subject' in Moon, B., Brown, S. and Ben-Perez, M. (eds) (2000) *Routledge International Companion to Education*, Routledge, London.

Foreword

The nature and form of initial teacher education and training are issues that lie at the heart of the teaching profession. They are inextricably linked to the standing and identity that society attributes to teachers and are seen as being one of the main planks in the push to raise standards in schools and to improve the quality of education in them. The initial teacher education curriculum therefore requires careful definition. How can it best contribute to the development of the range of skills, knowledge and understanding that makes up the complex, multi-faceted, multi-skilled and people-centred process of teaching?

There are, of course, external, government-defined requirements for initial teacher training courses. These specify, amongst other things, the length of time a student spends in school, the subject knowledge requirements beginning teachers are expected to demonstrate or the ICT skills that are needed. These requirements, however, do not in themselves constitute the initial training curriculum. They are only one of the many, if sometimes competing, components that make up the broad spectrum of a teacher's professional knowledge that underpin initial teacher education courses.

Certainly today's teachers need to be highly skilled in literacy, numeracy and ICT, in classroom methods and management. In addition, however, they also need to be well grounded in the critical dialogue of teaching. They need to be encouraged to be creative and innovative and to appreciate that teaching is a complex and problematic activity. This is a view of teaching that is shared with partner schools within the Open University Training Schools Network. As such it has informed the planning and development of the Open University's initial teacher training programme and the *flexible* PGCE.

All of the *flexible* PGCE courses have a series of connected and complementary readers. The *Teaching in Secondary Schools* series pulls together a range of new thinking about teaching and learning in particular subjects. Key debates and differing perspectives are presented, and evidence from research and practice is explored, inviting the reader to question the accepted orthodoxy, suggesting ways of enriching the present curriculum and offering new thoughts on classroom learning. These readers are accompanied by the series *Perspectives on practice*. Here, the focus is on the application of these developments to educational/subject policy and the classroom, and on the illustration of teaching skills, knowledge and understanding in a variety of school contexts. Both series include newly commissioned work.

This series from RoutledgeFalmer, in supporting the Open University's *flexible* PGCE, also includes two key texts that explore the wider educational background. These companion publications, *Teaching, Learning and the Curriculum in Secondary Schools: A reader* and *Aspects of Teaching and Learning in Secondary Schools: Perspectives on practice*, explore a contemporary view of developments in secondary education with the aim of providing analysis and insights for those participating in initial teacher training education courses.

Hilary Bourdillon – Director ITT Strategy
Steven Hutchinson – Director ITT Secondary
The Open University
September 2001

Introduction

This book is aimed at students in initial teacher training but may also be of use to newly-qualified teachers, those returning to teaching and practising teachers wanting to update their knowledge.

The book addresses contemporary issues in Design and Technology teaching and learning, although practising teachers will notice that some of the contemporary issues have been around for a while. As a relatively new subject on the secondary school curriculum, Design and Technology is still developing through discussion and practice, and this book hopes to make a contribution to the discussions. However, Design and Technology by its very nature is a subject that will never be fully defined, and it will continually change to take account of developments in science, industry and society. What can be achieved, though, is an agreement on the general principles underlying the subject, its nature and purpose, and its importance in the general education of all pupils. These are some of the issues addressed by this book.

The first section looks at the subject of Design and Technology from a number of perspectives. The opening chapter considers the broadest spectrum, the impact of technological developments on the whole of society. This chapter serves to show the breadth of what is covered by the term 'technology', the influences upon it and what it, in turn, influences. Although offered as an opening chapter, this may be one that is returned to at various points throughout the book, or when all other chapters have been read. Chapter 2 takes a more narrow perspective, to consider what Design and Technology is in the context of secondary school curriculums and Chapter 3 describes the development of the subject in schools. Chapter 4 looks at what is common among the different areas within Design and Technology, whilst Chapter 5 considers the subject from the pupils' perspective.

The second section turns to the teaching and learning of technology in schools. Chapter 6 looks at research into pupils' learning of the concepts and processes in technology, and those of teachers, and how these impact on the learning and teaching of the subject. Chapters 7 to 12 cover a range of issues which define the subject, some of which are still open to debate and discussion. The issues covered are: defining capability in design and technology, problem-solving, design, visual literacy, modelling and creativity. The final chapter in this section considers the relationship between Design and Technology and science.

Chapters 14 and 15 make up the section on assessing Design and Technology, and they cover important ground. Chapter 14 discusses what progression is in Design and Technology, what it looks like and how to build progression into teaching. Chapter 15 describes how assessment has developed in Design and Technology and how it is carried out in schools, with reference to statutory requirements and those of examination boards. Taken together these chapters give a good picture of how we can describe and assess pupil learning in the subject.

The fourth section takes a broader perspective and looks at social and cultural issues which have an impact on the subject. Chapters 16 to 20 discuss issues such as gender, values, citizenship and vocational relevance.

The final section in the book is concerned with the development of the teacher. Chapter 21 looks at the subject from an international perspective, to give the student and teacher a wider view of the subject within their own curriculum. Finally, in Chapter 22, there is a discussion of how teachers of Design and Technology can, through research in their own classrooms, contribute to the continuing development of the subject.

It is hoped that this book will inform and inspire student teachers and the newly qualified, and provide food for thought for practising teachers. Design and Technology is a subject that never stands still; its content changes continually as new materials and processes are developed. This means that teachers of the subject must be continually revising their subject knowledge, considering the issues which impact upon it and how the subject can be communicated effectively to pupils. Pupil learning should be encouraged through teaching which is relevant, stimulating and motivating and this can be done through teaching which is up-to-date and meaningful. This book hopes to contribute to the development of teachers who want to excite pupils about technology through their own excitement and knowledge of the subject, and who realize that they themselves will never stop learning about it.

Section 1

Design and Technology
in the curriculum

1   The immensity of technology

John B. Gradwell

This introductory chapter is included to encourage you to think about technology in its broadest terms, to consider the influence that technological developments have on society and the influences that society have on technology. Technology is described as a 'mode of activity' which has an important determining effect on society. The chapter describes perceived positive and negative effects, the need to be aware of these as new technologies are developed and the need to be aware of the consequences of decisions that are made. The author argues that decisions should be shaped by shared cultural values and that 'intelligent participation' of those affected should be encouraged. This serves to introduce the importance of education to allow this participation in technology decision-making, and you may wish to return to this chapter after reading the rest of the book and thinking about technology education in secondary schools.

[...]

Technology: a force that reshapes society

Technology represents a powerful mode of activity capable of shaping the entire universe, whether this be in matters of action, intellectual thought or material products. Ursula Franklin expresses technology's power by stating that it 'has acted to reorder and restructure social relations, not only affecting the relations between social groups but also the relations between nations and individuals, and between all of us and our environment' (Franklin 1990, p. 13). The tendency of technology to be the dominant organizer extends back to the early history of mankind as can be seen by the fact that each age is referred to in terms of its predominant technology: from stone tools to bronze ones followed by the iron age. In more recent times we have the agricultural revolution, the industrial revolution and the information age, each with a particular set of technological tools.

The reason why the name we have given to certain historical periods reflects the technology of that time is that each new technology does not simply add something to its environment: it fundamentally changes everything. Jacques Ellul illustrates this point using the clock tower as an example. The public clock tower made its appearance around the fourteenth century and private clocks in the sixteenth century. 'Time, which had been a measure of organic sequences, was broken and dissociated. Human life ceased to be an ensemble, a whole, and became a discon-nected set of activities' (Ellul 1964, p. 328).

Another common example is the printed book which appeared for the first time in the Western hemisphere during the fifteenth century. The production and dissemination of relatively inexpensive printed books, particularly the Bible, contributed immensely to the progress of literacy without individuals seeking the help of, or being influenced by, an intermediary. Thus fifty years after adoption of the printing press we did not have the original Europe plus the printing press: we had a radically different Europe: one where anyone who could read had access to Martin Luther's translation of the Holy Bible, and the ability to interpret for them-selves, as opposed to being told by church leaders, what it meant. Books provided access to knowledge, to learn from other cultures and thereby to restructure their lives along social or economic lines if they wished to do so. Books were jealously guarded with one's life, as was so magnificently illustrated in the film, *The Name of the Rose*, set in medieval Europe at the time of the Spanish Inquisition.

Clocks and books are just two examples of inventions that changed the world. There are many others including gunpowder, the magnet and the telescope. The telescope serves to point out how one invention, glass, whose original use was for window panes, can subsequently spur a range of other uses from jewellery to insula-tors to test-tubes. [...]

What appears clear when a technology enters the scene is that it:

- fundamentally alters the society or environment it enters
- spawns a multitude of subsequent inventions
- is adopted at a much faster rate nowadays than in previous times
- is likely to become a world-wide phenomenon due to our current state as a 'global village'
- may very well be more powerful than a previous technology
- has such a broad effect as to increase the need for checks to balance its growth.

The excesses of technology

With value judgements of this magnitude it is not surprising that certain groups have spoken or acted out against the advance of technology. The first widely recog-nized group to do so is referred to as the Luddites. Sale lists lessons to be learned from the Luddites:

1   Technologies are never neutral and some are harmful. Tools come with a prior history built in ... a conquering violent culture ... with the United States at its extreme.
2   Industrialism is always a cataclysmic process, destroying the past, roiling the present, making the future uncertain: growth, production, speed and novelty, power and manipulation.
3   Only a people serving an apprenticeship to nature can be trusted with

machines. The technosphere must re-establish some connectedness to the biosphere.

4   The nation-state, synergistically intertwined with industrialism, will always come to its aid and defence, making revolt futile and reform ineffectual.

5   But resistance to the industrial system, based on some grasp of moral principles and rooted in some sense of moral revulsion, is not only possible but necessary.

6   Politically, resistance to industrialism must force not only 'the machine question' but the viability of industrial society into public consciousness and debate. It is necessary to debate all the issues of the uncontrolled growth of technology (costs and consequences), winners and losers.

7   Philosophically, resistance to industrialism must be embedded in an analysis ... that is morally informed, carefully articulated and widely shared.

8   If the edifice of industrial civilization does not eventually crumble as a result of a determined resistance within its very walls, it seems certain to crumble of its own accumulated excesses and instabilities within not more than a few decades, perhaps sooner, after which there may be space for alternative societies to arise.

(Sale 1995, p. 261)

Quite an indictment, and yet historically the social effects have been equally dramatic. Just a few examples illustrate how widespread the effects, brought about by individuals, can be:

1   In the design of the parkways for New York State, Robert Moses intentionally specified that the bridges and underpasses be constructed quite low so as to allow only private cars to pass. All persons who travelled by bus were poor or black or both and therefore were barred from the parkland and its 'public amenities' (Franklin 1990, p. 71).

2   Hitler's dictatorship 'employed to perfection the instruments of technology to dominate its own people. The radio and public-address systems ... had helped to subject 80 million persons to the will of one individual. Telephone, teletype and radio made it possible to transmit the commands of the highest levels to the lowest organs where because of their high authority they were executed uncritically ...' (Herf 1994, pp. 127–8). [...]

3   The use of DDT in Borneo was designed to kill malaria-carrying mosquitos. It was successful in this regard, but it didn't kill roaches which accumulated DDT in their bodies. These were eaten by long-tailed lizards, called geckoes, and the DDT from the roaches hit the nervous system of the lizards who became less agile so the cats caught and ate them. When the cats died rats started moving in from the forests. Also the roofs of the houses began caving in as the lizards had been eating the caterpillars that made their meals from roof thatching (de Nevers 1972, p. 233). [...]

As noted previously those not convinced of the liberating powers of technology see their roots in Luddism, where the development of machinery becomes, for most of the working population, 'the source not of freedom but of enslavement, not of mastery but of helplessness, and not of the broadening of the horizon of labour but the confinement of the worker within a blind round of servile duties in which the machine appears as the embodiment of science and the worker as little or nothing' (Braverman 1985, p. 82). In other words the real-life, day-to-day consequences of the industrial revolution were epitomized in the societal and cultural disruptions, including displacement and dislocation, where little else counted save a total subservience to the machine. […]

As the technology becomes all pervasive, concerns increase. While the latest figures show that the internet includes over 36 million 'advertised' connected computers in over 200 countries and territories, there are simultaneously concerns about junk mail, fraud, false or dangerous information, propaganda, information explosion, personal security, security of intellectual property, censorship and domination by a superpower.

Technology's siren call

Granted there are those who see technology as an unmitigated blessing especially within a historical context. Few of us would deny that technology, until the seventeenth century, provided tools (the plough, waterwheel and windmill) to overcome backbreaking tasks, or served for defence or religious worship (construction of castles and cathedrals). However, times were different: the term 'global village' was unknown and the effects were largely local. […]

The effects of technology broadened from the eighteenth century onwards as did the approach to solving problems, settlers gradually moving from a position of battling with nature to understanding the science and technology involved in an efficient system. […]

Domination of nature had finally been assured in spite of man's puny physique. In fact what makes the argument for technological inventions so powerful for some is that man was inherently the least likely of all the animals to succeed, yet he had one superiority: a capacity to invent. So by extension, invention often takes precedence in our assessment of technology, especially during the nineteenth century when domination at the local level spread its siren call quickly promising leisure, comfort and speed in abundance. […]

If there remain any doubts about the ability of technology to woo the public and change society one only has to examine its most visible product: television. Borgmann describes television as 'the purest, i.e. the clearest and most attenuated, presentation of the promise of technology. It appears to free us from the fetters of time, space and ignorance and to lay before us the riches of the world in their most glamorous form' (Borgmann 1984, p. 142). And it does all this with no demands made on its viewers in terms of dress, transportation or manners. We are accepted as we are and we accord the technology the same reverence!

This same kind of comfort and satisfaction is experienced by individual consumers when operating many of the technical devices designed for leisure, including a video recorder or riding a snowmobile. Even at work satisfaction may be felt by a craftsperson touching and smelling walnut ready for its final finish or an engineer contemplating a finely tuned engine. At the time, each of these pleasurable incidents is likely experienced in a manner far removed from the society which it influences.

Finally, among those who see technology as the saviour of mankind there are those whose faith remains unshaken, providing that social effects are placed first and foremost. Buckminster Fuller believes that '... the unlimited energies of the universe capable of doing realistically unlimited work, thus producing realistically unlimited wealth, now need only social comprehension and orderly social initiatives for turning on the valves of unlimited wealth for all humanity' (Fuller 1969, p. 73).

Recognizing both positive and negative effects

In spite of, or perhaps because of, the 'successes' of technology, individual assessments of technology can take a number of forms. Several different categories are suggested including:

> The Doomsday School (the problem of environmental degradation is insoluble): the Minimalist School (environmental degradation is a minor problem compared to other issues): the socialist school (environmental deterioration is an inescapable consequence of capitalist 'exploitation'): the zero growth school (stop the growth of population and production): the austerity school (less consumption in order to conserve resources and reduce pollution): the priorities school (too much spending on government and too little on the environment).
>
> (Burke 1972, pp. 72–4)

To those who count themselves as belonging to a particular camp we can add those who are unsure of what to think. Their uncertainty stems partly from the fact that they have always lived in a technological age with various possibilities and probabilities of change and in spite of all of it we always seem to muddle through. There is also the reality that technological policies have been determined mainly on an *ad hoc* basis and have focused on immediate, not future choices. In addition it is hard to quantify the values inherent in technology in the same way that one can quantify other aspects of technology such as the dates when inventions occurred. While it is easy to state that a Singer sewing machine was invented in 1851 or Ford started mass production in 1903, no similar definitive record of dates exists for when ethical or moral discussions and decisions were taken.

Experiencing both positive and negative views of technology may lead one to a middle-of-the-road position based on the idea that technology is a two-edged sword; it provides material comforts and benefits but it can change social patterns and values, leading to confusion and despair. Each innovation, regardless of its positive side may also have a negative impact, this impact increasing in direct proportion to the number of societies in which it takes root.

Even within a given population, technology will affect some people adversely while benefiting others. The resultant tendency is for individuals to see themselves as members of a particular group (Table 1.1), which may take a stance for or against prevailing technology. However, the inherent complexity and unexpected secondary results suggest that we cannot simply add costs versus benefits of a given technology to arrive at a balance sheet.

What we, as individuals, can do is to recognize technology's dual nature. It is not a dichotomous being but a creature, dressed in shades of grey, or even, at times, a chameleon. … Technology must not be taken for granted, neither must it be conceived, celebrated and promoted without being first thought about. This is not a simple task. While techniques are relatively easy to transmit, a value system is acquired far more slowly.

Technology today

The most pervasive technologies today are electronic based. As the cost of artificial memory continues to decline, electronic devices proliferate and affect our lives in an exponential manner. All products and services have the potential of being changed to gather information about our lives, value preferences, needs and wants and to respond to these data whether we request it or not. It is a technological world that is highly complex and interwoven into all aspects of our lives. It begs the question as to whether the scale and intricacy of technology in the political, economic and cultural aspects of our lives transcends the current competence of the average citizen.

Certainly the rate of change brought about by technology has increased exponentially in the past two centuries, increasing the need for public awareness and dialogue. As Burke states, 'Until the past few decades, most technological and social changes were gradual and affected only a small percentage of the population at any given time. The rate of change was slow enough for man to adapt – the physiological and anatomical characteristics of his body underwent alterations to fit the new circumstances, and so did his mental attitudes and social structures. But now the environment is changing so rapidly that the process of biological, mental and social adaptation cannot keep pace. A tragedy of modern life is that the experience of the father is of little use to his children' (Burke 1972, p. 187). Furthermore it is not a simple case of a constant reduction in the time between major developments but rather one that is complicated by several major innovations happening simultaneously.

One of the most powerful developments is 'machine intelligence'. Mechanical products are rapidly changing by incorporating 'chip' technology. Microchips enable all products to become knowledge-based products by incorporating data and information. These products automatically provide information to the users enabling them to do things better or to work smarter (Davis and Bodkin 1994). The operative point here is that *all* products can be changed to become knowledge

Table 1.1 Visionaries in different settings

Social dilemmas	Industrialists	Technologists	'Luddites'	'Greens'
Toxic substances Pollution Environmental effects	Pollution happens but the economy benefits	Technology will cure the problems	The sources of pollution should be eliminated	Invent non-polluting alternatives
Resource exploitation	Build in obsolescence and create new needs	New methods are more efficient and therefore worthwhile	Use renewable resources only	Ensure items have a second use (not discarded)
Matching culture to a society	It is a global society and everyone has to catch up	Advanced nations will solve problems for third world countries	Not necessary to follow industrial nations: find a better way	Use local alternatives Appropriate technology
Effects on workers	More technology is inevitable	More technology equals a better type of job	Say 'no'. Don't let technology displace workers	Consider the workers first
Consumerism	More products equal a better standard of living	More products equal more leisure time	Focus on what is good in the present	Focus on a simpler life

products or smart products. Various parts of a car, from the engine to the tyres, can be programmed to feed the driver with information about their condition and suggest means to correct problems, if any. Food products could transmit cooking instructions to equipment and nutritional information to the consumer. Televisions could be programmed to recognize your preferred type of entertainment and select it automatically for you each week. By giving your credit card information upon entering a store you could receive a printout of products that are personally interesting to you based on your previous shopping habits. Sensors embedded into every type of machinery could tell us when a part is about to break down. Your VCR could search an internet video library and create a library of all the movies on your favourite topic. In other words smart products will be able to adjust to your preferences, or to certain pre-programmed conditions or to changing circumstances and to provide the products or information that each of us appears to need or want.

Ensuring balance in technology

Where does this knowledge lead us? How can we, as individuals, connect our abilities to practise (using the technique) with a sense of values (providing evaluation and direction)? In attempting to make connections we can draw from other fields

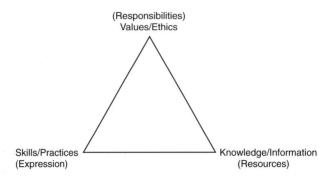

Figure 1.1 The triangle of technological inquiry

such as medicine where knowledge plus skills plus values/ethics are intimately intertwined. We should also focus our thoughts on one of the strongest structural shapes, the triangle, in order to recognize the equality of importance of the three parts which should be included in all technological inquiries. Using the three points shown in Figure 1.1 a particular inquiry could start from any one of the three points and progress to the others, ensuring that social relevance and ethical decisions are always a controlling factor.

In technological practice it would appear that knowledge and skills are readily acquired. However, determining who bears the responsibility for what happens to the culture is more elusive. It includes 'knowing what culture is, what its characteristics are, what it means to a society, and what the processes of change are. It is not enough to be a competent technician, morally fortified with the unquestioned assumptions of goodness of one's profession. One must be a responsibly competent technician, aware that any technical improvement has social and economic consequences that may or may not be deleterious. The responsible technician is the one who is able to help adapt scientific technology and methods to the ecological, social and economic environment of the developing country, but does not think that good consists in leading others to do things as he does' (Foster 1994, p. 268).

Technologies cannot operate outside of a particular culture. Culture means the basic rules by which we live together and the way of life we share. It is the totality of our beliefs and system of values. Each part, whether we speak of tools or techniques or industries or institutions, plays only a part and cannot be allowed to reinvent the whole without adequate forethought. Only by consciously controlling our evolution, rather than leaving it to chance, can we be assured that there will be a planned future in store. We must give at least equal thought to this part of the big picture as we currently give to the other two parts. 'Rather than deciding whether one technical device is more efficient than another, decisions would focus on whether a given device improved the possibility of individuals reaching their full potential as human beings, served a prestated society purpose, and contributed to the long-term dynamic stability of the ecosphere' (DeVore 1980, p. 348).

The equal partnership being proposed for values and ethics of technology with resources and skills reflects the revolution in which we are engaged. Following the agricultural and industrial revolutions, our current information revolution is even more complex and extensive. Also its sphere of influence is far wider. ... New technologies, because they never occur in isolation, can bring about many effects, as widespread as replacing workers, invading one's privacy, causing an overload of information and depersonalizing relationships. Viewed from the perspective of secondary and subsequent changes, the entry of a new technology is more than throwing a pebble into a lake with its ever-widening circles. It is as though the pebble breaks on entering the water into an unknown number of sharp fragments, each of which is capable of reaching multiple targets.

Today's technology can be even more far reaching. As great as the influence of the internal combustion engine has been, the computer chip is far more versatile and intrusive. It has a potential of creating new devices but, of considerably greater importance, the likelihood of being embedded into almost everything technical and biological, including ourselves. By invading our private space, in the guise of increased efficiency, our lives are being reshaped. [...]

Technology's checks and balances

To deal with the increasing invasiveness of technology one approach is to attempt to return to times when society was supposedly cleaner and safer. Even if poverty were rampant, it is argued that life was at least based on solid values. But rejection of modern technology and reversion to rural ways of living is not the answer. ... Many of the finest products of our culture, from cathedrals to musical instruments to the Hubble telescope, are the result of the prevailing technology of a given period. Instead, we must focus on the priorities which ensure that concerns of meeting basic human needs for all are met prior to the esoteric 'wants' of an already technologically satiated society. But what are the basics? [...]

A manifesto of consumer rights is useful in considering what rights are important for the general public. Papanek (1984 p. 339) includes the rights to:

1　Safety, to be protected from hazardous goods
2　Information, not to be misled by lack of information or misinformation
3　Basic services, fair prices and choice and access to a variety of products and services
4　Representation, to be consulted and to participate in decisions affecting consumers
5　Be heard and to have access to an ombudsman
6　Consumer education
7　A healthy and safe environment.

This list is just one that could be used as a starting point for discussion. The main point is that the notion that whatever technology ... could do, should be done, is simply unacceptable. Every challenge we face is not necessarily one that should be turned over to technology. The viability of democracy depends on justice and enforcements of limits to power; likewise technology must have its limits.

What is the counterbalance to unbridled technological advance? Are morality, public opinion, the constraints of our culture or our social structure sufficient obstacles? Can 'control of nature' be replaced by a desire for 'control of technology'? Can we live in harmony with technology rather than encouraging it to conquer the world? These questions can be partly answered by our desire to distinguish true and false needs. ... 'False needs are those which are superimposed upon the individual by particular social interests in his repression: the needs which perpetuate toil, aggressiveness, misery and injustice ... The result then is euphoria and unhappiness. Most of the prevailing needs to relax, to have fun, to behave and consume in accordance with the advertisements, to love and hate what others love and hate, belong to this category of false needs' (Marcuse 1972, p. 76).

True needs are evident when we consider the tenets of prudence, ecology and decentralization, goals which may not be easy as, even when one nation sets up stringent controls, production can move across national boundaries where no constraints exist. The result of this global production and market place is that policy-setting power has been moved upwards, beyond the reach of an individual state. At the Earth Summit in Rio de Janeiro in 1992, one hundred and forty-three nations put the world's environment 'in the hands of a new Global Environmental Facility, effectively controlled by the G-7 nations and administered by the World Bank, whose primary mission is to be continued industrial development with cursory ecological constraints' (Sale 1995, p. 222). This may partly explain why technology may be harder to control than people. ...

Quite obviously there is an element of uncertainty in visioning the future, partly due to the complexity of what happens when a new technology interacts with the processes already inherent in a society. Technology can indeed be a web of interactions capable of replacing workers, invading one's privacy, creating a dependence and depersonalizing relationships. In case this statement seems alarmist, consider the 1992 statement by the United States Union of Concerned Scientists who are anything but alarmist or self-interested. In 1992, this group, in a statement endorsed by a hundred Nobel laureates and 1,600 members of national academies of science around the globe, proclaimed a 'World Scientists' Warning to Humanity' stating that the present environmental assault and population increase cannot continue without 'vast human misery' and a planet so 'irretrievably mutilated' that it will be unable to sustain life in a manner that we know' (Sale 1995, p. 229).

Self-fulfilment for an individual will come through giving quality of life to all the world's citizens rather than a personal desire for more consumer goods. Why do we seek to be the sole owners of consumer goods? 'Few tools in our society are designed for communal (or shared) ownership. If they were designed for sharing rather than for individual use, we believe they would change structurally, mechanically and in material composition' (Papanek and Hennessey 1977, p. 27). Questions of this nature do not imply that one is renouncing technology but rather finding a middle way between materialistic self-centredness and traditionalistic self-righteousness. This is the type of question that should be asked. Indeed the first step towards rationalizing technology is to formulate appropriate questions such as:

- What are our expectations about goods designed to increase health, security and freedom from want?
- Can we produce enough surplus to allow freedom to pursue goals other than production?
- Can we avoid excesses and provide for the less fortunate?
- Are we living in an age where there is a culture of consumption and acquisition which is forever expanding?
- Could a 'public project or loan be evaluated by whether it: 1. promotes justice; 2. restores reciprocity; 3. confers divisible or indivisible benefits; 4. favours people over machines; 5. is a strategy that maximizes gain or minimizes disaster; 6. whether conservation is favoured over waste; and 7. whether the reversible is favoured over the irreversible'?

(Franklin 1990, p. 126)

These are points that lead us to consider optimal conditions for human society on earth, the parameters of global and ecological systems, the limits of our resources and finally the limits of human beings. Furthermore we should not be surprised if these questions lead us to visions rather than short-term goals, to attitudes rather than skills and to human values as opposed to techniques.

From eureka to spaghetti to blackbox

Determining the optimum time to ask these questions is crucial. It cannot be at the point when a product is in full use in society because, in spite of any shortcomings it may have, people will be depending on it. Also at this point the technology is likely to be operating automatically and its inner workings or structure are hidden from view. It is therefore at a point largely beyond control.

Let us consider at what stage decisions concerning technology adoption should be made. The movement towards the point where a product functions autonomously happens in three stages which I shall call:

Eureka (invention), Spaghetti (participation) and Blackbox (automation).

All modern technologies pass through these stages. At the first stage a cry of excitement follows the invention of a new process or product. At the second stage, trying out various alternatives often means that the general public and manufacturers alike participate in hooking up components or making modifications until it is in a form that is adopted by many people. By the time the third stage has been reached the product has become part of our culture and is accepted to the degree that it is almost invisible. These three stages can be readily illustrated by using a number of common examples, shown in Table 1.2.

If anyone has doubts about the eventual movement to the third stage which, due to its complicated nature, effectively takes the technology out of our control, consider this advertisement for something as mundane and 'simple' as your local mobile 'phone':

Table 1.2 The three stages of technological adoption

	Eureka	Spaghetti	Blackbox
Cars	Benz	Customizing Tuning, repairing	Integrated circuits
Clocks	Pendulum Escapement Balance spring	Grandfather clock Wind-up alarm	Quartz crystal Electronic alarm
Computers	ENIAC	Assembling comps. Programming	Speech recognition
Telephones	Bell	Plug-in exchanges	Cell phones
Photography	Niepce	Home developing	Digital cameras
Money	Coins	Bank notes	Debit cards/Smart cards
Toilets (W.C.)	Harington	Flushing mechanism	Excrement analysis and direct contact with physician

> It sets its ring tone and voice to suit my surroundings
> Snooze alarm included
> There are 35 different ring tones and tunes
> All my missed, received and dialed calls get time-stamped
> Its faceplate changes colours with the light
> It uses an extended lithium-ion battery
> It lets me identify different callers with different rings
> I program its calendar with call, birthday and divorce date reminders
> It has a built-in calendar and currency converter
> And 4 stimulating games
> Plus … it also vibrates!

Let us examine where control or decision-making concerning technology adoption take place in this model. Technology is an evolutionary process starting with invention, which could be likened to the principle of mutation and selection in plants and animals. Invention is a form of mutation in that an unexpected direction suddenly happens. This is the exciting eureka point. In the second stage the general public becomes involved in using, selecting, trying out and modifying the invention. In today's world of electronics the device may be wired to a number of other devices, hence the term 'spaghetti' to describe this phase.

In the days of mechanical technology it may have appeared that people were content to remain at this second stage. There was a certain fascination in knowing what was contained inside an object and being able to maintain and repair it when necessary. However, with today's digital technologies, opening up a 'blackbox' tells the eye nothing. The binary on–off nature of digital technologies is totally at odds with earlier adjustable mechanical technologies which appealed to the senses.

It would appear that the more a product becomes 'smart' and approaches the third or blackbox stage, the more the user abdicates control. The idea that consumers may consciously or subconsciously be asking for products that are out of their control may seem to be an anathema to those of us more familiar with a mechanical age (or even those educators sold on the problem-solving method) but it is a sobering reality. We as teachers assume that drivers need to know how their car functions; however, I would propose that most don't know and don't care to know. Their interest in any technology is not based on knowing how it works but knowing that it will help them do a task easier and faster than previously. When viewed in this light we understand that technology systematically withdraws devices from our competence and care by making objects maintenance free, discardable or blackbox-complicated and that there is public complicity in this direction. In the opinion of R. B. Fuller most of modern technology falls into this category.

> Better than 99% of modern technology occurs in the realm of physical phenomena that is sub or ultra to the range of human visibility – for example, the dynamically operating functions of the transactions of information-processing within blackboxes of visibly wired static circuitry are entirely invisible ... We can see the metal parts of an airplane ... but there is nothing to tell us how relatively strong those metals are in comparison to other metals ... World society has throughout its millions of years on earth made its judgements upon visible, tangible, sensorially demonstrable criteria. We may safely say that the world is keeping its eye on the unimportant visible one percent ... significant functions are invisible.
>
> (Fuller 1969, p. 275)

It is evident that at a certain point, that being the blackbox stage, technologies are largely hidden from view, and hence beyond our informed decision-making. Also it is equally obvious that very few people have decision-making power at the point of invention. It therefore becomes obvious when and where decisions should be made. There is a critical window of opportunity at the 'spaghetti' stage when one has the opportunity to evaluate an item against what it was originally designed to do, or not to do; when one can decide whether a particular technology is desirable. These considerations can only be made at the 'spaghetti' stage as it is the sole time that many people are involved in trying, testing and modifying the technology.

The importance of questioning any technology at this stage arises partly from the realization that once a technology enters into a culture, at the blackbox stage, it is there to stay. One cannot pull the plug on bank machines or any other widely adopted technology. It is also partly based on unforseeable secondary effects such as may happen when a technological object has far-reaching social and environmental consequences. Technology 'recognises no self-limiting principle – in terms, for instance, of size, speed or violence. It therefore does not possess the virtue of being self-balancing, self-adjusting, and self-cleansing' (Schumacher 1974, p. 122). Nor does it provide us with any hints as to how it should be evaluated.

Who should control technology?

So who bears the responsibility? In what type of form should people have the occasion to debate? With what degree of awareness will decisions be made? How can we provide a system of checks and balances to ensure that technological development does not go forward virtually of its own inertia, resisting any limitation? How can we ensure that humans have full, conscious choice and that they are responsible for choices made at each step in the sequence of change? […]

Whenever social or technological planners think they are using their power for the good of all, whether that be in a major social revolution or the introduction of a product by a multi-national corporation, history has proven that seemingly moral intentions have their corrupt sides. Relying on corporations to police themselves is not recommended by Toffler as 'Some individual corporations are economically larger than the countries in which they operate … Multinationals operate their own intelligence networks, fleets of planes and banks of computers. For all practical purposes they carry out their own foreign policy, often independently of their country of origin' (Toffler 1975, p. 12). However, this does not necessarily mean that corporations or other groups are against regulation, rather that they have not found an effective means: 'Indeed, the great earth-spanning corporations will soon find it in their own interests to support the creation of some form of transnational regulatory order. Like all large corporations, they despise and fear unpredictability. They will therefore come to support some form of stabilizing machinery' (Toffler, p. 76).

While there is public concern with technology there appears to be a lack of public discourse and decision-making. Will the result be a dissipation of public agitation or an action born out of frustration or even violence in the manner of Ned Lud and the Luddites who, two hundred years ago, destroyed textile frames? Alternatively can the level of discourse regarding technology assessment be raised? If so, what structure is necessary? Should citizens' groups, private associations or special interest groups be mobilized and if so, how?

Ensuring full participation is indeed a challenge, that is, the inclusion of all persons who are knowledgeable about certain issues, in the social and technical processes of developing, implementing and regulating a given technology. In any technological society we must preserve a plurality of centres where decisions can be made and where intelligent participation by all those affected is encouraged. Historically this would have been advisable, as C. P. Snow points out in relation to the industrial revolution when all so-called intellectuals, politicians and engineers were, at best, limited in their ability to effect change. 'Almost everywhere, intellectual persons didn't comprehend what was happening. Certainly writers didn't. Plenty of them shuddered away, as though the right course for a man of feeling was to contract out; some like Ruskin, William Morris and Thoreau and Emerson and Lawrence tried various kinds of fantasies' (Snow 1961, p. 26).

Galbraith contends that the 'individual has far more standing in our culture than the group … Individuals have souls; corporations are notably soulless' (Galbraith 1967, p. 60). Nevertheless our society is not particularly well structured for identifying, publicizing and resolving questions of a technological nature in public forums. It may take a change in the way the public perceives itself, not strictly as consumers, but as people who can exert influence and enjoy developing their own capacity to do so. [...]

Technology's final word

If there were ever any doubts that debating alternative futures is urgent then consider the predicted future for mankind with intelligent machines in a computer-controlled society where there could be mass unemployment, enforced leisure and all major decisions in the grasp of an élite. Are these ideas fanciful or are they probable? Tipler (1994) suggests that the Turing test of an intelligent machine (where it will respond to all questions in a manner undistinguishable from that of humans) is just around the corner. It is these machines that will help us colonize space. It is improbable that biological life can travel light years away to other planets, whereas it is much more probable that fertilized eggs would be placed in an artificial womb and the children raised by robot nannies. Reducing payload mass will be of prime importance in space exploration. Nanotechnology will make instrumentation very small and payload mass very tiny so that it can travel much faster. This will enable an interstellar probe to be launched within a few centuries. Cloning of the probe on site would enable the probe to make copies of itself after reaching the target stellar system. Colonization of space could begin by mid-twenty-first century. Even those who are considering staying on planet earth will eventually have to look elsewhere before the earth becomes vaporized.

Technology educators must recognize the immensity of the boundaries of their subject field. They cannot and must not avoid questions that will ultimately include the future of mankind. Among questions of the future will be one which asks whether we as humans insist that we are a chosen people or are just one step in evolutionary time where we will ultimately be replaced by intelligent machines who, like us, can think and feel. We will be able to 'stay alive' but only in a virtual sense, as emulations in computers of the future, just as long as the computers wish to allow us to do so! The difference between living and non-living matter will lose its meaning in a civilization that continues forever but in which *homo sapiens* is extinct due to limited abilities.

Note

Initial ideas for this paper were presented during the *International Working Seminar in Technology Education*, Washington, D.C., 25 September 1998.

References

Borgmann, A. (1984) *Technology and the Character of Contemporary Life: A Philosophical Inquiry*, Chicago: University of Chicago Press.

Braverman, H. (1985) 'Technology and capitalist control', in D. MacKenzie and J. Wajcman (eds) *The Social Shaping of Technology*, Milton Keynes: Open University Press.

Burke, J. (1972) *The New Technology and Human Values*, Belmont, CA.: Wadsworth Publishing.

Davis, S. and Botkin, J. (1994) *The Monster Under the Bed: How Business is Mastering the Opportunity of Knowledge for Profit*, New York: Simon and Schuster.

de Nevers, N. (1972) *Technology and Society*, Reading, Mass.: Addison-Wesley.

DeVore, P. (1980) *Technology: An Introduction*, Worcester, Mass.: Davis Publications

Ellul, J. (1964) *The Technological Society*, New York: Vintage Books.

Ellul, J. (1982) 'The technological order', in *Symposium Readings: Classical Selections on Great Issues*, Series 2, Vol. 2, Science Technology and Society, New York: University Press of America.

Foster, P. (1994) 'Technology education: aka industrial arts', *Journal of Technology Education* 5(2).

Franklin, U. (1990) *The Real World of Technology*, Concorde, Ontario: Anasi Press.

Fuller, R.B. (1983) *Critical Path*, London: Hutchinson.

Fuller, R.B. (1969) *Ideas and Integrities*, New York: Collier.

Galbraith, J.K. (1967) *The New Industrial State*, Boston: Houghton Mifflin.

Herf, J. (1994) 'Technology and twentieth century German conservative intellectuals', in Y. Ezrahi, E. Mendelsohn and H. Segal (eds), *Technology, Pessimism and Postmodernism*, The Netherlands: Kluwer Academic Publishers.

Marcuse, H. (1972) 'The new forums of control', in A. Teich (ed.), *Technology and Man's Future*, New York: St. Martin's Press.

Papanek, V. (1984) *Design for the Real World*, London: Thames and Hudson.

Papanek, V. and Hennessey, J. (1977) *How Things Don't Work*, New York: Pantheon.

Sale, K. (1995) *Rebels Against the Future: The Luddites and their War on the Industrial Revolution: Lessons for the Computer Age*, New York: Addison-Wesley.

Schumacher, E. F. (1974) *Small is Beautiful*, London: Abacus.

Snow, C.P. (1961) *The Two Cultures and the Scientific Revolution*, New York: Cambridge University Press.

Tipler, F.J. (1994) *The Physics of Immortality*, New York: Doubleday.

Toffler, A. (1975) *The Eco-Spasm Report*, New York: Bantam Books.

2   The nature and purpose of Design and Technology

Richard Kimbell, Kay Stables and Richard Green

Here we begin to look at technology in schools. This chapter explores what technology in schools is, its links with science and its relationship to knowledge, language and values – themes explored in more detail in other chapters. Whilst reading these views about technology in schools think about your educational experiences in technology and what technology is now in the schools you know.

This chapter is taken from a book called Understanding Practice in Design and Technology *and had the original title* Technology and Human Endeavour.

In this chapter, we discuss the *nature of technology* as a phenomenon that lies at the heart of what it means to be human. In technology, *homo sapiens* ('man the understander') meets *homo faber* ('man the maker') (DES/WO 1988). But underlying this powerful liaison of mind and hand is an infinitely more powerful force. For technologists are of necessity visionary – they imagine the impossible – they project forward from what *can* be done now, to what *might* be done tomorrow. They see things that are as yet unseeable except in their own 'mind's eye'. It is this visionary quality that has dragged the human race out of the primordial mire and placed it in a position of such supremacy that we can choose from a breathtaking range of possibilities. Shall we visit the moon today or shall we utterly destroy our planet?

The Polish scientist and philosopher Jacob Bronowski, when writing his magnificent tribute to the triumphs of humankind (*The Ascent of Man*), put his finger on this central defining characteristic of and motivation for technology:

> Among the multitude of animals which scamper, fly, burrow, and swim around us, man is the only one who is not locked into his environment. His imagination, his reason, his emotional subtlety and toughness, make it possible for him not to accept the environment but to change it. And that series of inventions, by which man from age to age has remade his environment ... I call ... *The Ascent of Man.*
>
> (Bronowski 1973)

Technology is essentially about satisfying human desires – for comfort, for transport, for power, for communication, for identity. It is built upon dissatisfaction; upon the tendency (some argue the compulsion) of humans constantly to seek to improve their lot. But equally it is built on the vision of those who say '... I can see a better way of doing that ...' Technology is a task-centred, goal-directed activity. It is purposeful and focused. Technology makes use of a wide range of bodies of knowledge and skill, but is not defined by them, for the *raison d'être* of technology is *to create purposeful change* in the made world. Something did not exist before, but now – as a result of human design and development – it does exist. We have wheelbarrows, wallpaper, widgets, waistcoats and warships because someone (or group) decided (for one reason or another) that they would be good things to have. We can do things with them that were impossible without them. This is technology.

But technology is not just about new things. We constantly try to make our latest model of wheelbarrow (or warship) better than our competitors. This too is technology and again it is a highly focused activity. It is also intensely value laden as should be clear from the use of the word 'better'. We might mean cheaper, or stronger, or longer lasting, or shorter lasting, or less damaging to the environment, or more damaging. All these are perfectly proper objectives that might make our whatever better than yours for the purposes we have in mind.

Technology and clients

Definitions of technology that allow us to distinguish between it and other human activities must therefore centre on this concept of purposeful change. The boundaries of technology are *not* set by our current practices and understandings in electronics or biochemistry or any other existing field of knowledge. The boundaries are defined by our human desires. These desires may arise through dissatisfaction with a current arrangement ('I really do need a better way of fixing punctures on my bike') or simply through an opportunistic response ('I can see a great way to use silicon chip technology to make singing birthday cards'). Few of us would have thought seriously about buying singing birthday cards – or even singing birthday-cake candles – but when they become available they become desirable.

So technology may be driven by the explicit desires of the user (for a better puncture-repair kit) or by the desires of the designer or the producer looking to exploit an opportunity. Probably some innovation results from a combination of these sources, where an interesting design idea meets a novel manufacturing opportunity to meet a real user need. *But in any event, any technological innovation arises from human desires and results in a change in the made world.*

Another fact of life in technological innovation is that – regardless of the *source* of the original desire – the purchaser is the ultimate decision-maker. Any given technological outcome only exists when there is an identifiable client-based need for it. This need may have been massaged by marketing experts or it may be a real fundamental need, but without it there will be no change in the made world. It matters not whether this need/desire is for Sidewinder missiles (very few clients but very wealthy ones – hence sufficient development and production money) or for cups and saucers (very many clients – hence a big market creating sufficient development and production money). In the Thatcherite 1980s this would typically have been characterized as technology being 'market-driven', but that phrase tends to disguise the fact that 'markets' are little more than collective human desires.

The Science Policy Research Unit (SPRU) at Sussex University conducted a detailed study of 'Industrial Innovation' – project SAPHO. It sought to identify and evaluate the factors which distinguished innovations which have achieved commercial success from those that have not. The first and most critical feature was – as we might properly expect from the above discussion – all about understanding the needs and priorities of the client or user.

> The clear-cut differences … were … (1) Successful innovators were seen to have a much better understanding of user needs. They acquire this superiority in a variety of different ways. Some may collaborate intimately with potential customers to acquire the necessary knowledge of user requirements. Others may use thorough market studies. However acquired, this imaginative understanding is one of the hallmarks of success. Conversely failures often ignored users' requirements or even disregarded their views.
>
> (SPRU 1984)

There are some classic design failures that illustrate the point. Clive Sinclair saw an opportunity to exploit an innovative power/transmission system for his famous C5 tricycle. But without a client-based need for it, it became a very expensive white elephant.

The process of technological innovation can work from both ends: from a user desire or from a designer/manufacturer desire. But the purchaser/user/client has the whip hand. If we decide that we do not want or need the new whatever, it is doomed to failure.

Technological and non-technological change

There are of course many kinds of user-focused, purposeful change going on around us all the time. Are they all technological? Or is there a further element in the definition of technology? At the next General Election there may be a change of government. If this were to happen, it would be an expression of 'user' opinion but not many of us would describe it as a technological change. We would rather call it a purposeful political change.

Technological change operates on the made world of products and product-based systems. Any 'made world' product innovation – from a wheelbarrow to a widget – is the product of technology. Political change will naturally impact upon these 'made world' changes, but this impact does not create or define the change. Politicians influence the climate within which we live, but they do not directly create our world. Technology does. The fact of technological change is manifest in the world around us: in houses, in trains, in garden centres. …

Non-technological change

On this definition, a change in the voting system itself (e.g. from 'first past the post' to 'proportional representation') would not be an example of technological change. It would presumably be intended to provide a better constitutional relationship between the electors and the elected. It might *incidentally* involve a new technological product (there are some wonderful electro-mechanical voting machines in the USA), but that is not the reason for the change. Re-designing the voting system is *not* intended to change the made world and therefore would not be a technological change.

Technological change

By contrast, a new adaptor that enables us to fix a hose-pipe to a tap without spraying water everywhere *would* be a technological change (and a very welcome one), since it is specifically intended to impact directly on our made world.

We recognize that this distinction has some fuzzy edges, but it is none the less important to make. And generally it is easy enough to make. We might argue about whether a new bit of software – a computer game, for example – is a product or a system (or both). But it is easy enough to agree that it is intended to create a change in our made world. So too was 'Mr Whippy's' squirting ice cream, Mary Quant's mini-skirt, and the British Aerospace HUD (head-up display) system of aircraft instrumentation. These technological changes are clearly distinguishable from other forms of change: from *political change* in the above example of proportional representation; from *economic change of* collectivist communism to individualist markets: and from *educational change* of selective to comprehensive schooling. Each may have had an impact on the made world of products and product-based systems, but that was not the driving purpose behind them and that is why we do not see them as technological changes.

Change and 'improvement'

The reader will have noticed that we have been careful to use the neutral word 'change' rather than the emotive one 'improve'. Technological changes are all intended to improve something for someone, but the inevitable fact of innovation is that there are winners and losers. We can get whiter than white clothes, but only by using detergent cleaners which irritate the skin of some people. We can have cars that go from 0 to 60 m.p.h. in 3.5 seconds, but only by consuming great quantities of lead-enriched hydrocarbon fuel. We can grow far more wheat by using nitrogen-rich fertilizing agents in the soil, but the nitrogen leaches out and affects our rivers. It seems almost as if there is a natural law that prohibits benefits without losses.

It is easy to identify the winners – since they are usually the clients that commission or induce the technological development. With the losers it is more difficult. Sometimes they are individuals, and sometimes whole eco-systems are at stake:

sometimes they emerge rapidly and sometimes the down-side does not make itself evident for years. And sometimes the winners are also the losers. The motorway speeds up our movement but only by encroaching on land that we formerly used as recreational space or farmland. […]

The eco-design movement is an interesting manifestation of the late twentieth century. As industrialized societies have increasingly sought to build a 'better' world, we have repeatedly been brought up short by the manifest failings in our efforts. Eco-design is an interesting response to the problem not just because it seeks to illuminate the grand scale of ecological matters but because of the tools that it has spawned. Environmental audit (EA) and life cycle analysis (LCA) are complex tools that have been developed – quite literally – to account for each decision that contributed to the design of a product.

Whilst the surface of this argument might be in terms of whether a metal or a fibre should be used for a given purpose, the irreducible bottom line of such arguments is only reached when we get to the values that inform the designer and the product. This is brought most sharply into focus when the retrospective EA and LCA tools are transposed into the more proactive life cycle design (LCD) tool. Here the designer is constantly forced to confront the meaning of 'better' and 'worse' not just at the technical level of the product, but also at the levels of production, marketing, use and disposal. As Layton points out:

> The technology does not have to be as it is. Other options have been available: what we encounter is the result of decisions which reflect the value judgments of those who shaped a development which was not inevitable.
>
> (Layton 1993)

Science and technology

The thrust of the early parts of this chapter has been to assert that the driving force behind technology and innovation is a desire to change our made world. We wish to improve things for ourselves. However, this view is somewhat at odds with a traditional assumption that technology is actually driven by science. Scientists discover things and then technologists apply them to human purposes. This argument (invariably propagated by scientists) has always appeared less than convincing to us since a moment's reflection on the history of technological endeavour reveals example after example of technology leading, rather than following, science. The Chinese built firework rockets in advance of any established theory of rocket propulsion; a functioning steam engine preceded the Laws of Thermodynamics; and Bell's telephone system depended on the electrical properties of carbon which were unknown to science at the time he used it. …

It seems self-evident that science can provide an immensely important resource for technology, but this resource is neither a sufficient nor even a necessary condition to guarantee technological innovation, and a useful analogy can be seen in the world of crime and detection. When a police officer investigates a murder, he or she looks for someone who had the *means* (a knife) to commit the dirty deed and the *opportunity* to use it (in the rhododendron bushes at the garden party). But most of all the search is for someone who has the motive (personal gain or revenge). In terms of technological innovation, science can only reliably provide the first of these – the means of technological advance. As for the second, we have only to reflect on the way technology strides ahead in wartime – because of the concentrated political/economic focus – to see that it too plays its part. But it is our hunger for improvement (in whatever way one wishes to define this) that provides the driving force of motive.

Moreover, if we want something badly enough, the evidence suggests that human ingenuity will find a way to do it even without the scientific means. The examples of the steam engine and the telephone illustrate that a heady combination of motive and opportunity was more than enough to overcome the difficulty of a lack of any formal scientific base for the innovations.

Science is a resource for technology – and that is all. As Layton eloquently describes it, it is a quarry to be mined rather than a cathedral to be worshipped in.

...

In case this debate appears a little arcane, we would do well to remember the damage that has been inflicted on engineering education in the UK by its too close association with science, especially in university circles. In official report after official report the universities are castigated for making engineering courses into quasi-science courses.

> Complaints commonly voiced, especially by employers, are that the education of engineers is unduly scientific and theoretical.
>
> (Finniston 1980, section 4.18)

> ... our overseas competitors are generally superior in the formation of engineers. This deficiency to a large extent reflects the relatively restricted and narrow conception of engineering as a branch of applied science ...
>
> (Finniston 1980, section 4.39)

> The engineering schools have not provided an education which is sufficiently distinctive from science and physics ... we have tended to produce second rate scientists.
>
> (Allen 1980)

> The whole burden of developing competent development engineers or design engineers at present falls upon industry itself.
>
> (The Corfield Report 1976, section 8.6)

The academic snobbery attached to pure study – in Layton's 'cathedral of science' – combined with the delusion that technological innovation naturally flows from such science, has been a major contributor to the undoing of Britain's manufacturing competitiveness. Engineering education in particular has been myopically focused on the scientific means for innovation rather than responding to a broader vision of technological innovation. As we have attempted to illustrate, this broader vision must incorporate the motives of human need and aspiration that are the real engines of technological advance.

The language of technological change

[...] Communication, and especially the link between language and learning, has a well-established place in our understanding of education. The philosopher Susan Langer described it in the following terms:

> Language is our prime instrument of conceptual expression. The things we can say are in effect the things we can think. Words are the terms of our thinking as well as the terms in which we present our thoughts, because they present the objects of thought to the thinker himself. Before language communicates ideas it gives them form, makes them clear and in fact makes them what they are. Whatever has a name is an object of thought.
>
> (Langer 1962)

Vygotsky makes a similar point:

> Reflection ... may be regarded as inner argumentation. We must also mention speech which is originally a means of communication with the surrounding people and only later, in the form of inner speech, a means of thinking ...
>
> (Vygotsky 1966)

For the purposes of this discussion, however, we should remember that languages are not only based on words; indeed, Vygotsky's analysis of signs and symbols as communicators takes us well beyond Langer's single-minded preoccupation with words.

In the technological world, it is these other forms of communication that become pre-eminent, but they operate in exactly the same way as Langer indicates.

> The history of engineering drawing demonstrates that the modelling methods available to designers do directly affect the thoughts they can think. Engineering drawing was a dramatic and powerful modelling tool that made possible a new relationship between management and manufacture and separated the process of design from the process of construction. It was at the heart of the industrial revolution and the new work relationships that it brought into being.
>
> (Baynes 1992)

Whilst this is true of engineering drawing, it is equally true of all the other communication techniques used in technology. Mathematical symbols and formulae enable us to think about things that would otherwise be impossible to conceptualize. Concrete modelling enables us to think about form and structure in ways that are impossible with the use of abstract formal representations. Sketching allows us to 'talk through' ideas with ourselves or with others. Workshop manuals are full of diagrams, drawings and photographs, not because the users cannot read, but because the language of images is so much richer than the language of words when one has to deal in technological matters.

Imagine the task of describing to someone how a door lock works. Imagine doing this without a door lock to point to and by using only words. It would be far more difficult than if one were also able to use diagrams. We need to be able to 'image' in our minds what is happening on the inside of the lock, so using images as the means of communication is far more efficient.

In the technological domain we might rephrase Langer (with apologies) as follows:

> Images are our prime instrument of technological expression. The things we can draw are in effect the things we can think. Models are the terms of our thinking as well as the terms in which we present our thoughts, because they present the objects of thought to the thinker himself. Before a drawing communicates ideas it gives them form, makes them clear and in fact makes them what they are.

Those who might doubt the validity of this transformation should read *The Art of the Engineer* (Baynes and Pugh 1981) if only for the fascinating account of the codification of engineering drawing and its central role in making possible the development of the steam engine.

> James Watt's personality, education and situation meant he was well fitted to codify drawing practice … he drew together the threads of architectural, technical, scientific, military and naval draughtsmanship to turn them into an effective means for design, development and production control … Watt executed all the drawings himself … step by step there evolved, from Watt's work alone, small groups of draughtsmen and finally well organized, recognisably modern drawing offices … [which became] the normal means for developing ideas and controlling production.
>
> (Baynes and Pugh 1981)

The language of technology is indisputably a concrete one – of images, symbols and models. Without this language it is just not possible to conceive of technological solutions.

Expressing ideas and developing ideas

The thrust of our argument above is that the use of a concrete language is essential to grapple with the concrete realities of technological innovation. But we need to go further than this – to examine how we *use* the language as a technological development tool.

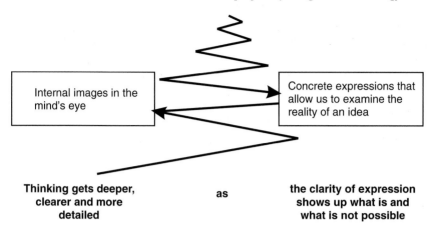

Figure 2.1   Interaction of internal images and expressions in drawings

One of our principal conclusions from the APU project concerned this critical relationship between the concrete *expression of ideas* and the *development of ideas*.

> ... the act of expression pushes ideas forward. By the same token, the additional clarity that this throws on the idea enables the originator to think more deeply about it, which further extends the possibilities in the idea. Concrete expression (by whatever means) is therefore not merely something that allows us to see the designer's ideas, it is something without which the designer is unable to be clear what the ideas are.
>
> (Kimbell *et al.* 1991)

Whilst this work for the APU was based on 'novice' technologists at school, an exactly parallel finding emerged at about the same time from the study of expert technologists – in this case Edison and Bell's work in developing the telephone – which was analysed in detail by Gorman and Carlson (1990) at the University of Virginia.

> ... the innovation process is much better characterised as a recursive activity in which inventors move back and forth between ideas and objects. Inventors may start with one mental model and modify it after experimentation with different mechanical representations, or they may start out with several mechanical representations and gradually shape a mental model. In both cases, the essence of invention seems to be the dynamic interplay of mental models with mechanical representations.
>
> (Gorman and Carlson 1990)

Gorman and Carlson's findings accord exactly with our own, which we summarize in Figure 2.1. We used the term 'iterative' to describe the interaction of the internal (mind's eye) images and their expression in drawings and models. Gorman and Carlson use a different term, 'recursive', but the point remains the same.

Our work for APU led us to the conviction that

> Cognitive modelling by itself – manipulating ideas purely in the mind's eye – has severe limitations when it comes to complex ideas and patterns. It is through externalised modelling techniques that such complex ideas can be expressed and clarified ...

> It is our contention that this inter-relationship between modelling ideas in the mind and modelling ideas in reality is the cornerstone of capability in design & technology. It is best described as 'thought in action'.

> (Kimbell *et al.* 1991)

Technological capability

As with all languages, its existence is no guarantee that we can all use it fluently. The fact that we have at our disposal a complex concrete language for technological developments does not guarantee that we can all be creative with it. We can use languages at many levels of sophistication and an important distinction is between using it *to understand and respond* and using it *to create new*.

The argument is as follows: When I am in France on holiday I am content to understand and respond in the language; to use it to buy goods in the market or to converse with local people over a drink in the bar. I do not aspire to explore the limits of the language by creating something new: a novel, poem or play. So too with technology we might just wish to use the language to understand and respond: to read the symbolic instructions in the car manual when we break down; or to understand and interpret the dress pattern in order that we can adequately follow its instructions. But equally we might wish to be more proactive with the language – using it to create new technological ideas and outcomes.

This is what we take to be the essential difference between *technological understanding* and *technological capability*. By 'capability' we mean that combination of ability and motivation that transcends understanding and enables creative development. It provides the bridge between what is and what might be. Specifically, in technological terms, it mediates between human desires and dissatisfactions on one hand and technical constraints and possibilities on the other.

... Technology has only recently emerged into the mainstream of the school curriculum. Thirty years ago it was an idealistic dream of a handful of pioneers, and even 15 years ago it was a minority activity bearing little resemblance to its current formation in the curriculum. At the heart of this new technology curriculum lies this creative technological capability that we seek to develop in all pupils. [...]

Summary

- Technology is a quintessentially human activity based on our desire constantly to improve our condition. It is an organized way of creating purposeful change.

- It is therefore centred on, and defined by, the needs/wants/desires of people, who will be the users of the outcomes of any given technological development. Technology is task-centred.
- But not all purposeful change is technological. To be technological, the change needs to impact on the 'made world' of products and product-based systems. Warships and widgets are technological but voting systems and new economic models are not.
- Whilst technology seeks 'improvement' (for someone) it invariably creates winners and losers. It is intensely value laden and usually driven by the values of those that commission the task.
- Technology can be resourced by any body of knowledge – but is not defined by them. Whilst a rich knowledge base is a valuable resource for technology, the possession of any body of knowledge is neither a sufficient nor even a necessary condition of technological development.
- The language of technology is dominantly a concrete one: of graphics, symbols and models. The development of technology has required the progressive sophistication of these concrete languages.
- There is a tight relationship between the expression of ideas and the development of ideas. It can be described as 'thought in action'.
- Technological capability is dependent upon a combination of abilities and motivations that empower us to create what has never formerly been seen. It enables us to bridge the gap between human aspiration and technical constraint.
- Technological capability is now at the heart of the school curriculum in the UK and we must examine why it is there and what it contributes to the education of young people.

References

Allen, Sir G. (1980) Engineering: Finniston and the future, *Times Higher Education Supplement*, 10 October, p. 1.

Baynes, K. (1992) The role of modelling in the Industrial Revolution, in: *Modelling: the Language of Designing*, Occasional Paper No. 1. Loughborough: Loughborough University of Technology.

Baynes, K. and Pugh, E. (1981) *The Art of the Engineer,* Cambridge: Lutterworth Press.

Bronowski, J. (1973) *The Ascent of Man,* London: British Broadcasting Corporation.

The Corfield Report (1976) *Product Design,* London: National Economic Development Office.

Department of Education and Science/Welsh Office (1988) *National Curriculum Design and Technology Working Group – Interim Report*, London: DES.

Finniston, Sir M. (1980) *Engineering our Future*, London: HMSO.

Gorman, M. and Carlson, B. (1990) 'Interpreting invention as a cognitive process: the case of Alexander Graham Bell, Thomas Edison, and the telephone', *Science Technology and Human Values* 15(2): 131–64.

Kimbell, R., Stables, K., Wheeler, T., Wozniak, A. and Kelly, V. (1991) *The Assessment of Performance in Design and Technology: The final report of the Design and Technology APU project*, London, Evaluation and Monitoring Unit, Schools Examination and Assessment Council (SEAC).

Langer, S. (1962) *Philosophical Sketches*, Johns Hopkins University Press. Baltimore, MD:

Layton, D. (1993) *Technology's Challenge to Science Education*, Buckingham: Open University Press.

Science Policy Research Unit (1984) *Project SAPHO – a report*, Brighton: University of Sussex.

Vygotsky, L.S. (1966) Psychological research in the USSR, in: Light, P., Sheldon, S. and Woodhead, M. *Learning to Think* (1991), Buckingham: Open University Press.

3 The coming of technology education in England and Wales

Robert McCormick

Having considered what technology is in schools, we now consider the subject in its historical context. An historical appreciation is important in helping to develop an understanding of why design and technology is as it is now. This chapter describes how technology was defined and constructed as the National Curriculum Working Group prepared and presented their reports, and how the subject developed through publication of the various Orders.

This chapter first appeared in Teaching Technology and has been updated by the author and myself to take account of developments in the National Curriculum.

Historical background[1]

Technology is often described as a new area of the curriculum, but there are historical antecedents which are important in understanding the current state of technology education. I will explore these antecedents by giving a brief overview of some of the strands that have contributed to the development of technology education, before going on to examine the developments that led to the National Curriculum for Technology. The contributing strands include craft, art and design, home economics, science and technology and society (STS). For each I will identify the traditions and some of the views that each contributes to technology education. It is onto these traditions that the National Curriculum was grafted, and from which teachers started as they tried to make sense of the curriculum proposals presented through the first Order for Technology (DES/WO 1990), and from which Design and Technology as it is now has evolved.

Craft

This tradition is not a single one and differs across time; two strands were important in England and Wales. One strand is (trade)craft stemming from the nineteenth- and early twentieth-century manual training, and emphasizing exercises to develop skills with tools. Another form of craft developed from Swedish *sloyd*, that in some forms became aligned with art. *Sloyd*, founded to keep village crafts alive in nineteenth-century Sweden, emphasized creativity and was popularized in England through women elementary school teachers. The tradecraft tradition has developed from wood to metal, from hand tools to machinery, but has been unable to continue to develop as technology did because the basic model of production was flawed, and because there is a limit to what can be done in schools (Medway 1989: 14–15). The craft model, of the single worker in control of the whole production process, does not reflect the teamwork found in industry. The failure of computer-controlled lathes to have a meaningful place in schools is an example of the difficulty of representing modern industrial practice. It is not a parallel of the ordinary lathe because it is a mass-production machine, and exercises which get students to programme its operation, or to use CAD/CAM links, often ignore the industrial context within which such machines are used. Flexible manufacturing systems, which are often responsive to one-off production (based upon a basic 'model'), are only accessible to pupils through three-dimensional models, computer simulation, video and factory visits. To some the answer to limitations of schools is a process approach, through problem-solving and design, in an effort to free the curriculum from a specific content (a specific technology). ...

But the difficulties that the craft tradition may have should not blind us to the important contribution it makes to how to teach skill development, use materials and manage individually-based project work. The emphasis of this tradition on finished products does, however, create problems for the development of modelling skills.

Art and design

There are three main inter-related groups (not all of them homogeneous), those from art and design, design education as part of general education, and craft, design and technology (CDT). In the nineteenth century two groups existed within art and design (Thistlewood 1989). One, the Society of Art Masters (SAM), was a hierarchical, subject-centred association of art school (male) principals dedicated to presenting drawing as an academic discipline, emphasizing classical draughtsmanship and design allied to industrial arts. The other, the Art Teachers Guild (ATG), contrasted strongly with SAM. It was mainly made up of female classroom teachers, and was egalitarian, individual-centred (child-centred) in its interests. Its ethos was to support those who considered the creativity, expression, invention and imagination of childhood as important. This, Thistlewood argues, was a by-product of the English Arts and Crafts Movement, with its concern for the spiritual value of craftwork. Industrial art to them suppressed free creativity. The successors to these two organizations combined in 1984 to form the National Society for Education in Art and Design (NSEAD), in a synthesis of their two approaches. NSEAD commented upon the National Curriculum for Design and Technology schools (NSEAD 1990; Steers 1990).

Those seeing design education as part of general education focused initially around the Royal College of Art and Bruce Archer, who was responsible for an enquiry into design in schools (RCA 1989). He viewed design as a third area in education, distinct from, but equal to the sciences and humanities (Archer 1979). It concerns doing and making and includes such things as technology, fine art, performing arts and useful arts; he represented technology as lying somewhere between science and design. As an interest group they are represented by the Design Council and, along with other groups, are represented on the Design Education Forum. This Forum impressed upon the working group which drew up the original England and Wales National Curriculum on Technology in schools the importance of seeing design, not technology, as the overarching curriculum activity (Steers 1990: 11–12). Such views have contributed to an understanding of design and, in particular, they offer a sophisticated view of design based on what professional practitioners do.

CDT developed under a number of influences, including that of design education (Penfold 1988: Ch. 4). The view of design which CDT has developed, epitomized by John Eggleston's work (Eggleston 1976), has been criticized by the art and design groups. These criticisms include: a mechanical view of design, expressed through various linear and circular staged models that fail to teach pupils the process, and do not reflect how designers think (Jeffrey 1990); a view of craft that emphasizes an outdated woodwork and metalwork view of making, rather than one which develops new ideas and designs (NSEAD 1990: 32); and the problem of modelling I mentioned earlier.

Home Economics

Domestic subjects first officially appeared on the curriculum in 1862, with 'plain needlework', followed in 1870 by 'cookery'. Their introduction was mainly due to the concern of social reformers for the living conditions and health of the poor, and the belief that these could be improved through education (East 1980, Jackson 1992). Their developments parallel those of craft: from needlework and cooking, which emphasized skills by following patterns and recipes, to textiles and food. Textiles work developed design approaches, while food included investigations along with a good deal of science. Like Craft, however, Home Economics focused on the development of skills and the production of well-finished single items. Until the advent of National Curriculum Technology little attention had been paid to mass-production techniques and the development of textiles and food products for mass sales.

Science

Having started with 'applied' beginnings in the nineteenth century (Layton 1973), science educators in England went through a post-war phase of emphasizing 'pure science', and were reluctant to support technology education (McCulloch, Jenkins and Layton 1985: Ch. 6). The Association for Science Education (ASE) then recognized the importance of technology education, as different from science education, and the role of science teachers in it (ASE 1988; SSCR 1987).

The concern to make science relevant has increased the interest in studying science in meaningful contexts, technology being one of these. Problem-solving therefore becomes important. Science brings to technology education: scientific investigation and experimentation methods including ideas of a 'fair test' (Harrison 1990); a knowledge and conceptual understanding essential to a technologist; the development of new science and technology areas such as biotechnology. ...

There were efforts to introduce science into technology teaching, through the *Modular Courses in Technology* (Schools Council 1981). Students could study a number of modules on electronics, mechanisms, structures, materials and pneumatics, before completing a more substantial project for GCE O level (i.e. covering what is now Key Stage 4).

Science, technology and society (STS)

This tradition stems directly from the desire to educate for citizenship and to control science and technology. It is one response, by those in science education who want to teach science in context, to avoid the irrelevance of 'pure science' and, by implication, to replace 'science for all' in schools by STS (Za'rour 1987: 731). The STS tradition has been responsible for developing value issues in relation to technology and, in particular, has developed teaching material and methods for discussing controversial issues, role-play activities and games (Solomon 1988: 272–3), methods more familiar to social studies teachers. This tradition also brings in a different kind of problem-solving from that of design and make, one which relates to decision-making about, for example, where to locate a power station.

The creation of the National Curriculum for Technology[2]

The first Statutory Order for Technology in the National Curriculum for England and Wales (DES/WO 1990) defined the Attainment Targets (ten levels of achievement against which children would be assessed) and the Programmes of Study (what they should be taught). As the first legal document to be issued it contained none of the rationale for the curriculum, nor any of the thinking that led up to it. This thinking, encapsulated in earlier reports, is another important antecedent, only some of which reached the teachers who have to implement it. All teachers received was the Order, and few ever saw the earlier documents. In this section, therefore, I will review some of the thinking that appeared through the earlier reports.

The initial moves

The Education Reform Act 1988 introduced the title of the foundation subject 'Technology' into the school curriculum, although previously HMI had defined a technological area of learning and experience (DES 1985).[3] As with all the subjects, a working group was set up to define the profile components and the Programmes of Study for the subject. The title of the working group was for 'design and technology' and its terms of reference issued in April 1988 included, along with similar terms given to other subject groups, 'design in all its aspects' (i.e. those not within technology) and 'information technology'. Initially primary level technology had been given to the Science Working Group, which had included it in its interim report, but the Design and Technology Working Group took it on.

The combination of 'design and technology' as a single title was used by the Working Group to indicate a unified activity; indeed they use the term 'design and technological activity'. Medway (1992: 68) puts the change from 'technology' to 'design and technology' down to pressure from the 'design lobby'. The Working Group recognized that there was an overlap: 'most, but not all design activities will generally include technology and most technology activities *will* include design' (DES/WO 1988: para. 1.5). However, this underplays the complexity of the rela-tionship. There are activities in both design and technology (separately) that do not overlap, and the relationship varies according to what is being designed. Thus in a product cycle (including market research, design, supply of parts, production) design as an activity is not the whole of the cycle, though where it begins and ends is not easily defined. Technology as an activity includes the 'design' phase, and also the supply and production phases. When an individual potter produces a product the phases may not be clear and modelling, prototyping and making run into each other. Here design and technology activity cannot easily be disaggregated. When an architect designs a building he or she will work only on a model (2-D or 3-D) and design is a distinct phase, but technology activity will be part of both the design and the construction of the building. The simplest way to resolve this is actually to use the word 'technology' (and technological activity) and assume that design is part of it. (See McCormick (1993) for a fuller discussion of the relationship.) There may be other aspects of design that are excluded, but they may be covered in other areas of the curriculum. At the time, of course, the Working Group was not neces-sarily defining *an* area of the curriculum. The first Order for Technology did not resolve the problem and there remains a puzzle, for me, as to whether there are *design* activities and *technological* activities, or only *design and technological* activities.

The place of information technology (IT) was also a difficulty. The Working Group in effect proposed a subject of 'design and technology', but that would have been in contravention of the Education Reform Act that used the title technology, and so eventually two profile components were created: *design and technology* and *information technology*. While this may appear a cosmetic change, it is one which caused problems for IT staff who in some schools might on the one hand be part of a technology team, but on the other see their responsibility for IT across the curricu-lum and hence outside the team. The decision certainly severed the connection between design and technology and computers and information technology as *a technology*; this effectively destroyed the subject technology.

The interim report

The Design and Technology Working Group produced an interim report late in 1988 (DES/WO 1988), which then went out for consultation before a final report was produced in 1989. The interim report contained some interestingly different statements from those which eventually formed the final Proposals and the Order itself. The first chapter in the *Interim Report* was a reflective discussion of the nature of design and technology, and education based on such activities. At this stage there was no implication that Design and Technology would be a separate subject; indeed the requirement to understand the effects of technological change implied strong cross-curricular links (Barnett 1992: 89). However, perhaps the most significant aspect was the definition of capability:

- pupils are able to *use* existing artefacts and systems effectively;
- pupils are able to make *critical appraisals* of personal, social, economic and environmental implications of artefacts and systems;
- pupils are able to *improve,* and extend the uses of, existing artefacts and systems;
- pupils are able to *design, make* and *appraise* new artefacts and systems;
- pupils are able to *diagnose* and *rectify faults* in artefacts and systems.

(DES/WO 1988: 17–18, my emphases)

This is a much wider range of aspects of capability than eventually found its way into the attainment targets, which really only focused upon the fourth of the ones above. In other words the interim report saw design as only one of *several* aspects of capability, and a more true reflection of technology in the world outside school, where design, important though it is, is undertaken by only a fraction of those working in technology.[4]

The final report

The Design and Technology Working Group produced their final report in the form of proposals to the Secretary of State (DES/WO 1989). These proposals took the form of an introduction spelling out some of the rationale for the subject, complete Attainment Targets (and associated Statements of Attainment) and Programmes of Study. The rationale was much less specific about the nature of capability than the interim report, presumably because the Attainment Targets (ATs) specified what capability meant. However, it was discussed in one paragraph, where yet another list of attributes, different from those of the interim report, were given:

- to intervene … to bring about and control change;
- to speculate on possibilities for modified and new artefacts … ;
- to model what is required;
- to plan … ways of proceeding and organize … resources;
- to achieve outcomes … which have been well appraised;
- to understand the significance of design and technology to the economy and to the quality of life.

(DES/WO 1989: para. 1.5)

Four ATs were proposed for the design and technology profile component and one for the information technology profile component. The design and technology ATs corresponded to identifying needs and opportunities for design and technological activities, generating a design proposal, planning and making the design, and appraisal of it (and the designs of others). For each of these ATs ten levels of Statements of Attainment (SoA) were defined. In addition the Programmes of Study (PoS) were defined for each of the Key Stages under sixteen headings and at ten levels! The headings included: materials, business and economics, aesthetics, structures, exploring and investigating, modelling and communicating, making, health and safety, energy, tools and equipment, systems, mechanisms, imaging and generating, organizing and planning, appraising, social and environmental. Not surprisingly there was a universal reaction against the complexity of the PoS during the consultation period that followed.

Besides the complexity of the proposals, one of the major problems was the difficulty in interpreting what some of the statements meant. They had been deliberately kept at a level of generality to try and avoid prescription but, even with examples, this meant that the various statements were somewhat abstract or vague (for example, AT1, Level 7: to devise an effective research strategy for investigating a specific context). There was also a confusion in the types of statements in the PoS compared with those in the ATs. The SoA in the latter were focused upon the process of designing and making, devoid of any particular content. The statements in the PoS were a combination of the two, some on process topics such as 'exploring and investigating' and some on content such as 'mechanisms'.

Finally, the most significant aspect of the proposals, from the point of view of implementation, was the idea that design and technology would be taught by teachers from subject areas of art and design, business studies, CDT, home economics and information technology. This implied bringing together teachers who had had no real contact in the past and, as there was no national curriculum subject for most of them (apart from art and design), put them under some pressure to cooperate.

The consultation report

Following the publication of the final report, the consultation process revealed a concern about the complexity of the structure (PoS), the difficulty in the language and the CDT bias. The National Curriculum Council (NCC) was given the task of conducting this consultation process and responding to it. Its position was much less independent of government than the Working Group and so it was mindful of both the responses to consultation and government concerns. The latter is evident in the foreword to their consultation report, which as Barnett (1992) notes was very much concerned with wealth creation and enterprise, whereas the Working Group had talked about a range of reasons for teaching technology in schools.

The need to reduce complexity and simplify language (because in many cases, especially primary schools, non-specialists were being addressed) resulted in the PoS having only four headings:

- developing and using systems;
- working with materials;
- developing and communicating ideas;
- satisfying human needs.

In fact these headings only superficially simplified the PoS, because the original statements under each heading had been retained and redistributed among the new headings. Thus 'developing and using systems' contained items from the original 'organizing and planning', 'structures', 'mechanisms' and 'energy'.

The ATs were much the same as before except that the idea of a specification was added to AT2, but as McCormick (1990b: 42) argues this was poorly interpreted in the SoA and not carried through to evaluation in AT4. One of the problems for the NCC was in trying to learn from the thinking developed by the Working Group over the time of its work. Not surprisingly the NCC misunderstood some of the ideas in technology, and 'specifications' was just such an example.

The NCC did, however, respond to the CDT bias and introduced examples that would appeal to Home Economics teachers. In so doing they set in motion a problem that was to be raised in the first years of implementation of the Technology National Curriculum, that is whether design-and-make activities could be extended to those including food. Thus examples included the design of a salad; in itself this is rather a ridiculous example of 'technology', although as part of 'design' there may be some rationale. Inasmuch as designing a salad is a model of, say, catering or industrial activity (e.g. supermarket retailing) then it is a good analogy, but taken on its own it simply says any activity can be conceived of as a 'design and technology' activity.

Subject by committee

Most subjects are created by a long process of development, perhaps involving universities. Technology, on the other hand, was created by committee. There were of course a variety of interest groups that had a vested interest in the outcome; I have already mentioned the 'design lobby'. The creation of the Design and Technology Working Group was an opportunity to sweep aside all the special interest groups that might have lobbied for their brand of design and technology and, by all accounts, Lady Parkes, who chaired the group, did just that. However, when it came to operationalizing the broad ideas on design and technology, which previously had taken up much of the first chapter of the interim report, the final report, as I have already noted, exhibited a CDT bias. In any case, even discounting the influence of pressure groups, the subject created by the committee is very sensitive to the composition of the committee. The listing in the final report (DES/WO 1989: 102) indicates that of this group only one member represented the world of practising technologists (Denis Filer from the Engineering Council), with another from 'business'. The other ten were, in one way or another, associated with education. It would be unfair to cast any aspersions on the work of the Group, which had an unenviable task, but it is not unfair to ask how such a group could come to grips with an area of activity with so few practising technologists in its number. Such groups should perhaps work more like parliamentary select committees, taking evidence in public and publishing it all, then we could see the sum total of expertise available. Whatever the considered view of the Working Group, the NCC then modified the ATs and PoS of the final report and, though we have access to the way they weighed up the evidence, we do not even know who was involved in drawing up the NCC consultation report. The NCC had to assimilate in a short period of time an understanding of the issues that the Working Group spent a year on. The NCC did an admirable job in taking into account responses to the final report, but how could it be expected to represent adequately the breadth and depth of technology in the short period of time it had?

The first Order for Technology

In March of 1990 the first Order was issued (DES/WO 1990) which did not differ substantially from the consultation report. Thus design and technology, as a component of technology, was launched into schools:

- strong on process (encapsulated in the ATs), but weak in content (not defined in the PoS);
- seeing the process in terms of a holistic design-based activity;
- recognizing value issues but scattering statements on this over a variety of levels and ATs;
- asking a diverse set of teachers to work together to provide a coherent area of the curriculum.

Although there was *Non-Statutory Guidance* (NCC 1991a) and in-service material to help teachers to implement the curriculum, they were not adequate to cope with the considerable task of getting teachers to take on the issues required. The difficulties were at the level of the staff team that had to implement the new curriculum, and at the level of individual teachers who had to use a rather vague document to plan their work and, more important, assess their pupils. Thus, for example, the Level 2 statement for AT1 was: 'ask questions which help them to identify the needs and opportunities for design and technology activity'. Assessing a pupil on the basis of this statement would prove different in each of the following starting points for an activity based upon the design of play equipment:

1   using existing play equipment identify needs and opportunities for the design of play equipment;
2   using the given beams and plastic drums identify needs and opportunities for the design of play equipment;
3   identify needs and opportunities for the design of play equipment (i.e. start with a 'blank sheet of paper').

Clearly the last of these starting points is the most open-ended and the demands all three make on pupils depend on any stimulus material that is provided. ...

The difficulties in implementation were revealed in an HMI report (HMI 1992) and in the NCC's own monitoring of the curriculum (NCC 1992). The political debate was also fuelled by a report prepared for the Engineering Council which opened with the statement, 'Technology is a mess' (Smithers and Robinson 1992). The culmination of this was a review process which resulted in another round of reports and draft legislation.

The revised Order

... The changes suggested by the review group of HMI and NCC officers tried to address the problems of implementation noted above, by reducing the number of SoA and PoS statements and clarifying the content (the skills and knowledge) to be taught. This resulted in two ATs, *designing* and *making*. However, each of these contained strands:

Designing
- investigating, clarifying and specifying the design task;
- modelling, developing and communicating design ideas.

Making
- planning and organizing making;
- using a variety of materials, components, tools, equipment and processes to make products safely;
- testing, modifying and evaluating.

On the face of it, it looked as if four ATs were replaced by five, except that the review group argued that originally there were twelve. Somewhere along the line I must have missed something – nowhere in the first Order is there any mention of strands. Although the NCC in-service materials (NCC 1991b) referred to strands they were not listed. No doubt the review group are referring to the strands created during the development of SATs, but these had no statutory place. What is a teacher to make of such informal and perhaps not universally shared knowledge? Despite this problem of the number of strands, the number of SoA was reduced by half (to 59!), so at least the Order was simplified.

The PoS identified the 'skills and knowledge which pupils should acquire' (DFE/WO 1992: 3) through establishing two core sections on *designing* and *making*, and five supporting sections:

- construction materials and components;
- food;
- control systems and energy;
- structures;
- business and industrial practices.

Control systems have a variety of elements, such as electrical/electronic, mechanical and pneumatic. At Key Stage (KS) 4 the elements, along with 'Construction materials' and 'Structures' or 'Food', were offered in various choice combinations depending upon whether a full course (10 per cent of curriculum time) or a short course (5 per cent) was being offered. Finally, a number of design-and-make tasks (DMTs) was suggested as the basis of teaching, with the number and content being specified for each Key Stage.

As in the first Order, there were the problems of 'subject by committee'. 'Food', as a section in the PoS, quite rightly preserved some of the home economics input to technology teaching, but what were we to make of the specific identification of textiles as a construction material? At Level 6 it was listed along with other generic groups of materials (timbers, metals, plastics, composites, etc.), but it was the only construction material that has a DMT specified for it in the proposals (DFE/WO 1992: 27). The purpose was clear: it ensured that those home economic teachers specializing in textiles could have some input. The cost of this was a degree of illogicality and the loss of textiles as a distinct technology, equivalent to that of 'food', which had its own section in the proposal.

This Order, however, was not the final version. In 1993 there was a review of the whole National Curriculum, including technology. Such was the confusion at the time over technology that, in 1994, the government announced that it was no longer a statutory requirement to teach technology at Key Stage 4. Many schools welcomed this and reverted to examination courses in CDT and Home Economics. Others continued with technology, knowing that it would be re-introduced later.

The report of the National Curriculum review was published in December 1993 (SCAA 1993) and became known as the Dearing Report, after its chairman. This report recommended clarification and simplification for the Programmes of Study for all subjects. Subject working groups were again convened and the recommendations for Design and Technology (note the change of title) were published in 1994 (SCAA 1994). These were accepted by the Secretary of State and became statutory in 1995 for Key Stage 3 pupils, in 1996 for Year 10 and in 1997 for Year 11.

The 1995 Order, now for Design and Technology, was better received than its predecessors. One major outcome of the review was the separation of Design and Technology and Information Technology, the latter now being recognized as a subject in its own right (currently renamed as Information and Communications Technology). Another major difference from earlier Orders was that there was now no requirement for schools in Wales to teach Design and Technology at Key Stage 4.

The Attainment Targets had Level Descriptors rather than Statements of Attainment, and these were reduced from ten levels to eight, plus one for 'exceptional performance'. Furthermore, the level descriptors applied only to pupils in Key Stages 1–3; those at Key Stage 4 were covered by examination syllabuses, which were now required to meet the demands of the Programmes of Study.

The Programmes of Study identified three main areas: designing skills, making skills, and knowledge and understanding. Knowledge and understanding was listed under six headings: materials and components; systems and control; structures (Key Stage 3 only); products and applications; quality; and health and safety.

There was a greater emphasis on the making of products, in response to criticisms of earlier Orders. However, it retained the problem of the inclusion of food by recommending that it be an 'optional area of study' at Key Stage 3. This was likely the result of representations from boys' schools, which generally have no provision for the teaching of Food Technology and for whom making food a compulsory element would be costly in terms of the provision of rooms, resources and staff.

There was also a statement that pupils should work independently and in teams, and that they should apply knowledge, skills and understanding not only as listed in the design and technology programmes but also, where appropriate, from art, mathematics and science. Pupils should learn through design-and-make assignments which, from Key Stage 3, should be in different contexts and materials including resistant materials, compliant materials and/or food (note the continuing lack of commitment to the use of food with design and technology). The assignments should also include work with control systems and structures. At Key Stage 4 the assignments should relate to industrial practices and the application of systems and control.

Dearing also recommended in the report that there be a moratorium on further changes in the National Curriculum for a five-year period, to allow schools to stabilize and consolidate. This was adhered to and design and technology experienced a relatively stable climate for a number of years, which allowed teachers to develop schemes of work that they could refine and improve.

National Curriculum 2000

In 1999 the latest review of the National Curriculum in England took place. The rationale for this was to allow the whole curriculum to respond to changes in society and the economy, and to be able to meet future needs (QCA 1999a). In the new curriculum there is, for the first time, a statement describing the distinctive contribution that each subject makes to the curriculum. For Design and Technology this reads:

> Design and technology prepares pupils to participate in tomorrow's rapidly changing technologies. They learn to think and intervene creatively to improve quality of life. The subject calls for pupils to become autonomous and creative problem solvers, as individuals and members of a team. They must look for needs, wants and opportunities and respond to them by developing a range of ideas and making products and systems. They combine practical skills with an understanding of aesthetics, social and environmental issues, function and industrial practices. As they do so, they reflect on and evaluate present and past design and technology, its uses and effects. Through design and technology, all pupils can become discriminating and informed users of products, and become innovators.

The Attainment Targets are reduced again, this time from two to one: design and technology. The level descriptions still only apply to pupils in Key Stages 1–3. These are not drastically different; they combine statements from the previous two ATs, but are much clearer and simpler.

The Programmes of Study now have one main heading, 'Skills, knowledge and understanding', with four strands 'to reflect the designing and making process' (QCA 1999: 7). These strands are: developing, planning and communicating ideas; working with tools, equipment, materials and components to produce quality products; evaluating processes and products; applying knowledge and understanding. The knowledge and understanding is further identified as: materials and components; systems and control; structures (Key Stage 3 only) and health and safety.

Again the Order states that pupils should learn through design-and-make assignments, these to include work in all materials. Also to be part of the curriculum are focused practical tasks and product analysis. There is a greater emphasis on the use of CAD/CAM, new technologies and materials and, at Key Stage 4, industrial practices and the effects of technology on society.

Creativity features more prominently in the 2000 Order than in earlier versions, with pupils learning to 'intervene creatively' and become 'creative problem-solvers' and 'innovators'. Questions have been raised, however, as to whether the National Curriculum framework and examination criteria encourage creativity, or whether they constrain it by setting up procedures which pupils must follow – and which creative pupils find stifling (see Chapter 10 for further discussion of this issue).

Interestingly, the consultation papers for the review of the National Curriculum (QCA 1999a: 127) and the Secretary of State's published proposals (QCA 1999: 7) both recommended the compulsory study of food at Key Stage 3. The latter document stated: 'The study of food has been made compulsory at Key Stage 3 to improve pupils' knowledge of health and hygiene relating to food. Offset against these benefits are the resource implications for the few schools which currently do not include food technology at Key Stage 3' (p.7). (These schools are likely to be the boys' schools referred to earlier.) By the time the final National Curriculum Orders were published, this compulsion had been reduced to 'The government believes that schools should be encouraged to look for opportunities to teach both food and textiles …' (QCA 1999c: 17). What, or who, one wonders, occasioned this change of heart?

Another change, less welcomed, was that schools in England can now elect to 'disapply' the National Curriculum for Design and Technology (or Modern Foreign Languages or Science) for pupils at Key Stage 4 under the following conditions: if they want to provide more time for 'work-related learning'; if pupils need to study fewer subjects in order to consolidate and make progress in other subjects; if pupils have strengths in other subjects and want more time to specialize in their studies.

Teachers of design and technology once more have to reconsider what National Curriculum Design and Technology is meant to be, and how they can plan their teaching to be motivating and interesting to pupils, relevant to their lives, and meet the new requirements.

Wales

Up to 1995 Wales followed the English National Curriculum requirements. In 1995 it was decided, as noted earlier, that it would no longer be compulsory for Key Stage 4 pupils to study Design and Technology, which became an optional subject.

Then, in 2000, the Qualifications and Curriculum Authority for Wales (ACCAC) and the National Assembly for Wales published the first Welsh National Curriculum. This document, with the earlier English versions as its historical roots, now refers to the subject as 'technology (design and technology and information technology)', with separate Orders for the two elements. The subject remains compulsory in Key Stages 1–3, but not Key Stage 4.

The historical roots of the programmes can be seen in what is offered, but there is some variation, although no rationale is given to explain the perceived purpose of design and technology in the curriculum or the principles on which decisions were made. The Programme of Study for each Key Stage begins with a focus statement which briefly describes what pupils will be taught. Interestingly, the content of the Programmes of Study are set out in reverse order to that in the English versions, with knowledge and understanding appearing first, then designing skills and finally making skills. From Key Stage 3 the knowledge and understanding is subdivided into two: systems and control; structures and materials. These seem to sit more easily with the teaching of resistant materials and electronics, but pupils are required to undertake investigate and evaluation tasks, focused practical tasks and design-and-make products which, taken together, should use a range of materials including food, metal, plastics, textiles and timbers. Pupils are also required to use CAD and CAM and have health and safety training.

The Welsh National Curriculum also identifies 'common requirements', cross-curricular elements which all subjects are required to cover, and the Programmes of Study indicate graphically where design and technology may contribute to these.

Reflections

Over the years of development we see how the subject area emerged first as the development of groups of teachers in craft-related subjects. These teachers developed the subject to reflect what they saw as the important educational qualities of the subject, along with trying to relate it to the world outside school. The intervention of the government, through the National Curriculum, took this development out of teachers' hands and put it into those of 'experts' and then 'curriculum officers' in the various forms of government curriculum agencies. Teachers were placed in the situation of receiving and learning a new curriculum. In time they did take more ownership of this curriculum and consultation and subsequent revision tried to reflect this, as well as to make the assimilation process easier. What remains, however, is to see how subsequent growth and development reflect classroom practice and an understanding of the pupils' experience of the subject.

Notes

1   This section of the article is taken from an earlier more extensive account of the evolution of technology education (McCormick 1990a), a shortened version of which is published in McCormick, Murphy and Harrison (1992).
2   This section is based upon a previously published article (McCormick 1990b). Barnett (1992) and Medway (1992) also give background account and analyses of various stages in the creation of the National Curriculum for Technology.
3   In fact the Assessment of Performance Unit had defined technology as one of the areas of their curriculum model that would be tested (APU 1982).
4   One of the main arguments of Medway (1992) is that the overemphasis on design in the National Curriculum was a symptom of the divorce between the curriculum and real technology.

References

Archer, B. (1979) 'The three Rs', *Design Studies* 1(1): 17–20.

APU (Assessment of Performance Unit) (1982) *Understanding Design and Technology*, London, APU.

ASE (Association for Science Education) (1988) *Technology Education and Science in Schools*, Hatfield ASE.

Barnett, M. (1992) 'Technology, within the National Curriculum and elsewhere', in J. Beynon and H. Mackay, *Technological Literacy and the Curriculum*, London: Falmer Press, pp. 84–104.

DES (Department of Education and Science) (1985) *The Curriculum from 5 to 16*, Curriculum Matters 2, an HMI series, London: HMSO.

DES/WO (Department of Education and Science) (1988) *Interim Report of the Working Group for Design and Technology*, London: DES.

DES/WO (Department of Education and Science and the Welsh Office) (1989) *Design and Technology for Ages 5 to 16: Proposals of the Secretary of State for Education and Science and Secretary of State for Wales*, London: HMSO.

DES/WO (Department of Education and Science and the Welsh Office) (1990) *Technology in the National Curriculum*, London: HMSO.

DFE/WO (Department for Education and the Welsh Office) (1992) *Technology for Ages 5 to 16 (1992) Proposals of the Secretary of State*, London: HMSO.

East, M. (1980) *Home Economics: Past Present and Future*, Allyn and Bacon.

Eggleston, S.J. (1976) *Developments in Design Education*, London: Open Books.

Harrison, M. K. (1990) 'Science in technology: technology in science', in *Proceedings of the 3rd National Conference Design and Technology Education Research and Curriculum Development*, Loughborough: University of Technology, Department of Design and Technology.

HMI (Her Majesty's Inspectorate of Schools) (1992) *Technology at Key Stages 1, 2 and 3*, London: HMSO.

Jackson, G. (1992) *Technology and Home Economics as related to the School Curriculum 5–16*, Research Report, Sheffield City Polytechnic.

Jeffrey, J.R. (1990) 'Design methods in CDT', in *Journal of Art and Design Education* 9(1): 57–70.

Layton, D. (1973) *Science for the People*, London: Allen & Unwin.

McCormick, R. (1990a) 'The evolution of current practice in technology education', paper presented to NATO Advanced Research Workshop 'Integrating Advanced Technology into Technology Education', 8–12 October, Eindhoven, Netherlands.

McCormick, R. (1990b) 'Technology and the national curriculum: the creation of a 'subject' by committee?', *The Curriculum Journal* 1(1): 39–45.

McCormick, R. (1993) *Teaching and Learning Design*, PGCE Pamphlet, Milton Keynes: Open University.

McCormick, R., Murphy, P. and Harrison, M.E. (eds) (1992) *Teaching and Learning Technology*, London: Addison-Wesley.

McCulloch, G., Jenkins, E. and Layton, D. (1985) *Technological Revolution? The Politics of School Science and Technology in England and Wales since 1945*, Lewes: Falmer Press.

Medway, P. (1989) 'Issues in the theory and practice of technology education', *Studies in Science Education* 16: 1–23.

Medway, P. (1992) 'Constructions of technology: reflections on a new subject', in J. Beynon and H. Mackay, *Technological literacy and the curriculum*, London: Falmer Press, pp. 64–83.

NCC (National Curriculum Council) (1991a) *Non-Statutory Guidance for Design and Technology*, York, NCC.

NCC (National Curriculum Council) (1991b) *Implementing Design and Technology at Key Stage 3*, York, NCC.

NCC (National Curriculum Council) (1992) *National Curriculum Technology: The Case for Revising the Order*, York, NCC.

NSEAD (National Society for Education in Art and Design) (1990) 'Current issues in art and design education: the NSEAD response to the Report of the National Curriculum Working Group for Design and Technology', *Journal of Art and Design Education* 9(1): 23–37.

Penfold, J. (1988) *Craft, Design and Technology: Past, Present and Future*, Hanley: Trentham Books.

QCA (Qualifications and Curriculum Authority) (1999a) *The review of the national curriculum in England: The consultation materials*, QCA: London.

QCA (Qualifications and Curriculum Authority) (1999b) *The review of the national curriculum in England: The Secretary of State's proposals*, QCA: London.

QCA (Qualifications and Curriculum Authority) (1999c) *The national curriculum handbook for secondary teachers in England*, QCA: London.

RCA (Royal College of Art) (1989) *Design in General Education: The Report of an Enquiry Conducted by the Royal College of Art for the Secretary of State for Education and Science*, London, Royal College of Art.

Schools Council (1981) *Teacher's Master Manual*, Modular Courses in Technology, Nottingham, National Centre for School Technology, Trent Polytechnic/Olive & Boyd.

Smithers, A. and Robinson, P. (1992) *Technology in the National Curriculum: Getting it Right*, London: The Engineering Council.

Solomon, J. (1988) 'Science technology and social courses: tools for thinking about social issues', *International Journal of Science Education* 10(4): 379–87.

SSCR (Secondary Science Curriculum Review) (1987) *Better Science: Making it Relevant to Young People, Curriculum Guide 3*, London: Heinemann/Association for Science Education.

Steers, J. (1990) 'Design and Technology in the National Curriculum', *Journal of Art and Design Education* 9(1): 9–22.

Thistlewood, D. (1989) 'The formation of the NSEAD: a dialectical advance for British art and design education', *Journal of Art and Design Education* 8(2): 135–52.

Za'rour, G. I. (1987) 'Forces hindering the introduction of STS education in schools', in K. Riquarts (ed.) *Technology Education: Science-Technology-Society. Science and Technology Education and the Quality of Life*, Vol. 2. Papers submitted to the International IOSTE symposium on world trends in science and technology education, Kiel University, West Germany: Institut für die Pädagogik der Naturwissenschaften.

4   Links across
Design and Technology

Marion Rutland

Chapter 3 described how Design and Technology has developed by drawing together different subjects. This chapter was specially commissioned as little has, as yet, been written on the general principles and issues which apply across the different material areas. Here we look at the commonalities and differences across these different areas, with a specific emphasis on Key Stages 3 and 4. Whilst reading this chapter think of how your own specialist area contributes to these general principles and issues, and how the different areas can build on their commonalities to give pupils a coherent Design and Technology experience. Many of the aspects covered in this chapter are dealt with more fully in other chapters, with this one serving to introduce the ideas and pull them together.

Introduction

Although Design and Technology is composed of several contributing areas there are common themes across these areas, which link them and make them coherent. This chapter explores some of these themes in order to help to develop an understanding of what the subject is.

It can be argued that if we, as teachers, fail to acknowledge:

- the coherent nature of Design and Technology
- that it is essentially a practical subject (DfE 1995)
- that 'design and technology prepares pupils to participate in tomorrow's rapidly changing technologies' (DfEE/QCA 1999: 15)

we could be in danger of losing the very essence of the teaching of the subject, and eventually of losing the subject area from the school curriculum.

The document *The Curriculum from 5–16* (DES 1985) included technology as an area of experience and learning and as a particular form of *problem-solving* concerned with bringing about change, of designing in order to effect control. Black and Harrison (1985) thought technology was not mere academic study, rather it was concerned with the human capacity for action, and was used when practical solutions to problems were needed. Ritchie (1995) emphasized that humans have from earliest times tried to control the world around them in order to survive and enhance the quality of their existence. They have done this by imagining new possibilities, putting their ideas into action and evaluating the outcomes. He, together with Johnsey (1998), saw the process of problem-solving as the essence of Design and Technology in the school curriculum.

Owen-Jackson (2000) argues that technology has both technical and social aspects. She suggests that technology can be seen through a vocational perspective as 'a competence', requiring a knowledge of things and how they work. On the other hand, it can be seen as 'a social phenomenon' worthy of study for its impact on the development of society. This reflects the view that design and technology is concerned both with *things* and with *people*. When a product is designed and made, whatever the material area, it requires technical knowledge, understanding and skills and the ability to consider the needs and background of the individuals using the product.

National Curriculum Design and Technology

The introduction of National Curriculum Technology in 1990 was a landmark, in that it became a compulsory subject which centred on the processes of designing and making. The previous chapter presents a fuller discussion of the development of National Curriculum Technology.

The latest National Curriculum Orders for Design and Technology in England (DfEE/QCA 1999: 15–20) state that:

> The subject calls for pupils to become autonomous and creative problem solvers, as individuals and members of teams.
>
> Through design and technology, all pupils can become discriminating and informed users of products and become innovators.
>
> They develop their understanding of designing and making by investigating products and finding out about the work of professional designers and manufacturing industries.

Design and Technology has its own distinctive knowledge, understanding and skills, but pupils are also required to apply the skills, knowledge and understanding from other subjects, including Art and Design, Mathematics and Science. It is stressed that Design and Technology has a capacity to motivate and stimulate pupils to develop their creativity and inventiveness to develop products to meet precise specifications. Solutions to initial problems may succeed in different ways: some may function well yet lack aesthetic appeal and some will be pleasing to the eye, yet not function as they were intended. The need for balance between function and aesthetic appeal, combined with the ability to design for themselves or a range of other people, presents pupils with many opportunities to improve and develop their products. These principles apply across all the focus areas of Design and Technology, including electronic products, food technology, graphic products, industrial technology, resistant materials technology, systems and control technology and textiles technology.

Design and Technology capability

How do pupils learn in this subject area? Banks (1995) sees technology as an active study, involving the purposeful pursuit of a task to some form of resolution that results in improvement (for someone) in the made world. Kimbell (Kimbell *et al.* 1996, and see Chapter 2) sees an essential difference between technological understanding and technology capability. He considers that *capability* is more complex than *understanding,* as it is a combination of ability and motivation that enables creative development. Capability bridges the gap between what is and what might be, taking into account human desires, dissatisfaction with technical constraints, and possible outcomes.

If we accept the idea that understanding is necessary, but that capability is a more complex activity or process then we might arrive at the following:

- Design and technology capability is knowledge and understanding of properties of materials, components and processes, and involves the ability to select and use the appropriate tools and materials to explore these properties for developing products. This statement applies to all the focus areas, though the materials, components and processes used will be specific to each area.
- Design and technology capability is demonstrated by using designing skills with the appropriate knowledge and understanding, and selecting the making skills needed to develop products. Many of the designing skills, for example brainstorming, attribute analysis, using mood boards, writing design briefs and specifications and modelling, are generic but others, and some making skills, will be specific to the individual areas.
- Product design and development occurs when pupils design and make by selecting materials, making design decisions, using making skills, modifying and evaluating. Such elements are common for product design (Figure 4.1), regardless of the material(s), processes and skills that pupils use.

Capability is discussed further in Chapter 7.

Problem-solving

A common question in the past has been, 'Does an understanding of the concepts of problem-solving and the design process help us when developing products in all of the specialist areas?' In addition some have asked, 'Are there specialisms that do not fit in?' Fisher (1989) sees problem-solving as involving critical or analytical thinking and creative thinking, which generates possible solutions, together with doing or acting for some purpose. The development and realization of a product is problem-solving, in that it requires critical and creative thinking to generate a range of ideas to fit the criteria of the brief before one idea is explored, extended, refined and finally developed.

However, when general problem-solving is used to deliver Design and Technology a number of issues arise:

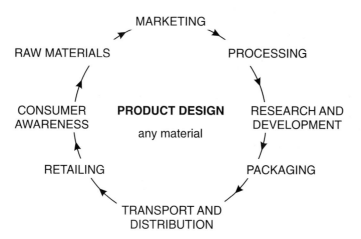

Figure 4.1 Elements of product design

Children may:

- lack the knowledge and understanding to carry through an activity
- only centre on their own experience
- not be able to move forward to new experiences
- not be able to think in a technological way if they are working in isolation at general problem-solving level.

Teacher may:

- be unsure of his/her role (when does he/she structure, intervene, facilitate?)
- be unsure of the optimum number of children that can be taught effectively by this approach
- feel de-skilled and unable to cope with the need for a range of knowledge and expertise
- be unsure how he/she can accommodate all the pupils' needs.

When teaching:

- where and when is the time to teach the required knowledge and skills?
- how can resources be managed effectively?
- how can the activity be broken into manageable pieces?
- there is a time element: problem-solving can take a long time.

The messages are that:

- there is a need for a balance between problem-solving and the acquisition of knowledge and skills
- activities need to be broken into manageable pieces for teaching and learning purposes.

Despite these apparent concerns, problem-solving is a way in which pupils can learn effectively across all the focus areas. Problem-solving is discussed more fully in Chapter 8.

The design process and designing

Early models of Design and Technology activity, and the Orders for Technology (DES 1990), provided a linear model of the design process, which started with a problem and progressed through linear steps to a final solution which is then evaluated. In practice, this model proved to need refinement as evaluation is carried out not just at the end of the process but is part of a continual process of refinement and modification. The linear process thus becomes a 'loop' or circle, as shown in Figure 4.2.

Examples of designing activities can be found in all the focus areas, including:

- In food technology pupils may develop a low cost, high energy product to sell at a student union bar. A range of dishes using different foods would be developed, made and evaluated for their cost, energy value and appeal, before one dish is chosen for further development as a prototype and taken through to the manufacturing stage. The focus areas of food and graphics may be combined to design and make a snack food together with promotional materials (Nuffield 2000).
- In resistant materials, a design brief could be based on the theme of 'Petshop parade' where pupils design and make a mechanical toy, to be sold in pet shops, that will amuse and intrigue (Nuffield 2000).
- In systems and control, pupils might work on the design brief 'Smart-card security'. This could combine control with graphics, to design and construct a smart-card-based security system to meet an identified need, for example, a model for a security door or a secure jewellery box. Alternatively, pupils could design and make an educational toy to meet an identified need, for example, a buzzer, sensor or beeper to control the movement of a toy or to be integrated into a board game (Nuffield 2000).
- In textiles technology the brief could be to design and make a simple personal carrying device (Nuffield 2000). This could be interpreted as bags used to carry particular items, such as lunch, gym kit, homework, CDs, etc.

For all of these products, pupils progress through the same stages of the design process, which is a constant process of investigation, development, evaluation and modification.

It is important to remember that a *creative* practical activity requires the interaction of mind and hand. The Assessment and Performance Unit (APU 1989) devised a way of looking at Design and Technology, where the interactive process between mind and hand was central. The Unit concentrated on the *thinking* and *decision-making* processes that took place and were more interested in *why* and *how* pupils choose to do things rather than *what* it is they choose to do. The APU saw

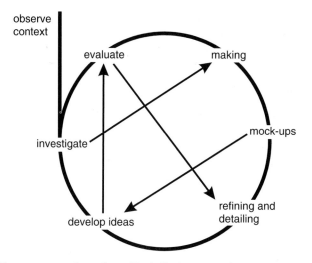

Figure 4.2 The interactive design loop (Kimbell 1986, in Banks 1994)

the essence of Design and Technology as the interaction of hand and mind inside and outside the head. Conceptual understanding and practical skills are both needed and are dependent on each other, so ideas conceived in the mind can be expressed in a concrete form that can be evaluated and further modified. (This idea is shown graphically in Figure 2.1.)

If pupils follow a recipe from a book, use a trade pattern to make a waistcoat or use a 'kit' to make a mechanical toy or an alarm system, they are simply copying what other people have designed and made. This involves little individual thinking; pupils are engaged in rote, mechanistic learning with little or no understanding of the concepts and knowledge underpinning the activity. Such pupils are not designing, being creative, thinking and making decisions: they are only *making*. It is not a problem-solving activity as it does not involve actionable knowledge, the interaction between thinking and doing or the intermeshing of thought and action (Watts 1994). Design and Technology requires pupils to be creative, to design and make their own products based on a sound knowledge of the working properties of materials and processes.

When working in any one of the focus areas pupils are using a range of knowledge about materials, understanding of concepts and designing and making skills. These come not only from the sciences, arts and mathematics but also from other areas of the curriculum. They are using the generic skills and processes to generate a range of design ideas, making design decisions and using specific skills to design and make quality products. The design process is central to designing and making in all focus areas, as are the stages of product design (see Figure 4.1). Knowledge and understanding of different materials will continue to develop from Year 7, to exploring them in greater depth in Year 8 and on to critically selecting materials in Year 9 (QCA 2000).

Thinking

The teaching of thinking skills has been identified in the National Curriculum (1999) as an important aspect of general education. The capability to 'think' is essential in Design and Technology, in order to design and develop new ideas. Our knowledge of thinking comes from two distinct traditions. Philosophy emphasizes the study of 'critical' thinking through the analysis of argument and the application of logic. Psychology looks at the study of the mechanisms of the mind and cognitive psychologists tend to emphasize creative thinking (Fisher 1989). Thinking involves 'critical' and 'creative' aspects of the mind, both in the use of reason and the generation of ideas. Fisher sees the aspects of the 'thinking' child as:

- psychological – the emotional child
- philosophical – the reasoning child
- biological – the physical child
- sociological – the social child.

All aspects have an important role to play in the process.

In Design and Technology both forms of thinking, critical and creative, are essential. A number of writers have suggested that success in the design process and the area of designing, or creative problem-solving, requires the application of the two very different modes of *divergent* and *convergent* thinking (Dodd 1983; Eggleston 1992). The former opens up the design brief and generates a range of ideas, i.e. it is creative, and the latter critically analyses and develops a chosen idea to a successful solution. The successful resolution of a design task involves the interplay of both modes.

Creativity

It can be argued that the ability to develop innovative and creative ideas is the most difficult concept to address for designers and teachers. In the educational arena, the Robinson Report, *All Our Futures*, considers that a national strategy for creative and cultural education is essential to unlock the potential of every young person. Creativity is defined as an 'imaginative activity fashioned so as to produce outcomes that are both original and of value' (DfEE 1999: 25).

In the context of Design and Technology, based on the above definition, designing and making is certainly a creative activity. Pupils 'learn to think and intervene creatively to improve the quality of life. ... They must look for needs, wants and opportunities and respond to them by developing a range of ideas and making products and systems' (DfEE/QCA 1999: 134). Whatever the material area they are working in, when pupils are asked to design and make we hope that this will help them to develop their creative skills.

Amabile (1996), an American psychologist, describes a framework for creativity which includes the inter-linked components of:

- domain or area skills of knowledge
- experience
- technical skills
- cognitive skills
- task motivation
- attitudes
- creative relevant skills, such as training and personality traits.

She links the framework to a process of problem or task identification, preparation, response generation, response validation and communication and outcome with the opportunity for feedback – a process that bears a striking similarity to the design process we work with in Design and Technology. Her original model (1983) was one of the first to take into account the combined effects of cognitive, personality, motivational and social influences on the creative process. Of particular interest to teachers, it emphasized the previously neglected role of motivation and social-environmental influences.

Elements of creativity

It would seem that there are four essential elements of creativity that Design and Technology teachers need to be aware of:

1   the person – early work on creativity from 1950 to 1980 focused on identifying a set of personality traits, abilities or characteristics of a creative person (Guilford 1950; Torrance 1962). Later work (Gardner 1982, 1983, 1993) focused on the cognitive, intellectual aspects of creativity. Gardner proposed a theory of seven (now eight) intelligences, i.e. 'multiple intelligences' of equal importance. He argues that an 'intelligence' enables a person to solve problems or make products that are of consequence in a particular cultural setting or community' (1993: 15)
2   product, i.e. one that is novel, original and appropriate (Amabile 1983)
3   domain, i.e. a set of opportunities within an area that has specialist knowledge and skills (Csikszentmihalyi 1990)
4   situation, environment and context, i.e. the social, environmental and cultural influences on creativity (Amabile 1996).

Creativity is the interaction between these elements with each one playing an important role for the Design and Technology teacher supporting creative activity in the classroom. Sternberg and Lubart (1999) argue that there are six resources needed for creativity: aspects of intelligence, knowledge, thinking styles, personality, motivation and the environment.

Developing creativity

So, we think we can identify the essential elements required to develop creativity in our pupils, but how do we use this knowledge successfully in the classroom?

There are some people who believe that creativity is a matter of semi-mystical talent that some people have and others do not. de Bono (1992) argues that this is confusion between artistic creativity, which is often not creative, and the ability to change concepts and perceptions. Fortunately for teachers there are people who agreed that creativity is teachable, usually through acquiring techniques relevant to particular parts of a creative problem-solving process (Torrance 1987; de Bono 1992).

There are a growing number of people, including de Bono (1992), who think that creative thinking skills can be improved through direct effort and attention. He sees a need for systematic techniques: for example, 'brain-sailing' or brainstorming, which are deliberate, controlled processes. He sees creativity as the way in which a self-organizing system integrates new information and uses it with old structures, patterns, concepts, and perceptions. The essence of creativity is how perceptions set up in one way can suddenly be reconfigured in another way. Humour is important as it indicates better than any other mental behaviour the nature of the information system that gives rise to perception (de Bono 1992).

Pupils can be encouraged to be creative if they take part in lessons where they use different strategies to generate a wide range of ideas (QCA 2000). These strategies can be grouped into six categories (Nuffield 2000) with a sequence of increasingly demanding tasks across a Year and a Key Stage:

1   investigating a context, writing design briefs and specifications
2   stimulating a wide range of ideas
3   developing aesthetic capability
4   modelling and testing ideas
5   presentation skills
6   evaluating products.

These groups include generic designing strategies such as:

Year 7

- using image boards
- brainstorming
- capturing and manipulating images

Year 8

- writing interview questions
- attribute analysis
- modelling with spreadsheets

Year 9

- evaluating outcomes – is it appropriate?
- modelling with CAD.

There are, in addition to these generic strategies, others which are more area-specific (Nuffield 2000). These include:

- drawing quick 3D views
- crating
- using nets
- using systems diagrams
- understanding feedback.

Lateral thinking – a tool for creative designing

Lateral thinking is when new thoughts or ideas are generated as an 'offshoot' or alongside the linear processes of thoughts generally followed. The term 'lateral' refers to moving sideways or off at a tangent across the established patterns instead of moving along them in a normal way (de Bono 1992: 15).

de Bono (1992: 313) has suggested a number of strategies that teachers could use to develop creativity in the classroom. They are:

- six thinking hats – each of six fundamental modes of thinking is given a hat of different colour. These can be switched at any moment by request or design.
- the creative pause – a brief pause to consider possible alternative and other ways of doing things.
- challenge – a creative challenge is the most fundamental process in lateral thinking, i.e. is this the only way of doing things? It also challenges the 'continuity' – i.e. no one has bothered to think about it, through complacency or because trapped by a sequence of our experiences. Basically it is a search for alternatives.
- the concept fan – this is useful for 'achievement' thinking and includes problem-solving and task completion. The concepts are used to cascade further alternatives.
- concepts – these are general methods or ways of doing things, expressed as broad, blurry, non-specific ways. It is useful sometimes to pull back from 'ideas' to discover the 'concepts' behind ideas.
- provocation and movement – these are needed to cut across accepted patterns. Movement is an active operation to move an idea forward.
- arising provocations – any statement, remark event not necessarily intended.
- escape provocations – the thinker looks at any point taken for granted and escapes, cancels, drops or does without it.
- stepping-stone provocation – an established set of provocations used without considering their effect.
- the random input – start at a different point to open new patterns. i.e. random words from a list.
- movement – an active mental operation. There may be general willingness to move forward but it is systematic and formal.

- the stratal – a sensitizing technique. Put together five unconnected statements about the situations to see what new idea emerges, i.e. on slips of paper to be drawn.
- the filament technique – basic requirements are listed and considered to create extended 'filaments' or strands. The context or creative focus of the problem is ignored.

de Bono's strategies can be used in different ways in Design and Technology, in any of the material areas. For example, when asking pupils to design for different user groups, in Year 7 they could design and make for themselves, in Year 8 when their knowledge, understanding and skills have developed they could concentrate on designing for clients, and in Year 9, they could concentrate on designing for markets (QCA 2000). Some of the above techniques could be used to help pupils generate ideas that they might not otherwise have thought of. Chapter 12 provides further thoughts on creativity in Design and Technology.

Design and Technology as a value-laden activity

Design and Technology is about the realization of appropriate solutions to human problems, with value judgements being made throughout the designing and making process. There is no value-free, neutral judgement (Riggs 1991). Pacey (1983) explored three aspects of technology, which he identified as *technical* – knowledge, skills and tools; *organizational* – economic or industrial; and *cultural* – values, ethics, beliefs and creativity.

As teachers we need to ask ourselves:

- What do we mean by values?
- What part do values play in Design and Technology?
- Are they important?
- How do we teach them?
- Should we teach them?

A number of writers have attempted to outline values that are relevant for consideration in Design and Technology (Layton 1992; Barlex 1993; Prime 1993; Martin 1996). They include:

- Economic – what are the costs, energy, labour, materials used?
- Moral and ethical – is the product likely to frighten, shock or offend anyone?
- Aesthetic – is the product pleasing to the visual senses?
- Social – is it acceptable to the target audience?
- Cultural – are the materials used and the final product appropriate for the people or country?
- Environmental – does the product take into account the use of non-renewable resources? What effect might it have on the immediate environment? Can it be recycled?

- Political – what are the political influences in developing a product?

Questions we would expect pupils to think about include:

- Whose needs are being met?
- What materials will be used?
- What methods of processing will be used?
- What are the costs involved?
- Is it culturally acceptable to the target group?
- Is it environmentally friendly?
- Who benefits from the activity – who are the 'winners'?
- Who lost out because of the activity – who are the 'losers'?

Considering values is an essential aspect of teaching Design and Technology. Each material area provides a range of interesting contexts in which to discuss and explore key issues. For example:

- in resistant materials, a knuckle-duster, mouse trap, pipe rack or ashtray might all seem to be technically sound products, but are they acceptable in society today?
- in textiles, investigating the traditional fabrics and patterns and the production of clothes in developing countries is a rich aesthetic, cultural, social and ethical context
- food introduces a range of issues including religion, culture, ethics, health and the environment.

Considering values is a strategy for making pupils, as future citizens, sensitive to the social, cultural, economic and environmental implications of the products designed and made. Values are discussed further in Chapter 18.

ICT

The increasing access to communications technology, for example, the internet and the National Grid for Learning, has a particular relevance for Design and Technology as it can provide a rich source of data for research and enables pupils to enhance their learning. Important skills which can be developed through using ICT include:

- interpreting, exploring and analysing information
- developing and displaying data and using computer modelling
- evaluating the role of software and ICT (QCA 2000).

There are many opportunities in all the material areas of Design and Technology to use generic software, for example:

- word processing to write reports which include pictures produced with a digital camera or scanner during the designing and making process
- Desktop Publishing (DTP) to present design thinking, using paint packages to illustrate folders, produce marketing materials and present design ideas
- spreadsheets for modelling activities, such as costing exercises, presenting data as graphs and complex production charts
- databases to capture data on, for example, the properties of materials, for analysis and retrieval
- multimedia for authoring on-screen presentations including sound and animation
- computer-aided design (CAD) to explore, develop, model and communicate design ideas using 2D Design and Pro DeskTop to design and produce 2D and 3D products
- computer aided manufacture (CAM) where design ideas produced, for example by Pro DeskTop, can be electronically sent to computer-controlled manufacturing machines such as through a lathe, cutter/plotter, milling machine or sewing machine
- electronics and control software and equipment to model and test design ideas and control systems, for example, printed circuit boards (PCB) which can be incorporated into other products.

It is important to remember that though generic software can be used in many ways across the different areas, subject specific software and equipment are also available. These include nutritional dietary analysis packages in food technology, a microcontroller on a single integrated circuit (chip), often called a Programmable Interface Controller (PIC) in resistant materials/control and systems, software such as 'Fitting Sew' CAD/CAM for drafting and making a sewing pattern block, and 'DesignaKnit' for designing knitwear in textiles.

Systems and control

An understanding of systems or 'systems thinking' helps pupils to understand complex situations and design complex products. A system is made up of a collection of parts that work together to do a job, such as control a switch for a light or bell, control the temperature of a gas fire or boiler, alter the settings of a music centre, control the processes of a drinks dispenser or those on a production line in a factory. The parts, or subsystems, of the system, which might be objects or people, are connected together within a system boundary. A systems diagram shows how the subsystems are connected together to make the complete system. It explains how a designer will break down the system into subsystems to see how inputs and outputs need to be arranged.

The fast food outlet example in Figure 4.3 illustrates how the *output* of one subsystem becomes the *input* of another, creating *feedback* of information. For example, if there is an increase or decrease in the number of people buying food, there is feedback from the service area to the cooking area telling them to produce

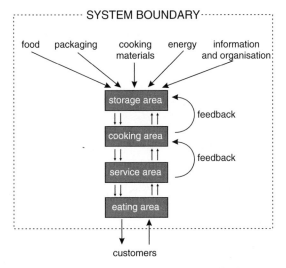

Figure 4.3 Systems diagram of a fast food service outlet (Nuffield Design and Technology Project)

more or less food. This type of feedback is called a *closed-loop system*, again a familiar control term. Additional terms used in industry are introduced, including *operator* and *user interface, human and machine interface.*

Conclusion

Having considered a range of issues in the teaching and learning of Design and Technology, to explore the commonalties and differences across the different areas, it is important to remember the advice given by Ofsted on good-quality teaching and learning in the subject (DFE 1995). In their inspections, observed standards of teaching are considered to be high in the following circumstances:

Teachers

- are enthusiastic about their subject
- are confident in own subject knowledge.

The lesson

- is well planned
- has clear objectives which are shared with pupils
- involves teachers observing pupils at work
- reflects teachers' knowledge of their pupils
- includes ideas suggested by teachers to stimulate pupils
- sets realistic deadlines
- provides opportunities for pupils to reflect
- encourages pupil to review and refine their work.

The teacher

- encourages pupils to try out ideas
- gives clear and carefully timed demonstrations of practical skills
- builds on past experiences
- takes opportunities to extend pupils' subject knowledge
- carries out monitoring year by year, with an analysis of the rate of progress to aid future planning
- uses assessment to identify strengths and weaknesses of teaching to inform future planning.

Much progress has been made since the introduction of Technology into the National Curriculum in 1990. There is now a better understanding of the common, unifying elements of the subject and an increased appreciation of the differences across the different contributing areas. However, the outcomes for the pupils as outlined above are fundamentally the same across all the areas of Design and Technology.

References

Amabile, T. (1983) *The Social Psychology of Creativity*, New York: Springer-Verlag.
Amabile, T. (1996) *Creativity in Context*, USA: Westview.
APU (1989) *The Assessment of Performance in Design and Technology*, London: SEAC.
Banks, F. (ed.) (1994) *Teaching Technology*, London: Routledge.
Barlex, D. (1993) 'The Nuffield approach to values in design and technology', *Design and Technology Teaching* 26(1).
Black, P. and Harrison, G. (1985) *In Place of Confusion: Technology and Science in the School Curriculum*, London: Nuffield–Chelsea Curriculum Trust.
Csikszentmihalyi, M. (1990) *Flow: The Psychology of Optimal Experience*, New York: HarperCollins.
de Bono, E. (1992) *Serious Creativity*, London: Harper.
DES (1985) *The Curriculum from 5–16*, London: HMSO.
DES (1990) *Technology in the National Curriculum*, London: HMSO.
DFE (1995) *Design and Technology in the National Curriculum*, London: HMSO.
DFE (1995) *Design and Technology – Characteristics of Good Practice in Secondary Schools*, London: HMSO.
DfEE (1999) *All our Futures: Creativity, Culture and Education*, London: DfEE.
DfEE/QCA (1999) *Design and Technology: The National Curriculum for England*, London: HMSO.
Dodd, T. (1983) *Design and Technology in the School Curriculum*, London: Hodder.
Eggleston, J. (1992) *Teaching Design and Technology*, Buckingham: Open University Press.
Fisher, R. (1987) *Problem Solving in Primary Schools*, Oxford: Blackwell.
Gardner, H. (1982) *Art, Mind and Brain*, New York: BasicBooks.
Gardner, H. (1983) *Frames of Mind*, New York: BasicBooks.
Gardner, H. (1993) *Multiple Intelligences: The Theory in Practice*, New York: BasicBooks.
Guilford, J. P. (1950) 'Creativity', *American Psychologist* 5: 444–54.
Johnsey, R. (1998) *Exploring Primary Design and Technology*, London: Cassells.

Kimbell, R., Stables, K. and Green, R. (1996) *Understanding Practice in Design and Technology*, Buckingham: Open University Press.

Layton, D. (1992) 'Values in Design and Technology', in Budgett-Meakin, C. (ed.) *Make the Future Work*, London: Longman.

Martin, M. (1996) 'Valuing products and applications', in *IDATER 96*, University of Loughborough.

Nuffield (2000) *Nuffield Design and Technology 11–14 Student's Book, Teacher's File*, (2nd edn), Harlow: Longman.

Owen-Jackson, G. (2000) *Learning to Teach Design and Technology in the Secondary School*, London: RoutledgeFalmer.

Pacey, A. (1983) *The Culture of Technology*, London: Blackwell.

Prime, G. (1993) 'Values in technology: approaches to learning', *Design and Technology Teaching* 26(1).

QCA (2000) *Design and Technology: A Scheme of Work for Key Stage 3*, London: QCA.

Ritchie, R. (1995) *Primary Design and Technology: A Process for Learning*, London: David Fulton.

Riggs, A. (1991) 'Values and technology education', *Design and Technology Teaching* 24(1).

Sternberg, R. and Lubart, T. (1995) *Defying the Crowd: Cultivating Creativity in a Culture of Conformity*, New York: The Free Press.

Torrance, E. P. (1962) *Guiding Creative Talent*, Englewood Cliffs, NJ: Prentice Hall.

Torrance, E. P. (1987) 'Can we teach children to think creatively?', in S. G. Isaksen (ed.) *Frontiers of Creative Research: Beyond the Basics*, Buffalo, NY: Bearly, pp. 189–204.

Watts, M. (1994) *Problem Solving in Science and Technology*, London: David Fulton Press.

5   Pupils' attitudes and perceptions towards Design and Technology

Dave Hendley

The research discussed in this chapter was undertaken by the author, with colleagues, over a period of five years following the introduction of Design and Technology as a statutory subject in the National Curriculum. They sought to investigate the attitudes and perceptions of pupils in Key Stage 2 (Year 6) and Key Stage 3 (Year 9) to Design and Technology, and to determine whether or not the introduction of a compulsory and pre-defined curriculum had any effect on pupils' attitudes. The work began in 1991 and their findings have contributed to our understanding of the subject from the perspective of pupils.

Introduction

There has been very little methodical investigation into pupils' attitudes to technology. Earlier research in this subject has been carried out by Smail and Kelly (1984a, 1984b), Nash *et al.* (1984), Whyte (1986), Moore (1987), Grant and Harding (1987), Ormerod and Waller (1988), Woolnough (1990), McCarthy and Moss (1990). Interestingly, all of these showed that girls were less inclined to study technology later in their school careers, when it was an optional subject, even though some research has shown that girls enjoy the subject as much as boys in the first three years of secondary education (McCarthy and Moss 1990). One conclusion is that career prospects for girls are not as high in technological areas and so girls will drop this subject in favour of those they perceive will give them 'better' job prospects. This is reinforced by Nash *et al.* (1984), who found that the factors which influenced the choice of technology at 14+ were parents and the pupils' career interests. Ormerod and Waller (1988) also found similar results. Much of the research, however, has combined science and technology, with the emphasis on the former. The Girls Into Science and Technology (GIST) project (Whyte 1986), for example, showed that the greatest discouragement to girls arose from the 'masculine' image of science and technology.

Kelly's (1988) research into pupils' options for the final two years of compulsory schooling showed that pupils opt for subjects mainly because of usefulness in getting a job, interest in the subject and ability in the subject. There was very little difference between boys and girls.

McCarthy and Moss (1990) carried out their research in one school in Wales, prior to the introduction of the National Curriculum in Design and Technology. They found that the choice of CDT at 14+ was dependent upon career choice; that value of the subject was perceived as greater by boys than girls; that girls found the subject to be more difficult than boys found it; and that Design and Technology was perceived as being intellectually more demanding than CDT.

Woolnough (1990) found that boys had a more favourable attitude to CDT than girls; that girls had a more unfavourable view of technology and its effects on the environment than boys; that those who had a member of the family with a job involving technology had a more favourable attitude to it than those who did not; that those who had a hobby or pastime with a technological aspect had less unfavourable views of it than those who did not; that those who needed technology in order to go on to their chosen course in higher education had a more favourable attitude to it than those who did not; and that those who had nine or more GCSE passes at Grade C or higher had a less unfavourable view of technology (and its effects on the environment) than those who had fewer.

Research into pupils' perceptions and their subject preferences at age 14 years reported that girls are less likely to want to continue with technology post 14 years (Rennie 1987). Nash *et al.* (1984) also reported that girls were unlikely to choose technology post 14 years due to the fact that they were 'ignorant' of the subject. The studies by McCarthy and Moss (1990, 1994) both concentrated on one element of technology, namely CDT. Their results indicated that pupils perceived the usefulness of the subject as one that would help them gain employment and that enjoyment of the subject is a major factor. The research carried out by Hendley *et al.* (1995, 1996) is the first major investigation into pupils' attitudes and perceptions towards Design and Technology as a statutory curriculum subject for all pupils from 5 to 16 years (5–14 years in Wales).

The Swansea Research

The research is divided into three distinct phases. The first phase was part of a wider project designed to investigate the attitudes of pupils in South Wales to Mathematics, English, Science and Design and Technology. The pupils who took part were selected from Key Stage 3, specifically Year 9 (age 13–14 years). Thirty-four schools and 4,263 pupils took part, representing 15.3 per cent of the total population of school children of this age in Wales (Welsh Office 1993). We can therefore generalize from this sample to the whole of Wales.

The second phase took a more qualitative approach and interviews were carried out with Year 9 pupils to determine which aspects of technology they liked best and least and whether or not they intended to opt for the subject in Year 10 (Hendley *et al.* 1996).

Drawing on the interview data, in the third stage it was decided to conduct a cross-phase study into pupil perceptions of what makes a good Design and Technology pupil. The target groups were pupils at the end of Key Stage 2 (Year 6) and those at the end of Key Stage 3 (Year 9) (Hendley and Lyle 1996).

Phase 1   Attitudes to Design and Technology

The first stage of the study was carried out with 1,282 pupils in nine comprehensive schools at the end of Year 8. All the pupils in the sample were asked to complete an attitude questionnaire. This asked them to register their responses to 48 statements about Design and Technology on a five-point scale from 'strongly agree' to 'strongly disagree'.

When the responses were analysed the statements which produced the strongest positive (strongly agree) response overall, from both boys and girls were:

- I like creating things in Design and Technology.
- I like Design and Technology because I really enjoy making things.
- Learning about computers is important.
- It is very satisfying to make something in Design and Technology.
- Design and Technology lessons are a waste of time.
- I find making things a waste of time.
- I hate working with tools in Design and Technology.

As can be seen, even though all the statements above produced strongly positive responses, some of the statements themselves are negative. In each case, boys' statements were generally more positive than girls'.

When analysed from a boys' perspective, the statements which produced the strongest positive response were:

- I find making things a waste of time.
- Learning about computers is important.
- I enjoy learning how to use machines in technology.
- I like creating things in Design and Technology.

When analysed from a girls' perspective, the statements which produced the strongest positive response were:

- I find making things a waste of time.
- I like creating things in Design and Technology.
- I enjoy choosing what I am going to make in Design and Technology.
- Design and Technology lessons are a waste of time.
- I haven't learnt anything new in Design and Technology this year.

Significantly, the statement that produced the strongest attitude in boys and girls strikes right to the heart of Design and Technology: if pupils find making things a waste of time it does not augur well for the subject.

The greatest differences between boys and girls were revealed in the following statements:

- I'm not very good at working with the machines and hand tools and I wish I didn't have to.

- I hate working with tools in Design and Technology.
- Learning about computers is important.
- I enjoy learning how to use machines in technology.
- I'm no good at Design and Technology.
- I hate making things because I'm useless.

In all these statements, boys were significantly more positive about Design and Technology than girls. In fact, in only one case was the response of the girls more positive than boys:

- I think we should have fewer Design and Technology lessons each week.

The statements producing the most negative responses (strongly disagree) overall were:

- I enjoy evaluating the work we have done.
- I like having the whole afternoon for Design and Technology.
- The problems they give you in Design and Technology are too difficult.
- I'm often bored in Design and Technology.
- I'm no good at Design and Technology.
- I would give up Design and Technology if I could.

In all these cases, girls were more negative than boys.

Certain sections of the scale were identified as having some common elements which reflected part of the spirit of the Attainment Targets in the Standing Orders. They were classed as: Designing; Making; Evaluating. In each of these groupings, boys' attitudes were more positive than those of the girls.

The numbers of pupils completing the questionnaire in each school were small and so the results school-by-school are less reliable. However, in two schools, the overall pattern of boys having a more positive attitude than girls was reversed. This is interesting because it indicates that general patterns of gender divisions in relation to attitude to technology are not universal. There is scope for more research to be undertaken to investigate various school practices in the teaching of technology in terms of their effect on boys' and girls' responses to the subject.

Further analysis revealed seven factors, six of which reflected some aspect of Design and Technology. The strongest factor which emerged was enjoyment (or not!) of the subject. Of the others, groups of statements relating to designing, making, research and perceived ability emerged.

Phase 2 Pupil perceptions of Design and Technology

Twenty-three boys and twenty-four girls were interviewed. They represented the complete spectrum of opinion from the questionnaire. The pupils were asked about the following:

- their three favourite and least favourite subjects in the curriculum
- the aspects of Design and Technology liked best and least
- their feelings about whether they would opt for technology if it were not in the compulsory curriculum in Key Stage 4, their ambitions after Year 11 and in 'ten or twenty years' time'.

Analyses of the results were carried out by overall score, then by gender.

Best and least liked subjects

Overall, Design and Technology came out second to English as best liked subject, above both sciences and Mathematics. When analysed by gender, boys liked Design and Technology best; girls placed the subject second to English.

When they were asked why they liked Design and Technology various reasons were given. The most common responses were about enjoyment of the subject and enjoying the teaching of the subject.

Design and Technology was most disliked by pupils who have a low attitude to the subject. The reasons for pupils disliking the subject can be grouped into dislike of the teacher, pupils considering themselves to be 'no good' at the subject, boredom, no use in getting a job, work in Design and Technology never being finished and comments about dislike of cookery (*sic*) and textiles (*sic*).

Aspects of Design and Technology liked best and least

When asked this question, pupils' responses broadly fell into three categories, relating to:

- practical skills /manufacturing
- drawing/graphics
- designing/creativity.

More girls than boys (approximately 3:2) made comments about enjoying learning practical skills. Boys' enjoyment of practical skills was fairly evenly spread across the disciplines within the subject. However, girls' enjoyment of practical skills is more slanted towards work with food and textiles, with work with wood coming third. A clear gender difference emerges in enjoyment of practical work in food with girls being far more positive. Significantly, there are no great differences in the other subject areas, including textiles.

Drawing and graphics skills learning were enjoyed equally by girls and boys. Designing/creativity was similarly enjoyed equally.

It was more challenging to group together aspects of Design and Technology liked the least, but some divisions can be made. Boys' perceived dislikes of Design and Technology were:

- lack of ability working with resistant materials
- a dislike of cookery (*sic*)

- a dislike of sewing (*sic*)
- the lack of relevance of writing.

Girls' perceived dislikes of Design and Technology were:

- sewing (*sic*)
- the quantity of written work
- the lack of point in learning home economics (*sic*).

The girls' perception that food was wasteful came from their views that what was done in these lessons was actually done at home. This point, put quite forcefully in some instances, is why bother doing something twice. The boys were more concerned with their lack of manual skills in working with resistant materials.

Will you opt for Technology in Key Stage 4?

(This applies to Wales only, where the subject is optional, not compulsory, at Key Stage 4.)

There were 11 boys and 10 girls who indicated that they would like to take Technology in Year 10, corresponding to approximately 50 per cent of the sample. The reasons ranged from employment prospects, enjoyment of the subject, wanting to specialize in a particular aspect, and ability within the subject. Enjoyment of the subject showed no gender split. However, the other categories showed marked differences: boys perceived Design and Technology to be an area where they had ability and where they could study to gain employment; girls perceived the study of particular aspects of Design and Technology (food and textiles) as desirable.

About half the boys and nearly 60 per cent of girls interviewed indicated that they would not wish to study the subject at GCSE level. The reasons given for this were split by gender. Boys had made decisions that they were not good at the subject and were not interested because it was not useful to help gain employment. Girls were more concerned about the restrictions imposed by their schools on which aspect of Design and Technology they might want to study.

What will you do after Year 11?

One girl stated positively that she wished to study textiles and CDT at college. Of the boys, seven stated that they had an intention of taking up either further study or a career which involved technology. Five of these were hedged with the statement 'if I am good enough'.

Vision in 10–20 years' time

Although most boys replied that they would be employed in some type of job or career, only five boys and one girl had a vision of doing anything in the area of technology, as the subject is perceived by them. The girl wished to become a clothes' designer, and three of the boys wished to work as electrical or electronic technicians or engineers.

Phase 3   What makes a good technology pupil?

A questionnaire was devised which included 26 statements which could be used to describe a good technology pupil (see Hendley and Lyle 1996). The statements were categorized for analysis but were randomly distributed for the questionnaire. The categories used in this research were statements about:

- aptitude for technology
- classroom interaction
- discipline
- outside influences.

Pupils were asked to pick nine statements which they considered best described a good Design and Technology pupil. They were not asked to rank them in any order of importance, simply to indicate which statements they felt were important according to the criteria. The list below shows the statements which gained over 50 per cent of the combined Years 6 and 9 pupils' votes, both boys and girls. These are:

- can design things
- can work safely
- can follow instructions
- can work with others
- can make things
- can plan their work.

These responses give a clear indication that pupils have thought about the different categories from which the statements were drawn. They have a perception of a good Design and Technology pupil as one who has an aptitude for the subject and is able to demonstrate skills in the processes associated with Design and Technology, both individual and interactional. They are also aware of outside influences, believing a good Design and Technology pupil wants to get a job in technology.

The ability to design things is clearly the most popular choice overall, perhaps indicating the change in emphasis brought about by the National Curriculum. The importance of being able to work safely has clearly been emphasized in schools. Significantly, the ability to work with others is given a high ranking.

Further analysis of the data reveals differences between the respondents according to age and gender.

There were no significant gender differences in responses for Year 6 pupils, with the exceptions of boys perceiving being good at Design and Technology useful for getting a job, and enjoying solving problems. Girls are far more willing to listen to other pupils' ideas. The most popular characteristic of a good Design and Technology pupil is identified as 'being able to work with others'. This is the top choice for both boys and girls. Very few respondents considered 'gender' as a characteristic of a good designer and technologist. Differences in emphasis appeared in the statements referring to 'can make things', 'is good at drawing', 'enjoys using computers' and 'enjoys solving problems'. These are all perceived by boys as having more importance. Girls perceive that 'can work safely' and 'can listen to the ideas of others' are more important characteristics.

There is little sign of gender difference in responses to statements with few votes. The ability to make assumptions and test them ranked very low with both boys and girls, as did predicting what might happen next and the ability to tell others what they have done.

The results show a remarkable degree of agreement between boys and girls in Year 9. Again, there was no real difference in perception of gender being a characteristic of a good Design and Technology pupil. Some of the statements are slightly differently prioritized by boys and girls. Out of all the statements only two divergences of opinion emerged. The boys prioritized 'listening to the ideas of others' more highly than girls did. The girls prioritized 'suggesting ways of improving their work' more highly than the boys did. The characteristics of 'can make assumptions and test them' and 'predicting what might happen next' keep their low ranking in Year 9.

Analysis revealed, however, some important differences in attitudes towards gender according to age. Year 6 boys were twice as likely as Year 9 boys to think being a boy was an important characteristic, although the percentages were low. Similarly, in Year 6 the number of girls who thought being a girl was an important characteristic was four times greater than the number of girls in Year 9 who thought this, although, again, the figures were low.

A very significant change between the Key Stages is the perception of the characteristic 'the ability to work safely'. This increases dramatically between Year 6 and Year 9. It seems likely that this reflects the fact that Design and Technology takes place in a workshop environment at Year 9, whilst few primary schools have separate facilities, with work taking place in the normal classroom. It may also reflect the greater emphasis on working with tools and machinery at Key Stage 3. However, this does not explain the fact that over half of girls in Year 6 chose safety as one of their nine qualities.

The quality of being able to enjoy using a computer also shows significant changes between the Key Stages with a drop in the importance of this characteristic in Key Stage 3. Computers are readily available in Key Stage 2 classrooms and their use is actively encouraged. However, it should be noted that using a computer is relatively more important to Year 6 boys than to the girls. Although computer access in Key Stage 3 is good – each school in the sample surveyed has at least one machine in the workshops – there is anecdotal evidence to suggest that its use is restricted due to constraints of time. Further, computers are used more regularly in a separate subject called Information Technology. Around a quarter of Year 9 boys considered computer use to be important which is over 50 per cent less than Year 6 boys. Similarly, only a fifth of the girls in Year 9 chose this quality, again showing a drop of nearly 50 per cent.

Some other interesting changes occur between the end of Key Stage 2 and the end of Key Stage 3. Almost three-quarters of the boys in Year 6 rated the ability to work with others, but this has dropped by half in Year 9. Anecdotal evidence suggests this might be due to pupils in primary school being encouraged to share work with each other, whereas in secondary schools the ability to work on their own is stronger. Key Stage 3 is also perceived as being a training period for national examinations and so pupils are encouraged to succeed by their individual efforts rather than as part of a team.

Similarly, the ability to follow instructions loses popularity between Year 6 and Year 9, whilst the ability to design things increases in popularity. This indicates that pupils are becoming increasingly aware of the process-based nature of Design and Technology, with the structure of their folio work becoming more important. Teachers also increasingly stress the need to present work well in Design and Technology. It is noteworthy to mention that the popularity of making things also increases as the pupils get older. This change is common between the sexes.

The quality 'can explain why something has happened' undergoes a slight change in emphasis between the Key Stages. The greatest change is seen in the perceptions of boys, with an almost three-fold increase.

Some gender differences occur between Year 6 and Year 9 concerning the statement 'can listen to the ideas of others'. There is an increase in emphasis in the boys' perceptions between Key Stages 2 and 3. Conversely, there is a decrease in emphasis by girls.

The quality of wanting a job using technology remains fairly constant between the two age groups. However, its ranking decreases with older pupils as other characteristics take precedence.

The ability to predict what might happen next, although not a strong choice, shows up an age imbalance for boys whilst girls were fairly consistent about this across the Key Stages.

The ability to think creatively and imaginatively is not ranked very high with pupils, although there is an increase with age and gender, with the boys showing the greater increase.

Another area where a significant change occurs is the ability to plan their work – a 30 per cent increase by boys and a 10 per cent increase by girls. This is probably due to the fact that girls are happier to plan work from an earlier age than are boys.

The quality of 'having an interest in the environment' ranks very low with both boys and girls in Year 9, which is a fairly dramatic change compared with Year 6 pupils, where many more thought it desirable. The characteristic 'can make a decision and live with it' also shows a similar change in emphasis between Year 6 and Year 9.

If we examine three of the statements which most closely relate to the association of Design and Technology with Science, we find that pupils overall give these a low priority:

- 'can predict what might happen next' increases between the Key Stages for boys, whilst girls' perceptions remain constant

- 'can use mathematics and science to solve a problem' remains fairly constant between Key Stages and genders
- 'can make assumptions and test them' has very low priority, but does become more important between Key Stages and between the genders.

This would suggest that pupils do not see a close relationship between qualities which are valued by Science and ones which help make a good pupil of Design and Technology. This contradicts the findings of McCarthy and Moss (1994) who report that technology is perceived by both genders as being similar to science- rather than craft-based subjects. However, this research was based at only one school and may reflect the values of staff and their interpretation of Design and Technology rather than being indicative of widely held values of pupils.

Conclusion

The review of this research suggests that there are lessons to be learned for all teachers of Design and Technology. Pupils are enthusiastic about the subject; however, they also experience frustration. Pupils enjoy making things, but many find this is a waste of time. They are not confident working with tools and feel frustration when they lack the skills to carry out the tasks and work is not completed. Pupils need to be encouraged to achieve: teachers can do this by ensuring pupils have enough time to complete their work and by teaching and reinforcing the necessary skills, knowledge and understanding to help pupils gain confidence and boost their self-esteem.

Career prospects are important to pupils and their parents. More 'real world' projects need to be incorporated into the curriculum, as these are seen by pupils as important in their daily lives. The work of product designers, interior designers, architects, furniture designers, engineers and so on could be incorporated into projects to help bridge the gap which exists between designing and making. When pupils are given design briefs which relate to a real problem they can see purpose in their work, which helps to increase motivation.

Gender is still an issue in Design and Technology despite the introduction of a compulsory curriculum for all from 5 to 16. The tendency for boys to choose resistant materials and systems and control and for girls to prefer food and textiles is still prevalent. However this is not an absolute and there are numerous examples of girls working successfully in resistant materials technology and boys in textiles and food. This is a practice which should be encouraged.

There is also the challenge of lack of confidence in the use of tools and machines by girls. This is reinforced by some teachers, either through allowing boys to 'show the girls how it's done' or by making girls unwelcome in the workshop. A similar challenge is present regarding their lack of confidence in the use of computers.

The ability to think creatively and imaginatively is not rated highly at all by the respondents to this research. This is a great concern; one of the main tenets behind designing is the capability to be creative, to use the imagination. The possible reasons for pupils' low rating of this could be the way in which they are taught to design, with their potential to work in a creative manner reduced due to constraints, usually budget related. Again, this is something which would benefit from further research.

Design and Technology is a subject that has great potential. Pupils see it as exciting and rewarding, they enjoy it and can see its usefulness. We, as teachers, need to harness that enthusiasm and creativity and use it to develop skills, which other subjects cannot provide.

References

Grant, M. and Harding, J. (1987) 'Changing the polarity', *International Journal of Science Education* 9: 335–42.

Hendley, D. and Lyle, S. (1996) 'Pupils' perceptions of design and technology: a case study of pupils in South Wales', *Research in Science and Technological Education* 14(2): 141–51.

Hendley, D., Parkinson, J., Stables, A. and Tanner, H. (1995) 'Gender differences in pupil attitudes to the national curriculum foundation subjects of English, mathematics, science and technology in key stage 3 in South Wales', *Educational Studies* 21(1): 85–97.

Hendley, D., Parkinson, J., Stables, A. and Tanner, H. (1996) 'Pupils' attitudes to technology in key stage 3 of the national curriculum: a study of pupils in South Wales', *International Journal of Technology and Design Education* 6: 15–29.

Hendley, D., Stables, A. and Stables, S. (1996) 'Pupils' subject preferences at key stage 3 in South Wales', *Educational Studies* 22(2): 177–86.

Kelly, A. (1988) 'Option choices for girls and boys', *Research in Science and Technological Education* 6(1): 5–23.

McCarthy, A.C. and Moss, D. (1990) 'Pupils' perceptions of technology in the secondary school curriculum: a case study', *Educational Studies* 16: 207–16 .

McCarthy, A.C. and Moss, D. (1994) 'A comparison of male and female pupil perceptions of technology in the curriculum', *Research in Science and Technological Education* 12: 5–13.

Moore, J.L. (1987) 'A technique for discovering pupils' ideas about technology', *CASTME Journal* 7(1): 1–9.

Nash, M., Allsop, T. and Woolnough, B. (1984) 'Factors affecting pupil uptake of technology at 14+', *Research in Science and Technological Education* 2(1): 5–19.

Ormerod, M.B. and Waller, J.E. (1988) 'Attitudes to craft, design and technology with some related factors and sex differences at 14+', *Research into Science and Technological Education* 6: 133–44.

Rennie, L.J. (1987) 'Teachers' and pupils' perceptions of technology and the implications for the curriculum', *Research in Science and Technological Education* 15: 37–52.

Smail, B. and Kelly, A. (1984) 'Sex differences in science and technology among 11-year old school children: 1 – Cognitive', *Research in Science and Technological Education* 2(1): 87–106.

Smail, B. and Kelly, A. (1984) 'Sex differences in science and technology among 11-year old school children: 2 – Affective', *Research in Science and Technological Education* 2(2): 61–76.

Welsh Office (1993) *Statistics in Education and Training in Wales: Schools*, Cardiff: Welsh Office.

Whyte, J. (1986) *Girls Into Science and Technology*, London: Routledge Kegan and Paul.

Woolnough, B. (1990) *Making Choices? An Enquiry Into The Attitudes Of Sixth Formers Towards Choice Of Science And Technology Courses In Higher Education*, Oxford: Oxford University Department of Educational Studies.

Section 2

Issues in teaching and learning Design and Technology

6   Research in learning technological concepts and processes

Alister Jones

This chapter offers a review of research, rather than a theoretical exploration, and introduces issues which are developed further in other chapters in this section. The research highlights what pupils' concepts of 'technology' are and their concepts of various aspects of technological processes. It also provides a discussion of how the concepts held by pupils affect their learning, and how teachers' concepts of technology affect their teaching, and, in consequence, pupils' learning.

In reading this chapter consider how the research discussed relates to pupils you know, your own concepts and how it might impact on your classroom practice.

Introduction

Technology education is a relatively new area of research and I would suggest there is a need to develop a coherent framework within which an analysis of student learning of technology concepts and processes can take place. ... While there is published research about what students do when involved in technological activities (e.g., Jones, Mather and Carr 1995; Kimbell *et al.* 1991; Kimbell 1994; and McCormick *et al.* 1994), there has been very little published work which analyses these findings in terms of the students' learning of technological concepts and processes. ... McCormick (1997) notes that there has been little empirical research in this area, and Layton (1994) highlights that there has been lack of a developed research base compared with science or mathematics education.

Technology education is concerned with complex and interrelated problems that involve multiple variables that are technical, procedural, conceptual and social (Hansen and Froelich 1994). The researching of learning in technology therefore needs to be multidimensional. This chapter will review research that I believe is useful in developing a coherent framework for the exploration and analysis of this learning, and finishes with a discussion of the implications for future research specifically in the area of learning technological concepts and processes.

The importance of concepts

Any concept a learner holds provides a framework from which to construct other concepts as well as determine courses of action (Mather 1995). This means that any existing concepts that students have will have a direct impact on their learning in technology. Concepts may be broadly taken to include dispositions that include inclinations, sensitivity and abilities (Perkins *et al.* 1993). These terms are defined in the following way:

> *Inclination* refers to the person's felt tendency toward behaviour X … *sensitivity* refers to the persons alert to X occasions … *Ability* refers to the actual ability to follow through with the X behaviour.
>
> (Perkins *et al.* 1993, p. 4)

Since learning is an active process, that is a behaviour, then the dispositional aspects of concepts appear crucial. The wealth of research data from science education on students' existing concepts indicates that conceptual knowledge significantly affects students' predictions, explanations and perceptions of phenomena and problems (Hennessy 1993). Students' concepts of technology and technology education will therefore directly influence their learning of technological concepts and processes. In addition, the classroom environment, student concepts of what it means to be a learner, teachers' concepts of technology and technology education, as well as curriculum directions will also all influence student learning in technology. This means, therefore, that students' and teachers' concepts of technology, including concepts of technological knowledge and processes, will impact on the way in which technological practice is undertaken in the classroom. For example, if a teacher has a concept of technology as craft (Black 1994), then that will influence the emphasis he or she places on task descriptions and classroom interactions. This will also determine what is considered to be technological knowledge and processes. For example, learning may be expressed as a progression of isolated skills, rather than a multidimensional technological activity. If a student has a concept of technology as being 'hi-tech', then he or she may seek solutions to technological problems that incorporate 'hi-tech' features which are not necessarily relevant, or part of an appropriate solution.

Students' technological practice and limited concepts of technology can affect the teacher's own perceptions of technology education, especially where the teacher's concept of technology is somewhat fragile in nature (Jones *et al.* 1995). It is therefore crucial to explore teachers' and students' concepts of technology to understand the way these will influence the learning of technological concepts and processes. …

Student concepts of technology and their impact on technological practice

Most of the work on student concepts of technology has been in relation to their perceptions of technology, using the Pupils' Attitude Toward Technology or PATT questionnaire (Raat *et al.* 1987), which was undertaken in 22 countries. The general findings of this research indicate that while students have a positive attitude to technology they generally have a limited concept of it. Students often perceived technology as being a recent phenomenon and as artefacts. Rennie and Jarvis (1994) also found that students tended to express technology in terms of modern artefacts, or useful products. Students generally did not consider the social context of technological practice. Mather and Jones (1995) found that younger students (5–6 years old) seemed more likely to link technology and people, compared with 9–13-year-old students who appeared to base their concept of technology on artefacts as distinct from people. These findings are in keeping with other similar studies (Burns 1992).

Research findings from New Zealand (Jones and Carr 1993; and Jones *et al.* 1995) show strong links between students' concepts of technology and their technological practice, that includes the learning and use of technological concepts and processes. However, as noted by Mather and Jones (1995) the interaction between concept and future learning is quite complex and dependent on a number of factors.

Where students' concepts of technology are broad then students are more likely to undertake their technological activities in a holistic fashion, that is showing links between the various stages in the process. Where students' concepts of technology were narrow then this constrained their technological practice and limited the potential for learning technological concepts and processes. Some students had slightly broader concepts of technology that included social aspects, but most students lacked a linking of the different aspects of the technological process. Mather and Jones (1995) also indicate that students' concepts of technology may be difficult to change (as the literature on conceptual change from other areas would support).

Research by Mather (1995) indicates that students' existing concepts of technology have a greater impact on their technological practice than do the associated teaching strategies. If students have limited concepts of technology then it could be assumed that this will limit their learning of technological concepts and processes. ...

Teachers' concepts of technology and their impact on technological practice

Teaching and learning of technology at the school level is often bound up with the initiation and the socialization of teachers into subject sub-cultural settings (Goodson 1985). These subcultures, according to Paechter (1991), represent reasonably consistent views about the role of the teacher, the nature of their subject, the way it should be taught and expectations of the students' learning. Paechter also points out that the teachers' beliefs about what was important for students to learn in their existing subject areas (prior to the National Curriculum), such as craft design and technology, home economics, art, were transferred to technology education. In Sweden, Lindblad (1990) found that primary school teachers in responding to developing a new technology curriculum formulated classroom experiences based on their past experiences. For example, art teachers made the technology curriculum into a design course and science teachers made it into a laboratory course. Research in New Zealand (Jones and Carr 1992; Jones *et al.* 1995) also suggests that secondary school subject subcultures were a strong influence on teachers' concepts of technology and subsequent classroom practice. Science teachers discussed technology in terms of applied science, social studies teachers focused on the effect technology has on society, English teachers discussed technology as an information tool and technical teachers' views of technology were primarily focused on specific skills and design and making artefacts. ... The subject background influenced teachers' perceptions of what could be described and validated as technological concepts and processes, and therefore what should be emphasized in student learning.

Subject backgrounds had a direct influence on the way teachers structured lessons and developed classroom strategies to teach technological concepts and processes. Teachers developed strategies to allow for learning outcomes that were often more closely related to their particular teaching subject than to technology hence affecting the student learning in technology. [...]

Differing understandings of technological knowledge and the impact on learning

As Layton (1994) notes, technology does not have a single well-established academic discipline in higher education but rather there is a multiplicity of technologies. There are also a number of interpretations of what is meant by technological knowledge. Technological concepts are not consistently defined in the literature. For students to undertake technological activities, knowledge and processes cannot be divorced. Therefore it is important to consider what are technological concepts and how these are learnt. [...]

Gardner (1995) notes that if technology is perceived as simply applied science then this ignores economic, social, personal and environmental needs and constraints. This will therefore limit students' learning of technological concepts. Technological knowledge is often identified as modified and tacit knowledge as opposed to abstract knowledge (Layton 1991). Within the literature technical knowledge or 'knowing that' is frequently used (Anning 1994; Barlex 1993; Donnelly, 1992), but there is little discussion of what this might be and how students learn it. Technology also generates its own knowledge and this needs to be made explicit to students (Gunstone 1994). Students need to learn the principles of technology and that these are knowledge bases in their own right.

... In applying abstract knowledge an intermediate step of translation is required. This is a difficult process and one that will be need to be taught to students. There are numerous examples, from the research by Jones, Mather and Carr (1995), of students having difficulty translating knowledge taught in alternative subject areas to technological problems. Kimbell *et al.* (1991) found that students often failed to produce a working prototype because of a lack of knowledge e.g., electronic knowledge. The ability to utilize knowledge was limiting student performance in technology. McCormick *et al.* (1994) also note that the student's inability to transfer knowledge was an obstacle in the technological activity. Transfer assumes that students have been taught the understanding of when and how to use that knowledge. Transfer within the domain does not always happen. ...

The impact of the curriculum on learning

Student learning of technological concepts and processes will be influenced by approaches supported by particular curriculums, at the national, school and classroom level. Curriculums (such as the English National Curriculum) provide the framework for possible learning and assessment outcomes and these will therefore influence the way in which students undertake technological problems. Most curriculums in technology are relatively recent and little research has been done documenting these influences. ... Kimbell (1994) points out that in the English and Welsh curriculum, capability is assessed in terms of processes, but knowledge and skills are presented in the Programmes of Study. This highlights a tension between what is taught and what is assessed. What is defined to be assessed gives clear messages to teachers, students and parents about what is considered important.

Hence a curriculum which separates knowledge and understanding, and skills and processes, will make the teaching and learning of technological concepts and processes even more difficult. [...]

The impact of the classroom culture on learning

The classroom culture and student expectations appeared to strongly influence the way in which students carried out their technological activities (Jones and Carr 1994). McCormick *et al.* (1994) also note that classroom management, classroom culture and teacher subculture can interfere with student learning in technology. Research indicates that learning is enhanced when students are involved in authentic activities (Brown *et al.* 1989). However, most classroom approaches do not reflect actual technological problem-solving which involves mainly adaptation and modification rather than starting from scratch (Hennessy *et al.* 1993). Research indicates that from 400 activities developed by teachers and students, very few of these activities reflected principles of technological practice (Jones and Carr 1993). This then limits the potential learning of technological concepts and processes.

Jones and Carr (1994) found, for example, that in many classes the expectation of the students was to make a model to present to the rest of the class. This expectation meant that the students did not need to undertake planning and design, and take into account appropriate measurements in solving their problems, nor did they see the need to carry out appropriate research. Although they were introduced to technological principles, their expectations meant these were largely irrelevant. This limited their approach to possible solutions. Another example was that of the students in a food technology class where the expectation was to make food. Since the purpose for many students was to make some food to present to the teacher, the students were not concerned with developing a realistic solution to their problem of packaging and marketing food, with carrying out research and evaluation, or taking into account technological principles. The students' expectation of what was an appropriate outcome in a particular class influenced the approaches they took, and what knowledge and skills they identified and used in a particular activity.

The assessment approaches and the task definition can also affect student practice and learning. Emphasis on particular summative assessment procedures in a
classroom may mean students might omit unsuccessful designs and ideas from
folders (Anning 1993) and not appreciate particular technological principles
involved in the development and design of technological solutions. Stables (1995)
highlights the way in which the culture of the school and the classroom influences
the amount of responsibility students are given in their design and technology
tasks. The openness of the activity can also affect student learning of technological
concepts and processes. The more open and loosely-defined the task might be (e.g.,
designing a playground), the more students can end up getting lost with the
multiple demands of the technological problem (Jones and Carr 1993; Jones *et al.*
1995; and Kimbell, 1994). For example, students may select a task where they
approach the solution in a superficial manner and not allow for technological principles to be incorporated. Students who tried to consider large problems often
concentrated on organizational aspects rather than developing and incorporating
technological approaches to their problems (Jones and Carr 1994). The opposite
situation is also true where if a task is closed (i.e. tightly defined), then this can
limit students' approaches and affect the potential to learn and incorporate technological principles. This is often found where students are constrained by a defined
design cycle, where resources and outcomes are identified. This can also limit innovative approaches that students might have to technological solutions and limit the
learning of technological principles, such as modifications, adaptations.

Aspects of learning technological processes

So far I have examined the concepts of technology, knowledge and curriculums
and classroom approaches and the way they impact on learning. This next section
examines technological processes, student concepts of these and the way they will
influence the learning of technological practice.

The identification, development and realization of a technological solution is a
complex activity that involves identifying needs and opportunities, exploring problems and constraints, gathering information from a variety of sources, using this
information appropriately, using a variety of techniques, exploring ideas, modelling
and testing, production and evaluating. These stages do not imply a linear process
but rather describe some of the features of technological processes. These stages
and processes are not generalizable or transferable but are operationalized within
particular contexts and technological areas reflecting particular technological
communities of practice. ...

Modelling

Modelling is a key feature of technological capability (Kimbell *et al.* 1991).
McCormick *et al.* (1994) define the three purposes of modelling as to evaluate, to
think through and to communicate, with 2D modelling important in forcing the
students to consider design details.

One of the features of technological capability that Anning (1994) identifies is that of communicating ideas through drawing. She notes that traditionally drawing skills have not been emphasized, and that drawing, sketches, and scribbling ideas are not traditionally encouraged. Young children have difficulty linking their drawings with 3D models and there is evidence that young children have difficulty representing scale, spatial orientation and overlap. Anning suggests that it is at about 9 years of age that students generally represent their design intentions accurately.

Jones *et al.* (1995) report that students often focused on making models as their technological solution. The 6–8-year-old students had difficulty with the idea of a model, often being confused between what is real and what is not. If the students were making the real thing then measurements, materials and equipment were considered to be important. These students could test out their constructions and make adaptations. In comparison, the students who made models saw little value in making measurements or thinking about appropriate materials. The focus on models as an end-product meant that students could include complicated components in their design without exploring the appropriateness of these components. Similarly for 11–15-year-old students who focused on models as an end-product, the considerations of elements such as materials and cost, were seen in terms of the model. When problems arose the students could dismiss them because a model could include features to overcome those problems. The students modified their designs to take account of the materials available to make models rather than considering appropriate materials for the end-product. The focus on cardboard models also meant that students' ideas about particular technological concepts were not challenged or learnt during their engagement in the activity. Where the initial focus was on making the real thing rather than a model, which meant that the students identified clearly who would use it, they also began to identify how they might carry out the task.

It is therefore crucial that students are aware of the concept and purposes of models and modelling in technological practice, rather than seeing them as an end-point in themselves.

Evaluation

Young children have a concept of evaluation as 'doing it again' and this influences this facet of technological activities (Anning 1994). Evaluation needs to be an integral part of the whole process; evaluation as an add-on exercise does not work. It is important to get students to talk about the changes they would make as an ongoing process. ... Jones and Carr (1994) found that students worked in a stepwise fashion rather than questioning and reflecting between and within the identifiable stages. ... In fact the parts of a technological activity might be done well but there were not sound links between the stages of the technological process. To develop such an understanding children need to be taught how technologists work, so that they see that evaluation is an integral part of technological practice. One way of providing this is for students to gain insight into the different technological communities of practice. Evaluation depends on the students' understanding of the link between the problems they define and the solution they seek (McCormick *et al.* 1994). If evaluation is not taught as being on-going and integral to technological practice there is little evaluation that occurs naturally in student technological practice.

Technological problem-solving

The pedagogy of technology has been seen as being active problem-solving, particularly in the UK (Donnelly 1992). It has been identified as having three key elements: holistic activity; design cycle; applying independent bodies of knowledge. Problem-solving is context-dependent so student learning of technological processes will tend to be context-dependent. The way in which the task is presented, the openness and the way in which the students identify and operationalize aspects of the problem will all influence student learning of technological problem-solving. Abstract knowledge needs to be reinterpreted in order to be used in the technological problem-solving. The way in which students prioritize the different aspects of the variables of the problem will influence what technological knowledge is actually required. This is also true for the processes and societal aspects they will need to consider.

McCade (1990) notes there are different forms of problem-solving in technology, e.g., design, troubleshooting and technology assessment, such as critically analysing the impacts of technology to predict outcomes and choosing the most appropriate outcome, and evaluating existing solutions. An understanding of the different types of problem-solving in technology can help students learn the process of problem-solving.

Design cycle and processes

The design cycle has been particularly strongly emphasized in technology education, especially in curriculum materials. Rennie *et al.* (1992) and McCormick *et al.* (1994) note there are problems with an over-emphasis on the design cycle. The design process assumes that students will be able to access and use knowledge from across the curriculum, yet there is no evidence for this happening (Jones *et al.* 1995). As mentioned earlier, problem-solving is context-specific, and involves the integrated use of knowledge that cannot be directly applied (Layton 1991). There are varying knowledge demands required for technological practice that are not always made explicit to students when a design cycle is over-emphasized. ... Where students had been taught a design cycle approach this was generally undertaken in a linear way with no reflection. The teaching of the design cycle without an equal emphasis on knowledge and reflection causes difficulties for the students. McCormick *et al.* (1994) indicate that the conceptual demands of a task are more influential than the procedural, and they stress the importance of developing global aspects before local skills. Pupils have commented they were often confused by the conceptual demand of a project and the lack of explicit process teaching. Teachers need to make the processes, their rationale and criteria explicit to pupils.

Evidence of these concerns about the teaching and learning of technological processes is provided by Jones *et al.* (1995). In the primary class (6–8 years) the students' processes were essentially linear (identification of the problem, formation of possible solution, design as a pictorial representation, gathering of resources, construction). Evaluation and reflection were not key features of the process and when it occurred it was not strongly linked to solving the originally-defined problems. Students often changed their ideas when unable to construct some aspect of their design. Students might modify their design to suit the materials available in a random fashion with no linking back to the original purpose (for example, making it smaller without consideration as to whether this would still solve the problem).

Jones and Carr (1994) found that when students had been taught a closely defined design cycle approach they followed this step by step in a superficial manner and there was no planned linking between the different aspects of the task (atomistic approach). Even though technological principles were introduced, students had difficulty translating these principles into a holistic multifaceted technological activity. The students generally did not examine existing technology as a strategy to solve their problem. The students' approach did not use systems but focused on the end-product.

When students did examine existing technology, and developed an understanding of its functions and operation and investigated modifications, they were able to develop an understanding of some technological principles and processes and were more likely to undertake a process that led to an appropriate solution. When students (11–15 years) were involved in an authentic, plausible activity there was more likelihood that they would learn about and incorporate technological processes in their technological practice. Those students who were being innovative asked questions, collected information, explored a number of ideas, considered systems and began to develop appropriate solutions. These students learnt technological knowledge and developed further understanding of technological processes.

McCormick *et al.* (1994) also highlight that it is important to deal with processes explicitly, otherwise students are dealing with apparently isolated tasks. A lack of understanding of the overall process means that students undertake the parts in isolation or follow the design process as a ritual (McCormick 1997). Students do not necessarily see the relationship between the different stages or problems of the task. Guidance must be given about how to evaluate; learning in technology does not happen by discovery. When technical skills are taught in isolation from the tasks to which they are to be applied, students have problems with transferring them to solve technological problems (Anning 1994; Jones and Carr 1993). Transfer needs to be taught directly in technological practice (Johnson 1997).

Implications for learning technological concepts and processes

This chapter indicates the need for a framework of technological knowledge and processes to be developed and for concepts both of and in technology to be explicitly identified and understood. There needs to be an understanding of the complexity of learning problem-solving in technology and an appreciation that the transfer and application of appropriate knowledge and skills do not necessarily occur in a simplistic fashion (Johnson 1997). ...

This chapter has outlined some research that contributes to a framework for the understanding of student learning of technological concepts and processes. Students' existing concepts of technology can limit their learning of technological concepts and processes. It is therefore essential that strategies are developed that broaden students' concepts of technology and technological practice. Teachers also have differing perceptions of technology and this directly influences classroom practice and subsequently the learning of technological concepts and processes. Teachers also need to develop a coherent understanding of technology and technological practice (Jones *et al.* 1995).

Within the literature there are differing interpretations of what technological knowledge is. This causes difficulties in defining technological concepts to be introduced to students. Technological knowledge needs to be acknowledged and this needs to be conveyed to students. Technology relies on multiple knowledge bases but can neither be identified nor reduced to them (Salomon 1995). A restricted view of technological knowledge limits student learning in technology by considering only some aspects. A more coherent picture of technological knowledge needs to be developed. The translation and transfer of knowledges and skills is required in technological practice, yet this causes the biggest obstacle for students. Teaching for transfer is difficult but there is some evidence that it is possible (Perkins and Salomon 1989).

Curriculums also influence student learning of technological concepts and processes. Where there is a separation between knowledge and processes this causes problems in student and teacher understanding of the inter-relationship between processes and concepts.

The appropriate classroom environment is crucial for the development of student learning of technological concepts and processes. Learning is enhanced when students are involved in authentic activities and where classroom approaches reflect technological practice, e.g., meeting needs, modification, societal aspects. When students are being innovative and taking risks with reflection there appears to be a greater chance of students learning technological concepts and processes.

Students have existing concepts of technological processes, such as problem-solving and design cycles, and the different aspects of that process, such as modelling, skills, planning and evaluation. These existing concepts affect current technological practice, as well as future learning of technological concepts and processes. Further research is required to further understand and change students' existing technological concepts.

Initial evidence suggests that there are changes in the students' technological processes when teachers and students have developed a more appropriate concept of technology (Jones *et al.* 1995). Students were more likely to carry out better research, take more factors into account and consider design a more integral part of technological activity. To create better links between the stages, students were also explicitly taught to reflect about the process they were undertaking, and to reflect about the links between the stages. Students were also encouraged to monitor the process they were developing. They were encouraged to be meta-cognitive and to consider appropriate knowledge in their technological process. However, this is only an initial study and further research in student learning needs to be undertaken.

To enhance student learning of technological concepts and processes it appears crucial that students and teachers develop an understanding of technology and technology education, and reflect on the nature of technological practice. [...]

References

Anning, A. (1993) 'Learning design and technology in primary schools', in R. McCormick, P. Murphy and M. Harrison (eds), *Teaching and Learning Technology*, Wokingham: Addison-Wesley Publishing Co.

Anning, A. (1994) 'Dilemmas and opportunities of a new curriculum: design and technology with young children', *International Journal of Technology and Design Education* 4(2), 155–78.

Barlex, D. (1993) 'The Nuffield approach to the role of tasks in teaching design and technology', in R. McCormick, P. Murphy and M. Harrison (eds), *Teaching and Learning Technology*, Wokingham: Addison-Wesley Publishing Co.

Brown, J. S., Collins, A. and Duguid, P. (1989) 'Situated cognition and the culture of learning', *Educational Researcher* 18(1), 32–42.

Burns, J. (1992) 'Student perceptions of technology and implications for an empowering curriculum', *Research in Science Education* 22, 72–80.

Donnelly, J. (1992) 'Technology in the school curriculum: a critical bibliography', *Studies in Science Education* 20, 123–56.

Gardner, P. (1995) 'The relationship between technology and science: some historical and philosophical reflections: part 2', *International Journal of Technology and Design Education* 5(1), 1–33.

Goodson, I. F. (1985) 'Social histories of the secondary curriculum', in I. F. Goodson (ed.), *Subjects for Study*, Lewes: Falmer Press.

Gunstone, R. (1994) 'Technology education and science education: engineering as a case study of relationships', *Research in Science Education* 24, 129–36.

Hansen, R. and Froelich, M. (1994) 'Defining technology and technological education: a crisis, or cause for celebration', *International Journal of Technology and Design Education* 4(2), 179–207.

Hennessy, S. (1993) 'Situated cognition and cognitive apprenticeship: implications for classroom learning', *Studies in Science Education* 22, 1–41.

Hennessy, S., McCormick, R. and Murphy, P. (1993) 'The myth of general problem solving capability: design and technology as an example', *The Curriculum Journal* 4(1), 73–89.

Johnson, S. D. (1997) 'Learning technological concepts and developing intellectual skills', *International Journal of Technology and Design Education* 7(1–2): 161–80.

Jones, A. and Carr, M. (1992) 'Teachers' perceptions of technology education – implications for curriculum innovation', *Research in Science Education* 22, 230–39.

Jones, A. T. and Carr, M. D. (1993) *Analysis of Student Technological Capability,* Vol. 2, Working Papers of the Learning in Technology Education Project, Centre for Science and Mathematics Education Research, University of Waikato, Hamilton, p. 148.

Jones, A. and Carr M. (1994) 'Student technological capability: where do we start?', *SAME papers* 1994: 165–86.

Jones, A. T., Mather, V. and Carr, M. D. (1995) *Issues in the Practice of Technology Education,* Centre for Science and Mathematics Education Research, University of Waikato, Hamilton, p. 125.

Kimbell, R. (1994) 'Tasks in technology: an analysis of their purposes and effects', *International Journal of Technology and Design Education* 4(3): 241–56.

Kimbell, R., Stables, K., Wheeler, T., Wosniak, A. and Kelly, V. (1991) *The Assessment of Performance in Design and Technology,* London: Schools Examination and Assessment Council.

Layton, D. (1991) 'Science education and praxis: the relationship of school science to practical action', *Studies in Science Education* 19: 43–49.

Layton, D. (1994) 'A school subject in the making?: the search for fundamentals', in D. Layton (ed.), *Innovation in Science and Technology Education,* Vol. 4, Paris: UNESCO.

Lindblad, S. (1990) 'From technology to craft: on teachers' experimental adoption of technology as a new subject in the Swedish primary school', *Journal of Curriculum Studies* 22(2), 165–75.

Mather, V. (1995) *Students' Concepts of Technology and Technology Education: Implications for Practice,* unpublished M.Ed. Thesis, University of Waikato.

Mather, V. and Jones, A. (1995) 'Focusing on technology education: the effect of concepts on practice', *SET Number 2 Item 9.*

McCade, J. (1990) 'Problem solving: more than just design', *Journal of Technology Education* 2(1).

McCormick, R. (1997) 'Conceptual and procedural knowledge', *International Journal of Technology and Design Education* 7(1–2): 141–59.

McCormick, R., Murphy, P. and Hennessy, S. (1994) 'Problem solving processes in technology education: a pilot study', *International Journal of Technology and Design Education* 4(1): 5–34.

Paechter, C. (1991) 'Subject subcultures and the negotiation of open work: conflict and co-operation in cross-curricular coursework', paper presented to St. Hilda's conference, Warwick University.

Perkins, D. N. and Salomon, G. (1989, 'Are cognitive skills context bound?' *Educational Researcher* 18(1): 16–25.

Perkins, D., Jay, E., and Tishman, S. (1993) 'Beyond abilities: a dispositional theory of thinking', *Merrill-Palmer Quarterly* 3(1): 1–21.

Raat, J. H., Klerk Wolters, F. de and Vries, M. J. de (1987) *Report PATT Conference 1987,* Vol. 1, Proceedings, University of Technology, Eindhoven, The Netherlands.

Rennie, L. and Jarvis, T. (1994) 'Children's developing perceptions about technology', paper presented at ASERA, Tasmania, July.

Rennie, L., Treagust, D. and Kinnear, A. (1992) 'An evaluation of curriculum materials for teaching technology as a design process', *Research in Science and Technological Education* 10(2): 203–17.

Salomon, G. (1995) 'Reflections on the field of educational psychology by the outgoing editor', *Education Psychologists* 30(3): 105–8.

Stables, K. (1995) 'Discontinuity in transition: pupils experience of technology in Year 6 and Year 7', *International Journal of Technology and Design Education* 5(2): 157–69.

7 Capability lost and found?

Robert McCormick

This chapter was originally presented as a lecture at a Design and Technology Association conference. It is a difficult chapter as it deals with the complex notions of problem-solving processes and design processes, and how these are linked. It describes different kinds of knowledge, not simply factual or conceptual but also procedural (knowledge that is demonstrated through action) and how knowledge is bound up in the situation or context in which individuals are working. The author argues that capability is a relationship between the processes of problem-solving and design, the knowledge brought to bear in these and the knowledge developed by them.

The lecture was first published in 1999, prior to the publication of the 2000 National Curriculum for England. Although there is no explicit use of the term 'capability' in the 2000 National Curriculum, the tripartite relationship and the development of pupils' capability is implicit in the statements used to describe the contribution of Design and Technology to the curriculum, and in what pupils will do. In the Welsh National Curriculum, the Focus Statement, which begins each Key Stage Programme of Study, states that pupils:

> *should be taught to develop design and technology capability through combining their Designing and Making skills with Knowledge and Understanding in order to design and make products.*

> *(ACCAC 2000)*

This mirrors the earlier English version and again contains the tripartite relationship.

In Northern Ireland, although the detail of the Technology and Design National Curriculum varies from that in England and Wales, the Attainment Target is entitled 'Technology and Design Capability'.

Introduction

The title of my lecture parodies Milton in his search for paradise. Technology education in its many guises in the UK has the idea of 'capability' embedded within it. Like Milton's search, there has been a search for capability's identity. The nature of capability has varied over time and among different advocates. Although capability has been central to the debate about technology education for the last 10

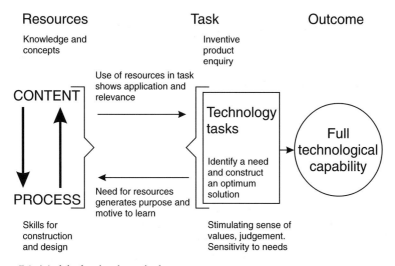

Figure 7.1 Model of technological education

years or so, we have vacillated in what we understand by the term. However, in the earlier versions of the National Curriculum, we find capability expressed as a tripartite relationship of designing, making and knowledge. The 1995 National Curriculum Programmes of Study for each Key Stage started with the statement:

> Pupils should be taught to develop their design and technology capability through combining their Designing and Making skills ... with Knowledge and understanding ... in order to design and make products.
>
> (DFE/WO 1995)

What remains unclear is just how the 'combining' takes place, an issue that has been present in all the models of capability that have emerged over the past 10 years. These models started with the recognition of the combination of process and content: for example, that of Black and Harrison (1985) shown in Figure 7.1. But they also emphasized the link between thinking and action. Black and Harrison saw capability in terms of being able 'to perform, to originate, to get things done, to make and stand by decisions' (Black and Harrison 1985, p. 6). It is the ability to act that is the predominant idea in capability. The APU model similarly linked thought and action through the model of the interaction of mind and hand (see Figure 7.2) and its model of capability reflected the link of process and knowledge, with the process being that of design (see Figure 7.3).

The role of using 'knowledge' has always been present in ideas of capability, but its relationship to 'the process' is ill-defined, as is how knowledge is used in action. Although we started with a clear focus on both action and the combination of knowledge and process, we have moved the focus to process alone, leaving the role of knowledge unclear. Paradise lost?

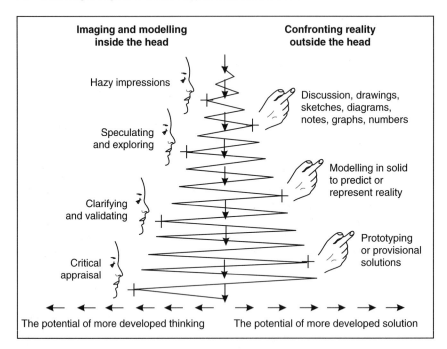

Figure 7.2 The interaction of mind and hand

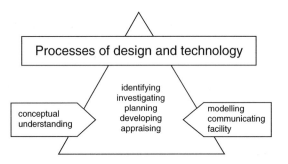

Figure 7.3 The dimensions of capability

I shall argue that we need to examine again what we mean by capability and in particular to try to locate the role of knowledge. This argument has a number of strands. First, that we cannot continue to use models of capability that rely on processes that exist independent of knowledge. Second, that the use of knowledge, particularly from science and mathematics, is more complex than the injunction in the National Curriculum presents it. Third, we need to examine the nature of the knowledge that is used in technological activity, and to explore qualitative knowledge. In presenting this argument I shall draw upon some of the research that my colleagues and I have undertaken at the Open University.[1]

Capability as process

The focus on processes within capability, particularly the design process, added important dimensions to technology education:

- giving pupils decisions and hence control over what they produce
- allowing opportunities for creative responses to situations
- reflecting an important element of technology in the world outside school
- providing a powerful motivational tool.

For those teachers who have some personal design experience, particularly in a professional design capacity, this approach offers a chance to deal innovatively with an approach to learning. For those less experienced, the warnings in the *Non-Statutory Guidance* for the National Curriculum (NCC 1990) and the APU report (APU 1991), to avoid treating the design process as a series of unchanging steps to be used in all situations, have not always been heeded. In our own work, where we have examined teachers' approaches to process at Key Stage 3, we found that the 'design process' is treated by some teachers as an algorithm: that is, as a series of steps that are used invariably in all situations. It is used ritualistically to structure pupil activity, but plays little part in the pupils' design thinking (McCormick, Murphy and Davidson 1994; McCormick and Murphy 1994: McCormick, Murphy and Hennessy 1994). Teachers will structure a series of lessons to correspond to each of the steps in the design process (first lesson is to identify a need, second, to create several solutions, third, to choose one solution and develop it and then make and evaluate). This not only takes away design decisions from pupils, but also misrepresents the way design may be carried out.[2] Inasmuch as the design process is seen as a problem-solving process, this corresponds with the findings from problem-solving studies in other domains.

The coincidence of problem-solving and design processes is, however, not accepted by all. Our interviews of teachers show various views of problem-solving and design processes, and of the relationship (Murphy *et al.* 1995):

1   some saw the two as synonymous (as in the Table below)
2   others saw a 'problem' as the starting point for a design activity, though they did not always ensure that pupils found it problematic
3   some even saw the design process as a planning process, providing pupils with a systematic sequence of activities to keep them on track.

Design	Problem-solving
Identify the need or opportunity	Define or clarify the problem
Creative alternative design ideas	Creative alternative solutions
Choose one idea and make or model it	Implement the best solution
Evaluate the product made	Evaluate the solution

Each of these approaches is defensible, but pupils are likely to meet all three from teachers of Design and Technology during their school career, with little explicit discussion to aid their understanding of the nature of the processes they are experiencing. Are they to assume that each approach is equivalent, or that they are just different things deserving the same name? Will pupils be involved in any discussion about the different approaches teachers take?

Where the problem-solving process was important, there was little attention to what pupils found problematic or to teaching pupils strategies or skills in problem-solving. Indeed the pressure on teachers to ensure that all pupils produce a successful product can mitigate against giving attention to supporting problem-solving (McCormick and Davidson 1996). Where design is seen as distinct, the attention to pupil learning fares no better. Kimbell and his colleagues concluded that, across the Key Stages in England, there was little continuity in the teaching of design and technology (Kimbell, Stables and Green 1996). Even where pupils at Key Stage 4 are involved in 'simulated technology' ('How real designers work', Kimbell *et al.* 1996 p. 46), earlier evidence (Jeffery 1990) indicates that the need to record it for assessment purposes leads to similar rituals to those that we observed at Key Stage 3. We need to replace rather mechanical views of such processes with those that are based on how children, and indeed real designers, actually work. There are, however, relatively few empirical studies of either problem-solving or design in the classroom, but this situation is changing.[3]

Problem-solving and the design process need to be seen as forms of knowledge about how to proceed. This *procedural knowledge* operates at a number of levels (McCormick 1997). At the lowest level are simple 'know-how-to-do' skills that are employed, for example, to use a solvent to adhere two styrene sheets along their edges. At a higher level there needs to be strategic procedural knowledge that determines the order things are to be done in. This knowledge includes the processes of design and problem-solving. Knowing how to evaluate a set of design alternatives can be learned as some form of procedural knowledge, but knowing *when* to do it requires higher-level knowledge: a more strategic approach. This kind of procedural knowledge is complex and requires close attention to support pupils and ensure they can learn to solve problems and design (Murphy and McCormick 1997). The APU model (Figure 7.3 above) steers us away from a simple sequence, but still leaves a complex process of knowing when it is appropriate to 'identify', 'investigate', etc. Just 'doing' design or problem-solving activities does not ensure they are learned, at least not with the relatively modest level of experience of design and technology lessons that can be given in the years of compulsory schooling.

In addition to the issue of understanding the nature of problem-solving and design processes and how to support them in the classroom, there is a more fundamental issue. This concerns the basing of any model of capability around a process, without paying adequate attention to the role of knowledge (factual and conceptual). There is substantial research on problem-solving which has established that treating it as an abstract process to be employed in any context is unhelpful. The crucial finding from decades of research is that problem-solving skill is dependent upon considerable domain knowledge (Glaser 1984 and 1992). Thus, rather than it being a general skill that can be employed with equal success in a variety of areas, it requires expertise in the context of its application. Models of capability that assume problem-solving or design are general transferable skills, whatever the particular context, do not represent how real problem-solving and design take place. Those who solve problems rarely resort to general processes. Research does not support the idea of general transfer of skills, nor does it support the teaching of problem-solving as an abstract general-purpose process (Hennessy, McCormick, and Murphy 1993). Models that see a complex interplay of processes such as 'identifying', 'investigating, 'planning', etc. are based on the requirement of the use of considerable conceptual knowledge.[4] Although they are more realistic they hide the complexity of the nature of this knowledge and how it is used.[5] The role of 'knowledge' then must be re-examined to find its place in capability.

Capability and knowledge

To understand the role of knowledge in capability we have to examine some fundamental ideas on learning, which in turn leads to an examination of the nature of knowledge. I will do this through first showing how knowledge is itself context-dependent, and then by examining how knowledge is linked to action. This of course relates well to models of capability that stress the importance of 'action'.

The importance of context

Researchers at the Harvard Smithsonian Institute for Astrophysics showed graphically how knowledge is linked to context in their work in high school science lessons. (This was shown in a BBC television programme *Simple Minds*.) A girl, who had done some work on simple electric circuits using standard science lesson equipment (battery, bulb, bulb-holder and wires), was interviewed following the lesson. Prior to this work in science she was able to connect up a battery to light the bulb using only wires. When, in the interview, she was given the materials she had used in the science lesson, she drew a circuit diagram that would get full marks in a test but, as she connected up the circuit, she insisted that the circuit needed the bulb-holder. Even when pressed by the interviewer, she said the circuit would not work without it, and was astounded when it did. Thus, when this girl learned about electric circuits, she associated bulb-holders as a necessary part of the circuit. Imagine this girl, before she had that misunderstanding corrected, going into a technology lesson where she would be confronted not with wires, bulbs and bulb-holders but with ceramic resistors and Printed Circuit Boards. What is she to make of these, and how is she to 'transfer' the ideas from the science lesson to the technology lesson? Not only are the physical items different, but the representations can be different: in science she will see a circuit represented in an abstract form as a circular path (albeit in the form of a square!), and its equivalent in technology would be quite different (Figure 7.4). There is an enormous amount of research in science education that indicates the difficulties that children have with learning abstract science ideas (e.g. Driver, Guesne and Tiberghien 1985; Osborne and Freyberg

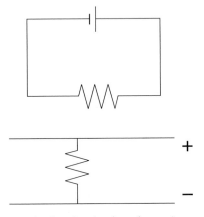

Figure 7.4 Circuits in science (top) and technology (bottom)

1985). It is unlikely, therefore, that pupils' understanding will be robust enough for them to be able to use that knowledge from science in other situations, such as in the technology class.

Similar issues arise with mathematical concepts. In technology the ideas in orthographic projection are based on mathematical ideas such as 'parallel' and 'perpendicular' lines. Technology teachers assume that they do not have to teach these basic concepts. However, research in mathematical learning indicates that pupil understanding of what 'parallel' means may be insecure. An APU study (Foxman *et al.*, undated) asked pupils aged 11 and 15 years the question in Figure 7.5.

The expected answer is option B but over 20 per cent of the 11-year-olds put a cross on more than one set of lines. They seem to have been distracted by factors such as three lines being present or lines of unequal length or lines angled to the edge of the page. These results confirm the findings of an earlier study by Kerslake (1979) with 10-year-olds, which concluded that the children had assumed equality of length to be a criterion for lines being parallel and had missed the point that the lines are always the same distance apart. Similar results were obtained in the APU study (undated) where pupils were asked to complete the sentence 'Two lines are parallel to each other if …' Only 30 per cent of 15-year-olds gave a response similar in meaning to 'the distance between them is constant'. Thus we have a situation where pupils' mathematical concepts are not robust even in the limited range of contexts they encounter in mathematical lessons: for example, the changing of the lengths or orientation of the parallel lines. Their problems are inevitably magnified when they encounter these in the more embedded situations typical of design and technology projects.

This complexity is evident when the knowledge is to be *used*, as is the case in the example of orthographic projection mentioned earlier. We have developed our work on problem-solving in design and technology projects to consider how the children use mathematics in design and technology projects (Evens and

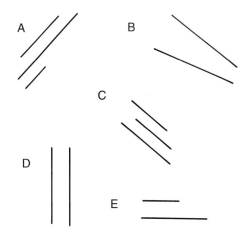

Figure 7.5 Evidence from an APU study of pupils' understanding of parallel lines. In which of the following – A, B, C, D or E – are the lines not parallel? Fifty-six per cent of 11-year-olds answered this question correctly. In a similar test, 82 per cent of 15-year-olds were successful

McCormick 1997, 1998). We have observed several teachers teaching orthographic projection. In observations of a teacher explaining how to make an orthographic projection we find, not surprisingly, that he focused on procedures. Some of his words indicated this:

> guidelines, all line up
> drop down (vertical lines)
> project the information round
> transfers the sizes.

This compares with the approach typical of mathematics classrooms, where the focus is on concepts (see Table 7.1).

We have characterized this difference in terms of the technology teacher's concern with *procedural knowledge* and the mathematics teacher's concern with *conceptual knowledge*. It is a common view that knowledge that is used (called by some, 'practical knowledge') is procedural in its nature (Sternberg and Cravso 1985).

Incidentally, it is also evident that one of the reasons that the technology teacher does not articulate concepts such as 'parallel lines' or 'perpendicular lines' is that these ideas are incorporated into the T-squares and set-squares, which are the tools used in this kind of drawing (but not used in mathematics). This is another illustration of the way knowledge is bound in with context (in this case, the tools). These observations about the use of knowledge become more understandable when we consider the nature of knowledge in relation to action.

Table 7.1 Comparison of terms used by technology and maths teachers in orthographic projection

Technology teacher	Mathematics teacher
guidelines, all line up	parallel lines
drop down (the vertical lines)	perpendicular lines
project the information round	reflection on line of symmetry
transfers the sizes	transformation

Knowledge and action

Most of us no doubt assume that knowledge is in the head and that we dig it out of our memory banks to use it for some task. There is, however, a collection of approaches to cognition and learning that argue that knowledge is integrated with activity, along with the tools, sign systems and skills associated with the activity. In this sense knowledge guides action, and action guides knowledge. A classic study of dairy workers illustrates this inter-relationship of knowledge and activity (Scribner 1985). One part of the study looked at how their various jobs (clerical, delivery or warehouse) affected how they thought about the dairy products, compared, for example, with consumers. Most consumers thought of the products in terms of 'kinds' (e.g. milk and cheese), whereas drivers thought about 'kind' and 'size' (e.g. quart), and warehouse workers in terms of 'kind', 'size' and 'location'. Each of the groups of dairy workers had their thinking organized by the kinds of activity they engaged in. But their knowledge also guided their action. When warehouse workers made up an order from an order form, they would group the items on the list to be brought for central loading in ways that reduced journey distance. They used the accumulated social knowledge that went into the layout of the warehouse and individual knowledge that reflected the current stacking arrangement. Observations showed that they would take very efficient travel paths in terms of distance, and would group items on the order form in ways that aided this efficiency. Looking at this from the point of view of learning (i.e. to be a dairy worker), Scribner (1985, p. 203) concludes that 'What you learn is bound up with what you have to do.' This explains the situation of the girl predicting the circuit operation with a bulb-holder: the activities and artefacts she worked with in science lessons determined what she learned about how circuits work. If she moved to technology lessons the different activities and artefacts would require different knowledge.

In cognitive psychology, those who deal with 'real-world' tasks see knowledge as the 'knowledge of devices or systems' (Gott 1988). In the area of 'real-world' tasks it is this 'device knowledge' that makes fault finding, for example, successful. The nature of such device knowledge may reflect as much the context of the device (e.g. its operation) as any abstract knowledge taught in science. For technologists this is important, not just because they deal with devices and systems (designing, making and repairing them), but because their conceptual knowledge will be linked to these devices and systems rather than to abstract concepts, as in science. The way knowledge is viewed (indeed what counts as knowledge) is determined by the actions associated with it. Thus, rather than seeing an electronic circuit in terms of a differential equation (a mathematical abstraction), engineers often see it in terms of Nyquist diagrams that reflect the effect of the components on the oper-ation of the circuit (Bissell and Dillon 1991). This is their 'device' knowledge that contrasts with mathematical knowledge. It also turns out that, as the complexity of devices increases, so does the importance of the interaction of device knowledge and procedural knowledge (Gott 1988, p. 120).

Taking stock so far, I have drawn attention to the importance of procedural knowledge, and its link with device knowledge. This latter knowledge stems from the fact that useful knowledge is embedded in objects, and related to action. This is the kind of knowledge that experts use in their problem-solving.

The qualitative nature of expert knowledge[6]

It is already well understood in the field of problem-solving, for example in physics, that experts always start to work on problems by thinking about them in qualita-tive terms (Glaser 1984). This stands in stark contrast to the way we start novices off on learning how to do such problem-solving: invariably with the figures and equations, working without much overall understanding of what they are doing. Chris Dillon, in his account of qualitative approaches used by experts, character-izes them by the degree to which they reflect the device (that is to be controlled or understood) on the one hand, in contrast to the mathematics (or science) model that could be used to represent the device's operation on the other (Dillon 1994). This in part reflects the device knowledge indicated earlier and in part the fact that in a practical situation the science cannot cope with the complexity involved.

Let me illustrate the kind of complexity where qualitative approaches are useful, and do this in the context of a simple mechanism. As part of our research into problem-solving in design and technology lessons at Key Stage 3, colleagues and I observed two 12-year-old girls working on a mechanism that was to be used to collect money for charity. The mechanism contains a number of components (Figure 7.6): a falling coin channelled (A) to hit a balanced beam (B) with an integral pendulum (C), with an off-set pivot (D) connected to a bird shape on the other side (E), that would rock to peck a tree trunk (F). There is an operational principle of the overall mechanism, which the pupils have to understand. Each of the components (e.g. the force exerted by the falling coin, the pendulum swing) could be understood with science, and made to operate successfully: for example, varying the distance of fall of the coin to allow enough momentum to be gained so that even a small coin would cause rocking; balancing the beam horizontally by altering the off-set pivot and counterweight, such that the beam would move on impact. Now the science of this is well beyond children of this age, and it would be likely that even a professional engineer would be hard pushed to put down all the quantitative science and mathematics to represent the operation of such a system as a whole. Of course it wouldn't be worth it! Any engineer would use qualitative reasoning to ensure a working mechanism. There would be some experimenting with the size of coins on simple beams to determine the amount of fall necessary, and similarly with the counterweight on the beam (the beam size is a function of the overall size of the money box), and so on. It might look like trial and error, but in fact it would be qualitative reasoning supported by a knowledge of science. However, it would be a level of science at a much simpler level than required for the full explanation of the operation of individual components. The reasoning is a combination of procedural knowledge and device knowledge, which seeks to explain how the initial fall of the coin works its way through the mechanism to end up in the desired effect of the bird pecking the tree.

The qualitative reasoning is not just a feature of the way an engineer might work, but also of how the two girls and their teacher worked. In our classroom research of this project we recorded their reasoning at three points. The first was at the beginning of the project when the pupils go to the teacher with their idea of a woodpecker that pecks a tree when money is put in the box. The teacher illustrates the rocking movement with his hand. As he does this he says, 'Transmit movement (from lever[7] to bird) to the front …', and then tells the pupils that they must lock the pivot to the lever 'to make sure it runs … (with the lever)'. Neither of these statements draws on much conventional science and the wording is close to the physical nature of the mechanism.

The second point we observed was when, later in the first lesson, the pupils started to model the mechanism in card, working from an example mechanism of a rocking boat. The girls try to decide on the positions of the components, including the bird, based on how much the beam moves for different-sized coins. At first one girl tries to locate the bird (cut out as a separate piece) relative to the tree trunk that she is trying to draw on the front cover sheet. She starts with the bird in its normal upright position and then rocks it, saying: 'It'll be in that position first of all, then it's going to go knock, knock.' (The 'knock' is the sound of the bird pecking the tree.) She then moves to the example mechanism and reasons about how it operates with different-sized coins:

P: It depends how much money they put in, because if it's a 50p, it's going to go 'dong' like that, so it's going to go really far.

P: Then if it's a 5p … it will still move … but only a little bit …

The girl uses language that reflects the object ('dong' – the sound a big coin makes), and it is qualitative in the way it describes the amount of movement ('really far', 'a little bit').

In the second week of the project, when they were making the actual mechanism, the pupils went to the teacher for help and he said they had to balance the beam. This was done with BluTack as the counterweight on the left-hand end of the beam (Figure 7.6). He used phrases such as:

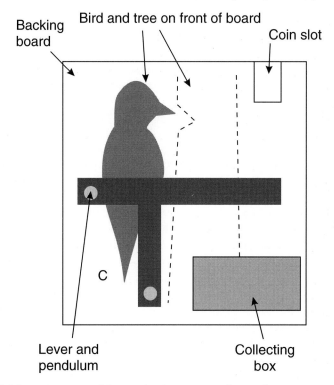

Backing board

Bird and tree on front of board

Coin slot

C

Lever and pendulum

Collecting box

Figure 7.6 The components of the woodpecker money collection box

> Balance that (lever) up with a bit of BluTack … stick another bit on it …

> The further over you get it (BluTack) … some more leverage … it's beginning to balance now.

There are some scientific ideas involved, but it is very qualitative, with language close to the operation of the mechanism.

Such qualitative reasoning could be improved if it was the focus of the learning. In the end the pupils are working out the effect of dropping different-sized coins, and the way that effect works its way through the mechanism. The teacher could encourage the pupils to follow his reasoning, and to explain to him the effect of dropping coins. The science that they used could be related to how certain effects can be changed (e.g. to increase 'sensitivity' of the beam to small coins), so that pupils could predict the likely effects of changes. This reflects the approach of the 'causal accounts' that Dillon (1994) describes as one kind of 'qualitative reasoning' that is being formalized as a way of dealing with complex situations. He also notes that these are the kinds of explanations of electronic circuits found in undergraduate texts, and our researches on design and technology have indicated similar teacher explanations for circuits in secondary schools (Levinson, Murphy and

McCormick 1997; McCormick and Murphy 1994). If such qualitative reasoning is so much a feature of technological thinking and action, then we should make sure that we try to develop pupils' abilities to use it.

The usual way in which we think about explaining devices and systems, such as mechanisms or electric circuits, is to use knowledge from science. There are a number of assumptions that underlie this. The first is that the science does indeed explain the devices. Layton (1993) has reminded us of Polanyi's idea of the *operational principle* which, according to Polanyi, determines how components in, say, a machine, fulfil their functions and combine in an overall operation that achieves the function of the machine (Polanyi 1962, p. 328). Layton contrasts this operational principle, as technological knowledge, with that of science: science, he argues, cannot contrive such a principle, but can explain the success and failure of it, and lead to improvement of it. This then sees science and mathematics in a supportive role, not a determining role, and the idea of technology as the 'appliance of science' is a misrepresentation of the situation. This is evident in the case of the mechanism of the money-box.

Capability found?

My argument has had a number of strands to get me to the point of seeing a role for qualitative knowledge within capability. First, I have tried to illustrate that early models of capability were based upon processes. This focus put knowledge to one side, and also characterized the process (design or problem-solving) in ways that did not do justice to its use in practice (by learners or experts). Expert problem-solving, for example, is based on rich knowledge of the context and the substance of the problem and its solution. Although it has a strong procedural element, it is not simply procedural. Where (conceptual) knowledge is assumed to be relevant (e.g. the use of science or mathematics), insufficient attention is paid to the nature of that knowledge. The context within which knowledge is learned and used has a profound impact on how it is conceived by individuals (learners and experts). Knowledge that is used by experts is not only tied to the context (device knowledge), but it is qualitative in nature. This links the conceptual knowledge to the procedural knowledge. Indeed the division of the two becomes less significant, as causal explanations are essentially procedural and yet indicate relationships that are typical of conceptual knowledge. As procedural knowledge is the substance of processes such as problem-solving and design, these processes cannot be seen in isolation from conceptual knowledge.

Thus we arrive at the situation where we must consider processes (procedural knowledge) as intimately linked with conceptual knowledge, and that also this conceptual knowledge is related to the objects in technology (e.g. the tools and devices): hence the use of the term 'device knowledge'. Qualitative knowledge, and with it qualitative reasoning about the devices in technology, are central to this view of knowledge. Qualitative knowledge is linked to action of all kinds, whether that be designing or solving problems.

I have argued for the importance of qualitative knowledge and the reasoning associated with it. Given this importance, we must teach this kind of knowledge, and ensure a greater role for it in teaching pupils to act technologically. Some of this teaching will be through pupils being helped in trying to understand devices (products and applications). When pupils are investigating or dismantling products they can develop ways of reasoning about the operation of these products. Some of this can be done through the more usual design-and-make activities, where making modifications to, or trying to establish, new products will give opportunities for reasoning, in the way the two girls did with their money-box. But ... we still have much to do to investigate what teachers and pupils currently do with regard to this kind of knowledge. Any experienced teacher will reason qualitatively quite naturally, and all they need to do is to make this more explicit, and to support pupils in developing this kind of reasoning. In some ways this may come more easily to them than the design processes that they are required to teach, especially where they are not expert practitioners of design themselves. We still have much to do in understanding how we teach design and problem-solving, and how qualitative reasoning links with these processes.

The way those involved in design and technology have refined their views on processes, albeit slowly, now needs to be developed to incorporate those of knowledge. My exploration of this kind of knowledge has sought to suggest that we should not look in the first instance to the abstraction of science and mathematics, but to the practical knowledge used by technologists. This search does not imply a swing from 'process' to 'knowledge', but the search for the relationship of the two. Nor does this imply that science and mathematics are to be ignored but that their role in the design and technology lesson may be more complex than assumed. For me this route would lead to the finding of that 'paradise', if that is indeed what it is.

Notes

1   In particular I will draw on work funded by the ESRC (*Problem solving in technology education: a case of situated learning?*), the Design Council (Mathematics by Design), and the Open University. I would like to acknowledge the work of Patricia Murphy, Marian Davidson and Hilary Evens, all of whom have contributed to the research, thinking and writing that formed the basis of this lecture. I would also like to acknowledge the help of Frank Banks, Gwyneth Owen-Jackson, and Frank Whiteman, all of who commented on an earlier draft.

2   Ofsted reports have highlighted the way lessons often leave pupils with no real decision making or creativity (e.g. Ofsted, 1995, p. 11).

3   When Murphy *et al.* (1995) reviewed the field they found relatively few; more recent studies have improved the situation (Doornekamp and Streumer, 1996; Kimbell, Stables and Green, 1996: Mioduser, 1998; Murphy and McCormick, 1997: Roden, 1997: Welch and Lim, 1998).

4   Science education has gone through a similar realization from the early days of process science, to the current position where 'process' is associated with particular conceptual areas. See Murphy and McCormick (1997) for a comparison of science and technology with regard to process.

5 'Knowledge' used in this general way refers to 'factual and conceptual knowledge', although, as it will become clear, even these categories are insufficient to explain the situation.
6 A version of this sub-section is published in McCormick (1999).
7 The teacher refers to the 'beam' as a 'lever', reflecting the kind of science terms with which the pupils would have been familiar.

References

ACCAC (2000) *National Curriculum, Design and Technology*, Cardiff: HMSO.

ACCAC (2000) *The School Curriculum in Wales*, Cardiff: ACCAC.

APU (1987) *Design and Technology Activity: A Framework for Assessment*, London: APU/ DES.

APU (1991) *The Assessment of Performance in Design and Technology*, London: Schools Examinations and Assessment Council.

Bissell, C. C. and Dillon, C. R. (1993) 'Back to the backs of envelopes', *The Times Higher Education Supplement*, 10 September: 16.

Black, P. and Harrison, G. (1985) *In Place of Confusion: Technology and Science in the School Curriculum*, London: The Nuffield-Chelsea Curriculum Trust/The National Centre for School Technology, Trent Polytechnic.

DFE/WO (1995) *Design and Technology in the National Curriculum*, London: HMSO.

DfEE/QCA (1999) *The National Curriculum Handbook for Secondary Teachers in England*, London: HMSO.

Dillon, C. (1994) 'Qualitative reasoning about physical systems – an overview', *Studies in Science Education* 23: 39–57.

Doornekamp, B. G. and Streumer, J. N. 'Problem solving in teaching/learning packages for technology', *International Journal of Technology and Design Education* 6(1): 61–82.

Driver, R., Guesne, E. and Tiberghien, A. (eds) (1985) *Children's Ideas in Science*, Buckingham: Open University Press.

Evens, H. and McCormick, R. (1997) *Mathematics by Design: An Investigation into Key Stage 3 – Report to the Design Council*, Milton Keynes: School of Education, Open University.

Evens, H. and McCormick, R. (1998) 'The use of mathematics in secondary school design and technology', paper in symposium, *The Use of Mathematics in Science and Technology Education*, British Educational Research Association Annual Conference, Belfast: 27–30

Foxman, D. *et al.* (undated) 'Assessment of Performance Unit' (APU), *A Review of Monitoring in Mathematics 1978–82 Part 1*. (No publisher or date given.)

Glaser, R. (1984) 'Education and thinking: the role of knowledge', *American Psychologist* 39(2): 93–104.

Glaser, R. (1992) 'Expert knowledge and processes of thinking', in D. F. Halpern (ed.) *Enhancing Thinking Skills in the Sciences and Mathematics*, Hillsdale, NJ: Erlbaum, pp. 63–75.

Gott, S. H. (1988) 'Apprenticeship instruction for real-world tasks: the co-ordination of procedures, mental models and strategies', in E. Z. Rothkopf (ed.) *Review of Research in Education* 15 1988–89: 97–169. Washington DC: American Educational Research Association.

Hennessy, S., McCormick, R. and Murphy, P. (1993) 'The myth of general problem solving capability: design and technology as an example', *Curriculum Journal* 4(1): 74–89.

Jeffery, J. R. (1990) 'Design methods in CDT', *Journal of Art and Design Education* 9(1): 57–70.

Kerslake, D. (1979) 'Visual mathematics', *Mathematics in School* 8(2): 34–35.

Kimbell, R., Stables, K. and Green, R. (1996) *Understanding Practice in Design and Technology*, Milton Keynes: Open University Press.

Layton, D. (1993) *Technology's Challenge to Science Education*, Buckingham: Open University Press.

Levinson, R., Murphy, P. and McCormick, R. (1997) 'Science and technology concepts in a design and technology project: a pilot study', *Research in Science and Technolgical Education* 15(2): 235–55.

McCormick, R. (1997) 'Conceptual and procedural knowledge', *International Journal of Technology and Design Education* 7(1–2): 141–59.

McCormick, R. (1999) 'Practical knowledge: a view from the snooker table', in R. McCormick and C. Pachter (eds) *Learning and Knowledge*, London: Paul Chapman.

McCormick, R. and Davidson, M. (1996) 'Problem solving and the tyranny of product outcomes', *Journal of Design and Technology Education* 1(3): 230–41.

McCormick, R. and Murphy, P. (1994) 'Learning the processes in technology', paper presented at the British Educational Research Association Annual Conference, Oxford University, England, September.

McCormick, R., Murphy, P. and Davidson, M. (1994) 'Design and Technology as revelation and ritual', in J. S. Smith (ed.) *IDATER 94 – International Conference on Design and Technology Educational Research and Curriculum Development*, University of Loughborough, Loughborough, pp. 38–42.

McCormick, R., Murphy, P. and Hennessy, S. (1994) 'Problem solving in Design and Technology: a case of situated learning?', paper presented at the Annual Meeting of the American Education Research Association, New Orleans, Louisiana, April.

Mioduser (1998) 'Framework for the study of cognitive and curricular issues of technological problem solving', *International Journal of Technology and Design Education* 8(2): 167–84.

Murphy, P., Hennessy, S., McCormick, R. and Davidson, M. (1995) 'The nature of problem solving in technology education', paper presented to the European Conference on Educational Research, University of Bath, England, 14–17 September.

Murphy, P. and McCormick, R. (1997) 'Problem solving in science and technology education', *Research in Science and Education* 27(3): 461–81.

NCC (1990) *Non-Statutory Guidance: Design and Technology Capability*, York: NCC.

Ofsted (1995) *Design and Technology: A Review of Inspection Findings 1993/4*, London: HMSO.

Osborne, R. and Freyberg, P. (eds) (1985) *Learning in Science: the implications of children's science*, London: Heinemann.

Polanyi, M. (1962) *Personal Knowledge: Towards a Post-critical Philosophy*, London: Routledge and Kegan Paul.

Roden, C. (1997) 'Young children's problem solving in design and technology: towards a taxonomy of strategies', *Journal of Design and Technology Education* 2(1): 14–19.

Schools Council (1982) *Problem Solving*, (Pupil book, Teachers' Guide and Workbook), Edinburgh: Oliver and Boyd/National Centre for School Technology.

Scribner, S. (1985) 'Knowledge at work', *Anthropology and Education Quarterly* 16(3): 199–206.

Sternberg, R. J. and Caruso, D. R. (1985) 'Practical modes of knowing', in E. Eisner (ed.) *Learning and teaching ways of knowing*, Chicago: National Society for the Study of Education, pp. 133–58.

Welch, M. and Lim, H. S. (1998) 'The effect of problem type on the strategies used by novice designers', in Smith, J. (ed.) *IDATER 98 International Conference on Design and Technology Educational Research and Curriculum Development*, Department of Design and Technology, Loughborough University.

8   The general problem-solving process in technology education
Myth or reality?

Sara Hennessy and Robert McCormick

This chapter picks up on an aspect of capability discussed in the previous chapter. It discusses what is meant by the term 'problem-solving' and looks at some research in the area. It raises a question of whether what is taken to be problem-solving in design and technology teaching is always so, a question that you might consider for yourself. The chapter ends with some considerations of the implications for teachers of Design and Technology.

The chapter originally appeared in Teaching Technology *and has been updated by the author for this edition.*

Introduction

'Problem-solving' is a much abused term in many areas of the curriculum, including technology. A basic confusion exists between *problem-based learning* and teaching *problem-solving methods*. Most areas of the curriculum give pupils problems to solve as one approach to learning, where the main purpose is to help pupils understand certain concepts or ideas in the subject. The actual *process* of solving the problem may be unimportant. In technology education, problem-based learning could be used to teach about mechanisms by, for example, setting a problem of transforming one kind of movement into another (perhaps dressed up in some 'realistic' context of someone needing to produce a toy with an electric motor to make the hair rise up and down on a puppet). This pedagogic strategy is very important because the learner is active and the problem makes the learning meaningful.

When teaching problem-solving methods, on the other hand, the processes involved in solving the problem are the focus, and understanding of concepts (*conceptual* knowledge) is usually of secondary importance. Those who are concerned to teach problem-solving consider it to be of more lasting relevance to pupils than content. Often they characterize problem-solving as some kind of idealized process involving the sub-processes of recognizing a problem, generating and implementing a solution, and evaluating the results. Knowledge of these sub-processes (*procedural* knowledge) is seen as applying across a variety of areas of the curriculum. In technology education, such a set of sub-processes is used to unite five previously separate curriculum areas (art and design, business studies, CDT, home economics and IT).

This approach depends upon some idea of a general problem-solving process that can be used in a variety of contexts and, if such a process exists, it is an important part of education. National Curriculum Technology intends to develop general practical capability, preparing pupils to 'become autonomous and creative problem-solvers' (DfEE/QCA 1999: 134). This idea of a general problem-solving capability is an attractive one, but is it just a myth? What is the evidence for a general problem-solving capability that can be taught, and that can be used in a variety of curriculum areas, and indeed in adult life? In this chapter we examine the evidence that derives from studying what both experts and ordinary people do in their everyday activity (what is called 'situated cognition'), and from the research in science education on children's 'alternative frameworks'. We also look at the specific difficulties of a process-based area such as design and technology, where the main concern is to learn to use the 'design-and-make' process.

Expert problem-solving

One obvious source for considering what we teach pupils about problem-solving is to look to see how experts solve problems. The sub-processes identified earlier for technology are based upon some idealized view of what experts do, but experts themselves disagree about this view (NEDO 1976). In fact, those who have studied how experts solve problems find that they do not follow a generalized decontextualized process (Glaser 1992). How experts work evidently varies according to the context in which they are working. In particular, they use considerable knowledge (much of it informal) about the problem area, and vary what they do according to the changing needs of particular problems. Significantly also, in actual work situations, experts work collaboratively, and have goals which they want to achieve and which they may even set. This makes the whole activity more meaningful to them.

Pupils in school (novice problem-solvers as they are called in the research literature) work in quite different situations from experts. They are not so goal-directed in solving a problem, nor do they work under the same constraints, and the task is less meaningful. More importantly, novices are continually working in unfamiliar contexts, where the nature of the problems and the knowledge required to solve them may not have been encountered before. Taken as a whole, the research on problem-solving challenges the idea of a general problem-solving process which is independent of the particular nature of the problem.

Situated cognition

Recent evidence from researchers taking a 'situated' perspective (predominantly in the area of mathematics learning) provides a similar challenge. This work spans several cultures and characterizes successful problem-solving strategies used in everyday life outside school. It has investigated mathematical capability in the workplace and in domestic life, documenting the craft apprenticeship of tailors in Liberia (Reed and Lave 1981), the everyday practice of arithmetic and manipulation of quantity relationships in grocery shopping, cooking, dieting and money management (Lave 1988), street vending in Brazil (Carraher, Carraher and Schliemann 1985, 1987), dairy workers' calculation strategies (Scribner 1984), and construction work (Carraher 1986). Researchers in this tradition have consistently found that concepts and relationships which appear complex to learners in a classroom context are dealt with inventively and effectively in everyday situations, and that problem-solving is structured into, and by, ongoing activity (Lave, Smith and Butler 1988). In other words, rather than applying some specialist procedure specifying how to solve a problem (e.g. identify the problem, generate solutions, etc.), people use a *variety* of methods that change appropriately according to the circumstances. Some key examples are as follows.

Most adults and children spontaneously invent their own, reliable mathematical procedures, and they rarely use the standard written methods outside school (Fitzgerald 1985; Shuard 1986). Two large-scale survey reports on adult numeracy have concluded that formal teaching lacks relevance to mathematics as commonly practised in daily life; many adults have forgotten those methods or they lack the confidence to use them (ALBSU 1983; Sewell 1982). By way of illustration, Lave (1988) has shown that personal methods are commonly invented and used successfully by adults in a practical situation (calculating the 'best buy' in a supermarket) with a very high degree of accuracy (98 per cent), whereas the same people solved only 59 per cent of similar calculations correctly in a written test. This finding, and that of Reed and Lave (1981), indicated that two distinct systems of arithmetic procedures and practices (symbol- or rule-based versus meaning-based) are functioning independently within the same culture, with different procedures and rates of success. This conclusion is corroborated by studies contrasting the calculation strategies employed by the same children selling produce in Brazilian street markets, in solving word problems and in computation exercises (Carraher *et al.* 1985; 1987). Similarly, construction workers have been found to demonstrate greater skill in applying proportional reasoning when interpreting blueprints than students who learned the principles in formal mathematics; the presence of physical objects in the builders' environment rendered the task more relevant to them (Carraher 1986).

Collectively this work shows that out-of-school problem-solving in mathematics can be sophisticated, but that it is intimately connected with the specific context, and it is the familiarity with this context that gives meaning to the activity. This contrasts with the school situation where mathematical operations are divorced from reality, have less meaning and hence appear more difficult. Skilled practical thinking varies to adapt to the changing circumstances of problems, and to the changing conditions while the problems are being solved (Scribner 1984). Formal procedures for solving problems are therefore largely unhelpful.

Constructivist research in science education

Students' mental models are similarly flexible and context-specific. Evidence for this comes from the wealth of research over the last two decades into 'alternative frameworks' in children's understanding of science (e.g. Driver 1989; McDermott 1984). There is conclusive evidence that children construct intuitive beliefs about natural phenomena (such as heat or forces) that conflict with the scientific view-point and that these beliefs are highly resistant to instruction and evidence to the contrary. These frameworks, and similarly lay adults' mental models of science and technology (Wynne, Payne and Wakeford 1990), often appear to be partial, inco-herent or internally inconsistent (Champagne, Gunstone and Klopfer 1985). This is because, as with everyday mathematics, pieces of knowledge or cognitive models (e.g. of electricity in a circuit) are being drawn upon flexibly and according to their appropriateness and usefulness in a *specific practical context*. These models provide a sensible framework for understanding and describing phenomena which fit with a person's existing beliefs and ideas about how the world works. For example, our common experience of moving objects is that they remain still unless we push them, yet we have to convince pupils that this model of motion is limited to a world with gravity and friction. Rather than such an Aristotelian view, we want pupils to use a Newtonian one that opposes their experience (i.e. to realize that a body con-tinues moving at a certain velocity unless acted upon by a force). In this sense pupils act in the same way as experts do, except that their models are derived from a different everyday experience. Research on problem-solving indicates the impor-tance of such models in understanding and hence solving problems (Glaser 1984).

The idea that we teach pupils correct conceptual models ('correct' because they have universal application and are shared by the scientific community) that they can then use in situations they meet in ordinary or working life ignores their experi-ence of alternative models that work in particular situations. Formal knowledge, such as that taught in science and mathematics, is not in a form that can simply be 'applied'. As Layton (1991) reminds us, formal scientific knowledge needs to be reconstructed, integrated and contextualized for practical action in everyday life. The expectation that pupils solving problems (such as they would encounter in technology education) can draw upon knowledge from other subject areas (e.g. sci-ence and mathematics) is therefore likely to be unrealistic. Work we have recently carried out at the Open University indicated that Year 8 pupils working on design and technology activities were unable to use, for example, elementary mathematics (e.g. simple arithmetic and geometric drawing) in their tasks (Evens and McCormick 1997), and confirms the informal work of Job (1991) on similar diffi-culties in using scientific knowledge.

In addition to the unrealistic demand for transfer of conceptual knowledge across curriculum areas, design and technology activities place a clear expectation upon pupils to assimilate an all-purpose 'design process' and apply it in up to five different subject areas which previously had little connection. However, the research on expert problem-solving and situated cognition points to the conclusion that the idea of a general problem-solving capability that can be used in a variety of contexts and subject areas has little empirical justification. The earlier discussion of the literature from cognitive psychology and situated cognition indicates that problem-solving in the areas of mathematics, science and technology will be differ-ent. Indeed, even within each of the three areas, particular problems and situations will require different approaches – that is, the implication of the doubt that research casts on a general problem-solving ability. However, this notion that there is such a general ability has a long tradition and there are instructional programmes specifically based upon it. What is the evidence for a general transferable problem-solving capability that can be taught, often independently of the prior acquisition of subject knowledge, and used flexibly in a variety of contexts? The next section examines this question.

Evidence for transfer

The development of programmes of instruction in higher order skills is based upon the assumed existence of universal cognitive skills of problem-solving and thinking. A well-known example is de Bono's CoRT (Cognitive Research Trust) Thinking Program. The CoRT programme uses generally familiar knowledge and is intended to foster problem-solving, interpersonal and lateral thinking skills, including metacognitive skills (i.e. reflecting upon one's own learning, planning a task, and apportioning time and resources) and a wide variety of idea- and solution-generation techniques and evaluation techniques. Although the programme has been widely used in the USA and elsewhere, very little systematic evaluation of it has taken place and there is minimal support for its lofty claims that students will transfer their new thinking skills to 'a variety of real-life situations' (de Bono 1985). While anecdotal evidence is often positive and short-term gains have been reported by Edwards (1991), the first substantial evaluation of de Bono's classroom materials by the Schools Council (Hunter-Grundin 1985) failed to demonstrate any significant transfer. Although there is some other evidence to support the notion of general cognitive skill development (Adey and Shayer 1994) the limitations of transfer theory and the importance of context in the application of knowledge and skills have increasingly been recognized and demonstrated empirically (Glaser 1984; Lave 1988).

In sum, research shows that what problem-solvers of all ages in everyday and workplace situations actually do and know depends on the context in which they are asked to work, and bears little relation to what goes on in the average classroom. Why, then, has the traditional classroom environment become an alien culture which lacks relevance to the everyday problem-solving practices and thinking which take place outside it?

Problem-solving inside and outside the classroom

The findings reported above are not altogether surprising when we explore the differences between problem-solving processes in classrooms and everyday situations. These differences include individual as opposed to group activity, the nature of incentives and the way problems and their solutions are formulated:

1   In school, a premium is placed upon what individuals can do by themselves and without external support (Resnick 1987). Yet teamwork is the norm in

practical settings outside school (especially in technological activity), where learning is characterized by the sharing of informal knowledge and the construction and negotiation of meaning (Wenger 1991).

2   The incentives outside school lead to learning that is self-motivated or commercially driven and the problems encountered are hence authentic and relevant to the learner rather than artificially constructed.

3   In school, many problems are pre-formulated and accompanied by the requisite data, whereas outside school, problems are seldom clearly defined initially and the information necessary for solving them must be actively sought from a variety of sources (Maier 1980).

4   Although the same subject topics arise in both contexts, the methods used are quite different; school mathematics relies heavily on paper and pencil, for instance, and the greatest premium is placed on pure thought activities – what individuals can do without the external support of books, notes, calculators or other complex instruments. In contrast, most mental activities and actions in everyday life are intimately engaged with the physical world with objects, events and with some form of tools. The resultant cognitive activity is shaped by and dependent upon the kinds of tools available (Resnick 1987).

The result of the differences between problem-solving inside and outside the classroom, and the devaluing of pupils' own informal knowledge, is that pupils are likely to ignore the formal methods taught in school. They secretly adhere to their own reliable and far more flexible, intuitive methods whilst presenting a 'veneer of accomplishment' (Lave, Smith and Butler 1988). This phenomenon is explored further below in the context of technology education.

Design and technology as a process-oriented curriculum

In England and Wales, the design and technology component of Technology in the National Curriculum previously defined capability explicitly in terms of the ability to employ the sub-processes of: identifying and clarifying tasks or problems; investigating; generating and developing solutions; evaluating (DES/WO 1990). These correspond to the kinds of general processes in the literature discussed earlier. Design educators maintain that these broad processes are universal, and proponents of this approach make great claims about the variety of potential outcomes. Examples include discovery, critical assessment, decision-making, problem-solving, planning, evaluating, reflecting and collaboration (deLuca 1992). In the first revision of the National Curriculum (DfEE/WO 1995) these sub-processes were subsumed, and capability was to be developed through the combination of designing and making skills with knowledge and understanding. In the English National Curriculum for 2000, capability is only implicit and is inferred as the application of knowledge and understanding to the development of ideas; planning; producing and evaluating products (DfEE/QCA 1999). These broader definitions, however, still encompass the sub-processes described above. Eggleston (1994) makes the claim that such skills will have a 'wide general applicability in the adult life likely to be experienced by the students'. Sellwood (1990) asserts that the value of the process approach lies in its structuring and organizing of thinking skills, and that it will ideally become second nature to pupils (and teachers) to organize a means of successfully achieving objectives which can then operate at all levels and in all situations. How realistic are these claims, especially in the light of the evidence examined earlier in this chapter?

The answer is far from clear. The only substantive published research was not based upon what pupils did, but upon the records of their design-and-make activity (sketches, notes, drawings, 3D models, prototypes and finished products), along with interviews with the pupils and their teachers (APU 1991). Our research at the Open University has investigated the way in which pupils work as they carry out design-and-make tasks. Although there has been no large-scale study of design and technology teachers' views of problem-solving, the many teachers we have interviewed exhibit a variety of views, especially with regard to its relationship to the design process. Some see design and problem-solving as synonymous in the correspondence of the steps used to represent each process. Others see design as often starting with a 'problem' (for example, how can we help to provide a physically disabled child with stimulating hand-eye coordination exercises?), but thereafter they are less concerned with a problem-solving process. It is likely that as pupils progress through their years of design and technology education they will come across teachers with different views on this, even in schools where the same design 'process' is used. This process is used to structure the pupils' progress through design-and-make tasks (Week 1: identify need; Week 2: create alternative designs, and so on). It is also fixed in the way design folders are constructed. Although this process can be a helpful structure it often does not reflect pupils' thinking about the design process or their problem-solving (whether they are seen as the same or different). It is treated as a ritual to go through (see McCormick, Davidson and Murphy 1994). So an over-emphasis on this process can lead to a 'veneer of accomplishment', where pupils appear to use a process (and hence have apparently learned it) but, in fact, may not have used it. (This is also evident in other subjects, such as mathematics.) Earlier work in design and technology has shown pupils omit unsuccessful designs from their project folders (Anning 1992) and describe a logical, systematic procedure rather than the actual development of design ideas (Jeffery 1990). The Hayes Report (1983) indicates that the 'veneer' extends to professional designers who can be observed to doctor their portfolios too, as a consequence of working under the same frustrating constraint of having to offer several alternative solutions to a design problem.

The problems that pupils solve, and the ways they approach them, are more varied than an algorithmic step-by-step process (see Murphy and McCormick 1997). For some pupils, problems are solved by turning to another pupil or the teacher for help; for others, problems are avoided (for example, by choosing a material that is familiar and which poses no problems in forming, etc.). When pupils go to a teacher with a problem, such as a circuit that doesn't work or a joining process that is complex, we have instances where teachers 'give' solutions, but do not make explicit their thinking to pupils. In other cases, teachers have encouraged pupils to think, either by asking a series of questions or presenting a range of solutions from which the pupil has to choose. It is, of course, rare to find design and technology classrooms where the design process is not taught explicitly. However, this is invariably done at the beginning of a project and in the abstract. In an effort to establish unity across a department, and to conform to a common assessment of the design process, pupils are taught the steps in an invariant way. Thus, in food technology, where a 'product development' approach might be more appropriate (systematic make, change and remake of the product), the design process is taught in the same way as in resistant materials. At some level the algorithm is useful, but research on procedural knowledge such as problem-solving indicates that some kind of reflection on that process is necessary. This reflection could be at various points in the process and could include discussions on the merits of one approach as opposed to another. For example, is a user test or a scientific experiment the most appropriate way of evaluating a product, or how much evaluation of existing products needs to be done at the initial stages of the process?

A critical insight derived from the situated cognition literature discussed earlier is that in rich problem-solving contexts, problems emerge out of dilemmas presenting a personal challenge. Learning arises when means are sought to resolve those dilemmas (Lave *et al.* 1988). Design and technology has greater potential than any other curriculum area for problems to be formulated in the context of authentic activity, so that pupils might engage in both reflective and active participation (two aspects identified as important by Kimbell *et al.* APU 1991). New or 'emergent' problems often arise during the course of design and technology activities, which present unique opportunities for learning through open-ended project work. (Thus, producing a stable structure for a kite might become for the pupil the 'problem' that emerges during construction, superseding the more global 'problem' presented by the teacher of creating a kite for a special occasion; see McCormick, Murphy and Hennessy 1994.) The popular idea that 'problem-solving' in technology must be confined to a holistic 'design-and-make' process is hence under challenge. Our position is that 'design-and-make' is instead a complex and iterative process of refining problems; various kinds of tasks, and stages within them, present different problems which require different approaches. According to Lave (1988), authentic problem-solving activity is commonly represented as a systematic sequence of recognizing a problem, representing it, implementing a resolution and evaluating the results. Unfortunately this ignores the multitude of ways of tackling a problem and the fact that some activities take place simultaneously or structure each other differently on different occasions.

Unfulfilled ambitions

To summarize, there appears to be a conflict between the problem-solving literature and the ambitious assumptions made in technology education, particularly that of a generally applicable design and problem-solving process. The research evidence casts doubt on any one general model of problem-solving, and design and technology activities may therefore not be fulfilling the ambitious aims of applicability of their proponents. The technology curriculum covers an impossibly wide range of activities and cannot prepare students for all kinds of future problem-solving, but is applicable only to those problems with related content (Medway 1992). Pupils have difficulty in operating with decontextualized knowledge, in using knowledge acquired in other subject areas and in bridging with problem-solving outside school. The present demand for pupils to conceive and develop an explicit design proposal bears no relation to expert practice and the demand for the artificial generation of several design ideas may be counter-productive. These demands could lead to children mechanically following a sequence of systematic procedures. To avoid this, more explicit attention needs to be given to developing students' problem-solving skills (Johnson 1987). 'Problem-solving' in technology is in fact much more than a straightforward sequence of 'design and make'; it requires a complex range of different approaches according to the changing nature and requirements of the activity undertaken, the information available, the stage reached and individual learning style. Rigidly fostering a single all-purpose process is inherently unproductive, and children need to realize that there are inevitably multiple ways to solve any problem.

A way forward?

Despite the evidence that most forms of everyday problem-solving require context-specific forms of competence, there is nevertheless evidence that global problem-solving strategies may also have a role to play. After all, situation-specific learning by itself can be very limiting, precluding transfer when familiar aspects of a task are changed. Decontextualized knowledge is potentially a powerful aid which helps us master complex situations and results in far greater flexibility.

A major implication of the research literature is that instruction needs to achieve a balance between subject matter knowledge, general problem-solving strategies and strategies for effective learning (Glaser 1984). Encouraging steps have indeed been taken in this direction in the form of the work on 'cognitive acceleration' across the curriculum through science learning (Adey and Shayer 1994), and a series of highly successful 'cognitive apprenticeship' programmes for mathematics and language learning (Palincsar and Brown 1984; Schoenfeld 1985). These promote situated learning by giving students the opportunity to observe, engage in, and invent or discover expert strategies in context. They also aim to extend situated learning to different settings, decontextualizing knowledge by explicitly conveying cognitive and metacognitive strategies for monitoring its use. The time is right to explore the potential of similar instructional approaches in other subjects such as technology. Johnson and Thomas (1992) have pointed out that apprenticeship programmes could easily be adapted for technological problem-solving, with teachers serving as role models for students, solving unfamiliar problems without fear of making errors or of encountering difficulties in finding solutions. Technology teachers could thereby show students how to collect and use information to solve technological problems and help them realize that not all problems have straightforward solutions.

Implications for the teacher

The above discussion yields several implications for educational practice in the context of the requirements of the National Curriculum. First, if teachers believe that the general design and problem-solving process is useful and can be transferred across many different contexts then they must endeavour to make it explicit. Children will *not respond* to a process approach otherwise. This has at least three consequences.

1   *Teachers must have a clear idea or model of the component processes involved and how they are inter-related*

Such an idea has to be developed in the knowledge that there is disagreement about the various models put forward. (See McCormick 1993 for a discussion of some of these models.) In particular, the degree of iteration in the process is controversial among engineers (NEDO 1976) and educators, who disagree about which models to follow and whose choices reflect their different motivations (e.g. working in industrial settings or developing creative potential in children). Unfortunately it is common practice to interpret the problem-solving sub-processes as ordered steps in a linear process (HMI 1992: 18), despite warnings in the *Non-Statutory Guidance* (NCC 1991) and in the first report of the APU Design and Technology Project (1987: 2.12):

> Used unsympathetically, the approach can reveal a greater concern for 'doing' all the stages in the process, than for combining a growing range of capabilities in a way which reflects individual creativity and confident and effective working methods (the 'ritual' referred to earlier).

A sympathetic approach may allow the use of a sequence of some sub-processes, but would encourage interaction and flexibility in their use.

2   *Teachers must attempt to structure and resource activities so that all pupils can exercise the sub-processes*

'Design-and-make' activities that always include a holistic process, with little or no focus on particular sub-processes (such as generating design ideas) are likely to make it difficult for pupils to build up their understanding of and skills at using the processes. We have already pointed out the importance of emergent problems, which may cloud pupils' view of the overall process. This, combined with the fact that activities stretch over a number of weeks, will tend to reduce the importance of the holistic process and fail to help pupils in exercising specific sub-processes that could be used at a variety of stages in their activity. Thus some activities should have a specific focus on particular sub-processes. For example, an activity could focus on evaluation, requiring pupils to draw up a specification and use it to evaluate their product. Such sub-processes can be introduced at different stages to show that they need to be used flexibly; an activity might begin by evaluating an existing product as a way of identifying a need in the market or to help generate ideas for a new design (in addition to using evaluation to assess alternative designs or finished products made by pupils).

3 There must be some method by which pupils are supposed to recognize, reflect on and use these sub-processes

This is essentially an issue of teachers talking about their teaching with pupils, who should be informed what the emphasis of the activity is and what the teacher is aiming to do. Self-assessment and group discussions about the process they have used could play a crucial role in getting them to reflect upon the sub-processes. If pupils are to learn about processes, they must be conscious of them and actively engage in developing their own capability in employing them.

The second teaching implication concerns the way knowledge is used in design and technology tasks. If pupils are required to be able to use scientific knowledge, for example, then some deliberate effort will be needed to facilitate and support this. Teachers must help pupils apply such knowledge in the context of a specific problem. At its simplest level, this means a teacher being aware in general terms of what science and mathematics pupils have encountered, and realizing that the inability to use this knowledge can prevent pupils from using the problem-solving processes (see McCormick, Chapter 7, for a discussion of the role of knowledge in design and technology). More problematic is the need to spend time with individual pupils when they appear to be stuck, helping them to access and use their knowledge. For most teachers there is only time to give a quick fix by telling a pupil what to do or 'providing' the knowledge, without being able to get pupils to make the transformation discussed earlier in this chapter.

Third, there is a need for pupils to develop 'metacognitive strategies', to 'think about their thinking'. In teaching mathematical problem-solving, Schoenfeld (1985) encouraged pupils to ask themselves questions about what they were doing, what they were trying to achieve and what they would do next. Continual asking of such questions eventually led pupils to internalize them and this improved their problem-solving performance. Requiring children to assess and monitor their own progress and performance in this way should help make pupils aware of what they are doing and why.

The fourth pedagogic implication follows up the idea of 'cognitive apprenticeship' introduced earlier. This requires pupils to be able to work with and observe an expert solving design and technology problems, or at least aspects of them. The expert could be the teacher undertaking design and technology activities, or an outside expert (designer or engineer) could be brought in to work with pupils so they can see how he or she works. In most design and technology classrooms, the teacher rarely takes part in activity, and usually only demonstrates particular skills rather than modelling problem-solving strategies. This is often to ensure that the pupil becomes involved in the task rather than just getting the teacher to do the work, but the result is that the pupils never see the teacher solving the kinds of problems they will encounter.

Apprenticeship can also take place in the context of peer interaction and collaboration. A situation where pupils are working together is both beneficial to learning and reflects most technological activity outside of school. To overcome the problems of individual assessment as part of a group, specific roles and division of labour may be necessary. Certain parts of the design and technology process become more significant in group work. For example, a pupil group acting as the market research department can draw up a specification that is used with a concept design team, a detailed design team, and a manufacturing group. Thus the specification acts as the common terms of reference for several teams, just as it does in industry. Similarly, the communication function of modelling (2–D or 3–D) can be exploited when, for example, the design team produce their ideas for the detailed design team, and the detailed design team produce manufacturing drawings. Discussions and negotiations in these kinds of situations will make more explicit many of the processes that design and technology teachers are anxious to encourage. The group work will provide a more meaningful engagement with these processes as a means to solving the problems as they occur within the 'design-and-make' task.

Finally, the most successful technology education programmes strive to promote pupils' 'ownership' of problems. These problems should be ones pupils want to solve, which are real and relevant *to them*, and for which they can take responsibility. This means providing opportunities for discovery and invention of problems, as well as solutions. We believe that 'problem-solving' must come to denote the resolution of meaningful problems and dilemmas in the context of guided social interaction and negotiation with teachers and peers.

To conclude, we would ask teachers to examine their own views on problem-solving in the light of the evidence we have presented. The fact that the research base on how pupils solve technological problems is as yet relatively weak means that teachers must carry out such an examination in a spirit of exploration.

References

Adey, P. and Shayer, M. (1994) *Really Raising Standards: Cognitive Intervention and Academic Achievement*, London: Routledge.

ALBSU (Adult Literacy and Basic Skills Units) (1983) *Literacy and Numeracy: Evidence from the National Child Development Study*, London: ALBSU.

Anning, A. (1992) 'Learning design and technology in primary schools,' in R. McCormick, P. Murphy and M.E. Harrison (eds) *Teaching and Learning Technology*, London: Addison-Wesley.

APU (1987) *Design and Technological Activity: A Framework for Assessment*, London: HMSO.

APU (1991) *The Assessment of Performance in Design and Technology*, London: Schools Examinations and Assessment Council, HMSO.

Black, P. (1990) *Implementing Technology in the National Curriculum: Key Issues in Implementation*, London: The Standing Conference on Schools' Science and Technology and DATA.

Carraher, T.N. (1986) 'From drawings to buildings', *International Journal of Behavioural Development* 9: 527–44.

Carraher, T.N., Carraher, D.W. and Schliemann, A.D. (1985) 'Mathematics in the streets and in schools', *British Journal of Developmental Psychology* 3: 21–9.

Carraher, T.N., Carraher, D.W. and Schliemann, A.D. (1987) 'Written and oral mathematics', *Journal for Research in Mathematics Education* 18(2): 83–97.

Champagne, A.B., Gunstone, R.F. and Klopfer, L.E. (1985) 'Instructional consequences of students' knowledge about physical phenomena', in L.H.T. West and A.L. Pines (eds) *Cognitive Structure and Conceptual Change*, London: Academic Press.

de Bono, E. (1985) 'The CoRT Thinking Program', in J.W. Segal, S.F. Chipman and R. Glaser (eds) *Thinking and Learning Skills*, Vol. 1, Hillsdale, NJ: Erlbaum.

deLuca, V.W. (1992) 'Survey of technology education problem-solving activities', *The Technology Teacher*, February: 26–30.

DES/WO (1990) *Technology in the National Curriculum*, London: HMSO.

DfE/WO (1995) *Design and Technology in the National Curriculum*, London: HMSO.

Driver, R. (1989) 'Students' conceptions and the learning of science', *International Journal of Science Education* 11(5): 481–90.

Edwards, J. (1991) 'The direct teaching of thinking skills', in G. Evans (ed.) *Learning and Teaching Cognitive Skills*, Hawthorn, Victoria: Australian Council for Educational Research.

Eggleston, J. (1994) 'What is design and technology education?', in F. Banks (ed.) *Teaching Technology*, London: Routledge/The Open University.

Evens, H. and McCormick, R. (1997) '*Mathematics by Design: An Investigation at Key Stage 3* (final report for the Design Council), Milton Keynes: The Open University.

Fitzgerald, A. (1985) *New Technology and Mathematics in Employment*, Birmingham: Department of Curriculum Studies.

Glaser, R. (1984) 'Education and thinking: the role of knowledge', *American Psychologist* 39(2): 93–104.

Glaser, R. (1992) 'Expert knowledge and processes of thinking', in D.F. Halpern (ed.) *Enhancing Thinking Skills in Sciences and Mathematics*, Hillsdale, NJ: Erlbaum.

Hayes Report (1983) *The Industrial Requirements of Industry*, A report commissioned by the DES and undertaken by Chris Hayes Associates and Keller Dorsey Associates, London, Design Council.

HMI (Her Majesty's Inspectorate of Schools) (1992) *Technology at Key Stages 1, 2 and 3*, London: HMSO.

Hunter-Grundin, E. (1985) *Teaching Thinking: An Evaluation of Edward de Bono's Classroom Materials*, London: Schools Council Publications.

Jeffery, J.R. (1990) 'Design methods in CDT', *Journal of Art and Design Education* 9(1): 57–70.

Job, G.C. (1991) 'The relationship between science and technology in the school entitlement curriculum', in M. Hacker, A. Gordon and M. de Vries (eds) *Integrating Advanced Technology into Technology Education*, Berlin: Springer-Verlag.

Johnson, S.D. (1987) 'Teaching problem solving', *School Shop*, February: 15–17.

Johnson, S.D. and Thomas, R. (1992) 'Technology education and the cognitive revolution', *The Technology Teacher* 51(4): 7–12.

Lave, J. (1988) *Cognition in Practice: Mind, Mathematics and Culture in Everyday Life*, New York: Cambridge University Press.

Lave, J., Smith, S. and Butler, M. (1988) 'Problem solving as an everyday practice', in J. Lave, J.G. Greeno, A. Schoenfeld, S. Smith and M. Butler (eds), *Learning Mathematical Problem Solving*, Institute for Research on Learning Report no. IRL88–0006, Palo Alto, CA.

Layton, D. (1991) 'Science education and praxis: the relationship of school science to practical action', *Studies in Science Education* 19: 43–79.

Maier, E. (1980) 'Folk mathematics', *Mathematics Teaching* 93: 21–3.

McCormick, R. (1993) *Teaching and Learning Design*, PGCE Pamphlet, Milton Keynes: Open University.

McCormick, R., Davidson, M. and Murphy, P. (1994) 'Design and Technology as revelation and ritual', in J.S. Smith (ed.) *IDATER94 – International Conference in Design and Technology Educational Research and Development*, Loughborough: University of Loughborough.

McCormick, R., Murphy, P. and Hennessy, S. (1994) 'Problem-solving processes in technology education: a pilot study', *International Journal of Technology and Design Education* 4; 5–34.

McDermott, L.C. (1984) 'Research on conceptual understanding in mechanics', *Physics Today*, July: 24–32.

Medway, P. (1992) 'Constructions of technology: reflections on a new subject', in J. Beynon and H. Mackay (eds) *Technological Literacy and the Curriculum*, London: Falmer.

Murphy, P. and McCormick, R. (1997) 'Problem-solving in science and technology education', *Research in Science Education* 27(3): 461–481.

NCC (1989) *Design and Technology for Ages 5–16: Proposals of the Secretary of State for Education and Science and the Secretary of State for Wales*, York: NCC.

NCC (1991) *Non-Statutory Guidance for Design and Technology*, York: NCC.

NEDO (National Economic Development Office) (1976) *The Professions in the Construction Industries*, London: NEDO.

Palincsar, A.S. and Brown, A.L. (1984) 'Reciprocal teaching of comprehension-fostering and comprehension-monitoring activities', *Cognition and Instruction* 7(2): 117–75.

Reed, H.J. and Lave, J. (1981) 'Arithmetic as a tool for investigating relations between culture and cognition', in R.W. Casson (ed.) *Language, Culture and Cognition: Anthropological Perspectives*, New York: Macmillan.

Resnick, L.B. (1987) 'Learning in school and out', *Educational Researcher* 16(9): 13–20.

Roazzi, A. and Bryant, P. (1992) 'Social class, context and cognitive development', in P. Light and G. Butterworth (eds) *Context and Cognition: Ways of Learning and Knowing*, Hemel Hempstead: Harvester Wheatsheaf.

Schoenfeld, A.H. (1985), *Mathematical Problem Solving*, Orlando, FL: Academic Press.

Schoenfeld, A.H. (1987) 'What's all the fuss about metacognition?' in A.H. Schoenfeld (ed.) *Cognitive Science and Mathematics Education*, Hillsdale, NJ: Erlbaum.

Scribner, S. (1984) 'Studying working intelligence', in B. Rogoff and J. Lave (eds) *Everyday Cognition*, Cambridge, MA: Harvard University Press.

Sellwood, P. (1990) 'The national project: practical problem solving 5–13', *Proceedings of the 3rd National Conference on Design and Technology Education Research and Curriculum Development*, Loughborough University of Technology.

Sewell, B. (1982) *Use of Mathematics by Adults in Daily Life*, Leicester: Advisory Council for Adult and Continuing Education.

Shuard, H. (1986) 'Primary mathematics towards 2000', *Mathematical Gazette* 70: 175–85.

Simpson, M. (1988) 'Improving learning in schools – what do we know? A cognitive science perspective', *Scottish Educational Review* 20(1): 22–31.

Wenger, E. (1991) 'Communities of practice: where learning happens', *Benchmark*, Fall: 6–8.

Wittrock, M.C. (1977) 'Learning as a generative process', in M.C. Wittrock (ed.) *Learning and Instruction*, Berkeley: McCrutchan.

Wynne, B. E., Payne, S.J. and Wakeford, J. R. (1990) *Frameworks for Understanding Public Interpretations of Science and Technology*, End of Award Report for ESRC grant A09250008.

9 The nature and nurture of design ability

Nigel Cross

The author of this chapter is a Professor of Design Studies and writes about design from a professional, rather than an educational, perspective. The chapter discusses what designing is, what designers think about designing and research on designing. The author suggests that all of us possess the ability to design, at some level, and that this can be developed through education. He argues that designing is not the same as problem-solving and that learning to develop design ability also develops personal qualities which are not addressed in other subjects.

The chapter is based on an article which originally appeared in the journal Design Studies *11(3).*

Introduction

Everything we have around us – our environments, clothes, furniture, machines, communication systems, even much of our food – has been designed. The quality of that design effort therefore profoundly affects our quality of life, and the ability of designers to produce efficient, effective, imaginative and stimulating designs is important to all of us.

This paper is in two parts. The first is concerned with the nature of design ability – the particular ways of thinking and behaving that designers, and all of us, adopt in tackling certain kinds of problems in certain kinds of ways. The second part is concerned with the nurture of design ability – that is, with the development of that ability through design education. My view is that through better understanding the nature of design ability, design educators may be better able to nurture it. I therefore see these two – nature and nurture – as complementary interests, and I do not intend to venture into those corners of psychology where fights go on over nature vs. nurture in the context of general intelligence. However, I shall try to make a claim that design ability is, in fact, one of the several forms or fundamental aspects of human intelligence. It should, therefore, be an important element in everyone's education.

I Nature

What do designers do

The most essential thing that any designer does is to provide, for those who will make the artefact, a description of what that artefact should be like. Usually, little or nothing is left to the discretion of the makers – the designer specifies the artefact's dimensions, materials, finishes and colours. When a client asks a designer for 'a design', that is what they want – the description. The focus of all design activity is that end-point.

The designer's aim, therefore, is the communication of a specific design proposal. Usually, this is in the form of a drawing or drawings, giving both an overview of the artefact and particular details. Even the most imaginative design proposals must usually be communicated in rather prosaic working drawings, lists of parts, and so on.

Sometimes, it is necessary to make full-scale mock-ups of design proposals in order that they can be communicated sufficiently accurately. In the motor industry, for example, full-scale models of new car bodies are made to communicate the complex three-dimensional shapes. These shapes are then digitized and the data communicated to computers for the production of drawings for making the body-panel moulds. Increasingly, in many industries, computerization of both design and manufacture is substantially changing the mode of communication between designer and manufacturer, sometimes with the complete elimination of conventional detail drawings.

Before the final design proposal is communicated for manufacture, it will have gone through some form of testing, and alternative proposals may also have been tested and rejected. A major part of the designer's work is therefore concerned with the *evaluation* of design proposals. Again, full-scale models may be made; product manufacturing industries use them extensively for evaluating aesthetics, ergonomics, and consumer choice, as well as for production purposes. Small-scale 3–D models are also often used in many industries – from architecture to chemical process plants.

However, drawings of various kinds are still the most extensively used modelling medium for evaluating designs – both informally in the designer's skilled reading of drawings and imagining their implications, and more formally in measuring dimensions, calculating stresses, and so on. In evaluating designs, a large body of scientific and technical knowledge can be brought to bear; and again computers are having significant effects through techniques such as finite-element structural analysis. This modelling, testing and modifying is the central, iterative activity of the design process.

Before a proposal can be tested, it has to be originated somehow. The generation of design proposals is therefore the fundamental activity of designers, and that for which they become famous or infamous. Although design is usually associated with novelty and originality, most run-of-the-mill designing is actually based on making variations on previous designs. Drawings again feature heavily in this generative phase of the design process, although at the earliest stages they will be just the designer's 'thinking with a pencil' and perhaps comprehensible only to him or her.

The kind of thinking that is going on is multi-faceted and multi-levelled. The designer is thinking of the whole range of design criteria and requirements set by the client's brief, of technical and legal issues, and of self-imposed criteria such as the aesthetic and formal attributes of the proposal. Often, the problem as set by the client's brief will be vague, and it is only by the designer suggesting possible solutions that the client's requirements and criteria become clear. The designer's very first conceptualizations and representations of problem and solution are therefore critical to the procedures that will follow – the alternatives that may be considered, the testing and evaluating, and the final design proposal.

Designers on designing

Although there is such a great deal of design activity going on in the world, the nature of design ability is rather poorly understood. It has been taken to be a mysterious talent. Dictionary definitions of design (as a verb) usually refer to the importance of 'constructive forethought', or, as Gregory (1987) puts it, 'Design generally implies the action of intentional intelligence'.

When designers are asked to discuss their abilities and to explain how they work, a few common themes emerge. One theme is the importance of creativity and 'intuition'. For example, the engineering designer Jack Howe has said:

> I believe in intuition. I think that's the difference between a designer and an engineer ... I make a distinction between engineers and engineering designers ... An engineering designer is just as creative as any other sort of designer.
>
> (Quoted in Davies 1985)

Some rather similar comments have been made by the industrial designer Richard Stevens:

> A lot of engineering design is intuitive, based on subjective thinking. But an engineer is unhappy doing this. An engineer wants to test; test and measure. He's (*sic*) been brought up this way and he's unhappy if he can't prove something. Whereas an industrial designer, with his Art School training, is entirely happy making judgements which are intuitive.
>
> (Quoted in Davies 1985)

Another theme that emerges from designers' own comments is based on the recognition that problems and solutions in design are closely interwoven – that 'the solution' is not always a straightforward answer to 'the problem'. For example, commenting on one of his more creative designs, the furniture designer Geoffrey Harcourt said:

As a matter of fact, the solution that I came up with wasn't a solution to the problem at all. I never saw it as that … But when the chair was actually put together, in a way it solved the problem quite well, but from a completely different angle, a completely different point of view.

(Quoted in Davies 1985)

A third common theme is the need to explore problem and solution together as the design process proceeds. The nature of design problems means that they cannot be solved simply by collecting and synthesizing information, as the architect Richard MacCormac (1976) has observed, 'I don't think you can design anything just by absorbing information and then hoping to synthesise it into a solution. What you need to know about the problem only becomes apparent as you're trying to solve it'.

Another common theme is the need to use sketches, drawings and models of all kinds as a means of making this design exploration, of making some progress when faced with the complexity of design. As the engineer-architect Santiago Calatrava has said:

To start with you see the thing in your mind and it doesn't exist on paper and then you start making simple sketches and organising things and then you start doing layer after layer … it is very much a dialogue.

(Quoted in Lawson 1994)

Given the complex nature of design activity, therefore, it hardly seems surprising that the structural engineering designer Ted Happold should suggest that 'I really have, perhaps, one real talent; that is that I don't mind at all living in the area of total uncertainty' (quoted in Davies 1985). If that seems a little too modest, there are certainly other designers who seem to make more arrogant claims, such as the architect Denys Lasdun:

Our job is to give the client, on time and on cost, not what he wants (*sic*), but what he never dreamed he wanted; and when he gets it he recognizes it as something he wanted all the time.

(Quoted in Birks 1972)

Despite the apparent arrogance, there is the truth in this statement that clients often do want designers to transcend the obvious and the mundane, and to produce proposals which are exciting and stimulating as well as merely practical.

From this brief review so far, we can summarize the major aspects of what designers do as follows. Designers

- produce novel, unexpected solutions
- tolerate uncertainty, working with incomplete information
- apply imagination and constructive forethought to practical problems
- use drawings and other modelling media as means of problem-solving.

Studies of designing

For some years now, there has been a slowly growing body of understanding about the ways designers work, based on a wide variety of studies of designing (Cross 1984). Some of these studies rely on the reports of designers themselves, such as those we have just seen, but there is also a broad spectrum running through observations of designers at work, experimental studies based on protocol analysis, to theorizing about the nature of design ability.

Such studies often confirm the comments of designers themselves, but try also to add another layer of explanation of the nature of designing. For example, one feature of design activity that is frequently confirmed by such studies is the importance of the use of conjectured solutions by the designer. In his pioneering case studies of engineering design, Marples (1960) suggested that:

> The nature of the problem can only be found by examining it through proposed solutions, and it seems likely that its examination through one, and only one, proposal gives a very biased view. It seems probable that at least two radically different solutions need to be attempted in order to get, through comparisons of sub-problems, a clear picture of the 'real nature' of the problem.

This view emphasizes the role of the conjectured solution as a way of gaining understanding of the design problem, and the need, therefore, to generate a variety of solutions precisely as a means of problem-analysis. It has been confirmed by Darke's interviews with architects (1979), where she observed how they imposed a limited set of objectives or a specific solution concept as a 'primary generator' for an initial solution:

> The greatest variety reduction or narrowing down of the range of solutions occurs early on in the design process, with a conjecture or conceptualization of a possible solution. Further understanding of the problem is gained by testing this conjectured solution.

The freedom – and necessity – of the designer to re-define the problem through the means of solution-conjecture was also observed in protocol studies of architects by Akin (1979), who commented, 'One of the unique aspects of design behaviour is the constant generation of new task goals and redefinition of task constraints'.

It has been suggested that this feature of design behaviour arises from the nature of design problems: they are not the sort of problems or puzzles that provide all the necessary and sufficient information for their solution. Some of the relevant information can only be found by generating and testing solutions; some information, or 'missing ingredient', has to be provided by the designer himself or herself, as suggested by Levin (1966) from his observations of urban designers:

The designer knows (consciously or unconsciously) that some ingredient must be added to the information that he already has in order to arrive at an unique solution. This knowledge is in itself not enough in design problems, of course. He has to look for the extra ingredient, and he uses his powers of conjecture and original thought to do so.

Levin suggested that this extra ingredient is often an 'ordering principle' and hence we find the formal properties that are so often evident in designers' work, from towns designed as simple stars to teacups designed as regular cylinders.

However, designers do not always find it easy to generate a range of alternative solutions in order that they better understand the problem. Their 'ordering principles' or 'primary generators' can, of course, be found to be inappropriate, but they often try to hang onto them because of the difficulties of going back and starting afresh. From his case studies of architectural design, Rowe (1987) observed:

> A dominant influence is exerted by initial design ideas on subsequent problem-solving directions ... Even when severe problems are encountered, a considerable effort is made to make the initial idea work, rather than to stand back and adopt a fresh point of departure.

This tenacity is understandable but undesirable, given the necessity of using alternative solutions as a means of understanding the 'real nature' of the problem. However, Waldron and Waldron (1988), from their engineering design case study, came to a more optimistic view about the 'self-correcting' nature of the design process:

> The premises that were used in initial concept generation often proved, on subsequent investigation, to be wholly or partly fallacious. Nevertheless, they provided a necessary starting point. The process can be viewed as inherently self-correcting, since later work tends to clarify and correct earlier work.

It becomes clear from these studies of designing that architects, engineers and other designers adopt a problem-solving strategy based on generating and testing potential solutions. In a laboratory experiment based on a specific problem-solving task, Lawson (1979) compared the strategies of architects with those of scientists, and found a noticeable difference:

> The scientists were [attempting to] discover the structure of the problem; the architects were proceeding by generating a sequence of high-scoring solutions until one proved acceptable ... [The scientists] operated what might be called a problem-focusing strategy ... architects by contrast adopted a solution-focusing strategy.

In a supplementary experiment, Lawson found that these different strategies developed during the architects' and scientists' education; whilst the difference was clear between postgraduate students, it was not clear between first-year undergraduate students. The architects had therefore learned their solution-focusing strategy, during their design education, as an appropriate response to the problems they were set. This is presumably because design problems are inherently ill-defined, and trying to define or comprehensively to understand the problem (the scientists' approach) is quite likely to be fruitless in terms of generating an appropriate solution within a limited timescale.

The difference between a scientific approach and a design approach has also been emphasized in theoretical studies, such as Simon's (1969), who pointed out that 'the natural sciences are concerned with how things are ... Design, on the other hand, is concerned with how things ought to be'. And March (1976) has categorized the differences between design, science and logic:

> Logic has interests in abstract forms. Science investigates extant forms. Design initiates novel forms. A scientific hypothesis is not the same thing as a design hypothesis. A logical proposition is not to be mistaken for a design proposal. A speculative design cannot be determined logically, because the mode of reasoning involved is essentially abductive.

This 'abductive' reasoning is a concept from the philosopher Peirce, who distinguished it from the other more well-known modes of inductive and deductive reasoning. Peirce suggested that 'Deduction proves that something must be; induction shows that something actually is operative; abduction merely suggests that something may be' (quoted by March, from Hartsborne and Weiss 1931–5). It is therefore the logic of conjecture. March prefers to use the term 'productive' reasoning. Others have used terms such as 'appositional' reasoning in contra-distinction to propositional reasoning (Bogen 1969).

Design ability is therefore founded on the resolution of ill-defined problems by adopting a solution-focusing strategy and productive or appositional styles of thinking. However, the design approach is not necessarily limited to ill-defined problems. Thomas and Carroll (1979) conducted a number of experiments and protocol studies of designing and concluded that a fundamental aspect is the nature of the approach taken to problems, rather than the nature of the problems themselves: 'Design is a type of problem solving in which the problem solver views the problem or acts as though there is some ill-definedness in the goals, initial conditions or allowable transformations'. There is also, of course, the reliance in design upon the media of sketching, drawing and modelling as aids to the generation of solutions and to the very processes of thinking about the problem and its solution. The process involves what Schon (1983) has called 'a reflective conversation with the situation'. From his observations of the way design tutors work, Schon commented that, through sketches, '[The designer] shapes the situation, in accordance with his initial appreciation of it; the situation "talks back", and he responds to the back-talk'. Design ability therefore relies fundamentally on non-verbal media of thought and communication. There may even be distinct limits to the amount of verbalizing that we can productively engage in about design ability. Daley (1982) has suggested that:

The way designers work may be inexplicable, not for some romantic or mystical reason, but simply because these processes lie outside the bounds of verbal discourse: they are literally indescribable in linguistic terms.

This review of studies of designing enables us to summarize the core features of design ability as comprising the ability to

- resolve ill-defined problems
- adopt solution-focusing strategies
- employ abductive/productive/appositional thinking
- use non-verbal, graphic/spatial modelling media.

Design ability is possessed by everyone

Although professional designers might be expected to have highly developed design abilities, it is clear that non-designers also possess at least some aspects, or lower levels, of design ability. Everyone makes decisions about arrangements and combinations of clothes, furniture, etc. – although in industrial societies it is rare for this to extend beyond making selections from available goods that have already been designed by someone else.

However, in other societies, especially non-industrial ones, there is often no clear distinction between professional and amateur design abilities – the role of the professional designer may not exist. In craft-based societies, for example, craftspeople make objects that are not only highly practical but often also very beautiful. They would therefore seem to possess high levels of design ability – although in such cases, the ability is collective rather than individual: the beautiful-functional objects have evolved by gradual development over a very long time, and the forms of the objects are rigidly adhered to from one generation to the next.

Even in industrial societies, with a developed class of professional designers, there are often examples of vernacular design persisting, usually following implicit rules of how things should be done, similar to craftwork. Occasionally there are examples of 'naive' design breaking out in industrial societies, with many of the positive attributes that 'naive' art has. In architecture and planning, there have been moves to incorporate non-professionals into the design process – through design participation or community architecture (Wates and Knevitt 1987). Although the experiments have not always been successful – in either process or product – there is at least a recognition that the professionals could, and should, collaborate with the non-professionals. Knowledge about design is certainly not exclusive to the professionals.

A strong indication of how widespread design ability is comes from the introduction of design as a subject in schools. It is clear from the often very competent design work of schoolchildren of all ages that design ability is inherent in everyone.

Design ability can be damaged or lost

Although some aspects of design ability can be seen to be widespread in the general population, it has also become clear that the cognitive functions upon which design ability depends can be damaged or lost. This has been learned from experiments and observations in the field of neuropsychology, particularly the work which became known as 'split-brain' studies (Gazzaniga 1970).

These studies showed that the two hemispheres of the brain have preferences and specializations for different types of perceptions and knowledge. Normally, the large bundle of nerves (the *corpus callosum*) which connects the two hemispheres ensures rapid and comprehensive communication between them, so that it is impossible to study the workings of either hemisphere in isolation from its mate. However, in order to cure epilepsy, some people have had their *corpus callosum* surgically severed, and became subjects for some remarkable experiments to investigate the isolated functions of the two hemispheres (Sperry *et al.* 1969).

Studies of other people who had suffered damage to one or other hemisphere had already revealed some knowledge of the different specializations. In the main, these studies had shown the fundamental importance of the left hemisphere – it controlled speech functions and the verbal reasoning normally associated with logical thought. The right hemisphere appeared to have no such important functions. Indeed, the right became known as the 'minor' hemisphere and the left as the 'major' hemisphere. Nevertheless, there is an equal sharing of control of the body; the left hemisphere controls the right side, and vice versa, for some perverse reason known only to the Grand Designer in the Sky.

This left-right crossover means that sensory reception on the left side of the body is communicated to the brain's right hemisphere, and vice versa. This even applies, in a more complex way, to visual reception; it is not simply that the left eye communicates with the right hemisphere, and vice versa, but that, for both eyes, reception from the left visual field is communicated to the right hemisphere, and vice versa. Ingenious experiments were therefore devised in which visual stimuli could be sent exclusively to either the left or right hemisphere of the split-brain subjects.

From experiments such as these, neuropsychologists developed a much better understanding of the functions and abilities of the right hemisphere (Blakeslee 1980). Although mute, it is by no means stupid, and it perceives and knows things that the left hemisphere does not. In general, this is the kind of knowledge that we categorize as intuitive. The right hemisphere excels in emotional and aesthetic perception, in the recognition of faces and objects, and in visuo-spatial and constructional tasks. This scientific, rational evidence therefore supports our own personal, intuitive understanding of ourselves, and also supports the (often poorly articulated) view of artists and many designers that verbalization (i.e. allowing the left hemisphere to dominate) obstructs intuitive creation.

It is now known that damage to the right hemisphere can impair brain functions that relate strongly to intuitive, artistic and design abilities. Recognition of this right-brain ability has been put to constructive use in art education by Betty Edwards (1979), who trains students to 'draw on the right side of the brain'. Anita

Cross (1984) has drawn attention to the relevance of the 'split-brain' studies to improving our understanding of design ability.

There is, of course, a long history of studies in psychology of cognitive styles, which are usually polarized into dichotomies such as

- convergent – divergent
- focused – flexible
- linear – lateral
- serialist – holist
- propositional – appositional.

Such natural dichotomies may reflect the underlying dual structure of the human brain and its apparent dual modes of information processing. Cross and Nathenson (1981) have drawn attention to the importance of understanding cognitive styles for design education and design methodology.

Design as a form of intelligence

What I have attempted to show is that design ability is a multi-faceted cognitive skill, possessed in some degree by everyone. I believe that there is enough evidence to make a reasonable claim that there are particular 'designerly' ways of knowing, thinking and acting. In fact, it seems possible to make a reasonable claim that design ability is a form of natural intelligence (Cross 1999), of the kind that the psychologist Howard Gardner (1983) has identified. Gardner's view is that there is not just one form of intelligence, but several, relatively autonomous human intellectual competences. He distinguishes six forms of intelligence:

1　linguistic
2　logical-mathematical
3　spatial
4　musical
5　bodily-kinaesthetic
6　personal.

Aspects of design ability seem to be spread through these six forms in a way that does not always seem entirely satisfactory. For example, spatial abilities in problem-solving (including thinking 'in the mind's eye') are classified under spatial intelligence, whereas many other aspects of practical problem-solving ability (including examples from engineering) are classified under bodily-kinaesthetic intelligence. In this classification, the inventor appears alongside the dancer and the actor, which doesn't seem appropriate. It seems reasonable, therefore, to try to separate out design ability as a form of intelligence in its own right.

Gardner proposes a set of criteria against which claims for a distinct form of intelligence can be judged. These criteria are as follows, with my attempts to match 'design intelligence' against them.

Potential isolation by brain damage   Gardner seeks to base forms of intelligence in discrete brain-centres, which means that particular faculties can be destroyed (or spared) in isolation by brain damage. The evidence here for design intelligence draws upon the work with 'split-brain' and brain-damaged patients, which shows that abilities such as geometric reasoning, three-dimensional problem-solving and visuo-spatial thinking are indeed located in specific brain-centres.

The existence of idiots, savants, prodigies and other exceptional individuals
Here, Gardner is looking for evidence of unique abilities which sometimes stand out in individuals against a background of retarded or immature general development. In design, there are indeed examples of otherwise ordinary individuals who demonstrate high levels of ability in forming their own environments – the 'naive' designers.

An identifiable core operation or set of operations   By this, Gardner means some basic mental information-processing operation(s) which deal with specific kinds of input. In design, this might be the operation of transforming the input of the problem brief into the output of conjectured solutions, or the ability to generate alternative solutions. Gardner suggests that 'Simulation on a computer is one promising way of establishing that a core operation exists'. Work in artificial intelligence on the generation of designs by computer is therefore helping to clarify the concept of a natural design intelligence.

A distinctive developmental history, and a definable set of expert, end-state performances
This means recognizable levels of development or expertise in the individual. Clearly, there are recognizable differences between novices and experts in design, and stages of development amongst design students. But a clarification of the developmental stages of design ability is something that we still await, and is sorely needed in design education.

An evolutionary history   Gardner argues that the forms of intelligence must have arisen through evolutionary antecedents, including capacities that are shared with other organisms besides human beings. In design, we do have examples of animals and insects that construct shelters and environments, and use and devise tools. We also have the long tradition of vernacular and craft design as a precursor to modern, innovative design ability.

Susceptibility to encoding in a symbol system   This criterion looks for a coherent, culturally-shared system of symbols which capture and communicate information relevant to the form of intelligence. Clearly, in design we have the use of sketches, drawings and other models which constitute a coherent, symbolic media system for thinking and communicating.

Support from experimental psychological tasks   Finally, Gardner looks for evidence of abilities that transfer across different contexts, of specific forms of memory, attention or perception. We only have a few psychological studies of design behaviour or thinking, but aspects such as solution-focused thinking have been identified. More work in this area needs to be done.

If asked to judge the case for design intelligence on this set of criteria, we might have to conclude that the case is 'not proven'. Whilst there is good evidence to meet most of the criteria, on some there is a lack of substantial or reliable evidence. However, I think that viewing designing as a 'form of intelligence' is productive; it helps to identify and clarify features of the nature of design ability, and it offers a framework for understanding and developing the nurture of design ability.

II Nurture

Learning to design

How do people learn to design, and on what principles should design education be based? Clearly, some development of design ability does take place in students – certainly at the level of tertiary, professional education, where we can compare the work of the same student over the years of his or her course. The crude, simple work of the first-year student develops into sophisticated, complex work by the final year. But the educational processes which nurture this development are poorly understood – if at all – and rely heavily on the project method.

Modern higher level design education owes much to the experimental work of the Bauhaus – the German design school of the 1920s and early 1930s – in particular, the radical 'basic course' introduced by Johannes Itten. As Anita Cross (1983) has suggested, many of the basic course's educational principles may well have been developed from the work of educational innovators such as Froebel, Montessori and Dewey. The Bauhaus also integrated design education with aesthetic cultures such as dance, theatre and music, as well as cultures of technology and industry. Itten himself incorporated physical exercises and dietary regimens in his courses, and required his students, for example, to swing their arms and bodies in circular movements before attempting to draw freehand circles. He and other tutors also encouraged tactile perception and the construction of collages from randomly-collected junk and other materials. From what we now know of the development of the thought-modes of the right hemisphere of the brain, these non-verbal, tactile, analogical experiences were intuitively correct aspects of design education.

Most of the Bauhaus innovations are now severely watered-down in conventional design education, usually retaining just a few vestiges of exercises in colour, form and composition. In fact, the increased attention on design education in recent years has exposed the lack of any clearly-articulated and well-understood principles of design education.

I would suggest that it is through understanding the nature of design ability that we can begin to construct an understanding of the intrinsic values of design education. For example, we can make a strong justification for design based on its development of personal abilities in resolving ill-defined problems – which are quite different from the well-defined problems dealt with in other areas of the curriculum. We can also justify the designer's solution-focused strategies and appositional thinking styles as promoting a certain type of cognitive development – in educational terms, the concrete/iconic modes that are often assumed to be the 'earlier' or 'minor' modes of cognition, and less important than the formal/symbolic modes. Furthermore, there is a sound justification in the educational value of design in its development of the whole area of non-verbal thought and communication.

The development of design ability

Although it may be present to some degree in everyone, design ability seems stronger in some people than others, and also seems to develop with experience. Experienced designers are able to draw on their knowledge of previous exemplars in their field of design, and they also seem to have learned the value of rapid problem-exploration through solution-conjecture. They use early solution attempts as experiments to help identify relevant information about the problem. In comparison, novice designers often become bogged down in attempts to understand the problem before they start generating solutions. For them, gathering data about the problem is sometimes just a substitute activity for actually doing any design work (Cross *et al.* 1994).

Another difference between novices and experts is that novices will often pursue a 'depth-first' approach to a problem – sequentially identifying and exploring sub-solutions in depth, and amassing a number of partial sub-solutions that then somehow have to be amalgamated and reconciled, in a 'bottom-up' process. They can also become 'fixated' on a particular solution possibility. Experts usually pursue predominantly 'breadth-first' and top-down strategies, and are more willing to reject an early solution when it is discovered to be fundamentally flawed (Smith and Leong 1998).

In contrast to the artistic, intuitive procedures encouraged by the Bauhaus, design education has more recently concentrated on teaching more rational, systematic approaches. Because skilled designers in practice often appear to proceed in a rather *ad hoc* and unsystematic way, some people claim that learning a systematic process does not actually help student designers. However, a study by Radcliffe and Lee (1989) did show that a systematic approach can be helpful to students. They found that the use of more 'efficient' design processes (following closer to an 'ideal' sequence) correlated positively with both the quantity and the quality of the students' design results. Other studies have tended to confirm this.

From studies of a number of engineering designers, of varying degrees of experience and with varying exposures to education in systematic design processes, Fricke (1996) found that designers following a 'flexible-methodical procedure' tended to produce good solutions. These designers worked reasonably efficiently and followed a fairly logical procedure, whether or not they had been educated in a systematic approach. In comparison, designers either with a too rigid adherence to a systematic procedure (behaving 'unreasonably methodically'), or with very unsystematic approaches, produced mediocre or poor design solutions. Successful designers (ones producing better quality solutions) tended to be those who:

- clarified requirements, by asking sets of related questions which focused on the problem structure
- actively searched for information, and critically checked given requirements
- summarized information on the problem formulation into requirements and partially prioritized them
- did not suppress first solution ideas; they held on to them, but returned to clarifying the problem rather than pursuing initial solution concepts in depth
- detached themselves during conceptual design stages from fixation on early solution concepts
- produced variants but limited the production and kept an overview by periodically assessing and evaluating in order to reduce the number of possible variants.

Conventional wisdom about the nature of expertise in problem-solving seems often to be contradicted by the behaviour of expert designers. But designing has many differences from conventional problem-solving, in which there is usually a single, correct solution to the problem. In design education we must therefore be very wary about importing models of behaviour from other fields. Empirical studies of design activity have frequently found 'intuitive' features of design ability to be the most effective and relevant to the intrinsic nature of design. Some aspects of design theory, however, have tried to develop counter-intuitive models and prescriptions for design behaviour. We still need a much better understanding of what constitutes expertise in design, and how we might assist novice students to gain that expertise.

Designing is a form of skilled behaviour. Developing any skill usually relies on controlled practice and the development of techniques. The performance of a skilled practitioner appears to flow seamlessly, adapting the performance to the circumstances without faltering. But learning is not the same as performing, and underneath skilled performance lies mastery of technique and procedure. The design student needs to develop a strategic approach to the overall process, based on some simple but effective techniques or methods (Cross 2000). What I hope we shall achieve through continued studies of the nature and nurture of design ability is that design education will become a reliably successful means for the development of design ability in everyone.

References

Akin, O. (1979) 'An exploration of the design process', *Design Methods and Theories* 13(3/4). Reprinted in N. Cross (ed.) (1984) *Developments In Design Methodology*, Chichester: Wiley.

Birks, T. (1972) *Building Our New Universities*, Exeter: David and Charles.

Blakeslee, T. R. (1980) *The Right Brain*, London: Macmillan.

Bogen, J. E. (1969) 'The other side of the brain II: an appositional mind', *Bulletin of the Los Angeles Neurological Societies*, 34(3).

Cross, A. (1983) 'The educational background to the Bauhaus', *Design Studies* 4(1).

Cross, A. (1984) 'Towards an understanding of the intrinsic values of design education', *Design Studies* 5(1).

Cross, N. (ed.) (1984) *Developments In Design Methodology*, Chichester: Wiley.

Cross, N. (1999) 'Natural intelligence in design', *Design Studies* 20(1).

Cross, N. (2000) *Engineering Design Methods: Strategies for Product Design*, (3rd edn), Chichester: Wiley.

Cross, N., Christiaans, H. and Dorst, K. (1994) 'Design expertise amongst student designers', *Journal of Art and Design Education* 13(1).

Cross, N. and Nathenson, M. (1981) 'Design methods and learning methods', in J. Powell and R. Jacques (eds) *Design: Science: Method*, Guildford: Westbury House.

Daley, J. (1982) 'Design creativity and the understanding of objects', *Design Studies* 3(3). Reprinted in N. Cross (ed.) (1984) *Developments In Design Methodology*, Chichester: Wiley.

Darke, J. (1979) 'The primary generator and the design process', *Design Studies* 1(1). Reprinted in N. Cross (ed.) (1984) *Developments In Design Methodology*, Chichester: Wiley.

Davies, R. (1985) 'A Psychological Enquiry into the Origination and Implementation of Ideas', MSc Thesis, Dept. of Management Sciences, UMIST, Manchester.

Edwards, B. (1979) *Drawing on the Right Side of the Brain*, Los Angeles: Tarcher.

Fricke, G. (1996) 'Successful individual approaches in engineering design', *Research in Engineering Design* 8(2).

Gardner, H. (1983) *Frames of Mind: the Theory of Multiple Intelligences*, London: Heinemann.

Gazzaniga, M. S. (1970) *The Bisected Brain*, New York: Appleton Century Crofts.

Gregory, R. L. (ed.) (1987) *The Oxford Companion To The Mind*, Oxford: Oxford University Press.

Hartsborne, C. and Weiss, P. (eds) (1931–5) *Collected Papers of C. S. Peirce*, Cambridge, MA: Harvard University Press.

Lawson, B. R. (1979) 'Cognitive strategies in architectural design', *Ergonomics* 22(1). Reprinted in N. Cross (ed.) (1984) *Developments In Design Methodology*, Chichester: Wiley.

Lawson, B. (1994) *Design in Mind*, Oxford: Butterworth.

Levin, P. H. (1966) 'Decision making in urban design', *Building Research Station Note EN 51/66*, Watford: BRS. Reprinted in N. Cross (ed.) (1984) *Developments In Design Methodology*, Chichester: Wiley.

MacCormac, R. (1976) *Design Is …* (Interview with N. Cross), BBC/Open University TV broadcast.

March, L. J. (1976) 'The logic of design', in L. J. March (ed.) *The Architecture of Form*, Cambridge: Cambridge University Press. Reprinted in N. Cross (ed.) (1984) *Developments In Design Methodology*, Chichester: Wiley.

Marples, D. (1960) *The Decisions of Engineering Design*, London: Institute of Engineering Designers.

Radcliffe, D. and Lee, T. 'Design methods used by undergraduate engineering students', *Design Studies* 10(4).

Rowe, P. (1987) *Design Thinking*, Cambridge, MA: MIT Press.

Schon, D. (1983) *The Reflective Practitioner*, London: Temple-Smith.

Simon, H. A. (1969) *The Sciences of the Artificial*, Cambridge, MA: MIT Press.

Smith, R. and Leong, A. (1998) 'An observational study of design team process: a comparison of student and professional engineers', *Journal of Mechanical Design* 120, December.

Sperry, R. W., Gazzaniga, M. S. and Bogen, J. E. (1969) 'Interhemispheric relations: the neocortical commissures; syndromes of hemispheric disconnection', in P. J. Vinken and G. W. Bruyn (eds) *Handbook of Clinical Neurology*, Vol. 4, Amsterdam: North-Holland.

Thomas, J. C. and Carroll, J. M. (1979) 'The psychological study of design', *Design Studies* 1(1). Reprinted in N. Cross (ed.) (1984) *Developments In Design Methodology*, Chichester: Wiley.

Waldron, M. B. and Waldron K. J. (1988) 'A time sequence study of a complex mechanical system design', *Design Studies* 9(2).

Wates, N. and Knevitt, C. (1987) *Community Architecture*, London: Penguin.

10 A visual literacy strategy
Why not?

Alan Howe

Though focusing on the primary curriculum, this chapter makes pertinent references to the links between Design and Technology and art and design. In exploring what is meant by 'visual literacy' some interesting ideas are introduced, they build on the previous chapter and may help teachers of design to think about their work from a different perspective. Some of the ideas are suggested for use in art lessons but could easily be adapted for product analysis or generation of design ideas.

In secondary schools it is not usually possible to integrate the ideas and approaches from these two subject areas, as the chapter suggests, but there is nothing to stop any teacher from extending her or his range of teaching strategies by drawing on good practice wherever it is found. You might consider how some of the ideas given in this chapter could be incorporated into your teaching.

Introduction

Can you think of two subjects in the primary school that have more in common than 'art (craft) and design' and 'design and technology'? Both are foundation subjects which pupils and teachers enjoy, and see as a contrast to 'academic' subjects. 'Making' activities are central to each subject; indeed it is sometimes difficult to define an activity in subject terms. …

You might say that the similarities identified above are simplistic or superficial. I am going to argue in this chapter that art and design and design and technology have a fundamental connection that has not been fully recognized or exploited. Between them, the two subjects facilitate the development of important, life-enhancing skills such as observation, aesthetic awareness, discrimination and critical thinking and furthermore they are best able to do this through a common rationale and approach to the development of visual literacy.

In this chapter I therefore hope to achieve the following:

- to define and offer a rationale for the inclusion of visual literacy within the primary curriculum
- to explore the connections between pedagogic frameworks currently in use to support the development of visual literacy skills in design and technology and art contexts.

So what is it to be visually literate?

> Young people who are visually literate have more control over their own work and are better able to understand, enjoy and discriminate between images and objects that appear both in familiar environments of the home and neighbourhood, and in less familiar places such as galleries and museums.
>
> (DES 1991: para. 3.19)

In the National Curriculum for England, in the Programme of Study for Art and Design, we have the statement that pupils:

> become more independent in using the visual language to communicate their own ideas, feelings and meanings.
>
> (DfEE/QCA 1999: 168)

This is a move from the 1995 Order, which stated:

> In order to develop visual literacy, pupils should be taught about the different ways in which ideas, feelings and meanings are communicated in visual form.
>
> (DFE 1995a)

Visual literacy is a somewhat problematic term. It is often taken as shorthand for the capacity to 'read' or 'interpret' or to 'find meaning in' the visual as opposed to textual world. Yet the analogy would suggest that the ability to manipulate a visual language to make images and artefacts which communicate meaning or message is also an aspect of visual literacy. Visual literacy will therefore entail thinking *critically* about the visual and perhaps making use of the information to inform one's own making activities.

Language has a broadly accepted 'correct' usage, whereas a whole set of valid alternatives is possible, and is yet to be possible, in visual communication. Raney suggests that:

> Coupling 'visual' with 'literacy' does two things. First, it introduces the metaphor of language, provoking debates about the value of linguistic metaphors for getting to grips with visual things … second, 'Literacy' suggests entitlement or necessity, and the need to seek out deficiencies and remedy them.
>
> (1999: 41)

Raney claims that by using the term, status is attributed to the visual in a word dominated world:

> [visual literacy] implies that the entire visible world is the purview of visual literacy … art education becomes a subcategory of visual education, art becomes a subcategory of visual culture, and visual literacy is what is needed to navigate around it.
>
> (1999: 44)

In the same terms, take design and technology as contributor to visual education so design becomes a subcategory of visual culture.

Visual awareness is another term in use. This does not go far enough. To be aware is a passive act, whereas within visual literacy there needs to be an active phase. It involves also the creation of the artefact.

Neither term is present in the latest versions (QCA 1999) of the National Curriculum for Art and Design or Design and Technology. The fact that a term is absent from these slim, vestigial documents should not be taken as a reason for thinking it unimportant. What we do find are a number of references in the curriculum documents to important aspects of education such as the need to encourage 'critical reflection', 'evaluation from a variety of perspectives' and 'exploration of meanings and interpretations'. Pupils should be 'engaging critically with a rapidly changing culture', developing an 'understanding of aesthetics and function' and 'asking and answering questions'. I will not provide you with exact references here – if you can work out for yourself which subjects are the source of each quote, then my argument for common ground between subjects is perhaps not a good one.

Let me clarify what I mean by this problematic term 'visual literacy'.

My usage of 'visual literacy' will encompass all the below. I would say that a visually literate person, when experiencing something that is primarily visual, would be able to say, in response to an artefact or art work:

> I am curious about this and I can learn something from examining this in a variety of ways.

This statement relates to the asking and answering of questions, to evaluating from a variety of perspectives:

- This relates to other things that I have seen.
- There are ways that I can describe and ways to classify this.
- The artist/designer/maker seemed to have these intentions.
- The artist/designer/maker will have been working under certain constraints or influences.
- The artist/designer/maker has worked in these ways.

These statements relate to the application of knowledge and understanding, of the aesthetic and functional in order to investigate roles and intentions.

This visually literate person would then go on to say: …

- I have a reasoned opinion on this – this is what I have found out and what I think.
- The visual can affect the way I feel – this is how I have been affected.
- What I have learnt can inform my own work.
- I could interrogate my own work in some similar ways.

These statements relate to the application of knowledge and understanding, the affective domain and critical thinking.

To illustrate this, carry out the following exercise:

> Mentally (or actually) choose a sculpture that you know well, and a textile artefact such as some clothing you are wearing, and apply to them the statements in the Table below.

Visual Literacy in an art context – looking at a sculpture	Visual literacy in a design and technology context – looking at a textile artefact
I can examine this sculpture in a number of ways such as …	I can examine this textile in a number of ways such as …
I can learn about the material, the process of making, the artist/maker, myself.	I can learn about the material, the process of making, the designer/maker, myself.
I can describe this sculpture in terms of formal elements, materials and techniques used in its creation, similarities with other works I have seen.	I can describe this textile in terms of form, function, materials and techniques used in its creation, similarities with other artefacts I have seen.
It seems that the maker was concerned with … intended to …	It seems that the maker was concerned with … intended to …
The maker may have been influenced by others working in a similar way and constrained by the limitations of the material.	The maker may have been influenced by others working in a similar way and constrained by the limitations of the material.
The sculpture has a certain effect on me – it has given rise to these thoughts and feelings.	The textile has a certain effect on me – it has given rise to these thoughts and feelings.
I have enjoyed looking at this sculpture and learnt something new.	I have enjoyed looking at this textile and learnt something new.
The knowledge I have gained can be used in my own work.	The knowledge I have gained can be used in my own work.

The ideas and insights derived from these statements are, I shall argue, important, worthwhile and relevant to pupils. Furthermore, there is potential to develop such skills in a number of subject areas, or in a cross-curricular way.

Why should the development of visual literacy be worthy of considerable curriculum time?

> Young people need to be visually literate … pupils can become visually literate by employing visual perception in the solution of a range of practical tasks and through regular reference to the work of others … Pupils' understanding of the

possibilities of visual language and of the variety of forms of expression available is significantly expanded through the study of the work of artists, craftworkers and designers.

(DFE 1991: para. 3.17)

We are in danger of over-emphasizing in our schools a limited number of ways in which we communicate and come to understand. The Qualifications and Curriculum Authority (QCA 1998) demands a 'broad and balanced' curriculum, yet time available to teach subjects beyond the core curriculum seems to be reduced with the current emphasis on the core subjects through the introduction of numeracy and literacy strategies.

The report from the National Advisory Committee on Creative and Cultural Education (NACCCE 1999) found that:

opportunities to promote creative and cultural education are being increasingly restricted by the cumulative effects ... of the National Curriculum.

(NACCCE 1999: para. 112)

The report goes on to argue that now, more than ever, it is vital to encourage all areas of young people's intellectual and personal capabilities and to recognize that doing this is not at odds with their academic development.

Many have argued that visual literacy is a 'basic' requirement if one is to understand the made world in the broadest sense, to include the built environment, art, artefacts, design, visual communications (graphics, advertisements), etc.

In *Datanews* (DATA 1999) there is a call that the National Curriculum should:

Enable pupils to become discriminating citizens and customers ... by having a better understanding of products and the associated values.

The article goes on to say that through design and technology pupils will:

develop skills in product analysis and evaluation and combine this with associated values related to social, environmental, spiritual, moral, aesthetic and economic aspects of products and systems.

Meanwhile the National Society for Education in Art and Design, in their publication *Manifesto for Arts in Schools* (Swift and Steers 1998), demand that there should be a clear rationale for the inclusion of the aspect of art education known as Critical Studies based on 'cultural transmission, real critical thought and reaction'.

Critical studies can be seen as a combination of studies in art history, art production, aesthetic, critical and contextual studies of art and design practice (Thistlewood (ed.) 1989) approached in such a way as to enrich children's own making. Taylor (1992) explains that:

The Critical Studies in Art Education (CSAE) Project demonstrated that this close relationship between the study of artists' work and pupils' own practice can open up a wide range of possibilities, rather than cause young people to produce predictable art because it was done in imitation.

(1992: 27)

Other projects such as 'Art in the Built Environment' (Schools Council 1982) and Arts 5–16 (Arts in Schools 1990) added weight to the shift in thinking and practice in order to include in the curriculum the so-called 'missing element' of critical study of art and artefacts. Arts 5–16 noted that:

Best practice in primary as well as secondary schools gives equal weight to developing young people's critical understanding of other people's work and their knowledge of different cultural practices and traditions.

The above initiatives were among the influences that resulted in the shape of the National Curriculum. A critical studies approach to teaching art at Key Stages 1 and 2 was implicit in the curriculum and the development of visual literacy one of its aims.

The connections between the disciplines of art critical studies and design and technology's 'product analysis' (DfEE/QCA 1999) may be clarified by reference to Michael Baxendall's (1985) book, *Patterns of Intention.* In the book he writes about two very recognizable products of the modern era – the Forth Bridge and Picasso's *Portrait of Kahnweiler*, drawing fascinating parallels between these two products of human imagination and endeavour. Crucially he seeks to explore the artist's or designer's intentions through analysis of the artefact or art work as a product of its time, place and culture.

Both are purposeful objects and are not necessarily different. The differences seem more of degree and of balance, particularly the balance of our interests and of our critical priorities.

(Baxendall 1985: 40)

Baxendall (1985) argues that in coming to understand the two objects, and ultimately the mind of the artist or designer from another time or culture, a common process of coming to an understanding is evident. Baxendall uses a structure to frame an analysis of the work of bridge builder Benjamin Baker, principal designer of the Forth Bridge, which can be summarized as:

The charge

In the case of the Forth Bridge, the charge, quite evidently, was 'Bridge the Gap'.

The brief

The brief, depends on specifics such as the location of towns, nature of traffic to use the bridge and the local weather conditions that a structure will need to withstand.

Causes of form

A certain number of solutions to a problem are usually possible. Baxendall describes these as 'cultural facts', i.e.:

- physical media available at the time, in this case steel as a new alternative to wrought iron
- historical precedence – designs, successes and disasters
- aesthetic taste – e.g. monumentality, elegance, decorative elements
- the decision-maker – the designer's preference, experience and knowledge.

Baxendall concludes by saying that given a three-cornered relationship between the solution, the problem and the possibilities then we can determine the intention of the 'decision maker'.

Turning to the work of Picasso, and a cubist portrait entitled *Portrait of Daniel-Henry Kahnweiler* (1910), Baxendall applies similar thinking. In some respects there are clear parallels. Causes of form, in the case of the painting, would be items such as the pigments and colours available (media), a new way of representing objects introduced by Cézanne, knowledge about African sculpture from a recent exhibition and the critical reception of Picasso's earlier work *Demoiselles d'Avignon* (precedence), a reaction against the preoccupations of the impressionists (aesthetic taste).

The charge and brief are more elusive to identify. In Picasso's era, the charge and brief were personally constructed within a cultural framework. In other words, no client is involved, no negotiation with others is needed and yet Picasso's contact with his society, his circle of friends and critics, the long tradition of painting as a human endeavour, will influence his work. Of course many artists do not have the luxury of constructing an entirely personal brief. More often concerns such as critical acclaim, commercial appeal, even the demands of a client will feature in many artists', craftworkers' and designers' work.

We have seen that objects as diverse as a bridge and a portrait can be understood using the same framework and by asking the same questions. In individual cases the concerns of the viewer may be different and the information that the object reveals will differ. To link them, can these objects be located along a continuum? At one end the output of the archetypal western twentieth-century artist working alone in his or her garret, via an individual commission produced by an artist or designer working for a client, on to a craftsperson producing traditional functional ware. A more sophisticated model might be a *visual field* in which artefacts and art works are located according to axes of brief (from internal

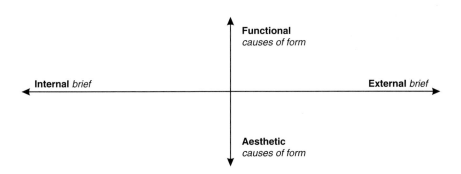

Figure 10.1 The visual field

to external) and causes of form (aesthetic to functional) – see Figure 10.1. It seems reasonable to suppose that objects or artefacts that can be located within this field can be interrogated using a common framework, although the location of the object and the interests of the interrogator will determine the parts of the framework that will be used.

Do we have a framework to interrogate objects within the visual field that can be used in school?

A brief review of some published frameworks offered to teachers to allow pupils to interrogate objects reveals the scope and limitations of current advice. Taylor (1986 and 1992) offers a framework of four types of questions that can be used with and by children. The four areas of concern represented are content, form, process and mood. They can be summarized thus:

- *Content*   e.g. what is the work about? What is its subject matter? Was the subject matter observed, remembered or imagined?
- *Form*   e.g. how has the work been arranged? Is this in keeping with its content? What kinds of colour schemes have been used? Are there recurring shapes, lines, forms, etc.? Is the work pleasing in parts or as a whole?
- *Process*   e.g. how was the work made and what was it made with? What materials, tools, processes and techniques were used? Where did the artist start? How long did the work take?
- *Mood*   e.g. does the work affect you? Does it capture a mood or feeling or emotion you have already experienced?

Taylor's approach has now reached the status of 'tried and tested'. In my experience it is effective in 'scaffolding' children's thinking and learning to aid the development of their knowledge and understanding of art (Howe 1995). Although very applicable for use by the generalist primary teacher the framework does not cover aspects of social, historical and cultural understanding but rather elicits a personal response drawing implicitly on prior experiences. It can be an effective springboard for the introduction of new knowledge by the teacher to move into socio-cultural analysis.

Taylor claims to have devised this framework in response to, among other things, another prevalent 'way of looking' – that of Feldman's (1970 – see Taylor 1992) Description, Analysis, Interpretation, Judgement model, seen as hierarchical and rigid. Taylor stresses that his model is not hierarchical, that each category might carry equal weighting or a judgement may be made about selecting categories to emphasize.

In Ritchie (1995) a framework of questions for design and technology contexts has headings of:

- Function.
- Process of making.
- Human factors (with values implicit).
- Aesthetics.
- Future developments (including evaluation of design success).
- Future evaluations (and connections with own making).

Approaches derived from Investigative, Disassembly and Evaluative Activities evident in DATA (1996) *The Primary Coordinators File* and DATA (1998) Planning into Practice can be summarized thus:

- relate to children's experiences
- focus discussion of artefacts/collection:
   on form related to function
   on variation of design solutions
   on application of technology
- encourage investigation of components, elements of system
- allow children to develop for criteria for own design. […]

So what does each framework emphasize?

We can see that each framework investigates different aspects of the made world and emphasizes different concerns, yet I argue that the artefacts they focus upon can all be located within the visual field defined in Figure 10.1. Taylor's framework is concerned with visual arts whose 'causes of form' are generally aesthetic in nature. Functions might be couched in terms of visual communication. Brief may be internal – as in fine art – or external in the case of book illustration. The intended scope of Taylor's framework in relation to the visual field can be represented thus (as in Figure 10.2) […]

Ritchie's list is concerned primarily with the functional/external quadrant of our field yet there are aspects of the aesthetic and internal.

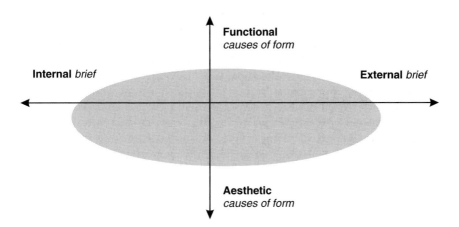

Figure 10.2 Locating Taylor's framework in the 'visual field'

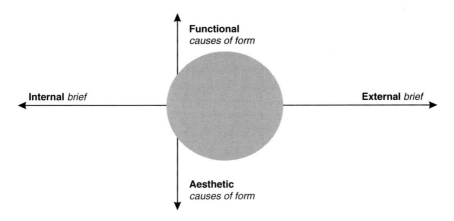

Figure 10.3 Locating DATA publications' concerns in the visual field

The concerns in the DATA Activities Sheets are primarily functional and lead-ing to an 'external' design brief. In some respects this is limiting and the framework needs to be refined and extended if aesthetic aspects of design are to be given due consideration (Figure 10.3).

We can see the frameworks have emphases and limitations yet none are mutu-ally exclusive. They are each capable of facilitating enquiry in the visual field and thus informing action.

Conclusions

The first aim of this paper was '*to define and offer a rationale for the inclusion of visual literacy within the primary curriculum*'. To know through the visual is a powerful way of knowing. Activities that develop visual literacy are worthwhile and desirable in a primary curriculum that purports to be broad, balanced and relevant. We have seen that such activities, such learning objectives, cannot be confined to a single subject in the National Curriculum. If we are to help children to understand how the way they feel is connected to or even *controlled* by those that can manipulate environments and artefacts we must go beyond subject boundaries. Critical, discriminating and questioning individuals, empowered to contribute to the made world, should be the eventual outcome.

The second aim was '*to explore the connections between pedagogic framework currently in use to support the development of visual literacy skills in design and technology and art contexts*'. A number of initiatives and curriculum developments have led to a variety of ways in which the made world, in its broadest sense, can be interrogated. All can be seen as belonging to a 'collection of strategies' that examine artefacts located within the visual field as defined. All rely on the skill of the teacher in their selection and application and are based on open-ended questioning in order to facilitate careful observation and the gaining of knowledge and understanding through engagement with the made world through the visual. A prerequisite of all is the need for children to draw on experiences of similar encounters with art and artefacts.

The strategies have emanated from two 'camps' or 'cultures'. I have attempted to show that there is much common ground between these with regards to visual literacy. ... If there is a discontinuity it is because the common features of approaches in design and technology or art have not been recognized. Educators and advisers need to help teachers identify the merits and appropriateness of the various strategies on offer. Integration is possible, if based on the notion of enquiry within the visual field. Yet ultimately, the teacher herself must reconcile advice that emphasizes different concerns if consistent and progressive teaching is to ensue.

Where next?

One question remains – how do we move forward from here? Gardner (1990) neatly sums up an educational approach that is difficult to argue against:

> If one wants to enhance an individual's understanding, the most likely route is to involve her deeply over a significant period of time with the symbolic realm in question, to encourage her to interact regularly with individuals who are somewhat (rather than greatly) more sophisticated than she is, and to give her ample opportunity to reflect on her own emerging understanding of the domain.
>
> (Gardner 1990: 17)

If we were to take Gardner's advice, it seems a number of things need to happen:

1   'Visual literacy' needs to remain in the primary curriculum. It should not be left out or until a later phase. The current trend to reduce the National Curriculum requirements of the foundation subjects seems to put this at risk. Those that believe such activity to be relevant and worthwhile need to continue to promote its importance. That will include advisers, subject organizations, such as DATA and NSEAD, and primary teachers themselves.

2   There needs to be a regular opportunity for children to consider the made and the visual in a structured way and to become familiar with different ways of looking and knowing. Any future statutory curriculum will need to be clear about this.

3   Children will need to be supported in developing their visual literacy by 'somewhat more sophisticated individuals' (the primary teacher), selecting and using appropriate strategies, which leads to …

4   The need to continue to introduce visual literacy strategies to teachers during their training and professional development. Indeed, returning to the previously cited NACCCE report (DfEE 1999), the committee has demanded that teachers should be trained to use methods and materials which help develop young people's creative abilities and cultural understanding. Common ground between approaches needs to be highlighted – anything other than that risks accusation of 'another thing' for teachers to consider. A *perception* amongst teachers that art and design and technology activities can contribute to a common goal needs to be fostered.

If that sounds like a call for a 'National Visual Literacy Strategy', then so be it.

References

Arts in Schools Project Team (1990) *Arts 5–16*, London: Oliver and Boyd.

Baxendall, M. (1985) *Patterns of Intention*, London: Yale University Press.

DATA (1996) *The D and T Primary Coordinators' File*, Warwickshire: DATA.

DATA (1998) *Planning into Practice*, Warwickshire: DATA.

DATA (1999) 'National Curriculum Review', *Datanews* 10, January: 1–5.

DFEE (1995a) *Art in the National Curriculum*, London: HMSO.

DfEE (1995b) *Design and Technology in the National Curriculum*, London: HMSO.

DfEE/QCA (1999) *The National Curriculum Handbook for Secondary Teachers in England*, London: DfEE/QCA.

Department of Education and Science (1991) *Art for Ages 5 to 14 Proposals of the Secretary of State for Education and Science and the Secretary of State for Wales*, London: HMSO.

Gardner, H. (1990) *Art Education and Human Development*, Los Angeles: Getty Center for Education in the Arts.

Howe, A. (1995) *An exploration into aspects of knowledge and understanding in art in the primary school*, MA dissertation, Bath Spa University College.

Morris, S. (1989) *A Teacher's Guide To Using Portraits*, English Heritage.

National Advisory Committee on Creative and Cultural Education (1999) *All Our Futures: Creativity, Culture and Education*, London: DfEE.

QCA (1998) *Maintaining Breadth and Balance at Key Stages 1 and 2*, Middlesex: QCA Publications.

QCA (1999) *The Review of the National Curriculum in England*, Suffolk: QCA.

Raney, K. (1999) 'Visual literacy and the art curriculum', *Journal of Art and Design Education*, 18(1): 41–47.

Ritchie, R. (1995) *Primary Design and Technology – A Process for Learning*, London: David Fulton.

Schools Council (1982) *Art in the Built Environment*, Essex: Longman.

Swift, J. and Steers J. (1998) 'A Manifesto for Art in Schools', *Journal of Art and Design Education*, 18(1):7–14.

Taylor, R. (1986) *Educating for Art*, Essex: Longman.

Taylor, R. (1992) *Visual Arts in Education*, London: Falmer Press.

Thistlewood, D. (ed.) (1989) *Critical Studies in Art and Design Education*, Essex: Longman.

11 The relationship between modelling and designing and making in Design and Technology

Jane Murray, updated by Gwyneth Owen-Jackson

Drawing on examples from the different material areas, this chapter explores the purposes of modelling in designing and making. Modelling aids in design generation, evaluation and design development and can precede making. Whilst reading the chapter think about how different forms of modelling can be used in your specialist area to develop pupils' learning.

This chapter is based on one written by Jane Murray for the reader, Teaching Technology, which focused on modelling with food, but has been expanded to include all the material areas.

To develop an understanding of the relationship between modelling and designing and making with any material it is necessary to explore the meaning of the term 'modelling'. A dictionary offers definitions of the term 'model', giving a variety of usages which cover a replica or representation of:

- a concrete object to show what it looks like or how it works;
- an abstract idea to make it more intelligible;
- a blueprint, design or plan for others to follow or imitate;
- different brands or versions of the same product.

This definition is referring to the word model as a noun; in design and technology the active form of 'modelling' is more commonly used. Modelling is a term used to embrace:

- modelling inside the head – cognitive modelling or imaging

and

- modelling outside the head – concrete modelling.

Modelling inside the head includes the activities of imaging thoughts and ideas and shaping and forming those ideas using images and representational forms. These representational forms might be mental pictures: in stills, in series or moving; in the spoken or written word; or using other forms of language, such as number or symbols.

Concrete modelling is the taking of the ideas inside the head and developing them outside the head by sketching, drawing, explaining, planning, exploring, experimenting and manipulating materials and communicating the ideas in a tangible form. Both forms of modelling can be used to develop ideas, explore what things look like or how they might work and test them. The tangible results of modelling outside the head are referred to as models, mock-ups or prototypes depending on their stage of development. The relationship between these two forms of modelling was developed by the Assessment of Performance Unit and has been described in earlier chapters; it is shown graphically in Figure 2.1.

Food is a material area in Design and Technology that initially created debate over whether it was a material that could be used for modelling. There is no conflict between the definitions given here and food. The dictionary definitions described earlier can be exemplified using all the materials in Design and Technology, including food, as shown in Table 11.1.

In relation to modelling, foods – like other materials – can be imaged in the mind and the images can be transformed, and food materials – like other materials – can be shaped, formed and represented through and with other materials and media.

The functions of modelling

The Assessment of Performance Unit design and technology project explored the concept of imaging and modelling, and the relationship with design and technology activities: 'As soon as we begin to perceive the outline of a task, pictures or images of solutions start to appear in our minds' (APU 1987). This relates closely to modelling inside the head, 'in the mind's eye', imaging, capturing and holding the images or 'temporary spatial displays' (Kosslyn 1978) and then manipulating and modelling them outside the head to produce tangible results. Modelling activity is a tight, iterative relationship between imaging and modelling as designing and making proceeds, and is at the crux of all 'practical' activity combining the human ability for thought and action. The concrete modelling fuels the ideas for further cognitive modelling which then need to be tried out in a concrete form.

When modelling in systems and control, for example, circuits can be designed and tested on the computer, and then refined, before being built. In textiles or resistant materials a product may be sketched out so that the image can be seen and developed before an actual physical product is made.

How do people engage in imaging of ideas with foods? Can these ideas be manipulated by cognitive modelling? The following quote shows the possibilities for imaging:

> Each wine we tasted was accompanied by an imaginary menu, described with much lip-smacking and raising of the eyes to gastronomic heaven. We mentally consumed ecrevisses, salmon cooked with sorrel, rosemary-flavoured chicken from Bresse, roasted baby lamb with creamy garlic sauce, an estouffade of beef and olives, a double loin of pork with spiked slivers of truffle.
>
> (Mayle 1990)

Table 11.1 Examples of modelling in different materials

	Resistant materials	Textiles	Systems and control	Food
A concrete object …	A mock-up of a product made in styrene	A toile	A mock-up of a system, such as a hand-drier	Any food product made
An abstract idea …	Annotated design drawings showing ideas for a product	Drawings of garments or textile products	A flow-chart showing the sequence for controlling a flashing light display	A spreadsheet showing nutritional analysis
A blueprint …	A production plan for a product	Instructions for making up a garment or product	A diagram of a printed circuit board	A recipe
Different brands or versions …	Varieties of CD holders	Varieties of hats	Varieties of electronic hand-held games	Varieties of flavoured soups

Try to use your own mind's eye to imagine the food on the table at a party for 6-year-olds. What type of snack foods will be on the table? What size and shape will the food be? What texture, what taste? Think of a novel food product that could be made to add to the table. Would this be savoury or sweet? What colour would it be, what texture?

This type of guided imagery could be used as a teaching strategy to help students appreciate the way in which they can engage in modelling designs. For example, in resistant materials pupils could be asked to imagine a futuristic or a themed home. What would its shape be? What materials might it be made from? What would the fittings and furniture look like? From this they could select one piece of furniture, such as a chair, and model their design of how it might look.

The functions of modelling discussed here are those which aid designing, but modelling can also be used as a tool for communication, including marketing the product.

Modelling as representation

The range of forms of modelling as representation includes language, both oral and written, and other symbolic forms: number, signs, notation, drawing and three-dimensional forms using available, substitute and specific materials. The form of model used will often depend on its purpose.

Modelling of thoughts, ideas or images is essential for demonstrating, developing, clarifying, expressing and communicating ideas with oneself and with other people. Taking the images that have been modelled inside the head to a point outside the head makes them more accessible for oneself and others to predict, to test, to confront, to transform and to appraise. What is expressed by modelling is a result of images in the mind; these are influenced by what can be expressed by modelling outside the mind.

Representative models can take different forms. In systems and control, for example, a computer simulation could be used to model how an actual system would work. In resistant materials or textiles a model could be a drawing, showing a product, a computer simulation or a mock-up. Mock-ups can be representative in different ways: they can be smaller than the actual product, such as a model bridge, simpler in construction, such as a car shell to show the shape, or parts of a product, such as a machine engine.

How can images of design ideas in food be drawn out of the mind and shared with others? Sketches of early ideas could be in the form of language, as in the spoken or written word, for example a description of the food to be sold in a new foreign-foods product range. Ideas for suitable foods could be described in the written or spoken word or through other forms of representation using number, symbols, drawings. As more detail emerges these might need the clarification of, for example, measurement, detail of appearance or make-up, as in a recipe.

Models can also be used to show aspects of a product that are not visible, for example a spreadsheet showing the nutritional analysis of a food product. By changing the ingredients it would be possible to model the nutritional changes. Spreadsheets can be used with textile or resistant materials products to model, for example, changes to weight or costings when using different materials. Other mathematical models are widely used in systems and control, for example formulae for resistance and capacitance. These are used to model the behaviour of electronic circuits and so how systems would perform.

Modelling and cognitive processes

Does this concept of modelling tie in with theories of cognitive development? Vygotsky wrote that words follow from objects in speech development. Language, signs and symbols are used for action, and have the potential for reverse action. Vygotsky also writes of the importance of tools in child development. By handling tools and mimicking tasks carried out by others the child learns through observation, action and thinking about what is being done.

> Consequently, the child's system of activity is determined at each specific stage both by the child's degree of organic development and by his or her degree of mastery in the use of tools.
>
> (Vygotsky 1978: 21)

This correlates very closely with the tight iterative process described by the APU and the way in which imaging and modelling is used by humans in order to imagine the world, image how it might be different and externalize these imagings through modelling using tools (including language, signs and symbols) and materials.

Modelling, particularly with computer-based diagrams and simulations, helps students to develop their imaging further. They can 'see' what would happen if they changed the size or shape of their design, used a different material or ingredient, or simply changed the colour or surface decoration.

Eisner writes about the importance of symbol systems in the 'process of concept formation':

> We can construct models of the world from which we can derive verbal or numerical propositions or from which we can create visual or auditory images. The point is that, while the sensory system provides us with information about the world in sensory form, our imaginative capacities – when coupled with an inclination toward play – allow us to examine and explore the possibilities of this information.
>
> (Eisner 1985: 204)

These writings on cognitive development serve to demonstrate the importance of modelling in relation to all concept formation, and in considering, rehearsing and engaging in practical activity – which is at the very heart of design and technology.

The visual sense is significant but the other senses are also used to observe, interpret and represent thought. Eisner points out that:

> Basic to the understanding of mind is the importance of understanding the functions that the sensory systems perform in the realisation of consciousness … Our sensory system performs an active role in this process by putting us in contact with the world.
>
> (Eisner 1985: 166)

Any material we use in design and technology interacts with the senses of sight and touch; food also uses our senses of taste and smell.

This is important for cognitive modelling, and responses to these senses can be represented in language and two-dimensional forms. In order to pursue the modelling 'outside the head' to develop design ideas and the function of modelling, materials must be used to bring the ideas into a form where they can be tested and modelled to a point of satisfaction in terms of the outcome being developed. The interaction between thought and action is enhanced by the use of real materials, as it enables the breadth of senses to be used and the possible outcome being represented to be appraised appropriately.

Modelling and teaching and learning

What are the issues and implications for teaching and learning concerning students and teachers? If modelling is fundamental to the development of capability in Design and Technology how should teachers address the issue of supporting students' development of modelling strategies?

An important aspect of modelling in Design and Technology is that both students and teachers need tangible evidence of cognitive modelling. Students use modelling to bring their ideas into the 'real world' and test them; teachers observe the modelling procedures for evidence of the conceptual modelling that the students have engaged in. However, there is a danger that the outcome of the modelling activity becomes the most significant part of the experience at the expense of the process. Modelling then becomes a series of prerequisite steps that students are expected to take to provide evidence for teachers.

The most important teaching and learning points must be that teachers encourage students to engage in imaging and modelling and support future situations by providing opportunities for observation, drawing upon as many experiences as possible. Modelling images in a rich range of representational methods and materials, not a sterile, hoop-jumping, linear route that merely requires conforming to a prescribed convention, is necessary. Gunstone writes of science:

> Traditional practical work has features which can inhibit the possibility of students restructuring personal theories … For these students, successful assembly of the apparatus became the only significant task. Once this was achieved the rest of the practical was completed in ritualised fashion, with little or no serious thought.
>
> (Gunstone 1990: 74)

This could equally apply to traditional school-based work in craft and home economics. Working to 'recipes' and methods prescribed for particular situations is not necessarily going to foster the imagination in designing either in resistant materials, textiles or food. Students need to be considering the properties and characteristics of materials and how they can use, develop, extend or change those properties or characteristics in the designing and making of 'new' products.

The wider concept of imaging and modelling is something that all teachers of Design and Technology need to embrace. The range of representational materials must be broad and appropriate for the actual materials being represented. Modelling serves the purposes of minimizing waste and expense in terms of materials as ideas are developed, trialled and tested; or finding out if the ideas that are being taken out of the head and into 'concrete' form will actually 'work'. This works differently with different materials: for example, with food, a product may meet the nutritional specification on the spreadsheet model, and the drawing of it may look fine, but it has to be smelt and tasted before you know if it is successful.

As Eisner notes:

> A particular symbolic system is useful for some types of information, but not for others and vice versa. Thus when we choose to become 'literate' in the use of particular symbol systems, we also begin to define for ourselves what we are capable of conceiving and how we can convey what we have conceived to others.
>
> (Eisner 1985: 125)

Conclusion

In conclusion, modelling is at the heart of design and technology. This is not just in its facility to enable students to image the world in which they live, consider changes and use thought and action in designing and making responses to these changes, but also in the development of understanding in relation to all the activities they are engaged in.

The iterative processes of thought and action, imaging and modelling inside and outside of the head are fundamental to design and technology when working with any of the materials identified in the statutory order. Food designers and technologists, like those working in other fields, engage in modelling when they image possibilities for new products and develop and test those images both inside and outside the head.

There are implications for teachers and for students. Students must develop the capacity to handle a range of images and use modelling strategies to do this, either by concentrating on snapshot images in the mind, or by encouraging the ideas to flow and synthesizing them, then communicating them. Teachers should take responsibility for setting up situations and activities that require students to think and be analytical, to give them opportunities for creating images and for modelling those images in a range of ways that are appropriate to the student, the intended audience, and the materials and outcomes being considered. This involves methods of teaching that contextualize activities, encourage creativity, support designing, reflecting and evaluating and the use of appropriate modelling strategies and representations.

Teachers of Design and Technology could benefit from appraising their understanding of the term 'modelling' as used in National Curriculum Design and Technology. The range of materials is broad and there are significant differences between all of them, which means that narrow definitions and interpretations of the terms used in designing and making are unhelpful and restrictive. It is essential that 'modelling' is interpreted in such a way to clarify its breadth, and that the interpretation encompasses the range of materials in Design and Technology, the range of methods of representation and the functions required from the activity of engaging modelling.

References

APU (Assessment of Performance Unit) (1987) *Design and Technological Activity: A Framework for Assessment*, London: DES.

Eisner, E. (1985) *The Art of Educational Evaluation: A Personal View*, London: Falmer Press.

Gunstone, R. F. (1990) *Reconstructing Theory from Practical Experience*, Oxford: Oxford University Press.

Kosslyn, S. M. (1978) 'Imagery and cognitive development: a teleological approach', in R. Siegler (ed.) *Children's Thinking: What Develops*, New York: Lawrence Erlbaum Associates.

Mayle, P. (1990) *A Year in Provence*, London: Pan.

Sparkes, J. (1993) 'Modelling', in R. McCormick, C. Newey and J. Sparkes (eds) *Technology for Technology Education*, Wokingham: Addison-Wesley in association with the Open University Press.
Vygotsky, L. (1978) *Mind in Society*, New York: Wiley.

12 Does the need for high levels of performance curtail the development of creativity in Design and Technology project work?

Stephanie Atkinson

Creativity is a quality which Design and Technology should be encouraging in pupils, but this chapter asks if it is actually doing so. The chapter reports a research study which looked at pupils' creative ability and their examination performance in Design and Technology, with some interesting results. I hope this chapter will lead you to consider how you can help pupils to develop their creative thinking through your teaching, whilst still enabling them to achieve examination success.

Introduction

[...] In recent years the critically important yet elusive topic of creativity has earned the serious attention of a great many psychologists, educators, politicians, and individuals in business and industry. Although psychological definitions of creativity have varied (Torrence 1988; Walberg 1988; Sternberg 1988; Ochse 1990; Mayer 1999), there is now, on the whole, common agreement on what creativity involves: '*bringing something into being that is original (new, unusual, novel, unexpected) and also valuable (useful, good, adaptive, appropriate)*' (Ochse 1990, p. 2). Researchers have all agreed that to be creative, creative thinking must take place. To be of value, that thinking needs to be critical. Creative thinking should integrate the fundamental aspects associated with thinking in general, which as Ryle suggested in 1949 is a polymorphous concept. It combines: recalling and imaging; classifying and generalizing; comparing and evaluating; analysing and synthesizing; deducing and inferring (Kamii 1980).

Thinking embraces many different kinds of activity which may have little in common. Psychologists have tended to study thinking by attempting to divide and classify types of activity which could be investigated separately. Lawson (1990) suggested that the most well used division was that between 'reasoning' and 'imagining', both of which he explained were obviously needed in the context of design activity.

Much has been written to suggest that thinking cannot be divorced from knowledge (Langley and Jones 1988; McAlpine 1988; Ochse 1990) and that learning is a necessity for the development of creativity (Torrence 1962; Gowan, Khatena and Torrence 1981; Kamii 1980; Perkins 1988; Ochse 1990). However, this form of learning should not necessarily be taken to mean learning to be creative, or learning to think creatively. Learning in this instance refers also to acquiring knowledge and skill within the area of a creator's speciality. Relevant skills, though not sufficient in themselves to produce creativity, have been shown to be crucial for its development (Gowan *et al.* 1981; Perkins 1988). A supportive learning environment has been seen by some as an important factor in encouraging creativity, although as McAlpine (1988) explained, that could deny the critical role played by cognitive challenge in creative thinking. He reminds the reader that it was the grit in the oyster that made the pearl.

Creativity in an educational context

The need for pupils to develop high order thinking and problem-solving skills throughout their education is now considered of paramount importance (Wu, Custer and Dyrenfurth 1996). Supported by government, business and educational leaders, the National Advisory Committee on Creative and Cultural Education (NACCCE) stated in their report that Britain's prosperity depended upon the educational system's ability to unlock the full potential of every young person (Robinson 1999). The report made particular reference to the importance of developing creative thinking skills, which it suggested could and should be taught in all schools, to all pupils. Other recent writers, such as Fritz (1998) and Lewis (1999), have added their support to the relevance of developing creative thinking skills. Fritz (1998) believed that these skills were a critical factor in an age that needed to focus on finding new directions, new ideas and new ways of being. Lewis (1999) in discussing the important link between high order thinking skills, problem-solving and the place of technology education in developing these skills, suggested that technology education could provide appropriate situations for pupils to come to understand technology whilst engaging in acts of technological creation. He believed that technology was in essence a manifestation of human creativity.

The research reported in this chapter has concentrated on pupil creativity at a stage in education when public examinations and the results achieved are considered of prime importance to both pupils and teachers alike. Educationalists would have us believe that the assessment used to judge pupils' work should not dictate the curriculum content (Task Group on Assessment and Testing 1987), rather it should be designed to develop capability and test competence (Secondary Examination Council 1986; Sutton 1991; Northern Examinations and Assessment Board 1993). However, the nature of assessment and its criteria has been shown to influence what is learnt and how it is taught (Atkinson 1997).

Important in this context has been the well established theory that creativity is promoted more by intrinsic than extrinsic rewards (Rogers 1959; Taylor 1960; Wallace 1985; Hennessey and Amabile 1988; Sternberg 1988; Simonton 1988). Unfortunately, external rewards or expectation of external rewards have been shown to dampen creativity (Gowan *et al.* 1981; Hennessey and Amabile 1988). Amabile (1985) suggested that in a classroom situation pupils were more likely to be creative when there was no expectation of a reward and that even thinking about extrinsic reasons for having to be creative lowered levels of creativity.

Design and Technology involves a complex integration of processes, concepts, knowledge and skills in such a way as to make it particularly distinctive within the school curriculum (Kimbell, Stables, Wheeler, Wosniak and Kelly 1991; DES 1992). The subject's ability to encourage pupils to develop creative, critical, analytical thinking and problem-solving skills, acquire practical and technological skills, whilst learning to cope with constant technological change, were all seen as important factors for the inclusion of Design and Technology as a core subject in the National Curriculum (DES 1987, 1989).

As the curriculum area has developed so has the use of design projects as a means of delivering and examining the complex concepts and subject content required (e.g. Design Council 1980; Kimbell 1982; Her Majesty's Inspectorate of Schools: Craft Design and Technology Committee 1983; National Curriculum: Design and Technology Working Group 1988; DES 1987, 1989; Kimbell *et al.* 1991; DATA 1995). In order to undertake this project work pupils have been expected to exercise logical procedural strategies, often referred to as problem-solving or design processes. Early followers of an 'intellectual approach' to these processes formulated their thoughts by using information gained from eminent creators who had examined and analysed their own thinking (Ochse 1990). During the past thirty years, the tendency to employ the term 'problem-solving' generically to include such diverse activities as coping with marital problems and finding faults in electronic circuits has led to generalizations that have often been unhelpful and inappropriate, particularly in the field of designing (Wu *et al.* 1996; Funke and Frensch 1995). ...

In the 1970s and early 1980s the term problem-solving was generally used to describe design activities carried out in Design and Technology in schools. However, by the end of the 1980s this general classification was deemed by many to be unhelpful. It was suggested that a more positive approach to project work was needed. It was believed that pupils should be encouraged to identify needs or opportunities, rather than see everything as a problem to be solved (DES 1990).

Traditionally, the creative process that designers have used has been described as a number of specific sub-activities such as researching, specifying the problem or need, generating ideas, making and evaluating. The relationship between these sub-activities and the whole process have been described in the form of a number of process models (e.g. Kimbell *et al.* 1991). In schools the early models were simple (see Figure 12.1a). These models described the process as linear (Schools Council 1975). As teachers have become more experienced in working with the models and as the subtlety of the process has become more apparent, so each model has become increasingly complex (e.g Layton 1991; Kimbell *et al.* 1991; Custer 1995) (see Figure 12.1b).

Since the early 1990s, in line with research into problem-solving activities, those looking specifically at design processes used in schools have become increasingly concerned at the models being adopted (Kimbell *et al.* 1991; Department for Education (DfE) 1992; Hennessey, McCormick and Murphy 1993; Chidgey 1994; Shield 1995; Custer 1995). Whilst all agreed that pupils needed to use logical approaches to their design activity, and that a single design process model could

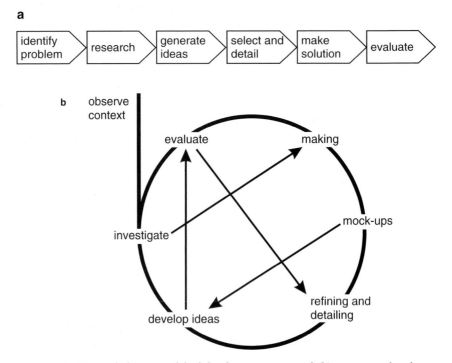

Figure 12.1   (a) simple linear model of the design process and (b) more complex design process model in the form of an interacting design loop

Source: Kimbell 1987, p. 10

not suit all situations, confusion existed between the contrasting models proposed by those from differing design backgrounds. Some suggested that a scientific, mathematical route was the way forward (e.g. Smithers and Robinson, 1992); others believed a loose framework to guide designing, rather than a straitjacket, was more appropriate (Department for Education and Science (DES) 1987). Lawson (1990) believed that it was only by using flexible procedures that creative, innovative thinking would be encouraged. Archer and Roberts (1992) explained that most real world problems encountered were 'ill-defined' and were therefore not resolvable by scientific or mathematical methods. Lewis (1999) added his support suggesting that while some problems lent themselves to algorithms, many others responded only to heuristics. Custer (1995) classified design and problem-solving activities in terms of their complexity and goal clarity. He believed that not all such activities were of equal creative merit. He explained that problems that warranted an inventive process needed divergent thinking and creativity, whilst troubleshooting processes generally required convergent thinking and an application of established procedures.

Archer and Roberts (1992) believed that pupils ought to be encouraged to use appropriate short-cut creative approaches and that these should be instinctive and emanate from intuition, guesses, inspiration or even accidents. Denton (1992), in support of the use of appropriate subsets of the process, suggested that in order to do so pupils needed to be taught how to design effectively and think creatively. However, recent research into design activity in an educational context (e.g. Atkinson 1994, 1995, 1997; Hennessey *et al.* 1993; Saxton and Miller 1996) would suggest that pupils have been left to discover and develop their own understanding of design procedures simply through 'doing' the activity. There has been little evidence gathered of pupils being taught 'how' to design or 'how' to think more creatively. One theory that may explain why this has been the case is that many of the concepts that lie close to the heart of design are not understood or shared by the majority of teachers (Atkinson 1995, 1997; Thistlewood 1997; Hopper and Downie 1998; Fritz, 1998; Hopper, Hepton and Downie 1999).

Unfortunately in Design and Technology, the terms used to describe the sub-activities in a simple linear design model have been used as units for assessment in the GCSE Design and Technology examination. This has tended to prevent flexibility which has in turn stifled creativity amongst many pupils (Atkinson 1995). In order to achieve high marks teachers have encouraged pupils to provide evidence of each stage of the assessed process, whether it was appropriate to the efficient design of an artefact or not. ...

Delivering creativity in schools has generated mixed feelings amongst practitioners. In primary schools creativity has always been welcomed as a crucial aspect of a young person's educational development. In the past its delivery has not been seen as problematic. However, more recently external pressure on primary teachers has meant that creativity can no longer be considered a feasible priority within the primary sector of education (Gardner 1995).

The drop in the creative ability of pupils once they reached secondary school age has been well documented since the 1960s (e.g. Torrence 1962; Gowan *et al.* 1981; Guilford 1981). The early reasons given for the decline were usually associated with developmental phenomena. [...]

Creativity, it has been suggested, encourages pupils to question, innovate, change direction and challenge. Unfortunately these characteristics create a difficult environment for schools and teachers to manage (Gardner 1995). Both Torrence (1981) and Gardner (1995), referred specifically to a lack of teacher support for developing creative thinking during secondary education. They both indicated that teachers on the one hand accepted the importance of developing creative thinking whilst at the same time striving to make pupils conform to behavioural norms which mitigated against any such development.

In researching the area of creativity in an educational context, the complex pattern of factors that affect a pupil's learning and performance whilst designing have been well rehearsed (Naughton 1986; DES 1989; Kimbell *et al.* 1991; NCC 1993; Atkinson 1994). There are those attributes that pupils bring with them – their gender; general ability; cognitive style; personal goals; knowledge base; curriculum experience – and the attributes of the task itself – its contextual location; its structure; its likely demands upon the pupils. In the context of Design and Technology the complex relationship between all these factors and such external forces as culture, context, parental and teacher expectations cannot be underestimated. Set against this complex background the question of whether the need for high levels of performance in Design and Technology examination project work curtailed the development of high order thinking skills, such as creativity, was examined.

The research study

The group of pupils in this study was part of a group used in a four-year project regarding pupil motivation in Design and Technology. [...]

Data were collected prior to the start of the GCSE Design and Technology coursework project, during the project and once the project was finished. A questionnaire ascertaining each pupil's perception of their ability to perform in, and enjoyment of, Design and Technology project work was given to the pupils at the beginning of the academic year.[1] Observation and informal interviews were then used to monitor the pupils' progress throughout the designing and making of their project. On completion of that work a two part creativity test, a summative questionnaire and a goal orientation index were completed by each pupil. Data concerning the school's internal, moderated mark for each Design and Technology project were also collected.

The Creativity Test

This was in two parts; the first section was used only to stimulate the pupil's creativity and was not scored. It was taken from De Carlo's *Psychological Games* (1983). In the original test there were 30 circles illustrated, each containing images for the viewer to interpret. De Carlo suggested that there were no 'right' answers, only witty, daring or unusual interpretations. In the creativity test used in this research project only 12 of the circles were selected as the researcher did not wish the unscored section of the test to take too long. The second section was based on the then unpublished PhD work of Oxlee (1996). In his test the subjects were presented with a sheet of paper on which 12 squares were drawn. Inside each square there were three marks, two short straight lines and one short curved line. Each square had the same three lines placed in identically the same positions (Figure 12.2).

The subjects in the sample were then each asked to produce twelve different images/pictures, either abstract or representational, utilizing all three lines in each composition. There were concerns over the test's validity as it had so recently been developed by Oxlee, although, after careful consideration, it was deemed appropriate to testing creativity in the context of design activity as it required flexible, divergent, thinking with a response that was drawn rather than written.

The test was administered once the pupils had completed their project work. ... Pupils were asked to work as individuals with no reference to each other's work. They were told that it was the variety which was important, not the quality of drawing. The pupils were also asked to give the individual images titles if they believed it was appropriate (see Figure 12.3 for examples of several pupil-created images).

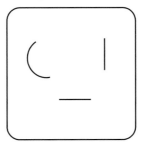

Figure 12.2 An example (not full size) of the square and lines around which the pupils created their images in the second part of the creativity test

On completion of the test each pupil's images were photocopied, coded and
cut into the twelve individual images. Similar images from the total sample were
then grouped together in piles (e.g. all the illustrations showing cups, mugs and
glasses were placed in one pile, all the full-faced humans in another, etc.).
Twenty-five separate piles were formed. Each pile was then counted. The piles
were then placed in rank order. A score was given to each pile, with the one
having the least responses in it being given the highest score of '19'. This score
decreased as more and more images were counted in a pile. The pile with the
most was given the score of '1'. A score of '0' was given to squares that had no
pupil input on them. Any piles that had the same number of responses in them
were given the same score. The score for an image in a pile was then credited to
the correct pupil using the pupil code on the back of each response. The twelve
scores (one for each image) were then added together to provide a final individual pupil score for creativity. Pupils with high scores were considered more
creative than pupils with low scores. [...]

Results

The relationship between levels of pupil creativity and pupil performance

Scores achieved in the creativity test and percentages awarded for the completed
project work were scrutinized for all the pupils. The mean percentages for performance when grouped by level of creativity provided the expected result: the higher
the level of creativity the higher the mean score for performance. [...]

Table 12.1 reports the raw data concerning levels of creativity and performance
for individual pupils within two groups, those who achieved high marks and those
who achieved low marks. These results indicated that 33 per cent of those who
achieved high marks were less creative, whilst 40 per cent of those who only gained
low marks were highly creative. The unexpected results within Table 12.1 have
been highlighted in bold. [...]

One of 44 cups, mugs or glasses

One of 20 full faced humans

One of 18 full faced animals

One of 17 skylines with either the
sun or the moon

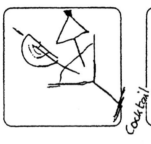

One of 16 side views of a face

One of 14 balls plus a foot

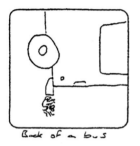

One of 11 back ends of a car, lorry or bus

One of 5 glasses, vases drawn in this way

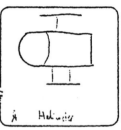

One of 5 helicopters

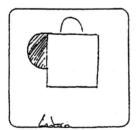

One of 3 lanterns or torches drawn in
this way

One of 3 people skating

The only plan view of a cooker although
2 others used plan views of roads

Figure 12.3 Some examples (not full size) of pupils' created images

Table 12.1 Raw data illustrating creativity scores and percentages achieved in the examination project work. The unexpected results are in bold text (*n* = 27)

High marks				Low marks			
Rank order	Mark %	Creativity score	Rank order	Rank order	Mark %	Creativity score	Rank order
01	98	98.0	40	36	40	145.0	12
02	95	175.0	03	37	33	157.5	08
03	94	173.0	04	37	33	56.0	48
04	90	99.0	39	40	32	141.0	13
05	88	183.5	01	39	32	115.0	33
06	84	137.0	14	41	28	93.5	41
07	83	151.0	10	42	26	125.0	23
08	78	120.0	25	43	24	118.0	32
09	78	155.5	09	44	23	84.0	43
10	72	80.5	45	45	21	147.0	11
11	70	70.0	46	46	20	130.5	18
12	66	180.5	02	47	18	160.0	07
				48	14	104.5	37
				49	11	81.0	44
				50	7	171.5	05

The relationship between creativity, performance and personal goal characteristics

In order to analyse the relationship between personal goal characteristics, creativity and performance, individual pupils' strengths and weaknesses regarding personal goal characteristics were calculated using the goal orientation index data. Two separate analyses were carried out. In the first analysis the individual scores for a pupil's ability to 'reflect', 'plan' and 'act' were computed. From this data the mean scores for those pupils who were high performance/low creativity (Group A) and those who were high creativity/low performance (Group B) were calculated and compared.[2] The results indicated that a pupil's ability to 'act' remained fairly constant across both groups whilst those who were not creative achieved higher scores in their ability to 'reflect' and 'plan' than pupils who were highly creative. These results are reported in Table 12.2.

The second analysis scrutinized the individual pupil scores achieved for each of eight personal goal categories. These were then placed in rank order. From this data the top two personal goal strengths and bottom two personal goal weaknesses for each pupil could be ascertained. Table 12.3 reports the two most frequently occurring strengths and the two most frequently occurring weaknesses for both groups.

The results indicated that a large proportion of the highly creative pupils (Group

Table 12.2 Goal orientation data for two sub-sets of pupils. Those who were High performance/Low creativity (Group A) and those who were High creativity/Low performance (Group B)

GROUP A *High performance/Low creativity*		GROUP B *High creativity/Low performance*	
Higher mean score for goal orientation	246.250	Lower mean score for goal orientation	214.500
Lower mean score for acting (max. 91 min. 52)	71.500	Higher mean score for acting (max. 91 min. 52)	73.167
Higher mean score for planning (max. 103 min. 53)	86.250	Lower mean score for planning (max. 103 min. 53)	71.333
Higher mean score for reflecting (max. 99 min. 53)	88.500	Lower mean score for reflecting (max. 99 min. 53)	70.000

Table 12.3 Goal orientation data for two sub-sets of pupils. Those who were High performance/Low creativity (Group A) and those who were High creativity/Low performance (Group B). The data illustrates the two most common strengths and the two most common weaknesses for each sub-set of pupils

GROUP A *High performance/Low creativity*	*No. of occurrences*	GROUP B *High creativity/Low performance*	*No. of occurrences*
The two most frequently occurring strengths			
Setting goals	3	Recognizing opportunities	5
Completing the work	3	Selecting strategies	4
The two most frequently occurring weaknesses			
Selecting strategies	3	Completing the work	6
Pushing on with the process	2	Organization	3

B) in the sample were generally able to recognize opportunities and select suitable strategies, whilst they tended to be poor at completing their work and general organization. On the other hand, many of those pupils who were not creative (Group A) were aided by their ability to set themselves goals and complete their work. Their personal goal weaknesses supported their low creativity results in that the two most commonly featured weaknesses were concerned with their inability to select suitable strategies and be able to push forward with the process involved in the task.

The relationship between creativity, performance and pupil perception of their enjoyment of designing and their belief in their ability to perform

Data collected in the questionnaire given to the pupils before the project work commenced indicated that there was a considerable difference between those pupils who were not creative (Group A) and those who were creative (Group B) when they were asked whether they would be able to design using the design process model that their teachers advocated for their project work. Only 34 per cent of pupils in the highly creative group believed that they would be able to work within the prescribed model, whilst all the pupils who achieved high marks although they were not creative believed that the adopted model would not cause them a problem. …

The data from the questionnaire also indicated that 50 per cent of those in the highly creative group already disliked design activities before the start of their examination project and that 75 per cent of those in the 'low creativity' group could also be found in this category. …

The relationship between creativity, performance and pupil motivation

Analysis of the data for Groups A and B concerning levels of motivation indicated a considerable difference between the two groups. All pupils who belonged to Group B became de-motivated during their project work even though they were highly creative. Of those belonging to Group A none was found to be de-motivated during or at the end of their project. …

As a second indicator of maintained pupil motivation, the number of pupils in Groups A and B who finished their project work by the hand-in date was scrutinized. … Only 34 per cent of highly creative pupils finished their projects by the due date whilst 75 per cent of pupils with low levels of creativity finished their projects on time.

The relationship between creativity, performance and scores for each aspect of the project work

The data displayed in Table 12.4 indicate that at each stage of the process the pupils who were not creative (Group A) achieved higher mean scores for their work than those pupils who were creative (Group B). […]

Discussion

In a GCSE Design and Technology project that ostensibly requires innovative, creative thinking and high levels of performance, the analysis of data concerning levels of creativity and performance provided results consistent with published literature (e.g. Walberg 1988; Osche 1990). The relationship between creativity and

Table 12.4 The mean scores achieved by the two groups. Those who were High performance/Low creativity (Group A) and those who were High creativity/Low performance (Group B) with regard to each aspect of the project work

GROUP A High performance/Low creativity		GROUP B High creativity/Low performance	
Higher mean scores for each aspect of the process	Mean score	Lower mean scores for each aspect of the process	Mean score
Spec and analysis	3.5	Spec and analysis	2.0
Research	3.5	Research	1.2
Early ideas	3.0	Early ideas	1.2
Detailing	3.5	Detailing	1.8
Planning for manufacture	2.2	Planning for manufacture	1.3
Manufacture of product	3.2	Manufacture of product	1.8
Quality of product	2.5	Quality of product	1.0
Ongoing evaluation	2.8	Ongoing evaluation	1.0
Final evaluation	2.5	Final evaluation	0.7
Skills found in folio		*Skills found in folio*	
Drawing	2.0	Drawing	1.5
Writing	3.8	Writing	1.8
Overall presentation	3.5	Overall presentation	1.7
Design understanding evidenced in folio	2.2	Design understanding evidenced in folio	1.3
Mean score for all aspects of the process	2.938	*Mean score for all aspects of the process*	1.408

performance was positive. The higher the level of creativity the higher the level of performance was found to be in the project-based assessment. The difference in performance between those who achieved high scores and those who achieved low scores in the creativity test was significant. This result supports two main assertions: examination project work is supported by creativity; examination project work supports the development of creativity. However, the statistics hide two key facts. Firstly, 40 per cent of those who achieved poor marks for their design projects were highly creative. Secondly, at the other end of the performance scale, 33 per cent of the pupils who achieved high marks had been categorized as 'not creative'.

In looking at the observation sheets for these individual pupils it became apparent that a number of possible reasons for these results could be highlighted. These mainly centred on the process that pupils were required to use whilst designing. The importance of the GCSE result for both a pupil and their Design and Technology teacher was seen to influence the model of designing adopted. In order to achieve high levels of pupil performance, teachers studied the examination assessment criteria carefully and allowed the units of assessment to dictate the way they presented the design process to their pupils. The result was that pupils were seen to adopt inflexible and ritualistic models that did not allow for risk-taking in order that they could provide evidence that would meet each unit of assessment. Creative, innovative thinking played little part in the process that they used.

Notes

1 A questionnaire was also given to pupils prior to them beginning their project work. It assessed pupils' perception of their enjoyment of designing and making and their perceived ability to be successful and creative when designing.
2 For the purpose of all the remaining analyses only pupils from the 'unexpected results' sub-group were used. These were divided into: Group A ($n = 4$), those pupils who achieved high performance although they were identified as having low levels of creativity; Group B ($n = 6$), those pupils who performed poorly even though they were highly creative.

References

Amabile, T. M. (1985) 'Motivation and creativity: effects of motivational orientation on creative writers', *Journal of Personality and Social Psychology* 48, 393–99.

Archer, L. B. and Roberts, P. (1992) 'Design and technological awareness in education', in P. Roberts, L. B. Archer and K. Baynes, *Modelling: The Language of Designing*, Design: Occasional Paper No. 1, Design and Technology, Loughborough University, Loughborough.

Atkinson, E. S. (1994) 'Key factors which affect pupils performance in technology project work', in J.S. Smith (ed.), *IDATER 94*, Design and Technology, Loughborough University, Loughborough. 30–37.

Atkinson, E. S. (1995) 'Approaches to designing at Key Stage 4', in J. S. Smith (ed.), *IDATER 95*, Design and Technology, Loughborough University, Loughborough, 36–47.

Atkinson, E. S. (1997, *Identification of Some Causes of Demotivation Amongst Key Stage 4 Pupils Studying Design and Technology*, PhD thesis, Newcastle University, Newcastle-upon-Tyne.

Chidgey, J. (1994, 'A critique of the design process', in F. Banks (ed.), *Teaching Technology*, Routledge, London, 89–93.

Custer, R.L. (1995) 'Examining the dimensions of technology', *International Journal of Technology and Design Education* 5(3), 219–44.

DATA (1995) *Guidance Materials for Design and Technology – Key Stage 3*, The Design and Technology Association, Wellsbourne.

De Carlo, N. A. (1983) *Psychological Games*, Guild Publishing, London.

Denton, H. G. (1992) 'The Design and Make task (DMT): some reflections on designing in schools', in J. S. Smith (ed.) *IDATER 93*, Design and Technology, Loughborough University, Loughborough, 70–73.

Department of Education and Science and Welsh Office (1987) *Craft, Design and Technology from 5 to 16: Curriculum Matters 9*, HMSO, London.

Department of Education and Science and Welsh Office (1989) *National Curriculum, Draft Order for Technology*, HMSO, London.

Department of Education and Science and Welsh Office (1990) *Technology in the National Curriculum*, HMSO, London.

Department for Education and the Welsh Office (1992) *Technology for Ages 5 to 16 (1992)*, HMSO, London.

Design Council (1980) *Design Education at Secondary Level* (Design Council Report), The Design Council, London.

Fritz, A. (1998) 'Creativity: from philosophy to practice', Keynote Address: *IDATER 98*, internet site: http://www.21leam.org/cats/testing/fritztxt.html.

Funke, J. and Frensch, P. A. (1995) 'Complex problem solving research in North America and Europe: an integrative review', electronically published article on Internet: www.psychologie.uni-bonn.de/allgm/mitarbei/privat/funke-j/fu and fr-cps.htm.

Gardner, H. (1995) 'Creativity: new views from psychology and education', in C. Joicey (ed.), *Royal Society of Arts Journal*, May, 33–42.

Gowan, J. C., Khatena, J. and Torrence, E. P. (1981) *Creativity: Its Educational Implications* (2nd edn), Kendall/Hunt, Iowa.

Guilford, J. P. (1981) 'Developmental characteristics: factors that aid and hinder creativity', in J. C. Gowan, J. Khatena and E. P. Torrence (eds) *Creativity: Its Educational Implication* (2nd edn), Kendall/Hunt, Iowa, 59–71.

Hennessey, B. A. and Amabile, T. M. (1988) 'The conditions of creativity', in R. J. Sternberg (ed.), *The Nature of Creativity: Contemporary Psychological Perspectives*, Cambridge University Press, Cambridge, 1–38.

Hennessey, S., McCormick, R. and Murphy, P. (1993) 'The myth of general problem-solving capability, Design and Technology as an example', *The Curriculum Journal* 4(1), 74–89.

Her Majesty's Inspectorate of Schools: Craft Design and Technology Committee (1983) *CDT: A Curriculum Statement for the 11–16+ Age Group*, FIMI, London.

Hopper, M. and Downie, M. (1998) 'Developing Design and Technology capability – rhetoric or reality?', in J. S. Smith and E. W. L. Norman (eds), *IDATER 98*, Design and Technology, Loughborough University, Loughborough, 54–9.

Hopper, M., Hepton, B. and Downie, M. (1999) 'Supporting the development of creativity and innovation – further issues examined as part of an extended curriculum development initiative', in P. H. Roberts and E. W. L. Norman (eds), *IDATER 99*, Design and Technology, Loughborough University, Loughborough, 97–106.

Kamii (1980) 'Teaching thinking and creativity: a Piagetian point of view', in A. Lawson (ed.), *The Psychology of Teaching for Thinking and Creativity*, Association for the Education of Teachers of Science, 29–58.

Kimbell, R. A. (1982) *Design Education – Foundation Years*, Routledge, Kegan Paul, London.

Kimbell, R., Stables, K., Wheeler, T., Wosniak, A. and Kelly, V. (1991) *The Assessment of Performance in Design and Technology -The Final Report of the APU Design and Technology Project 1985–91*, School Examinations and Assessment Council/Evaluation and Monitoring Unit, London.

Langley, P. and Jones, R. (1988) 'A computational model of scientific insight', in R. J. Sternberg (ed.) *The Nature of Creativity: Contemporary Psychological Perspectives*, Cambridge University Press, Cambridge, 177–201.

Lawson, B. (1990) *How Designers Think: The Design Process De-mystified* (2nd edn), Butterworth Architecture, London.

Layton, D. (1991) *Aspects of National Curriculum Design and Technology*, National Curriculum Council, New York.

Lewis, T. (1999) 'Research in technology education: some areas of need', *Journal of Technology Education* 10(2), 41–56.

Mayer, R. E. (1999) 'Fifty years of creativity research', in Robert J. Sternberg (ed.), *Handbook of Creativity*, Cambridge University Press, Cambridge, 449–60.

McAlpine, D. (1988) *Creativity: Thinking Processes and Teaching Implications*, paper presented at 4th Annual National Association for Curriculum Enrichment and Extension (NACE) Conference, Nene College, Northampton.

National Curriculum Council (1993) *Technology Programmes of Study and Attainment Targets: Recommendations of the National Curriculum Council*, NCC, New York.

National Curriculum: Design and Technology Working Group (1988) *National Curriculum, Design and Technology Working Group, Interim Report*, HMSO, London.

Naughton, J. (1986) 'What is "technology" anyway?', in A. Cross and B. McCormick (eds), *Technology in Schools*, Open University Press, Milton Keynes, 2–10.

Northern Examinations and Assessment Board (NEAB)   (1993) *General Certificate of Secondary Education: Design and Technology Syllabus for 1995*, NEAB, Newcastle.

Osche, R. (1990) *Before the Gates of Excellence: The Determinants of Creative Genius*, Cambridge University Press, Cambridge.

Oxlee, J. (1996) *Analysis of Creativity in the Practice and Teaching of the Visual Arts With Reference to the Current Work of Art Students at GCSE Level and Above*, PhD Thesis, Newcastle University, Newcastle-upon-Tyne.

Perkins, D. N. (1988) 'The possibility of invention', in R. J. Sternberg (ed.) *The Nature of Creativity: Contemporary Psychological Perspective*, Cambridge University Press, Cambridge, 362–85.

Robinson, K. (ed.) (1999) *All Our Futures: Creativity, Culture and Education*, report from National Advisory Committee on Creative and Cultural Education. Department for Education and Employment, London. Electronically published article on the Internet: http://www.dfee.gov.uk.

Rogers, C.R. (1959) 'A theory of therapy, personality, and interpersonal relationships, as developed in the client-centred framework', in S. Koch (ed.) *Psychology: A Study of a Science* 3, McGraw-Hill, New York, 184–256.

Ryle, G. (1949) *The Concept of Mind*, Hutchinson, London.

Saxton, J. and Miller, S. (1996) 'Design and designing: what's in a word?', *Journal of Design and Technology Education* 1(2), 110–16.

Secondary Examination Council (1986) in Kimbell, R. (ed.) *G. C.S.E, C.D.T.: A Guide for Teachers*, Open University Press, Milton Keynes.

Shield, G. (1995) 'The process approach: a dilemma to be faced in the successful implementation of technology in the National Curriculum', in J. S. Smith (ed.) *IDATER 95*, Design and Technology, Loughborough University, Loughborough, 187–94.

Simonton, D. K. (1988) 'Creativity, leadership, and chance', in R. J. Sternberg (ed.) *The Nature of Creativity: Contemporary Psychological Perspectives*, Cambridge University Press, Cambridge, 386–426.

Smithers, A. and Robinson, P. (1992) *Technology in the National Curriculum. Getting It Right*, Engineering Council, London.

Sternberg R. J. (1988) 'A three-facet model of creativity', in R. J. Sternberg (ed.) *The Nature of Creativity: Contemporary Psychological Perspectives*, Cambridge University Press, Cambridge, 125–47.

Schools Council (1975) *Education Through Design and Craft*, Edward Arnold, London.

Sutton, R. (1991) *Assessment: A Framework for Teachers*, NFER–Nelson, Windsor.

Task Group on Assessment and Testing (1987) *National Curriculum Task Group on Assessment and Testing*, DES, London.

Taylor, D. W. (1960) 'Thinking and creativity', *Annual New York Academic Sci.* 91, 108–27.

Thistlewood, D. (1997) in J. S. Smith (ed.), *IDATER 97*, Design and Technology, Loughborough University, Loughborough.

Torrence, E.P. (1962) *Guiding Creative Talent*, Prentice-Hall Inc., Englewood Cliffs.

Torrence, E. P. (1981) 'Identification and measurement: non-test ways of identifying the creatively gifted', in J. C. Gowan, J. Khatena and E. P. Torrence (eds) *Creativity: Its Educational Implications* (2nd edn), Kendall/Hunt, Iowa, 165–200.

Torrence, E. P. (1988) 'The nature of creativity as manifest in testing', in R. J. Sternberg (ed.) *The Nature of Creativity: Contemporary Psychological Perspectives*, Cambridge University Press, Cambridge, 42–75.

Walberg, H. J. (1988, 'Creativity in learning', in R. J. Sternberg (ed.), *The Nature of Creativity: Contemporary Psychological Perspectives*, Cambridge University Press, Cambridge, 340–61.

Wallace, B. (1986) 'Creativity: some definitions: the creative personality; the creative process; the creative classroom', *Gifted Education International* 14, 68–73.

Wu, T. F., Custer, R. L. and Dyrenfurth, M. J. (1996) 'Technological and personal problem solving styles: is there a difference?' *Journal of Technology Education* 7(2), electronically published article on the Internet: http://scholar.lib.vt.edu/ejournals/JTE/jte-v7n2/wu.jte-v7n2.html.

13 The relationship between Design and Technology and Science

David Barlex and James Pitt

This chapter begins by exploring what 'science' is and what 'technology' is, and how they are related in general terms, before going on to consider their relationship within secondary education. The authors then propose three models for a closer relationship between the two subjects, although acknowledging the practical difficulties involved.

In reading this chapter consider whether the principles could be applied elsewhere: for instance, Design and Technology also has links with Mathematics and with Art. The framework used in this chapter could be usefully applied to other areas.

The source of this chapter is a booklet, Interaction, the Relationship Between Science and Design and Technology in the Secondary School Curriculum, *which was commissioned by the Engineering Council and the Engineering Employers' Federation. The aim was to develop a more appropriate relationship between the two subjects. The full report includes the views of the education community; these are not included here due to limitations of space, but are worth reading. Details of the full report and executive summary are given in the references (Barlex and Pitt 2000).*

There is, in the minds of the public, an intimate connection between science and technology. Frequently the concepts of 'science' and 'technology' are conflated. In many newspapers or broadcasts the words are used almost interchangeably. 'Scientists' are usually blamed when a technology goes wrong or people get scared – whether it be at Chernobyl or over genetically modified foods. When people are asked to identify the contributions of science to civilisation, they think in terms of products – the steam engine, inoculation, the car, antibiotics, the mobile phone. These, of course, are equally the products of technology and design. ... Much scientific research is driven by the need for new or better products, whether these be materials, artefacts or systems; one could say that technology is the motor of science. To some extent the public perception accurately reflects a situation in which there is a dynamic, robust and useful interaction between science and technology.

The situation in secondary schools seems to be very different. The design and technology curriculum, where pupils learn technology, may be unconnected with the science curriculum, with scant communication between staff in the science and design and technology departments, let alone any joint planning or common projects. Hence topics which arise in both curriculums may be taught in both subject areas with no connections being made by either teachers or pupils, a situation that leads to wasted time and the loss of valuable opportunities for enriching pupils' learning. At a more fundamental level, pupils develop knowledge and understanding and skills in a fragmented way that fails to empower them. [...]

What is science?

The path towards a scientific view of the world began in western Europe almost 1000 years ago. In early medieval times knowledge was received from authority. Robert Grosseteste (1175–1243), Bishop of Lincoln, was among the first to reshape the medieval world view in a way that laid open the possibilities of empirical science. Roger Bacon (1214–1292), an English monk, took the view that the advancement of knowledge is best served by observation, experiment and measurement as well as by reasoning. Galileo Galilei (1564–1642) developed mathematical models to give insights into the motions of objects. The idea that knowledge proceeds through observation and measurement became established (Taton 1957; Crombie 1996).

Scientific activity provides explanatory knowledge. Scientists deal with hypotheses and empirical laws. In their search to explain and predict, they seek patterns and relationships between variables. If after repeated, focused experimentation, they consistently fail to disprove an hypothesis, they tentatively offer it as an empirical law. But these laws are really 'best fit' descriptions of the patterns that have been observed. In time, they will be modified or discarded altogether.

Scientists also deal with concepts and models. These too are constructs – ways of making sense of the natural world. Their value to the overall body of scientific knowledge rests in their power of explanation and prediction. They, too, have a limited shelf-life.

Finally, scientists work with theories. Theories are generalising constructs, linking different areas or aspects of scientific knowledge.

Although science does have its small, logical steps, in which dispassionate people gradually advance knowledge, the milestones in the history of science have been set down by individuals with commitment and creativity, thinking divergently, apparently illogically, and by huge leaps of the imagination. A new hypothesis might seem irrational at first. But its proponents, and those opponents who take it seriously, try systematically, using rigorous scientific method, to explore the implications of accepting the hypothesis, and try to disprove it. Thomas Kuhn (1996) clarified this in his work on scientific revolutions using the phrase 'paradigm shift' to describe the effect of developing a new and groundbreaking theory. Lewis Wolpert (1993) argues that scientific thinking is a special mode of thinking which is 'unnatural' and which runs counter to common sense.

He points out that the world is not constructed on a common-sensical basis, and that scientific ideas are usually counter-intuitive, outside everyday experience and not acquired by the simple inspection of phenomena. [...]

What is technology?

Technology has a longer history than science. Humans have always had technology. Since the start of civilisation we have processed raw materials and fashioned artefacts, to make life better. We have also developed systems to achieve our goals. This was as true of stone age hunters who learned how to cut flint, and who had techniques for cornering prey, as it is today for third millennium people who enjoy the benefits of technologies of clean water supply, controlled fertility and communications. Being 'technological' is part of what makes us human. Many writers have tried to unravel the complexity of technology. Here is a snapshot of typical views.

David Layton (1993) is critical of an 'internalist' history of technology, which consists only of a chronological account of inventions, plus how they work, were modified and applied. He argues that artefacts do not appear out of nowhere; that they are developed as the result of whole series of decisions, which in turn are based on certain values among the decision makers. He cites Stephen Kline who describes four uses of the word 'technology':

1   Hardware or artefacts: non-natural objects, of all kinds, manufactured by humans;
2   Socio-technical systems of manufacture: all of the elements needed to manufacture a particular piece of hardware: the complete working system including its inputs – people, machinery, resources, processes – and the legal, economic, political and physical environment;
3   Technique, know-how or methodology: the information, skills, processes and procedures for accomplishing tasks;
4   Socio-technic system of use: a system using combinations of hardware, people (and usually other elements) to accomplish tasks that humans cannot perform unaided by such systems – in order to extend human capacities.

(Layton 1993: 27–8, after Kline 1985)

[…] So complex is technology that it is difficult if not impossible to write a simple, agreed definition. Paul Black and Geoffrey Harrison have produced a useful statement which captures its all pervasive nature.

Technology is the practical method which has enabled us to raise ourselves above the animals and to create not only our habitats, our food supply, our comfort and our means of health, travel and communication, but also our arts – painting, sculpture, music and literature. These are the results of human capability for action. They do not come about by mere academic study, wishful thinking or speculation. Technology has always been called upon when practical solutions to problems have been called for. Technology is thus an essential part of human culture because it is concerned with the achievement of a wide range of human purposes.

(Black and Harrison 1992: 51–2)

This reinforces the points made by all other writers. Technology is much more than just artefacts and any attempt to look at the relationship between science and technology must consider these wider issues. […]

Kenneth Benne and Max Birnbaum (1978) clarify the different aims of scientific and technological activity as follows:

> The aim of the scientist is to produce tested knowledge. The aim of the engineer or technologist is to transform knowledge into techniques and artefacts for which there is a human demand. Scientists operate within the domain of knowledge. Engineers and technologists operate within the domain of practice.
>
> (Benne and Birnbaum 1978: 13)

[…]

A framework for analysing the relationship

One possible view is that there is no distinction between science and technology. Indeed this view is closest to the popular view in this country, in which science and technology are both associated with artefacts. This is unhelpful as it does not acknowledge the fundamentally different aims of scientific and technological activity.

Paul Gardner (1994) offers a framework for analysing the relationship between science and technology. He proposes four possible models.

1   Science precedes technology. Technological capability grows through applied science – thus as scientific knowledge expands, so does technology. This view of *technology as applied science* (or TAS) is widely held, and clearly some key technological advances have been made possible through scientific discoveries. An example is the development of the first camera. Without an understanding of optics and light-sensitive materials the invention of the plate camera in 1850 would not have been possible.

2   Science and technology are independent disciplines or domains, with different goals, method and outcomes. This *demarcationist view* suits some practitioners and curriculum developers. It is possible to find examples of designers practising in total ignorance of the scientific explanations of the working properties of the materials they use, and of theoretical scientists advancing knowledge from armchairs. … In a similarly disconnected way the designers of the electronic systems that are embedded in many modern artefacts – microwave ovens, washing machines, mobile 'phones, television sets and radios – need to understand very little if any of the solid-state physics that underpins the workings of the microelectronic components involved. A thorough appreciation of performance characteristics suffices.

3   In the *materialist view*, technology is seen as historically and ontologically prior to science. Technology precedes science. Indeed, scientists cannot push

forward conceptual development without the tools, instruments and other artefacts created by technologists. The steam engine developed by James Watt in the late eighteenth century provided the basis for the industrial revolution and a national rail transport system, yet the theory of heat engines was not developed by Sadi Carnot until well into the following century.

4   Finally, there is the *interactionist view* in which science and technology are seen in a dialectical relationship, with each informing and being challenged by the other. This view recognises their differences but also their inter-relationships, with neither science nor technology being seen as the dominant partner. In some ways, the first three views can be subsumed into the fourth view for particular instances of different technologies at different times. The history of the development of the camera illustrates this to some extent. There is a *technology as applied science* starting point with the invention of the plate camera; a *demarcationist view* as the evolution of the camera is propelled by the need for better means of developing and printing images; and a *materialist view* when digital technology makes the use of light-sensitive film and chemical processing unnecessary.

The *interactionist view* has the advantage of resolutely refusing to prefer the 'academic' over the 'practical' – or vice versa – and of acknowledging that, as humans, we are as much *homo faber* as we are *homo sapiens*. It rejects the hand/mind dualism that has bedevilled education in this country for far too long, and provides a basis for science and design and technology curriculums which could develop the whole person.

Gardner's models provide a simple yet effective means of considering the relationship between science and technology. ...

We take it as self-evident that school-based education should serve the process of humanisation in each individual and in society as a whole. This is not the only function of education. We need also to be pragmatic about how we give children the means to become active participants in the world they find when they leave school. We need to keep in mind economic, social and political goals. But we must not forget that the curriculum to which children are entitled must enable them to become more fully human. Both science and technology contribute towards our humanity.

Science helps us to make sense of our place in the world and universe, but only in combination with contributions from other disciplines, history and art for example, and from spiritual and philosophical thought. Through technology we transform our surroundings so that we have the time and resources to develop to our full potential.

In the most recent version of the National Curriculum for England (DfEE and QCA, 1999) each subject has a statement describing its distinctive contribution and justifying its importance in the curriculum. These statements also help to clarify the differences between subjects. It is important to remember that they have been written at a time when it is thought that the curriculum must be efficient and that there should be little if any duplication between subjects. So it is not surprising that they pay little if any attention to areas of potential overlap between the subjects. The statement for science reads:

> Science stimulates and excites pupils' curiosity about phenomena and events in the world around them. It also satisfies this curiosity with knowledge. Because science links direct practical experience with ideas, it can engage learners at many levels. Scientific method is about developing and evaluating explanations through experimental evidence and modelling. This is a spur to critical and creative thought. Through science, pupils understand how major scientific ideas contribute to technological change – impacting on industry, business and medicine and improving quality of life. Pupils recognise the cultural significance of science and trace its world-wide development. They learn to question and discuss science-based issues that may affect their own lives, the direction of society and the future of the world.
>
> (DfEE/QCA 1999a: 102)

The statement is consistent with the nature of science and scientific activity as described earlier and there is an acknowledgement that a relationship exists between science and technology. Interestingly, the statement is accompanied by a quote from the science writer Colin Tudge, who points to the limitations as well as the strengths of scientific knowledge:

> Science does not tell us everything that we want to know about life, or all we need to know. But it does provide us with the most robust information about the way the universe works that has so far become available to us.
>
> (DfEE/QCA 1999a: 102)

The statement for design and technology reads:

> Design and technology prepares pupils to participate in tomorrow's rapidly changing technologies. They learn to think and intervene creatively to improve quality of life. The subject calls for pupils to become autonomous and creative problem solvers, as individuals and members of a team. They must look for needs, wants and opportunities and respond to them by developing a range of ideas and making products and systems. They combine practical skills with an understanding of aesthetics, social and environmental issues, function and industrial practices. As they do so, they reflect on and evaluate present and past design and technology, its uses and effects. Through design and technology, all pupils can become discriminating and informed users of products, and become innovators.'
>
> (DfEE/QCA 1999a: 134)

… Intrinsic to this concept of technology is that of design – or the act of designing – although the words 'design' and 'designing' are not used other than in the phrase 'design and technology'.

Gunter Ropohl is in no doubt as to the significance and uniqueness of this activity:

> The engineer, developing and designing a novel technical system, has to antic-
> ipate the object to be realised through mental imagination. He has to conceive
> of a concrete object which does not yet exist, and he has to determine spatial
> and temporal details which cannot yet be observed, but will have to be created
> by the designing and manufacturing process. No wonder that this capacity of
> imagining objects which are completely unknown up to the very moment of
> invention has been regarded for a long time as a miraculous art, and even to-
> day the understanding of so-called creativity is not yet satisfactory. The fact is
> that engineers produce knowledge about not existing objects, and this know-
> ledge is usually represented by mental images rather than by discursive
> statements. ...
>
> (Ropohl 1997: 69)

He is clear that this view of 'creating novelties' applies to all areas of design or practical creativity – fashion design, architecture, product design, graphic design and so
on – as well as the many branches of engineering.

Debating the purpose of science education

It is fortuitous that, while we were considering the relationship between science
and design and technology, the Nuffield Foundation published *Beyond 2000: science education for the future* (Millar and Osborne 1998). The report paints a picture
of a secondary school science curriculum that has lost its sense of purpose and its
effectiveness.

> ... fails to sustain and develop the sense of wonder and curiosity of many
> young people about the natural world ...
> ... an over-emphasis on content which is often taught in isolation from the
> kinds of contexts which could provide essential relevance and meaning ...
> ... lacks a well articulated set of aims or an agreed model of the development of
> pupils' scientific capability over the 5–16 period and beyond ...
> Assessment is based on exercises and tasks that rely heavily on memorisation
> and recall, and are quite unlike those contexts in which learners might wish to
> use science knowledge and skills in later life.
> ... little emphasis, within the science curriculum, on discussion or analysis of
> the scientific issues that permeate contemporary life ...
>
> (Millar and Osborne 1998)

Debating the purpose of design and technology education

Design and technology is a new subject and as such is open to misunderstanding
and misinterpretation. It was introduced into the school curriculum in 1990, as
something radically different in intention from the aims of those subjects that were

its forebears, principally home economics, and craft, design and technology. Most parents and many teachers had very little understanding of this new subject. To help them, and as a direct response to their mystification, DATA (the Design and Technology Association), in conjunction with the DfEE, in 1996 issued a leaflet for parents and teachers in which the purpose and characteristics of the subject were explained (DATA and Department for Education and Employment 1996). In the section 'Why design and technology?' they state that learning design and technology at school

> … helps to prepare young people for living and working in a technological world. Children learn the technical understanding, design methods and making skills needed to produce practical solutions to real problems. D&T stimulates intellectual and creative abilities and qualities of commitment and perseverance. It enables young people to relate personal experience to the work of commerce and industry, to understand how design and technology affects our lives, and contributes to the use and development of technology in our society through informed participation. The subject is of value to everyone in understanding the made world, integrating knowledge acquired in other subjects and out of school, preparation for the citizen and for working life.
>
> (DATA and Department for Education and Employment 1996: 21)

The original National Curriculum Working Group clarified the unique purpose of design and technology as to enable children and young people:

> … to operate effectively and creatively in the made world. The goal is increased 'competence in the indeterminate zones of practice'.
>
> (Design and Technology Working Group 1988: 31)

When this was written in 1988 it meant virtually nothing to those who were required to teach the subject. But it is easy to see that this vision has survived the sometimes turbulent curriculum history of the last ten years and is strongly reflected in the statement describing the distinctive contribution of Design and Technology to the current National Curriculum. And it deserves to be noted that during this time design and technology teachers have made outstanding progress in establishing a new subject and teaching it effectively in the classroom. The number of lessons classed by Ofsted as 'good' has been rising steadily (Ofsted 1998). […]

The impression conveyed by the Orders

The texts of the current National Curriculum make some effort to provide information about links between subjects. In the Programme of Study for each subject there are notes in the margins that show how the subject might be related to other subjects. …

At Key Stage 3 the Science Programme of Study notes six links to mathematics, three links to English and thirteen opportunities for using information communication technology (ICT). For Single Science at Key Stage 4 the Science Programme of Study notes ten links to mathematics, three links to English and thirteen opportunities for using ICT. For Double Science at Key Stage 4 the Science Programme of Study notes fourteen links to mathematics, three links to English and twenty-three opportunities for using ICT. Sadly there are no links made with Design and Technology at either Key Stage 3 or Key Stage 4.

At Key Stage 3 the design and technology Programme of Study notes one link to mathematics, two links to English, four opportunities for using ICT, one link to art and design and one link to science. At Key Stage 4 the design and technology Programme of Study notes just two opportunities for using information communication technology (ICT) and no other links (DfEE/QCA 1999).

Clearly scant regard is being given to the relationship between science and design and technology. There is no encouragement for science teachers to look at the design and technology Programme of Study and only the smallest of inducements for design and technology teachers to look at the Science Programme of Study. In terms of Paul Gardner's models, the view from the National Curriculum Orders is almost exclusively demarcationist. [...]

How pupils might use each subject to enhance the other

Using science for design and technology purposes is not a simple process. John Staudenmaier notes that 'before scientific concepts can contribute to technological knowledge they must be appropriated and restructured according to the specific demands of the design problem at hand' (1987: 104).

David Layton (1993) asks how school science teachers can provide a science education 'which assists children to develop progressively a view of the natural world as scientists have constructed it, whilst at the same time servicing the needs of children engaged in specific technological tasks'.

He proposes that, in interacting with scientific knowledge, the student designer/ engineer/technologist might need to treat it in one or more ways:

- Adjusting the level of abstraction ... The technology student, 'having reached an understanding of science at a high level, (has) to be able to climb down the ladder of abstraction and judge where to stop, i.e. to recognise which level is most appropriate for a specific technological purpose' (1993: 58).
- Repackaging the knowledge. 'The 'problems' which people construct from their experiences do not map neatly on to existing scientific disciplines and pedagogical organisations of knowledge. What is needed for solving a technological problem may have to be drawn from diverse areas of academic science at different levels of abstraction, and then synthesised into an effective instrumentality for the basic task in hand' (1993: 58).
- Reconstruction of knowledge – the creating or inventing of new concepts which are more appropriate to the practical task in hand than the scientific ones.

- Technological knowledge has to be contextualised. Science knowledge is decontextualised, abstracted, built on unreal, perfect models – indeed this separation of general knowledge from particular experience is one of science's most successful strategies. Technological knowledge has to take the earth as it is, where ball bearings are not perfect spheres, levers can bend.

As Layton says, 'Solving technological problems necessitates building back into the situation all the complications of 'real life', reversing the process of reductionism by recontextualising knowledge' (1993: 59).

This theme recurs throughout the literature. Scientific knowledge needs to be transformed before it can be useful to designers and engineers. […]

Clearly any development of the relationship between science and design and technology in the secondary school will need to take this thinking into account.

Much less has been reported about how pupils might use design and technology in science. If pupils are given the task of designing experiments, it is obvious that they may need to design and make the necessary equipment as well. This is not a common experience in either secondary or primary schools but one current example exists: the designing and making of a field studies kit to enhance powers of observation (Scottish Technology Education Project 2000). In this activity pupils investigate the behaviour of convex lenses, develop an intuitive understanding of magnification and use this to design and make a magnifying glass, a microscope and telescope.

The first Attainment Target for Science in the National Curriculum concerns scientific enquiry (QCA/DfEE 1999: 16–17). The Programme of Study at both Key Stage 3 and Key Stage 4 describes the investigative skills that pupils should be taught. These involve using a range of equipment and materials including the use of sensors for data logging. There is an interesting if limited opportunity here for cooperation between science and design and technology teachers. […]

Restraints in the current situation

The relationship between science and design and technology is being hampered in the following ways.

- A demarcationist view of the relationship between science and design and technology is encouraged by the National Curriculum and prevails in schools, in direct contrast to the relationship between science and technology in the world outside school.
- Science and design and technology teachers have an interest in developing pupil's ability to reflect on their own practice but as yet do not cooperate in developing pupil's metacognitive skills.
- Mental modelling is an essential component of both science and design and technology but teachers are not sharing approaches or expertise.
- Curriculum materials designed to encourage pupils to use science in design and technology lessons appear to have had little impact on classroom practice.

- Curriculum materials designed to enable science teachers to use technological contexts to motivate students and improve learning appear to have been only little used.

These restraints are important because they identify the issues which must be addressed if a more productive relationship is to be developed. [...]

Here we present a justification for a closer relationship between science and design and technology and discuss the appropriateness of three possible models. Finally we identify barriers to progress in forming an appropriate relationship.

The relationship between science and design and technology in school is one of separate, almost totally unconnected and unrelated existence. This is in stark contrast to the perception and reality of the relationship between science and technology in the world outside school where a variety of dynamic relations coexist. We believe that a closer relationship between science and design and technology in the secondary school curriculum is important for these reasons:

- Each subject requires pupils to be reflective on their practice. In the case of science this is in the area of developing and testing hypotheses; in the case of design and technology it is in the area of designing and making. A difficulty in developing reflective practice in science is that there is often very little concrete evidence to reflect on. Investigations are seldom iterative with the opportunity for second or third thoughts in the light of what the pupil has found out and how the pupil found it out. The way in which pupils in design and technology generate concrete evidence for reflection will be of interest to science teachers. A consistent approach to encouraging reflection across both subjects would enhance pupils' metacognition. In addition the process of developing and testing a hypothesis is a useful model for the investigations pupils may need to carry out during designing and making, particularly during fair testing, and the practical competence acquired through designing and making is of great use in devising and executing successful experiments in science.
- Each subject requires pupils to visualise within the mind's eye that which cannot, or has not yet, been seen. This mental modelling, or imaging, is central to designing and explaining many phenomena in scientific terms. In both subjects these internal mental models need to be made concrete and refined through external realisation. Within science Ofsted has reported the difficulties experienced by less able pupils in engaging with concepts (Office for Standards in Education 2000). Within design and technology Ofsted has reported that designing skills lag behind making skills (Office for Standards in Education 1998). A consistent approach to enabling pupils to visualise within the mind's eye would aid progress in both these areas of concern.
- Pupils can use the technical knowledge and understanding acquired in science to good effect in justifying technical design decisions in design and technology. If the technological purpose for acquiring such technical knowledge and understanding is made explicit to pupils in the first place i.e. you can use what

you find out to make better design decisions, such investigations become authentic and are much more likely to be taken seriously by the pupils. Co-operation in this area can also have the effect of encouraging the use of common language, common analogies and an appropriate level of detail across the two subjects, thus avoiding misconceptions and regression.

- Pupils find the use of technological contexts in science lessons intriguing and motivating and an aid to developing technical understanding. A consideration of modern products provides authenticity for science content. An extension of this to Design and Technology lessons enables this conceptual content to be seen in the wider context of design decisions where far more than technical issues have to be considered.

We believe that concentrating on these areas of general interest to both disciplines provides a good basis for linked practice which would enhance transfer and synergy.

We endorse the idea of an interactionist relationship between science and design and technology and have identified three possible models for such a relationship – coordination, collaboration and integration.

Concerning coordination

We consider this to be a useful first step in moving towards a closer relationship between science and design and technology.

This involves teachers in each subject being *au fait* with the work carried out in the other and planning their curriculums so that the timing of topics within each subject is sensitive to each other's needs. The technical language and explanatory analogies used in both subjects can be developed by teachers working together so that in areas of known difficulty pupils will not become confused and there should be evidence of gains in conceptual understanding in both subjects. This can be extended to include common expectations in the use of discussion and rapid, rough sketching in both subjects as a means of recording and visualising. Again these should be utilised to tackle areas of known difficulty, designing in design and technology and recording investigations in science, for example. The effect of this coordination should be monitored in terms of the gains experienced by the pupils in both subjects.

Concerning collaboration

We consider this to be a natural extension to successful coordination. This involves the teachers in each subject planning their curriculums so that some, but not all, activities within each subject are designed to establish an effective relationship in the four areas of mutual concern that have been identified.

In the case of developing reflective practice teachers can require pupils to comment on their progress in both science and design and technology using a common framework and ask the pupils to compare their progress with a view to enhancing their metacognition so there is an improvement in setting and achieving realistic goals in both subjects.

The common approach to visualisation developed through coordination can be extended to involve a wider range of techniques with which both sets of teachers are familiar and able to use fluently with pupils. The result of this collaboration should be that pupils will be able to articulate their ideas in both subjects much more easily so that the focus of discussions with teachers and other pupils becomes the nature of the idea and its viability or significance.

In the case of using technical knowledge and understanding learned in science the teachers might identify just two designing and making assignments in the Key Stage where the design decisions are significantly dependent on concepts learned in science. In Science lessons the pupils could carry out investigations with the intention of learning about matters important for the design decisions they will need to make. This will involve both conceptualising and reconceptualising their science understanding and improving the quality of their technical design decisions. Clearly the majority of designing and making assignments will not be this science-dependent and it would be inappropriate to force-fit science investigations into them.

In the case of using technological contexts the teachers might identify a set of attractive modern products that can be used across science and design and technology. A common approach to underlying important concepts entailing appropriate language and analogies would be worked out. In addition to being motivating this provides an efficient way of teaching a wide range of difficult ideas.

Concerning integration

We consider this to be an inappropriate form of the relationship. Science and design and technology are so significantly different from one another that to subsume them under a 'science and technology' label is both illogical and highly dangerous to the education of pupils. Both are necessary and from their individual positions can enhance each other. Science is essentially explanatory in nature whereas design and technology is aspirational. And in order to meet those aspirations design and technology needs to use knowledge, skill and understanding from a wide variety of disciplines other than science – aesthetics, ergonomics, the realities of industrial production, marketing and the requirements of sustainable development are all necessary to bring a product into the world. Links with science need to be appropriate but they are not sufficient; without links to other subjects design and technology is impoverished. Design and technology is the area of the curriculum that enables students to intervene creatively to improve the made world. As such it is essential that design and technology is neither deflected from this main purpose nor diluted in its effectiveness by a shotgun marriage.

So for these reasons we recommend that in developing an interactionist relationship between science and design and technology, schools should limit themselves to coordination and collaboration.

Barriers to progress

Tunnel vision induced by the National Curriculum is a major barrier and has led to a situation where science and design and technology teachers know very little about each other's curriculum. Members of the design and technology community were emphatic that the real gains in establishing a rationale for their subject and an effective pedagogy must not be put at risk in developing a better relationship with science. It is important that both areas of the curriculum should benefit from any links that are forged and that if teachers are to work towards a more appropriate relationship between the subjects then these benefits must have currency in the current climate of raising standards. In-service training would be an essential element of any move towards a more appropriate relationship and within this there must be the opportunity for the subject communities to learn about each other's subject and priorities.

Recommendations for improving the situation

In recent years the Engineering Council and the EEF (Engineering Employers' Federation) have provided robust and effective support for the place of design and technology in the education of *all* pupils until the end of Key Stage 4. We see promoting the development of coordination and collaboration between science and design and technology in the secondary school curriculum as a logical and necessary extension of this activity. Implicit within this is a vigorous opposition to any notion of an integration of the two subjects. To provide a situation in which science and design and technology teachers can work together within secondary schools will require a range of partnerships between those who can support this initiative. We see the following bodies and organisations as natural and significant partners in the joint ventures that will be required to meet our recommendations:

> Association for Science Education
> Department for Education and Employment
> Department for Trade and Industry
> Design and Technology Association
> Design Council
> Engineering Council
> EEF (Engineering Employers' Federation)
> Nesta
> Office for Standards in Education
> Qualifications and Curriculum Authority
> Royal Academy of Engineering
> The Royal Society.

References

Barlex, D. and Pitt, J. (2000) *Interaction, the Relationship between Science and Design and Technology in the Secondary School Curriculum*, Engineering Council and Engineering Employers' Federation. Full report and executive summary available from Engineering Employers' Federation, Broadway House, Tothill Street, London, SW1H 9NQ, www.eef.org.uk, Engineering Council, 10 Maltravers Street, London, WC2R 3ER, www.engc.org.uk.

Barlex, D. and Carré, C. (1985) *Visual Communication in Science*, Cambridge: Cambridge University Press.

Bath Science 5–16 materials (1992) Walton-on-Thames: Nelson.

Benne, K. and Birnbaum, M. (1978) *Teaching and learning about science and social policy*, Boulder, CO. USA: ERIC Clearinghouse for Social Studies/Social Science Education/Social Science Education Consortium.

Black, P. and Harrison, G. (1992) in McCormick, R. *et al.* (eds.) *Teaching and Learning Technology*, Wokingham, England: Addison-Wesley Publishing Company, in association with the Open University, Milton Keynes.

Darwin, C. (1859) *The Origin of the Species*, London: Methuen.

DATA and Department for Education and Employment (1996) *Design and Technology?*, DfEE: London.

Design and Technology Working Group (1988) *National Curriculum Design and Technology Working Group INTERIM REPORT*, London: Department for Education and Science and Welsh Office.

Department for Education and Employment/Qualifications and Curriculum Authority (1999) *The National Curriculum for England*, London: DfEE/QCA.

Department for Education and Employment/Qualifications and Curriculum Authority (1999a) *Science – The National Curriculum for England*, London: DfEE/QCA.

Department for Education and Employment/Qualifications and Curriculum Authority (1999b) *Design and technology – The National Curriculum for England*, London: DfEE/QCA.

Gardner, P. (1994) 'Representations of the relationship between science and technology in the curriculum', *Studies in Science Education* 24: 29–47.

Kline, S. J. (1985) 'What is technology?', *Bulletin of Science, Technology and Society* 5(3): 215–18.

Kuhn, T. (1996) *The Structure of Scientific Revolutions*, Chicago: University of Chicago Press.

Layton, D. (1991) 'Science education and praxis: the relationship of school science to practical action', *Studies in Science Education* 19: 34–79.

Layton, D. (1993) *Technology's Challenge to Science Education – Cathedral, Quarry or Company Store?*, Buckingham and Philadelphia: Open University Press.

Kimbell, R., Stables, K., Wheeler, T., Wosniak, A. and Kelly, V. (1991) *The Assessment of performance in design and technology: Final Report*, London: Schools Examination and Assessment Council.

Millar, R and Osborne, J. (1998) *Beyond 2000: Science Education for the Future*, London: Kings College, School of Education.

Mitcham, C. (1994) *Thinking through Technology: The Path between Engineering and Philosophy*, Chicago: University of Chicago Press.

Nuffield Co-ordinated Sciences materials (1988) Harlow: Longman.

Nuffield Design and Technology Project materials (1995) Harlow: Longman.

Office for Standards in Education (1998) *Secondary Education 1993–97 – A Review of Secondary Education Schools in England*, London: The Stationery Office.

Office for Standards in Education (2000) *Progress in Key Stage 3 Science*, London: The Stationery Office.

Pacey, A. (1983) *The Culture of Technology*, Oxford: Basil Blackwell.

Royal College of Arts Technology Project materials (1997) London: Hodder and Stoughton.

Salters' Science Focus materials (1999) Oxford: Heinemann.

Scottish Technology Education Project (2000) *Primary Technology*, Scotland: Scottish Consultative Committee on the Curriculum.

Shayer, M. (1999) 'Cognitive acceleration through science education II: its effects and scope', *International Journal of Science Education* 21(8): 883–902.

Staudenmaier, J. (1985). *Technology's storytellers: Reweaving the Human Fabric.* Cambridge, MA, and London: Society for the History of Technology and the M.I.T. Press.

Technology Enhancement Programme (TEP) resources (1994) London: Engineering Council.

Wolpert, L. (1993) *The Unnatural Nature of Science*, London: Faber and Faber.

Section 3
Assessing learning

14 Progression towards capability

Richard Kimbell, Kay Stables and Richard Green

In thinking about assessment, we have to think again about what we consider 'achievement' to be in Design and Technology. What is it that we want pupils to learn and how do we know what they have learnt? This chapter considers how 'quality' can be identified in pupils' work and how progression in their work can be identified. In doing this it covers some of the key areas in Design and Technology that have already been discussed in earlier chapters – planning; modelling and making; design; evaluating; knowledge and skill; and communication. This chapter should help you to think more clearly about how you can plan for progression in pupils' learning.

This chapter appears in Understanding Practice in Design and Technology, *where it looked in detail at Key Stages 1–4. The pressures of space in this volume demand a heavily edited version of the original. Accordingly, edited versions of Key Stages 2–4 are included here; many of the classroom examples and illustrations, and text related to these, have been removed.*

In this chapter through the case study projects we shall outline some *overview characteristics* of pupil performance to exemplify what we mean by quality work at each Key Stage. We use this to build an overview picture of progression.

Through case study materials we shall identify a series of *facets of performance* that we believe to be central to the development of children's capability. We shall exemplify:

- investigating
- planning
- modelling and making
- raising and tackling design issues
- evaluating
- extending knowledge and skills
- communicating.

In each case we shall define and exemplify each of these facets of capability and identify some key indicators of quality. We shall then show how this quality progresses across the Key Stages.

Finally, we shall examine some of the common issues that emerge as being particularly significant for the development of capability.

Capability across the Key Stages

We see capability in Design and Technology as going beyond *awareness* of technology and *competence* in handling knowledge and skills to '*being* a technologist', engaging in creative action, and operating both reflectively and actively in the process of designing and making. In looking at the way individual children have responded to Design and Technology challenges it has been clear from the start that some young children operate *procedurally* in a remarkably capable way; they do this within their own levels of experience which inevitably imposes limitations on the knowledge, skills and understanding they can bring to bear on the task. But, at the level of a 6-year-old, they demonstrate capability.

Through looking in more depth at these 'capable' children, we have sought to unpick some key issues for the progression of capability. Over the next few pages we present brief case studies of learners. These case studies have a dual function. First they allow us to illustrate the differences and similarities of children of different ages operating effectively, and second they allow us to highlight the facets of capability that we make the focus of the subsequent part of this chapter.

Case Studies

Capability at Key Stage 2: Leanne (Year 6)

Leanne's class were making model powered vehicles. They discussed types of energy that could be used and were shown how to use 'Jinks' corners to make a basic frame. While other children took more straightforward routes, Leanne decided that she wanted to make a roundabout, despite everyone (including her teacher) saying this was very ambitious. Leanne rose to the challenge and started by *modelling* her initial idea, drawing it out on paper and labelling it. While she considered aesthetic *user issues*, her main focus was on *making issues*. She had ideas for using weights and pulleys to power the roundabout and *investigated* this by trial and error and by reading Lego Technic instruction sheets. She *planned* her constructing in a step-by-step chart and by completing a plan-and-review diary in each session (see Figure 14.1).

Leanne engaged in extensive problem-solving to complete her roundabout. She *evaluated* through review sheets and discussion, showing herself to be resourceful and persistent as she strove between action and reflection. She generally worked with a *street level* of understanding although with energy systems she developed this through the project to a *working knowledge* of gears, pulleys and weights. She used various forms of communication such as discussion, sketching and planning charts, producing her project report with use of Information Technology.

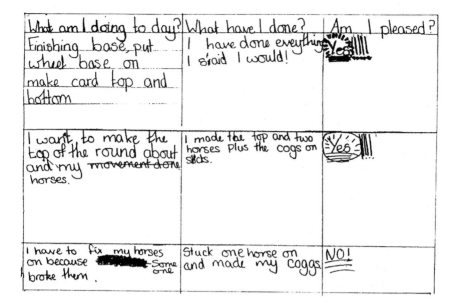

What am I doing to day?	What have I done?	Am I pleased?
Finishing base, put wheel base on make card top and bottom	I have done everything I said I would!	Yes
I want to make the top of the round about and my ~~movement done~~ horses.	I made the top and two horses plus the cogs on sticks.	Yes
I have to fix my horses on because ~~Someone~~ broke them.	Stuck one horse on and made my coggs.	NO!

Figure 14.1   Leanne's plan and review chart

Capability at Key Stage 3: Hien-Huy (Year 9)

Hien-Huy was designing and making a high-energy snack bar for his end of Key Stage 3 Design and Technology assessment. From the outset he considered *user issues* in tandem with *making issues* (see Figure 14.2). For example, he thought (regarding users) about nutritional needs and wanting an easily divided bar. He also considered (regarding making) the ingredients and ways of cooking and shaping the product. He *investigated* existing recipes and, from these and his own previous experience, produced a range of his own ideas, each of which was prototyped and *evaluated* in order that he could choose the most effective solution (see Figure 14.3). Ideas were *modelled* through both drawing and *making* trial bars, and modifications were made following ongoing *evaluations*. These were carried out to criteria which allowed him to address *user issues* in some depth. *Planning* involved organising his ingredients, the method by which he proposed making the bar, and detailed time planning to ensure that he reached the required stages in the time provided.

The development of the final bar involved a high level of refining and detailing, through which Hien-Huy showed *working knowledge* of materials, energy systems and meeting people's needs. He demonstrated good making skills and a range of communication skills, including making notes, flow charts, sketches and labelled drawings.

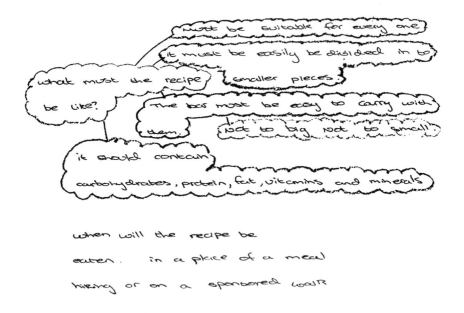

Figure 14.2   Hien-Huy's initial brainstorm

Capability at Key Stage 4: Stephanie (Year 10)

As part of a thematic mini-project, Stephanie created a brief focused on a company that wanted 'to provide a collection of fashion items based on the theme of the fair-ground'. She proposed a range of ideas and then developed one item (a beach bag) as a prototype. Working concurrently on ideas for the fabric and the bag she considered *user issues* such as what the bag would carry and the need for making the fabric visually exciting. She also dealt with *making issues* relating, for example, to ways of using fabrics, threads, dyes and paints to translate her fabric design ideas. She *investigated* ways of applying colour to fabric both by collecting information on techniques and through hands-on exploration. She also explored types of fasten-ings from books and what was available in catalogues and in the shops. In *planning,* she considered ways of using her time – identifying those aspects where she needed expert help or the use of particular resources in the school. She consciously planned other work to be carried out elsewhere. Ideas were *modelled* through sketches, exploring repeat patterns, producing tests samples and making paper patterns. *Evalu-ation* was carried out through ongoing review and reflection as ideas were tried and developed. She produced a detailed final evaluation, carried out to a school pro forma, including direct reference to National Curriculum attainment targets.

Stephanie worked autonomously, drawing on previous experience and seeking out new knowledge as required. Ideas were detailed and developed through a clear process of action and reflection. She demonstrated well-developed making skills

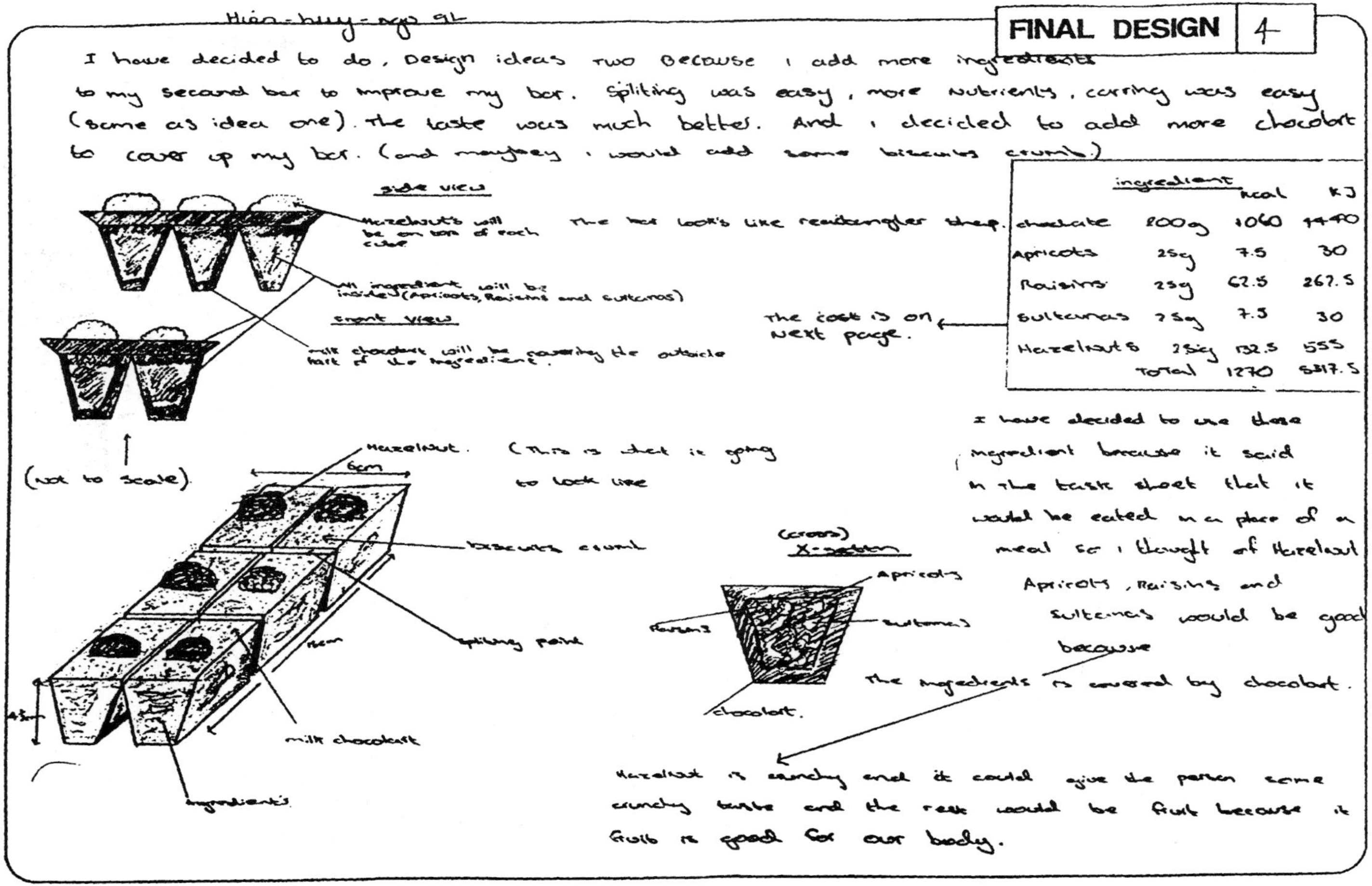

Thin bunny age al

I have decided to do, Design ideas two because I add more ingredients to my second bar to improve my bar. Splitting was easy, more nutrients, carring was easy (same as idea one). The taste was much better. And, decided to add more chocolate to coat up my bar. (add more because I would add some kilocalories (kcals))

ingredient		kcal	kJ
chocolate	200g	1060	4440
Apricots	25g	7.5	30
Raisins	25g	62.5	267.5
Sultanas	25g	7.5	30
Hazelnuts	25g	132.5	555
total		1270	5417.5

side view

hazelnuts will stick out of each.

all ingredients will be inside (Apricots, Raisins and sultanas)

front view

milk chocolate will coat all of the ingredients covering the outside.

the red lines like route number that. The cost is on next page.

I have decided to use these ingredient because it said in the taste sheet that it could be eaten in a place of a meal so, I thought of Hazelnut, Apricots, Raisins and Sultanas could be good because

Hazelnut

splitting point

sesame seeds

milk chocolate

hazelnut is crunchy and it could give to person some crunchy taste and the rest would be fruit because it gives is goods for our bodies.

(this is what is going to look like)

(not to scale)

(cross) X-section

the ingredients to covered by chocolate.

Apricots
Sultanas
Raisins
Chocolate.

Figure 14.3 Final ideas for the snack bar

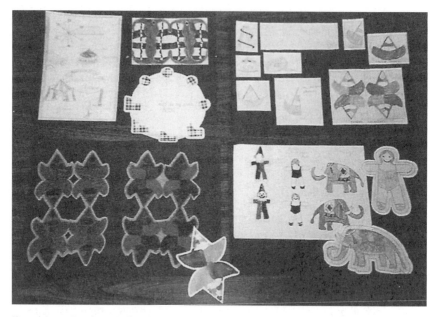

Figure 14.4 Stephanie's developing ideas presented as a project report

and *working knowledge* of materials, aesthetics and meeting people's needs. She used a range of communication techniques in a responsive way, mounting her ongoing work to produce an informative project report (see Figure 14.4).

We shall now look at the various facets of performance that we consider contribute to capability, and how these develop across the Key Stages.

Investigating

What is investigating?

Investigating is any activity which involves pupils in collecting information which is directly relevant to their task. This could be achieved from a wide range of sources, including books, CD-ROMs, experiments with processes, materials tests, conversations with, demonstrations by, or questions to the teacher or any other expert. It occurs at any point in a project.

Quality investigating includes:

- children drawing on their own experiences;
- making appropriate and relevant use of a range of reference and support materials, including books, magazines, videos, CD-ROMs, artefacts/handling collections, etc.; talking to their peers and looking at each other's work;

- making use of group and class discussion about issues relevant to the activity;
- testing the feasibility of their ideas;
- using 'hands-on' testing of materials;
- making visits to investigate real situations;
- interviewing relevant people, e.g. clients and other 'experts'.

Progression in investigating is supported by:

- providing a rich and varied supply of resources – including visits, outside speakers, etc.;
- providing opportunities for pupils to discuss with each other and the teacher;
- setting and structuring a task which involves the pupil in considering the needs of the user;
- helping pupils to settle onto a task with an appropriate degree of challenge (i.e. ensuring the project is demanding without being beyond the pupil's capability);
- encouraging pupils to be discerning and selective, and only investigate and record information of direct relevance to their project.

Key issues for progression in investigating

Key Stage 2

At Key Stage 2, children should be encouraged to imagine, early on in the activity, what problems they may encounter and what information they may need. Considering *user* and *making issues* should help focus this. The gathering of relevant information can usefully be encouraged by investigating existing products or situations; by making good use of other pupils and/or adults through asking pertinent questions; and by using books and other information sources to support their investigations. For example, a Year 5 class, designing information leaflets for a local leisure site, investigated and discussed a range of existing information leaflets, from many sources, to identify good and bad features. Combining information from different sources encourages children to be more discerning.

Key Stage 3

At Key Stage 3, even where tasks are tightly defined and there is a much increased teacher input, it is still important for pupils to consider users, to gather information about their tastes, preferences and needs and to use these in their designing. There should also be a clear link between new skills introduced by the teacher and the investigation of their application by the pupil.

Pupils need to increase their repertoire of techniques of investigating and learn to apply these in a responsive way – gathering information that is genuinely needed. In order for pupils to tackle such research effectively, both user and manufacturing needs should be presented in a tangible form.

Key Stage 4

At Key Stage 4, it is critical that investigations continue to be directly related to informing decisions about the user and manufacturing issues. Pupils should be able to identify for themselves the aspects of their designing that requires investigating, and then, building on the range of strategies introduced in earlier Key Stages, carry out research both in depth and with rigour.

Planning

What is 'planning'?

Planning is any activity which involves working something out in advance of doing it. It occurs at any point in a project, e.g. pupils might plan an investigation, a making process, or a field test of a finished product.

Quality planning includes:

- discussing work as an ongoing part of the process;
- considering time as a resource – and planning its use as a whole and within each phase of the project;
- working out the manufacturing issues before starting construction (e.g. types and amounts of materials, methods of shaping, joining, finishing, etc.);
- careful marking out of materials to ensure accuracy and avoid waste;
- having a view of what the final outcome will be like and how it might be achieved.

Progression in planning is supported by:

- encouraging pupils to think things through, take responsibility, and make their own decisions about ways to proceed throughout the activity;
- providing opportunities for pupils to discuss their projects, formally and informally, with each other as they proceed;
- helping pupils to set down their intentions early on in the activity, either through drawing or writing;
- making pupils aware of the time available, and of the time required for particular processes;

- helping pupils to develop strategies for allocating time to the whole activity and its component parts;
- setting intermediate deadlines so that, within a long project, timescales are shorter, more immediate, and therefore more manageable;
- developing an appreciation that a design folder is a working document, and that planning is integral, ongoing and important, not a retrospective presentation exercise.

Key issues for progression in planning

Key Stage 2

The main emphasis in Key Stage 2 is still the 'plan' drawing. But the almost continual discussion (in pairs or group work) of what is required helps to push the activity forward. However, consideration starts to be given to more complex factors such as the availability and appropriateness of resources, the most effective sequence of activities, and the overall use of time. These can be helped by the use of diaries, logs and pro forma planning sheets.

Another activity which helps pupils begin to consider longer term planning is writing 'To do' lists.

The teacher's role is to monitor discussion, to focus it where necessary, and to suggest strategies to support the pupils' decision-making about time and resources.

Key Stage 3

Pupils in Key Stage 3 devote less time to planning than in any of the other Key Stages. The teacher-directed nature of many of the tasks means that much of the responsibility for planning is removed from the pupil. In Years 7 and 8 planning tends to be short term and aimed at achieving the immediate task in hand.

Although the planning of time is usually controlled by the teacher, it is possible to build on pupils' primary experiences of planning, by discussing the targets to be managed during the lesson. This encourages pupils to take responsibility for achieving them. If pupils can be encouraged to utilise their increased knowledge of materials and techniques when planning the use of limited time, then this should help develop skills needed for managing longer, independent projects in Key Stage 4. It is commonplace in Key Stage 3 for project checklists (which detail the aspects to be considered or recorded in folders) to be given out at the start of an activity. These do help pupils to develop a view of the whole activity, but they also tend to encourage retrospective working rather than forward-looking planning.

Key Stage 4

With longer and more pupil-directed activities, the opportunities for planning reappear and the need for it becomes self-evident. The teacher's main concern (and usually a major difficulty) is getting pupils to accept responsibility for managing the project and for completing it by the given deadline. Dated time planners, time lines drawn on the blackboard, and 'days remaining' discussed at the start of each lesson, are all examples of strategies used to try to promote an understanding of the project schedule as a whole. However, even with these devices, pupils still find it difficult to allocate their time effectively. Regular reviews, formal and informal, may be a more effective way of getting pupils to focus on what has been done and what still needs to be achieved. 'Slip charts' can be helpful here, planning (on one side) what needs to be done in each session to complete the project and (on the other) reflecting on what was *actually* done. This identifies the 'slippage'.

Pupils appear more comfortable dealing with the shorter-term planning for making, probably because that is what planning typically meant for them at Key Stage 3. Working drawings, cutting lists and templates are produced prior to manufacture.

Modelling and making

What is modelling and making?

Modelling involves the *manifestation* or expression of ideas in order to *develop* ideas. Pupils use two-dimensional and three-dimensional modelling techniques to generate, explore, develop, modify and detail their ideas in the form of discussions, drawings, models, mock-ups and prototypes. 'Making' of the final prototype does not necessarily involve the developmental function of modelling, but is rather the final expression of the design solution.

Quality modelling and making include:

- pupils talking, discussing (with the teacher, and/or each other in pairs and groups), writing, drawing, and making their ideas;
- hands-on experimenting with materials;
- developing and detailing ideas to the stage where they will work and can be made;
- having a 'big picture' overview of their idea from the start, and then being able to identify and tackle it piece by piece;
- working to clear criteria;
- combining models with drawings and notes to communicate ideas effectively;
- selecting and using 2D and 3D approaches as appropriate;
- selecting and using appropriate materials and production techniques.

Progression in modelling and making is supported by the teacher:

- having a wide range of materials, including construction kits, with which pupils can experiment;
- getting pupils constantly to think and talk about their ideas in relation to agreed criteria for the activity; teaching pupils a range of appropriate drawing, modelling and making techniques;
- providing opportunities for a variety of modelling and making techniques to be used within projects.

Key issues for progression in modelling and making

Key Stage 2

As problems become more complex and require more sophisticated solutions there is a need to develop pupils' conceptual understanding about materials and to extend the range of communication techniques such as discussing, drawing and making.

Key Stage 3

There is a complete change of approach at Key Stage 3 with much less time devoted to developmental modelling (of any kind) and much more focus on making through the instruction and practice of techniques. The approach of modelling is often more formalised ('produce 4 design ideas on this sheet') with ideas being collected from research material and with the emphasis on drawing as the main modelling tool. Pupils are then typically expected to 'select their best/favourite idea for making'.

Using mock-ups and models as a means for *developing ideas* is far less common in Key Stage 3 than in Key Stage 2, but where it happens it can be very effective since the range of materials and techniques is so much expanded. This approach combines the best of the 'playful' qualities of the designer (a really important element of capability) with the rigour that is required of specialist material use.

Key Stage 4

The approach retains much of the formality of Key Stage 3, but becomes more responsive as a result of the individualised nature of the projects. Ideas are developed and modelled in response to the evaluation of real needs and problems as they arise. The initial stages of the process are almost exclusively conducted through drawing and this is then followed by what appears to be a fairly common pattern – sketch, 3D model, detailed working/engineering drawing, manufacture, modify where appropriate.

Design issues for the 'user' and for 'making'

What are design issues?

By *user issues* we mean those design issues which relate to the way in which the final designed outcome interacts with users. A child designing and making an educational board game from fabric may be concerned with user issues such as how the game will be played, what will be learned, how it (and the playing pieces) could be stored and how it is kept clean.

By *making issues,* we refer to the design issues concerned with realising the outcome being designed, such as those to do with techniques, tools and materials. The making issues in the board game might involve, for example, what technique to use to attach a pocket for the counters; how to make the fabric stiff enough to stay flat in use but remain flexible enough to be rolled up for storage, and so on.

Design issues arise constantly throughout a project.

Quality consideration of design issues includes:

- considering the user needs and impact of the designing at each stage of decision-making;
- demonstrating ability to *compromise and optimise* to achieve an effective outcome;
- children using knowledge of making *as a springboard* for design ideas;
- children using knowledge of making *to evaluate* and support decision-making as they develop their design ideas;
- children *choosing and using materials and tools appropriately* to use good quality outcomes that work.

Progression in considering design issues is supported by:

- setting tasks in contexts that have a *balance* of user and making issues;
- assisting the learner to engage with the context and take *ownership of and responsibility for* the task;
- helping the learner to keep sight of, and address, the user needs *throughout the project*, including when making decisions about making;
- encouraging learners to use the most *efficacious technique*, material or tool rather than the easiest or most obvious;
- ensuring that learners are introduced to new techniques at the time they are called for;
- helping learners to develop new techniques through 'hands-on' experience;
- supporting children to develop an awareness of the fullest range of issues that are both manageable and challenging for them at their stage of development.

Key issues for progression in design issues

Key Stage 2

At Key Stage 2, Design and Technology tasks should continue to present a broad range of user and making issues. Where it is linked to other curriculum areas (e.g. history) the opportunity to design (rather than just to replicate) should be encouraged. For example, children designing and making 'shoes fit for royalty' in a topic on Tudors and Stuarts identified issues such as luxury and status, creating footwear that was highly decorated with 'jewels' and embroidery. They also considered more utilitarian issues, wanting the shoes to fit and be easy to put on.

Encouraging children to consider a wide range of user issues, and designing for 'real-life' situations helps to raise the need for *compromising and optimising*. Children designing information leaflets for a new local leisure facility, and safety wear for bike riding, handled a range of consumer issues and had to balance the conflicting demands of fashion against safety.

When dealing with making issues, children should develop a greater concern for the *accuracy* demanded by their more sophisticated ideas and more complex designs. A wider range of techniques will be called for, which can be developed through a judicious mixture of problem-solving and teaching.

Key Stage 3

Whilst the principal Key Stage 3 agenda is strongly influenced by introducing new knowledge and skills, the user and making issues should still be focused. Important user issues identified in the early stages of a project (for example, through brainstorms) need to be kept in sight throughout the project. It is all too easy for pupils to forget them as they get immersed in the making techniques.

Years 8 and 9 should provide increasing opportunities for pupils to use newly acquired knowledge of making as a springboard for ideas. Pupils should be encouraged to handle making issues alongside user issues to improve their skills in optimising.

Key Stage 4

Year 10 marks a transition from the relatively closed briefs of Key Stage 3 to the much more open, personally constructed briefs in Year 11 GCSE project work. Pupils need to develop the confidence to take responsibility for their tasks, identifying and addressing design issues as independently as possible.

Year 11 projects are frequently challenging, placing great demands on pupils. Maintaining a grip on all the design issues is critical, and grappling with them requires confidence, perseverance and a developed skill in compromising and optimising.

Evaluating

What is evaluating?

Evaluating is an activity which allows the pupil to make a judgement or decision about aspects of the design as it develops, or to reflect on the strengths and weaknesses of the design once it has been completed. It occurs constantly throughout projects.

Quality evaluating includes:

- identifying clear criteria for judgement;
- pupils discussing with each other ways of overcoming problems;
- pupils commenting on their own work and the work of others as it goes along;
- constantly considering alternative solutions and ways of working;
- using evaluation sheets to review progress and comment on the overall success of the product;
- being disciplined in the collection of evidence, e.g. with questionnaires and opinion surveys;
- summative evaluations of the product success against the design criteria;
- basing decisions on a wide range of available evidence, including prior knowledge, testing, trial and error, etc.;
- using different kinds of evidence – distinguishing fact from opinion etc.;
- resolving conflicting demands to produce an optimum solution.

Progression in evaluating is supported by the teacher:

- creating specific opportunities for pupils to discuss work one-to-one with them, within groups, and as whole-class activities;
- prompting pupils to develop design criteria at the start of an activity;
- prompting pupils constantly to compare their products against these criteria;
- encouraging children to keep these criteria under critical review so that they can be modified as the project develops;
- encouraging pupils to consider the user of the product, and ensuring that this is a key factor in its evaluation;
- helping pupils develop techniques for gathering reliable data for evaluation;
- guiding project selection to ensure an appropriate level of challenge;
- allowing pupils to take responsibility for as much of the project as possible;
- teaching pupils a range of strategies to evaluate their work.

Key issues for progression in evaluating

Key Stage 2

Key Stage 2 pupils have considerable ownership of tasks and autonomy of decision-making in activities and therefore the evaluation which occurs is a natural and critical response to their developing ideas.

More formal evaluation strategies begin to be taught, with pro-forma planning and evaluation sheets and structured group and whole class evaluation sessions, all of which can help pupils check the success of their work when compared to the design criteria.

Pupils are also becoming more aware of the design-and-make process and how its effectiveness can vary.

Key Stage 3

At Key Stage 3, since there is less autonomy in decision-making (and often less ownership of the tasks), evaluation is too often seen as a necessary burden at the end of the project rather than as a critical developmental force throughout a project. If the level of decision-making is superficial (because the task does not allow room for it), then there is relatively little to be lost through inadequate evaluation. But if the pupil has to make major decisions about the appearance, function, materials and construction, then inappropriate choices have immediate and very tangible consequences for the overall success of his or her solutions.

Overall Key Stage 3 has the least evaluation of all the Key Stages, with Years 7 and 8 having less than Year 9 where the activities are becoming somewhat less directed. Most evaluation occurs summatively, and the ongoing evaluation that does exist typically relates to the processes and quality of manufacturing.

Formal written evaluations at the completion of the activity tend to be treated uncritically and are often regarded as of little relevance, though some pupils in the UTA study were able to describe the importance of this part of the activity in helping their thinking, decision-making and designing.

Key Stage 4

Evaluation at Key Stage 4 almost matches the amounts conducted in Key Stage 2, but unlike this earlier Key Stage, where it is spread relatively evenly throughout the activity, the vast majority is conducted towards the end. There is evidence in Year 10 of a growing awareness of the importance of ongoing evaluation, although much of it still tends to be of a trial-and-error nature. Self-assessment sheets were frequently used to encourage evaluation of the process and the product.

In Year 11, pupil-selected projects allow the pupils to take full ownership and control of projects, and therefore they realise the critical importance of making the correct decisions. Pupils are often in the position of making decisions for which there is no known, certain answer.

Through the misconceptions of many GCSE examination formats, the vast majority of marks for evaluation in design folders tend to be awarded for summative rather than ongoing evaluation, and the final page of the folder almost becomes a ritual to be completed rather than an important aspect of the whole process. Nevertheless, it can be enormously strengthened by drawing evidence from external sources with expertise in the area.

Extending knowledge and skill

What do we mean by extending knowledge and skill?

The knowledge and skill we are specifically concerned with within Design and Technology is that which can be used to make things work:

- to work technically – the materials, components and techniques applied and the systems created;
- to work for people (ergonomically)
  - creating outcomes that fit people
  - both physically and in their day-to-day lives;
- to work aesthetically – the form outcomes take, their quality and the impact this has on our senses and our sensibilities.

In the APU project (Kimbell *et al.* 1991) we constructed a simple way of judging the level at which knowledge and skills were being used:

- at a *blackbox low level* of operation, e.g. where a pupil says something will work 'by clockwork' or that the material needed is 'grippy stuff', or that something should be 'joined', with no further details to qualify the proposal. Things work as if by magic.
- at a *street level* of operation, where knowledge is consistent with that held by the person in the street, but not developed by exposure to specific teaching and learning in Design and Technology.
- at a *working knowledge level,* where specialist Design and Technology knowledge or skill is developed and applied with understanding to fit the particular requirements of a proposal.

We will use these terms to refer to development and progression in this area across the Key Stages.

Quality extension of knowledge and skill includes:

- operating at a level appropriate to the stage in designing – blackbox may be appropriate when preliminary ideas are flowing in a divergent way, but working knowledge will be necessary when the detail of the designing and making is being considered;
- working from what you know, through what you need to know to the acquisition and application of new knowledge and skill;
- operating through first principles to identify ways of resolving a task;
- using knowledge and skill to make good-quality outcomes, fit for their purpose;
- applying established aspects of knowledge and skill in new settings.

Progression in knowledge and skill is supported by:

- hands-on experimentation and problem-solving, resourced by judicious prompting and questioning from the teacher;
- hands-on activity to reinforce, practise and clarify new knowledge or skill;
- drawing on children's previous experience, transferring knowledge, skill and understanding into new settings;
- children reflecting on what they know and can do and how they can make best use of this;
- encouraging children to take responsibility for both the thinking and doing involved in their task;
- providing pupils with opportunities to take control of their learning;
- pupils constantly being required to think ahead about the areas of knowledge and skill with which they will need to come to terms;
- encouraging children to leave their 'comfort zone' of established knowledge and skills to tackle challenges and force them into new areas.

Key issues for progression in extending knowledge and skills

Key Stage 2

At Key Stage 2, children need to be involved in more complex designing and making that will push the knowledge and skill demands towards working knowledge in the specific areas of their project. A common Key Stage 2 model for development is where problem-solving is blended with teacher inputs when the children get 'stuck'.

Building on previous understanding and introducing new knowledge and skill at critical moments is important. It is vital that pupils are engaged in designing and making that is just within or just beyond their reach. This challenges them constantly to extend into new understandings in order to achieve success.

Key Stage 3

In Year 7, knowledge and skill are introduced in an intensive way, and generally in bite-size chunks of working knowledge. In order to ensure that pupils develop understanding along with knowledge and skill, it is important that new knowledge and skill are introduced at a point where pupils can take responsibility for applying them in their designing and making. It is also important that pupils are involved in Design and Technology tasks that require them to draw on previous understanding.

Knowledge and skill that are introduced by direct teaching and followed by hands-on experience to explore them can ensure that pupils receive quality information. However, in order for it to get beyond 'inert' (lifeless) knowledge it is important that such teaching is linked to the pupil's 'need to know' for the project, and with the opportunity and requirement for the pupil to take some responsibility for its application in the project.

Key Stage 4

At Key Stage 4 pupils should be given increasing responsibility to manage design projects. This requires them to draw on previous understanding and seek out new knowledge and skill as demanded by the task.

Individual projects in Year 11 present a wealth of opportunities for pupils to consolidate previous learning and develop real depth of understanding through the demands in their tasks. Teachers of this age group are well aware of the potential growth in some pupils at this stage. Development should be promoted across the Key Stage by encouraging pupils to take responsibility for achieving their design intentions throughout all project work, pushing rigorously at getting ideas to work. In facilitating the pupil, the teacher has the tricky job of providing support without creating dependence. We observed some amazing examples of this – teachers providing half answers dripping with clues that enabled the pupils to take them forward independently. This enabled pupils to glory in their personal success when they made it work, unaware of the subtlety of what the teacher had done.

Communication

What is communication?

Communication has two different aspects in Design and Technology:

- communication to clarify and develop ideas
- communication to *record and present* ideas.

These two dimensions form the focus of the work described here at each Key Stage.

Quality communication includes:

- the many kinds of drawing, modelling and discussing that supports design thinking and the development of ideas;
- the use of drawing and modelling to enable pupils to transform ideas into different arrangements;
- the exploitation of the different strengths of each form of communication:
    - verbal communication for speed;
    - graphic communication for style and relationships between parts;
    - construction drawing for detail and precision and concrete modelling to test if it all fits together;
- presenting ideas and outcomes with clarity and skill.

Progression in communication is supported by:

- encouraging pupils to engage in dialogues as a natural part of designing, using sketching, discussion and other forms of modelling;
- introducing drawing and modelling skills and formal conventions when they will directly support the designing;
- encouraging pupils to record work in such a way that it supports consolidation and reflection;
- providing pupils with a repertoire of communication 'tools' and encouraging them to use these appropriately.

Key issues for progression in communication

Key Stage 2

At Key Stage 2, planning, drawing and discussing tend to be used interactively as pupils clarify and develop their ideas. As children develop more complex ideas, they should be encouraged to use separate models to explore and communicate their thinking. Where children were making a model supermarket for their museum exhibition, they needed to model their ideas for display cabinets to sort out both the proportions and ways of fixing the units to the floor. With the group of children designing public information leaflets, before any drawing took place, they modelled (by paper-folding) their ideas for folding the leaflets and for laying out the information.

Preparing a project report is valuable, and good use can be made of information technology for the presentation of both text and drawings. Encouraging pupils to use logs, diaries and planning sheets is a useful way to encourage reflection, both through the project and at the end of it.

Key Stage 3

At Key Stage 3 pupils are typically introduced to more formal methods of communicating, both for the development and the recording of ideas. This can be important in helping them address the increasing complexity in designing and making. This has been found to be most effective when formal skills have been introduced directly in relation to a design development function, for example introducing orthographic drawing when pupils would otherwise be struggling to work out the dimensions of a 3D product. Encouraging pupils to keep a project folder can be useful for consolidation and reflection and can help pupils develop a pride in their work, but pupils must see a genuine need for folder work in terms of the design development if it is not to become a superficial and retrospective recording, masquerading as more immediate reflection.

Key Stage 4

At Key Stage 4 project folders take on even greater significance as they increasingly are seen as providing evidence of the pupils' design thinking for assessment purposes. In order that time is spent productively, it is important that all folder work genuinely supports the development of the project, and that pupils use communication techniques appropriately. Such a responsive approach was witnessed in one school where work was carried out as appropriate to the immediate needs of development (through rough sketches, samples of printing, collections of visual resources, etc.) and then mounted onto a set of presentation boards telling the story of the project. This method produced an effective record of the project that the pupils felt had not taken an undue amount of time.

It is important that pupils develop free-hand drawing skills to express, develop and clarify their ideas. They should also value them, and not feel that they need to be redrawn 'neatly' for examination purposes. Sketching in a notebook, folder or sketch book can be a personal monologue (thinking with oneself) and it often forms the centre of a dialogue between teacher and pupil as ideas are explained, explored and developed. As the project moves forward, these quick freehand sketches need to be supplemented with more formal and detailed styles of communication that allow ideas to be examined more rigorously. But sketching, discussing and 3D modelling should continue to be encouraged.

Some principles of progression

In this chapter we have attempted, through the use of UTA case study material, to show examples of design and technology capability in each of the Key Stages. We have also explored a range of processes, knowledge and skills which are the constituent parts of that capability. It is only by coming to understand the role and interrelationship of these individual elements that it is possible to clarify what represents a quality piece of work. It also then becomes possible to see how teachers can plan a progressive and coherent experience that may help pupils to develop towards capability.

However, it should be apparent that there are some overarching issues which directly affect performance in a number of these aspects of capability, and it is these that we shall summarise here.

More seems like less

Progression might seem a straightforward concept – you learn something, then you learn a bit more, then a bit more, and so on. Through this process of accumulation, our knowledge, skill and understanding grows and we become more competent and capable. One of the sad facts about progression, however, is that the more we learn about something, the more we realise what we do not know. This uncomfortable truth can come to children at a very young age. Penny Munn, in researching children's understanding of reading, found that in a nursery of 4-year-olds at the start of the year all said they could read. By the end of that year only a small number still maintained they could read. The others had all come to see that there is more to reading than sitting on dad's lap looking at a book and having a story! (Munn 1995). So a critical component of progression involves the conscious realisation that we cannot do something, or at least that it is more complicated than we first thought. It thereafter requires that we put ourselves in the firing line, operating with uncertainty and taking on new challenges.

Concrete and abstract challenges

We believe that one of the defining characteristics of Design and Technology is that it enables pupils to gain access to complex concepts through concrete means. We argue that this concrete access enhances pupils' learning opportunities, and over the years, many educational writers have made this point for us. From Piaget (1958) (who distinguished 'concrete' and 'formal' operations), to Bruner (1968) (who distinguished between enactive, iconic, and symbolic modes of operation) and Donaldson (1978) (who argued for an 'activity' model of curriculum), we have become increasingly aware of the importance of concrete, first-hand experience for children struggling to make sense of newly-introduced concepts. This has recently been taken a stage further by Rogoff (1990), whose arguments about 'situated cognition' suggest that children's learning is not of generalised qualities but is specific to the concrete context within which they learn it. To be able to generalise such learning would therefore be a mark of progression. This is further illuminated by the work of Clare and Rogers (1994) who established the importance of 'metacognitive' reflection in progression. As children are encouraged to think back over their work and turn tacit concrete operations into explicit understandings, they can make them more robust and more transferable to new situations.

All of this underlines the tight and complex interrelationship between concrete activities and pupils' progression in learning and this relationship can be seen at work in these case study materials.

Sequential and organic models of progression

It has frequently been argued that progression is sequential: first learn to do X and then it is possible to do Y. It appears to be common sense, and in Design and Technology this argument has been used to justify the view that children must *first* learn the essential tool skills, and *then* (and only then) can they decide how they might want to use them on projects of their own. More recently, it has been recognised that such 'basic skills' programmes completely ignore the need for children to see (as early as possible) the necessary connection between means and ends. To learn a collection of isolated, decontextualised skills will not help children to recognise when they need to deploy them. Accordingly a different paradigm of progression might be advocated and it would start from a very simple principle. Anything that pupils are expected to be able to do at the age of 16, they need to be getting started from the very beginning. As Bruner puts it:

> Any idea or problem or body of knowledge can be presented in a form simple enough so that any particular learner can understand it in a recognizable form.
>
> (Bruner 1968)

This model of progression suggests that learning amounts to progressively peeling layers of consequence and meaning. A 6-year-old can understand anything at a 6-year-old level, and a 16-year-old can understand the same thing at a much deeper level. This is after all how we manage the questions that our children ask about human reproduction. An answer that we might give to a 6-year-old will only last for a while, and we progressively have to make our answers more complex as their understanding deepens. It is easy to see how such a principle might apply to Design and Technology. If cutting and forming sheet materials is an important concept, it is easy to exemplify through 6-year-old levels of making as well as 16-year-olds levels. The materials and the tools might be different but the concepts of cutting and forming can be common. Similarly, if the liquids-into-solids transition is important to understand and experience, chocolate and jelly make excellent media through which to introduce it in an immediate form with very young children.

If we wish children to progress, we need to present them with activities and challenges that enable them progressively to peel these layers of understanding of the technological world. Again this has emerged through the case studies. All the pupils (for example) have a view about how materials behave and how they can be manipulated and joined. As they get older, these same concepts are being explored, but in progressively greater depth.

Balancing risk

Learning in schools presupposes teaching, since teachers have generally more expertise than the children they teach. However, one of the most difficult skills that our student teachers have to learn is how to restrain themselves from telling children how to do things. They have to learn to rein in the natural tendency to give children answers all the time, and rather encourage the children (through questioning and other techniques) to work out a solution for themselves. Any experienced teacher knows that receiving pre-digested truths from the teacher is far less demanding on children (and hence less extending of their intellect) than helping them to struggle to formulate such truths for themselves.

This is just as true in Design and Technology as it is in any other area of the curriculum. However, once again in Design and Technology, the significance of it may be more immediately apparent. The basic *modus operandi* in Design and Technology is to use techniques of 'designing' and/or 'problem-solving' and here it is patently necessary for children to operate at a level of uncertainty. They are put in pursuit of a solution that has not been pre-packaged for them, and many different solutions might work. This is potentially stressful and certainly a risk-taking environment. Teachers could remove this stress and eliminate the risk by using their expertise to give them all the answers, but that would destroy the whole purpose of the exercise. As Dewey puts it:

> A difficulty is an indispensable stimulus to thinking, but not all difficulties call out thinking. Sometimes they overwhelm and submerge and discourage … A large part of the art of instruction lies in making the difficulty of new problems large enough to challenge thought and small enough so that in addition to the confusion naturally attending the novel elements, there are luminous familiar spots from which helpful suggestions may spring.
>
> (Dewey 1968)

Children's progress relies centrally on the teacher's expertise in manipulating the level of challenge in tasks and in striking a balance that requires pupils to take risks – but only those that are carefully calculated to be manageable. This point has emerged clearly in the case studies, particularly in the contrasted models of teaching and learning in Key Stages 2 and 3.

Discussion (verbal modelling)

The way in which discussion can enhance pupils' performance was initially highlighted by the APU research findings (Kimbell *et al.* 1991). The UTA findings completely confirmed this critical role, but also highlighted that it was only primary pupils who regularly and consistently make use of it. In primary schools the technique is used formally and informally, as pupils discuss with each other:

- what they are doing;
- why;
- how they are going about it;
- what they have completed so far;
- what they need to do in the future;
- the problems that they have encountered;
- the ways in which they have overcome them; and
- the success or otherwise of their work.

Secondary pupils find themselves in a very different position. Partly because of the individualised nature of much project work and partly because of the pressure to teach knowledge and skills in a limited amount of time, it is very rare to see Key Stage 3 and 4 pupils making use of a technique that was at one time second nature to them. Consequently, the majority of secondary pupils are denied access to a vital tool which can help them clarify their thinking and develop both the active and reflective aspects of capability.

It is worth recalling the pupils' response to the questionnaire that was returned by all pupils after they had completed their APU activities. We had used a series of strategies in the activities and we asked pupils to rate them in terms of how helpful they had found them. The response in relation to the discussion session speaks volumes:

No help	8.60%
Some help	34.32%
Very helpful	56.21%
No response	0.87%

Total sample 1288 pupils

(Kimbell *et al.* 1991: section 8)

This was from a group of 15-year-olds with almost no recent experience of using the technique. There are few things in life that are certain, but one of them is that the occasional use of paired and/or small group activities, and the use of short but structured discussions to review progress, will enormously help pupils to make progress in their work.

User issues

The consideration of user issues has an enormous impact on a number of aspects of capability. If they are ignored, or only treated in tokenistic fashion, the performance of the pupil is likely to be seriously impaired. When the pupils realise that, as well as designing and making X to do Y, they are also doing this for the person(s) Z, the activity takes on a whole new level of meaning. If the outcome is to be successful it now has not only to do Y, but it has also to do it to the satisfaction of Z. Consequently, the user dimension has to be considered at every stage of the process:

- setting the design criteria which the outcome has to fulfil;
- collecting useful and relevant research information;
- evaluating ideas as they are modelled and developed;
- and testing and evaluating the outcome.

Key Stage 3 is an anomaly when it comes to user issues. Here the consideration of the user comes second to the demands of making, and to the development of new skills and knowledge. The UTA project suggests that, although there are very few Key Stage 3 activities where user issues are completely ignored, it is equally true that there are very few where user and making issues are treated in a balanced or integrated way. In many cases all it requires is to stress the importance of the user, and not allowing this to be lost as the activity progresses; in others, it may require a re-appraisal of how the activity is presented – or even how it is designed.

Working through materials

In every Key Stage, without exception, it is possible to see the importance of pupils working 'hands-on' with materials:

- to investigate and model their ideas;
- to evaluate alternatives;
- to establish the suitability of a material for the job;
- to develop an understanding about material properties; and
- to help clarify and consolidate their grip on new knowledge.

The ability to push ideas forward by trying them out in a concrete way is one of the unique features of Design and Technology activity, because pupils are confronted with the consequences of their decisions in a very tangible form. Reflection is enhanced and complemented by action, and it is the teacher's role to try and ensure that the pupil has the necessary opportunities and skills to do both.

Ownership of the task

It is self-evidently a good thing that pupils should take ownership of the tasks on which they are engaged. The earlier in the activity that pupils can take on this ownership, the more effective will be their overall response, since personal interest and involvement will drive them forward. Pupils should be encouraged to make their own informed decisions, and to take responsibility for the planning and organisation of the activity, for these are both necessary attributes of capability.

This is most difficult to achieve in Key Stage 3, where the teacher is seeking to retain control of the project in order to use it to teach some specific elements of knowledge and skill. This is particularly true at the beginning of this Key Stage in Year 7, where the increased amount of teacher direction, and the knowledge/skills-driven nature of the tasks seriously limits the opportunities for pupils to demonstrate autonomy and develop ownership of the activity. Once again, this breaks a progression which starts at Key Stage 1 with pupils naturally empathising with the users of their design work, and finishes at Key Stage 4 with pupils simulating 'real' technology in projects which they have chosen, and for which they can see a real purpose. It is a real challenge to Key Stage 3 teachers to find ways of working within these constraints which will provide increased opportunities for pupils to feel that they can exert some influence over the activity. This can be assisted by setting tasks in user-rich contexts and encouraging the pupils to take responsibility for the planning and management of their work within the framework of constraints established by the teacher.

The transition from Key Stage 2 to Key Stage 3

From the UTA project observations, it became clear that in many respects Key Stage 3 represents a discontinuity in the progressive development of design and technological capability.

We are not saying that the nature of Design and Technology activities in Key Stage 2 is better than that in Key Stage 3, or vice versa, just that they are different. And *very* different. But having identified here some characteristic and effective ways of working in these Key Stages, it may be worth considering how the best practice of each could be incorporated into the other. For example, secondary teachers might benefit from seeing how their primary colleagues organise groups, encourage pupils to discuss their work, integrate user and making issues, and take responsibility for planning and organising their work. Equally, primary teachers might gain from seeing how new skills and knowledge are taught through secondary project work, and the range of strategies employed for generating, developing, recording and evaluating ideas and outcomes.

Above all, there appears to be a need for primary and secondary teachers to meet, talk, observe, review each other's teaching methods, and learn to take the best from each other's approaches. This is obviously not a quick, easy or cheap exercise to organise or implement, but if it were possible, if only on a limited scale, the results would surely be worthwhile.

Summary

- Through specific case study projects we outline some *overview characteristics* of pupil performance to exemplify what we mean by quality work at each Key Stage, enabling us to build a picture of progression.

- Through selections of case study materials, we identify a series of facets of performance that we believe to be central to the development of children's capability. We exemplify and discuss:
    - investigating
    - planning
    - modelling and making
    - design issues (user and making)
    - evaluating
    - extending knowledge and skills
    - communicating.

  In each case, we define and exemplify each of these facets of capability and identify some key indicators of quality. We then show how this quality progresses across the Key Stages.
- Finally we examine some broad principles and common issues that emerge as being particularly significant for the development of capability.

References

Bruner, J. (1968) *Towards a Theory of Instruction*, New York: W.W. Norton.

Clare, D. and Rogers, M. (1994) 'The process diary: developing capability within National Curricula design and technology – some initial findings', IDATER 94, J.S. Smith (ed.) Loughborough: Loughborough University of Technology.

Dewey, J. (1968) *Democracy and Education*, New York: Free Press.

Donaldson, M. (1978) *Children's Minds*, London: Fontana.

Kimbell, R., Stables, K., Wheeler, T., Wozniak, A. and Kelly, V. (1991) *The Assessment of Performance in Design and Technology: The Final Report of the Design and Technology APU project*, London: Evaluation and Monitoring Unit, Schools Examination and Assessment Council (SEAC).

Munn, P. (1995) 'What do children know about reading before they go to school?', in P. Owen and P. Pumpfrey (eds). *Children Learning to read: International Concerns: Vol. 1*, London: Falmer Press.

Rogoff, B. (1990) *Apprenticeship in Thinking: Cognitive Development in a Social Context*, Buckingham: Oxford University Press.

15 Assessment of Design and Technology

Richard Kimbell

This chapter reflects critically on the development of assessment policy in Design and Technology over the last 20 years, and the effects on teacher practice. After reading about the history of assessment practice, think about current practice in your school. The author proposes the need now for the development of national standards, which will begin with school-based and local standards: how can your school, your practice, contribute towards this proposal?

The material in the chapter was originally selected and re-organized from two publications by the author (Kimbell 1992, 1993). The chapter first appeared in Teaching Technology *(Banks 1994): for this current volume it has been revised and updated, and now includes material from 'Assessing Technology' (Kimbell 1997).*

There are three central arguments in this chapter:

1   Assessment policy and practice in Design and Technology became, over the 20 years from 1970 to 1990, increasingly concerned with details and specifics and less concerned with broad judgements. The emergence of a crude reductionist approach to criterion-referenced assessment will be illustrated through three brief case studies.
2   The progressive atomization of assessment – exemplified in the National Curriculum [hereafter NC] – demanded practices that were inappropriate and cumbersome; lacking validity in terms of the established principles of the discipline; lacking reliability (judging by the evidence from research); and lacking manageability (any teacher will tell you).
3   In order to avoid these pitfalls, it was found to be important that teachers incorporate holistic approaches into their NC assessment practice. Approaches have been developed that make sense of detailed diagnostic assessment within the context of a holistic overview.

The progressive atomization of assessment

My first case study is drawn from a pioneering CSE course in the early 1970s[1], which was the first course explicitly to identify the process of designing as the basis

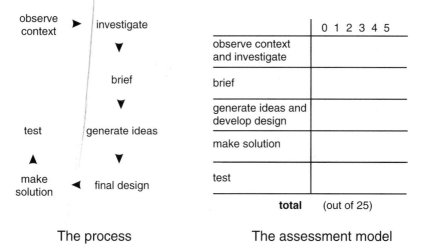

	0 1 2 3 4 5
observe context and investigate	
brief	
generate ideas and develop design	
make solution	
test	

total (out of 25)

The process   The assessment model

Figure 15.1 The process of design made explicit in an assessment model

for assessment. It created a seven-stage process that began with a general investigation of the context from within which a design brief might emerge, and ended with an evaluation of the outcome of the design and development process. This staged process was converted into an assessment scheme within which all the stages became – in turn – the focus of explicit assessment, as shown in Figure 15.1. For the first time, the whole of the design and technological activity was being assessed instead of simply the practical outcome of it.

The stages of the process were assessed on a sliding scale from 0 (no real attempt) to 5 (comprehensive grasp of the capability). The final mark out of 25 was therefore seen as a measure of whole capability. It was, in fact, a fine example of norm-referenced assessment, for the practice of teachers was typically to rank-order their pupils and then distribute the order across the mark range, on the assumption that the best pupils should get top marks and the worst should get the bottom marks. This tendency to distribute pupils around a norm was reinforced by the paperwork that described 3 as being 'average' with 2 and 4 being respectively below and above average. The marking was of necessity qualitative, with very few guidelines to inform the process of setting standards.

My second case study is from the first generation of National Criteria GCSE syllabuses in 1986–87.[2] The lineage of the assessment scheme is quite obvious, the stages of the design process once again being the basic structure of assessment. However, one of the fundamental tenets in the development of the GCSE was that norm referencing of the sort that was commonplace in the old GCE and CSE examinations was unhelpful because it did not identify in clear and positive terms *what pupils were capable of doing*. By contrast, the GCSE General Criteria were specific in requiring examinations that ensured proper discrimination and provided opportunities for pupils '... to show what they know, understand, and can do' (DES 1985: para. 16).

The candidate's evaluation;

0 – has not been attempted;
1 – is irrelevant;
2 – is relevant but superficial;
3 – represents an honest attempt to appraise his or her work but lacks objectivity and is either incomplete or not altogether relevant
4 – is complete and largely relevant but lacking in objectivity
5 – is thorough, objective, relevant and concise; it would provide a useful source of reference for later material

Figure 15.2 A five-point scale with descriptors

Here was a clear imperative to draw up a set of criteria that would enable us to remove for ever the concept of 'average' performance. Rather, the quality of capability that was to be assessed was *defined* at different levels of excellence, and pupils could then be assessed by the teacher identifying which descriptor applied to each pupil. If a pupil got 4 out of 5 for 'evaluating' it was not simply because she was nearly (but not quite) at the top of a rank order of other pupils, but rather because she was capable of doing the defined requirement of level 4.

> ... the performance required to achieve a particular mark is therefore specified in advance in the list of criteria on the form. It is therefore both more precise and more useful in a situation in which it is impossible for one teacher to know exactly what norms will be used by another teacher ... the norms are encapsulated in the criteria.
>
> (Secondary Examinations Council (SEC) 1985: 38)

Looking back at the CSE example we can see that this GCSE model of assessment is intended to be a more refined tool. As an illustration, the assessment of a pupil's 'evaluation' has – once again – a five-point scale, but this time each point on the scale is identified by a unique descriptor (Figure 15.2).

Clearly, these descriptors were intended to aid the teacher in deciding at which level to place the pupil, and also to serve as a focus for discussion in the moderation process. In theory, the criteria attempted to embody the received wisdom of what excellence entailed, thereby supporting the process of assessment. In practice, however, they represented little more than the best guess of what the chief examiner thought might be important. They were often arbitrary, ill-informed or little more than normative statements, such as '... thorough ...' (how thorough?).

In November 1989 the National Curriculum Order for Technology was finally ratified as a foundation subject, and it provides my third example. The Statutory Order sought to lay out, for the first time, a comprehensive description of the

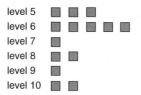

Figure 15.3 The spread of level descriptor statements for AT4 – 'evaluating'

progression of capability that was required between ages 5 to 16, both in terms of the Programmes of Study (PoS) that teachers would use in school courses and the Statements of Attainment (SoA) that pupils would seek to achieve through those programmes.

The original (1990) version defined four Attainment Targets (ATs)[3], again reflecting the process of design and development, and the SoA were intended to provide a comprehensive criterion-referenced assessment scheme within those ATs. It is interesting to note that there were 118 such SoA, each intended to describe a specific quality at a particular level. The simple (1970) sliding scale (0–5) had become a mass of 'can-do' assessment statements to which the teacher had merely to say 'yes' or 'no'. The NC had in effect created a digital assessment scheme in place of the former analogue approach.

For the purposes of comparing the three case studies, it is interesting to contrast the NC SoA for 'evaluating' (AT4) with the assessment criteria for the same quality under the former (CSE and GCSE) arrangements. The National Curriculum levels that are equivalent to GCSE are levels 5–10 and – just for AT4 (evaluating) – there were fourteen separate descriptors, spread across the levels as shown in Figure 15.3.

To place a pupil in one of these six levels (5–10) the teacher had to make 14 individual yes/no judgements against the SoA. We had gone from (in 1972) one single judgement of capability in evaluating to (in 1986) a choice of one 'best fit' descriptor from 5 possibles, then (in 1990) to a series of 14 independent yes/no decisions that had then to be processed into an answer – see Figure 15.4. In order to achieve clarity in measuring pupils' work, the units of assessment have become smaller and smaller and they have been reduced (like the Grand Old Duke of York) to one of two states – up or down; yes or no.

These three case studies are by no means the only ones (or even the most extreme ones) that I could have chosen to illustrate the trend towards detailed, atomized assessment. Significantly more extreme versions existed. The Graded Assessment scheme for CDT, for example, maps out hundreds of assessment boxes to be ticked when single or multiple skills have been demonstrated by pupils.

The big question of course was whether it produced a better (fairer, more reliable, more informative, more manageable) assessment system. It is tempting to believe that converting complex judgements into digital (yes/no) classifications will produce the same crispness and clarity in assessment that it achieves with the digital processor in my amplifier. But let us examine for a moment the problems involved.

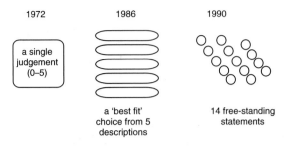

Figure 15.4 The progressive atomization of assessment over 20 years

The limitations of atomized assessment

The first difficulty centres on the problem of losing sight of the wood while trying to count the trees. It's a bit like doing a jigsaw. If you pick up a single piece of the puzzle it tells you very little about the whole picture and even less about the quality of that picture. Small, individual judgements make sense only if they are contextualized by a wider field of vision.

A second difficulty lies in the fact that in these categorical (yes/no) assessments, it is by no means obvious how to distinguish between a 'yes' and a 'no'. It involves a calibration exercise to decide the quality threshold at which a 'no' becomes a 'yes'. In a sub-aqua examination I had to demonstrate that I could tread water for one minute with my arms above my head. The instructor tells me that the results of this test are usually clear – you sink or you don't sink. It is (generally) good digital data. But few school-based assessments are so clear-cut.

The following statement is from the 1990 National Curriculum Order and required that pupils be able to:

> use specialist modelling techniques to develop design proposals.

How are we supposed to calibrate the achievement threshold for such a statement? At what level of capability does a 'no' becomes a 'yes'? Does it refer to a 5-year-old squeezing out some Plasticine, or to an 8-year-old experimenting with a Lego mechanism, or to a 15-year-old modelling a stage set? In reality, of course, design-ing *at all levels of capability* involves a degree of modelling. But a digital, categorical assessment system requires that all pupils be put into one of two camps – the mod-ellers and the non-modellers. Any decision here will not only be arbitrary, it will be misleading. It will imply that the 'non-modellers' cannot model their ideas, when in reality it will mean that their modelling facility has not reached the arbitrary threshold level.

A third difficulty is amply demonstrated in my three examples simply by noting the *number* of assessments that need to be made. It follows that as the units of assessment get smaller and (supposedly) more precise, they have also to get more numerous in order to cover the same ground. The price of atomization is prolifera-tion and an interesting parallel can be found in the engineering toolbox.

The go/no-go gauge is a precisely ground instrument that gives a clear (yes/no) answer to a simple question, 'Is this bar 20mm diameter?' If the gauge fits snugly on the bar the answer is 'yes'; if it does not then the answer is 'no'. It is a very limited instrument that is only capable of supporting that one single decision. For effective engineering, therefore, you need a great store full of them, all of slightly different sizes. Go/no-go gauges are not really measuring devices at all, but are *checking* devices. The 20mm diameter gauge is not used to measure whether a bar is 10, 15, 20 or 25mm diameter; it is used as a precision check exclusively on bars that are known to be (or supposed to be) 20mm diameter. Effective use of go/no-go gauges therefore depends on a prior *judgement* about the size of the bar. A skilled fitter could make far more efficient use of these gauges than an unskilled one.[4]

The point of the story is merely to indicate that a system based on atomized, categorical assessment can only sensibly work if the operator (teacher) is able to make a prior overview judgement and hence select the appropriate criteria of validation.

A fourth difficulty concerns the extent to which individual judgements necessarily interact in the assessment of capability. It's a bit like judging the quality of an omelette. However good the eggs are – and the herbs, and the butter, and perhaps the cheese – the key question is how well they are blended to work together and enhance each other. To treat the judgements as independent points to be scored is seriously to misjudge the interdependence of the elements that go to make up technological capability. Do we not know when we have eaten an exquisite omelette?

The effect in schools

Assessment in the early days of the National Curriculum became a nightmare. With four ATs and 118 SoA to be charted for every pupil, the period was marked by a proliferation of different designs for assessment and recording forms, as schools, LEA advisory teams and others sought desperately to find ways to help teachers to record this mass of data. The assessment forms got bigger and bigger; and the boxes on them got smaller and smaller. And this mass of assessment minutiae became more and more meaningless.

A case study I observed in Essex involved a pair of teachers assessing the work of their Year 9 pupils in two classes. They started with an enormous assessment sheet which contained boxes for all the SoA, and they spent hours ticking the boxes for the 43 pupils. They then started on the arithmetic. They aggregated the SoA ticks into AT scores, then they aggregated the AT scores to Profile Component (PC) scores and then finally to subject scores. Then they ranked the pupils by their performance. It was a meticulous and thorough piece of work. But at the end of it they started to question the result: 'Jane *can't* be better than Joanne' – 'Peter *must* be better than Patrick.' They had a clear sense of who (overall) was better than whom. And this intuitive sense was not confirmed in the assessments. So what should they do?

They couldn't adjust the PC scores because they were mathematically derived from the AT scores. They couldn't adjust the AT scores because they were mathematically derived from the SoA scores. All they could do was go back to the SoA ticks. So they did. And they changed them. Having formerly said 'No' (because

Peter was judged *not* to have used appropriate graphic techniques) they now recorded a 'Yes' (he *did* use appropriate graphic techniques). By some selective adjustments of this kind – and after lots of supplementary re-aggregation – the two teachers got the answers that they felt were appropriate for their pupils. It took an entire afternoon and evening. Eight hours. Sixteen teacher hours. And rather than leaving them professionally extended and satisfied with a good job done, it left them angry, frustrated and convinced they would never go through that ridiculous procedure ever again.

The problems I have identified above were the root cause of this fiasco. First, the digitization of assessment, the removal of sliding scales and their replacement with simplistic yes/no assertions. And this was fatally compounded by the preoccupation with detail (SoA ticking) at the expense of the big picture of overall quality.

An alternative approach

In the light of our previous research experience for APU (Kimbell *et al.* 1991), it was evident that the holism of Design and Technology projects can be reflected in an equivalent holism in the assessment procedure. Quite apart from any educational argument, we established through the APU research that, in Design and Technology, teachers are at their most reliable when assessing the whole and are least reliable when assessing the bits.

Accordingly, in our work with schools during this troubled period, we developed an assessment procedure that prioritized holistic assessment. The approach required that the teacher's *first* judgement should be an overall measure of the quality of a student's project, effectively 'pitching' straight for an overall PC level. We then invited teachers to identify the strengths and weaknesses of the work by indicating how the AT levels might vary from this overall score (some elements of the work might be really strong and others relatively weak). Finally we asked teachers to check these AT levels by validating them against the details of the SoA, illustrated in Figure 15.5. It should be noted that one of the distinct advantages of working this way round was that it reduced the SoA to a meaningful and manageable number – i.e. those in the level that had been 'pitched' – and (as a cross-check) those one level up and one level down.

Rather than seeing SoA as front-line criteria for assessment they become backstop validation devices. Our procedure used them to cross-check a judgement that had already been made – and for which we were seeking confirmation. The assessment process must start with whole judgements and work *towards* detail. It must not start with detail and work towards the whole.

In 1991, in the APU final report we put the case as follows:

> It is our view that SoA judgments would be more reliable if placed within a broader frame of reference through the AT and the PC … We are drawn therefore to a procedure that starts with big pictures (PC) moves to more restricted ones (ATs) and ends with the detail … If the SoA judgments do not confirm the overall judgment, then there is clearly something wrong. Either

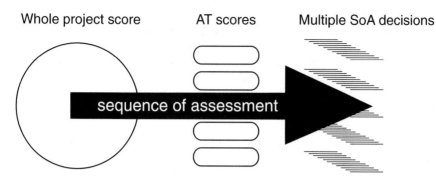

Whole project score   AT scores   Multiple SoA decisions

sequence of assessment

Figure 15.5   Assessing from whole project to ATs to SoA

the overview judgment is wrong or the interpretation of the detail of SoA is wrong. In either event the process of reconciliation is likely to be more just and accurate if it is operated from both ends – iteratively, rather than simply by assuming that the SoA is naturally right and the PC naturally wrong … (since) … our data suggest that the reverse is more likely to be the case.

(Kimbell *et al.* 1991)

At the heart of this process lay the challenge of making the initial 'pitch', and we knew that we would need to provide some support mechanisms to enable teachers to do this. We therefore developed a series of 'level guides' summarizing the things to look for and the critical components of capability at that level.[5]

The central thrust of my argument at the time was that in assessing technological capability, the requirement to operate exclusively on the basis of detailed, itemized criteria (SoA) was fundamentally unsound. It created a superficially simple (tick-box) system, but the crude reductionist methodology created enormous problems for the assessment of an integrated capability. In practice therefore it was bound to be (and was subsequently shown to be) unhelpful, unmanageable and unreliable.

The move towards holism

In the ten years that have followed the initial introduction of the Design and Technology National Curriculum we have witnessed a quite remarkable transformation in assessment policy. And this transformation has been towards holism. In 1990 and 1991 the Schools Examination and Assessment Council (SEAC) would not contemplate the model of assessment outlined above. The key reason for this was that it involved the heretical notion that teachers would have to make *professional judgements* about children's level scores, rather than have them derived from aggregated (and testable) SoA scores.

In the subsequent years there have been two major steps towards holism. The first was the progressive reduction of ATs in the Statutory Order for Design and

Technology, from four in 1990, to two in 1995 ('designing' and 'making'), and finally to one in 2000. Instead of looking at (and trying to assess) multiple bits of capability, teachers can now take a view of whole capability.

But perhaps the more important step has been the change of policy regarding SoA. This was triggered by a letter dated 4th November 1993 sent to all Chief Education Officers and to all schools. It was sent jointly from the new head of SCAA (Ron Dearing)[6], the Office of the Chief Inspector of Schools [Wales] (Roy James) and the founding head of Ofsted (Stewart Sutherland). The letter was sent following the shambles of that summer's SATs tests, which had been almost universally rejected by schools, and marked the final realization that the assessment model enshrined in the original National Curriculum was deeply flawed. In particular, the letter enshrines a complete reversal of the former SEAC policy on how *Statements of Attainment* were to be viewed; on the need for *evidence* to justify assessments; and on the role of teachers' *professional judgements*. It contained the following section:

> The essential points we would like to convey are as follows:
>
> - In those subjects which have statutory teacher assessment in 1994, the aim should be to arrive at an *all round judgment* of the level a pupil has achieved in each attainment target.
> - There is *no need to assess against every statement of attainment individually* or to record those assessments on a tick-list: teachers need only consider whether the knowledge, understanding and skills displayed by a pupil correspond *on the whole* more closely to the statements of attainment at one level than another.
> - When it comes to substantiating their judgments, teachers do not need to keep detailed evidence to support the assessment they have made of every child ... they need only collect a school sample of pupils work that exemplifies attainment at each level ... How teachers record pupils' progress is, of course, a professional matter for schools to decide.
>
> (Sutherland/Dearing/James 1993; author's italics added)

The 'of course' must have seemed a bit rich to Chief Education Officers and teachers who had just experienced five years in which the very idea of them exercising any kind of professional judgement over such matters had been systematically eliminated. That apart, however, the letter not only reflects a good deal of common sense but also signalled a quite new assessment regime.

In the subsequent seven years we have come full circle. I started this chapter by documenting the progressive atomization in assessment practice that took place between 1970 and the launch of the National Curriculum in 1990. The extreme point that it reached in 1991, 1992 and 1993 tested to the very limit the patience and professionalism of all teachers. I end the chapter by documenting a progressive withdrawal from this position, starting from the date of the letter from Sutherland, Dearing and James in 1993. Moreover, this letter demonstrates the very welcome realization on the part of SCAA[7] and Ofsted that good assessment inevitably involves teachers' professional judgement. This new regard for the professionalism of teachers was reflected in the 1995 revision of the National Curriculum, particularly for Design and Technology. Writing in May 1994 at the time of the SCAA consultation on the revision, I described it as 'Not so much a workshop manual, more a professional guide', and went on to make the following observation:

> It was with some relief that I read through this new D & T Order (May 1994). Its principal strength is that it appears to mark a return to professionalism, to the view that teachers understand about teaching and learning and can be trusted to behave sensibly and appropriately in the interests of their pupils. This is in marked contrast to former versions which took delight in specifying the curriculum – and how to teach it – in minute detail.
>
> (Kimbell 1994)

For assessment, this involved teachers using 'baskets of descriptors' to identify AT levels directly, without the need to derive them from lists of SoA 'hits'. The formerly separate SoA had been reworked into composite level statements that were not unlike the 'level guides' that APU had been using with teachers in our work. It was a very welcome transformation of policy. And then, in the 2000 revision, the two ATs were finally amalgamated into one and the level statements again went through a redrafting and consolidating process. Teachers are now really able to take a view of whole capability in Design and Technology.

However, whilst I recognize the significance of this reversal of the drift towards atomization in assessment, I also recognize that one of the principal consequences of this realignment of the assessment regime has not been fully recognized or addressed.

One of the purposes of a National Curriculum is that we should have national standards – not local idiosyncratic ones – so to have teachers making professional judgements in their individual schools can only be a first step in the assessment process. Initially, teachers' judgements will be informed by the standards that each individual teacher thinks appropriate in the light of their experience of their pupils. The challenge thereafter is gradually to transform these idiosyncratic individualized standards into something more generalizable. This is a formidable task that requires teachers' individual judgements to be compared and contrasted within schools so as to arrive at *school* standards of performance. These are the standards that Sutherland, Dearing and James saw as emerging from the portfolio or 'school sample of pupils work that exemplifies attainment at each level'. But the process needs to go further, for I believe that we should have required schools to compare and contrast their standards with those of other local schools so as gradually to arrive at *local* standards. Finally, we should have required local areas to collaborate into regional groups to generate regional and ultimately national standards of performance. In the process of reconciling disagreements amongst teachers at any of these levels (the school, the local area or nationally), exemplification material can be really helpful – feeding into the debate that is *founded upon teachers' own views of standards in their schools.* The challenge – for national assessment purposes – was to move from teacher-centred standards towards nationally-agreed standards that are understood and valued by *all* teachers. This of course required investment in collaborative moderation activities both within and across schools in order to share, generalize and ultimately universalize the *meanings* of the criteria: the *standards* to apply. I am aware that such cross-school moderation is already happening in some local areas, supported (usually) by the LEA.

The bottom line is that teachers do not just *apply* standards that they are given from elsewhere (SEAC or SCAA or QCA). The fact is that teachers have a critical role in calibrating, sharing and ultimately validating such standards.[8] Accordingly, if we are seriously concerned with raising standards in technology, and in having secure assessments of those standards, then it is the *understanding* of teachers, the *experience* of teachers and the *practice* of teachers that we should be supporting and enriching.

Notes

1   A 'Design Studies' syllabus developed through the North Western CSE Examination Board.
2   The Northern Examination Association syllabus for CDT: Design and Communication.
3   The 1990 Attainment Targets were: Identifying needs and opportunities; Generating a design; Planning and making; Evaluating.
4   It is interesting to reflect on the fact that as the engineering workforce became more educated (or at least more literate and numerate) the extremely limited go/no-go gauges disappeared in favour of more flexible measuring devices (vernier gauges and micrometers) that adapt to the size of the bar and yet render just as much precision.
5   For more details of the processes involved, and the underpinning APU research, see Kimbell (1997).
6   SEAC was renamed the Schools Curriculum and Assessment Council (SCAA) and absorbed the role of the National Curriculum Council (NCC).
7   SCAA has subsequently been renamed the Qualifications and Curriculum Authority (QCA) and has absorbed the role of the National Council for Vocational Qualifications (NCVQ).
8   For a fuller debate on the role of teachers in generating standards, see Kimbell, Chapters 5–6 (1997).

References

Banks, F. (ed.) (1994) *Teaching Technology*, Buckingham: Open University Press.
DES/WO (1987) *The National Curriculum – A Consultative Document*, London: DES.
DES/WO (1988) *Task Group on Assessment and Testing – A Report*, London: DES.
DES (1988) *Interim Report of the Design and Technology Working Group*, London: HMSO.
DES (1989) *Technology in the National Curriculum*, London: HMSO.
Kimbell, R. A. (1992) 'Assessing technological capability', in the Proceedings of the International Conference on Technology Education (INCOTE 92), Weimar, Germany.
Kimbell, R. A. (1993) 'Progression in learning and the assessment of pupil attainment', in D. Layton (ed.) *Innovations in Science and Technology Education*, Paris: UNESCO.

Kimbell, R. A. (1994) 'Not so much a workshop manual – more a professional guide', *Design and Technology Times*, May, Salford University.

Kimbell, R. A. (1997) *Assessing Technology*, Buckingham: Open University Press.

Kimbell, R., Stables, K., Wheeler, T., Wozniak, A. and Kelly, V. (1991) *The Assessment of Performance in Design and Technology: The Final Report of the APU Design and Technology Project 1985–91*, School Examinations and Assessment Council: Evaluation and Monitoring Unit.

Satterly, D. (1989) *Assessment in Schools*, Oxford: Blackwell.

Secondary Examinations Council (SEC) (1985) *Craft Design and Technology GCSE; A Guide for Teachers*, Buckingham: Open University Press.

SEAC/EMU (1991) *Profiles and progression in science explorations; Assessment matters No 5*, SEAC/COI.

Stables, K. (1992) 'Issues surrounding the development of technological capability in children in their first years of schools (ages 5–7)', in the Proceedings of the International Conference on Technology Education (INCOTE 92), Weimar, Germany.

Sutherland, S. Dearing, R. and James, R. (1993) 'Recording Pupils' Achievement' – a letter to CEOs and schools, London: SCAA/Ofsted and Office of Her Majesty's Chief Inspector of Schools.

Section 4

Social and contextual issues

16 Gender and Design and Technology education

Jan Harding

The next two chapters need to be read together. This one looks at the historical development of Design and Technology, and how this may have influenced perceptions of it. Consideration is given to how girls responded to Design and Technology when it was first introduced and how girls can be encouraged to participate and achieve in Design and Technology activities. Both chapters should encourage you to consider your own practice, in planning and teaching, in relation to the gender issues identified.

Technology in the curriculum

Technology is a relative newcomer to the curriculum of secondary schools. Its arrival, and its discrimination from technical education, are a recognition of the pervasive influence of technology on modern life and the prosperity of nations. This requires populations who are skilled in living with, managing and contributing to technological development.

But the form that technology education should take continues to be controversial, not only in the UK, but also in other parts of the world. Inevitably, the final outcome is dependent on the views of dominant pressure groups but it also relies on skills, identities and self-perceptions within the available teaching force, existing accommodation and equipment and related programmes offered in the past.

The antecedents of technology education in England and Wales are threefold: applied science courses (taken by pupils considered to be academically able), handicrafts (offered to younger pupils and pursued by the 'less able') and computing, which entered the curriculum on an *ad hoc* basis as computers became available in schools. McCulloch *et al.* (1985) documented the power struggle between 'science' and 'craft' for the heart of technology education in the 1960s and 1970s. Meanwhile the nature of 'handicrafts' was changing with the growth of 'Design and Technology', in place of woodwork and metalwork, for the more able pupils at what is now Key Stage 4. More recently Design and Technology has expanded to include elements of home economics and textiles.

A gendered history

All three antecedents of technology have been sex differentiated in the past. They

Table 16.1 Selected examinations entries and results for boys and girls at 16+ in England 1982 and 1992

| | 1982 CSE[1] examination | | | | | 1982 GCE 'O' level[2] examination | | | | |
| | Entries | | | % Grade 1 | | Entries | | | % Grade A–C | |
	Boys	Girls	% Girls	Boys	Girls	Boys	Girls	% Girls	Boys	Girls
English Language	327685	326939	49.9	11.2	18.3	234262	277690	54.2	51.7	57.5
Mathematics	228312	247032	52.0	16.5	14.2	173341	151323	46.6	60.4	51.9
General Science	44134	33192	42.9	5.9	6.4	3153	3163	50.1	51.9	44.3
Physics	123134	31021	20.1	14.0	14.8	134622	49286	26.8	60.4	61.4
Chemistry	63032	46236	42.3	16.4	15.5	87074	58651	40.2	63.0	60.1
Biology	61838	146032	70.2	14.6	12.8	83601	151061	64.4	59.3	51.1
Technical Drawing	92641	4932	5.1	15.8	13.4	57694	3227	5.3	43.9	37.9
Woodwork	61084	1718	2.7	12.1	11.2	14477	239	1.6	57.7	51.5
Metalwork	57680	685	1.2	12.4	12.0	12397	118	0.9	61.7	46.6
Design and Technology	—	—	—	—	—	13670	594	4.2	60.1	57.2
Domestic Subjects	12218	124561	91.1	4.3	13.3	1655	47658	96.6	35.5	60.6

Notes
1 CSE Certificate of Secondary Education, designed for less academic students
2 GCE General Certificate of Education, used for more academic pupils; offered at O and A level

Table 16.2 GCSE entries and results

| | 1992 GCSE[1] examination | | | | |
| | Entries | | | % Grade A–C[2] | |
	Boys	Girls	% Girls	Boys	Girls
English Language	245149	243598	48.9	45.9	61.8
Mathematics	231511	228880	49.7	44.9	43.0
Science (Single)	46246	51139	52.5	16.5	22.2
Science (Double)	147244	144192	49.5	44.7	44.1
Physics	35845	16146	31.1	69.2	73.7
Chemistry	30105	21358	41.5	71.6	68.6
Biology	25687	30367	54.2	70.0	61.4
Craft, Design and Technology	133352	36458	21.5	35.8	46.6

Source: Examination Boards Survey, supplied by the DES in 1983, and the DFE in 1993.

Notes
1   GCSE General Certificate of Secondary Education which replaced CSE and GCE 'O' level in 1988. All these examinations were/are usually taken at 16+ after five years of secondary schooling.
2   CSE Grade, GCE 'O' level Grades A–C and GCES A–C are accepted towards matriculation for entrance to university education; in popular culture these are 'passes'.

have been the most strongly gendered of all curriculum areas. McCulloch *et al.* (1985) point out how the discourse surrounding technology education in the 1960s and 1970s focused exclusively on boys. Entries at O and A level in Engineering Science, Electronics and Modular Technology in the 1980s were overwhelmingly from boys, until the TVEI programme required that efforts should be made to avoid sex-stereotyping where these subjects were included in the TVEI programme.

Statistics for 1982 shown in Table 16.1 showed only 2.7 per cent of CSE and 1.6 per cent of O level Woodwork entrants were girls; for Metalwork the figures were 1.2 per cent and 0.9 per cent, and for Technical Drawing 5.1 per cent and 5.3 per cent. The participation of boys in Domestic Subjects was 8.9 per cent for CSE and 3.4 per cent for O level.

A survey of more than 50 schools in two LEAs in the same year showed that, in what is now Key Stage 3, only 25 per cent of schools included continuous strands of CDT and Home Economics for all three years. The most common form of organisation was a compulsory rotational scheme of 'taster' courses in 'creative studies' for the first year of secondary schooling. The courses were of 8 or 9 sessions and included CDT, Home Economics, Art and, sometimes, Music. Optional courses would then be offered in the second and third years. The offering of choice inevitably resulted in sex differentiation of CDT and Home Economics as gender stereotyping operated on the choices made (Harding 1989).

The examination entries for 1992 (see Table 16.2) show that some progress had been made in breaking down stereotypes: 21.5 per cent of CDT entries for GCSE were girls and 13.8 per cent of Domestic Subjects entries were boys, with girls gaining a higher percentage of grades A–C in both.

At A level 24.8 per cent of entrants in Technology were girls, who also had a higher pass rate (see Table 16.3). These entries and pass rates are comparable to those in Physics that year, although the volume of entries was considerably less. [...]

Merely to make a subject compulsory does not necessarily result in gender-fair curricular experiences, as a number of studies in mathematics have shown (e.g. the HMI 1989 survey, and the Girls and Mathematics Project, Walden and Walkerdine 1985).

Computing, or Information Technology, has but a brief history in schooling in England and Wales, but it has become gender-stereotyped. Before computers were available in schools and homes women formed more than 30 per cent of students in undergraduate Computer Science courses, but over the 1980s their participation dropped to less than 10 per cent. Culley (1986) discusses some of the factors associated with girls' lesser participation in computing in schools; these include teacher expectation, boys' dominant behaviour, girls' limited access to computers at home and the nature of available recreational software.

Does it matter?

In discussing this question Head (1980) makes three points: one is an equal opportunity argument – women's earnings are considerably less than men's, which is partly due to their lack of technical qualifications, and in the year 2000 this is still true; another relates to skills shortage – although girls and women have the ability to work within science and technology, few qualify to do so; and the third relates to the nature of technology education – this has been presented too often as intensively narrow and divorced from human concerns. Within this framework girls have been defined as deficient. Head claims that the failure to attract girls is a failure of technology education, not a failure of girls.

If we look more closely at this last point we can ask: whose world views are more usually represented in the practice of technology and in its presentation for learning? The answer seems to be those of men and boys. A review of women in science, engineering and technology (HMSO 1994) shows that very few women are in positions to influence decision-making, and presentation methods have evolved in the context of mainly men teaching mainly boys.

Because society currently maps different roles onto men and women and expects different behaviours from them, males and females tend to develop different value systems and world views. Concerns of males include achievement, leadership, control and independence; those of females include care, nurturance, relatedness and personal responsibility. If women do not work within technology the values associated with them will not be strongly represented in technological development, which puts people and the planet at risk.

Although girls experience disadvantage more often in technology education

Table 16.3 Selected A level entries and results for males and females in England

	1982					1992				
	Entries[1]			% Passes		Entries[2]			% Passes	
	Males	Females	% Females	Males	Females	Males	Females	% Females	Males	Females
English Literature[3]	19003	44386	70.0	58.5	73.1	20062	44859	69.1	85.9	87.6
Mathematics[4]	70090	26626	27.5	66.5	68.5	31525	16972	35.0	77.2	78.8
Biology	17855	25596	60.0	68.0	67.8	12506	20419	62.0	80.6	79.3
Chemistry	30615	16420	34.9	73.7	73.1	17926	12634	41.3	82.3	82.2
Physics	44469	11259	25.3	68.9	70.1	23530	6680	22.1	80.4	82.0
Technology	—	—	—	—	—	6152	1528	24.8	77.7	82.1

Notes
1 Source: Examinations Boards Survey, supplied by the Department of Education and Science in 1983. No age range is given, but candidates are referred to as 'boys' and 'girls'.
2 Source: Department for Education Statistical Bulletin, No. 15/93. Candidates aged 18 years or over.
3 1992 figures show an aggregation of Language and Literature available as separate subjects.
4 Aggregation of six mathematical subjects: 'Pure and Applied' contributed 66 per cent of candidates in 1982.

than do boys, the gendered nature of expectations can also put boys at a disadvantage. The APU Report (SEAC 1991) cites one boys' school in which the pupils refused to develop an interactive toy for a baby. In what follows, the ways in which boys and girls may differ in their responses to curricular presentations will be explored.

Facilitating girls' participation and success in technology education

The Assessment of Performance Unit (APU) was set up within the DES (Department of Education and Science) in the late 1970s, to establish standards of performance in the major subjects of the curriculum at ages 11, 13 and 15. The APU Design and Technology, a latecomer to the scheme, operated only in the second half of the 1980s, with a brief to monitor the capability in design and technology of 15-year-old pupils. It defined design and technology as '*a purposeful, task-related, activity that results in 'improvement' in the made world*' (while recognising that the concept of improvement was problematic, depending on a set of shared values). The 'activity' was divided into sections for the purpose of assessment, short tests being devised to assess capability within these. Some clear gender differences in performance emerged (SEAC 1991).

Using reflective skills

It was found that tasks requiring reflection (e.g. the identification of a need, or the evaluation of a product) enabled girls to participate with confidence and to demonstrate good capability, whereas 'active' tasks favoured boys.

Recognising context

In general, girls outperformed in a 'people' context and boys in an 'industry' context; no clear gender difference was found in an 'environment' context. Context also differentiated between boys and girls in APU science surveys. Murphy (1990) reported:

> Typically girls tend to value the circumstances that activities are presented in and consider they give meaning to the task. They do not abstract issues from their context. Boys as a group conversely do consider issues in isolation and judge content and context to be irrelevant.

[...]

Valuing the social context

In particular the social context supports girls' performance and their readiness to be involved. In the early 1970s Ormerod reported that the perception that science has social implications correlated with girls' choice of science but not with boys'.

An analysis of girls' and boys' entries over a three year period to a National Design Prize Competition showed that while they worked on similar devices the problem they had identified differed: boys were working to improve the device (a technical problem) whereas for the majority of girls the problem was perceived to be one of human need which could be met by use of the device (the social context) (Grant and Harding 1987).

The Tasmanian Education Department placed their computer education in a social, rather than a science or mathematics, context by providing training initially for social science and humanities teachers, In addition, the rich resource of the detailed database for convicts sent to Van Diemen's Land (Tasmania) in the nineteenth century captured the girls' interest and they were as enthusiastic in their use of computers and software to question the database as were the boys.

Recognising complexity

The reluctance girls show in abstracting aspects of a problem from its context means that they often recognise a greater complexity in a given situation. This is referred to several times in APU reports. For example:

> (Girls) were often cautious in their entry into a situation, wanting to know how, why and who it was for. While studying and designing the minutiae they were constantly seeking to keep the implications of the whole in view, and for some this complexity became intolerable to the point where they capitulated.
>
> (SEAC 1991: 120)

Perhaps this is why it was also found that a tight structure to the activity supported girls' performance. On the other hand, a loose task, one in which they could decide meanings and priorities, also favoured girls. For example, the loose task that asked pupils to suggest areas where new or improved products or systems could be designed for the garden was structured in seven steps by the following instructions: *Brainstorm different situations (5 mins); Put down all your design ideas (25 mins); List all the things the product will do (5 mins); Plan all stages (25 mins); List what you need to know to carry out your plan (15 mins); Write a design brief (10 mins).*

The openness of the original task allowed pupils to develop ownership of the problem by reflecting on the gardener's need, but the tight structure provided a framework within which complexity was controlled without being denied.

On the other hand, a tight task but loose structure supported boys. An example was the requirement to develop a device to enable a drilling operation to be executed quickly and repetitively. Although the task involved a child's toy (a hobby horse), it was set in an industrial context and its closed, technical nature inhibited girls' performance, but not that of boys. Additionally, the exercise included more than an hour of unstructured 'free modelling' time, in two blocks. Girls' lesser familiarity with technical tools also contributed to their low performance in this task. The task administrator reported that girls tended to confine themselves to the safety of paper and pencil development (SEAC 1991: 125).

These findings highlight a further complexity that teachers need to recognise: the way a number of factors interact to influence pupils' performance to produce gender differentiated outcomes.

Differing teaching and learning styles

Following the Nuffield Science Projects of the 1960s and 1970s a study of teaching styles and related pupil attitudes to, and achievement in, science was carried out. Three teaching styles were identified: the Informer (I), the Problem Solver (II) and the Inquirer (III). Style I was the least successful, even in knowledge gains. Style II (a style wherein the teacher dominates) was used more by men than by women teachers; in it pupils were publicly challenged to hypothesise solutions to problems from data given verbally or from experimental work. This style was most successful in generating knowledge. Style III was more pupil-controlled, in which pupils investigated problems, often formulated by themselves, in small groups. It was used more by women than by men teachers, it produced the highest levels of achievement in problem-solving tasks, its knowledge gains were close to those of Style II and it was the only style in which the pupils' attitudes to science showed positive gains over a year. It was particularly successful with low achieving girls (Galton 1981). Girls were reported to dislike Style II and to prefer Styles I or III. As these are very different, this outcome was puzzling, but Galton suggests both Styles I and III do not require girls to 'go public' in a context where boys may make disparaging comments. They also provide less interaction with the teacher. Some studies in other parts of the world have also shown that girls prefer to work in a group, independent of the teacher, in science and technology, but others suggest girls show a marked teacher dependence. A possible explanation is that in a more teacher-controlled classroom, if the teacher's style, or the conceptual framework used, is alien in any way, the pupils will switch off or resort to rote learning or dependency. This may occur more for girls in a subject area which has evolved in a male-dominated context and is more usually taught by men.

An investigation in Denmark which required 'top junior' classes to solve problems in small groups, using a computer, found that boys preferred to work individually, negotiating time on the computer, whereas girls preferred to work collaboratively, exploring verbally a number of ideas relating to the problem. The APU survey (SEAC 1991) also found this gender difference in collaborative working.

Barriers to participation and achievement

Some barriers may be deduced from the evidence given above. Problems may be created for girls by disregarding the special (and valuable) skills they employ in the learning process. Other specific examples of barriers are given below.

Girls' attitudes?

If girls' attitudes to science and to technology are interpreted as negative, this will be conveyed to them in a number of ways by comment and by attempts to change their attitudes without changing the ways science and technology are presented. Most surveys of attitudes to technology conclude that girls' attitudes are less positive (more negative) than boys'. The Equal Opportunities Commission stated in a leaflet entitled 'Equal Opportunities in TVEI': '... *unless special measures are taken, the negative attitudes towards technology which girls already reveal, will undermine the objectives of TVEI*'. As Head (1989) suggests, those special measures should be addressed to technology education. But Grant and Harding (1987) propose that girls' attitudes to technology, with their reservations about some applications and their perception of the complexity of real problems (not often allowed for in questionnaire surveys), should be regarded as the more positive approach. If we make this conceptual change we are more likely to work with girls through their views of the world.

Teachers' behaviour

The GIST project found that most science and technology teachers regarded girls' low participation in science and technology as unproblematic, and not a serious professional issue (Whyte 1986: 257). This assumption still holds in many parts of the country. Many teachers have different expectations of girls than of boys. I find that teachers participating in in-service training on equity issues will consistently counsel Denise differently from Denis, using the same pupil profile. The GIST Project found the same outcome for the exercise (Whyte 1986). Spear showed that teachers given copies of pupils' work in science graded it higher and predicted a brighter future for a pupil if it carried a boy's name, than if the same piece of work bore a girl's name (Spear 1984). It is a sobering exercise to reflect on how such expectations are daily conveyed to boys and girls through comment and attitude. The GIST project also observed men teachers using what may be called mildly flirtatious behaviour to jolly girls along and create rapport, thereby reinforcing gender differences in the classroom (Whyte 1986: 28).

A number of classroom interaction studies have shown that teachers generally spend more time interacting with boys than with girls. The GATE project found that this was not always the case. The following pattern was observed in workshops: if a boy approached a teacher with a problem, the teacher would most likely give the boy verbal advice, but if a girl asked for help, the teacher would be more likely to go with the girl to her piece of work and carry out the required procedure for her, thereby compounding her sense of helplessness.

Boys' behaviour

Many of the classroom interactions observed in laboratories and workshops in the GIST project seemed to have the effect of 'edging girls out' (Whyte 1986: 25). In class discussion boys tended to call out their contributions while girls kept to the rule of raising their hand to answer. Boys would mock a wrong answer from a girl or groan at a right answer. Boys used equipment to generate aggressive play, using ray boxes as ray guns, spring balances as catapults and magnets for tug-of-war. Where resources were in short supply it was mainly the boys who elbowed their way to acquire them.

The negative effect of boys' behaviour on girls' participation has also been identified in Young Engineer clubs (Blackman and Brown 1993). One girl reported:

> We have done really well as a school in winning prizes in technology. I am the only girl in our team that won the awards. So a lot of attention has been focused on me since we won the awards. But the thing is I actually left the team. I had to go. It was so weird being surrounded by all these men and boys. At first it didn't seem to matter, but then it was upsetting me. They would do all the work. Do all the good, most difficult jobs. They had first choice of what to do. They said (the boys) 'do this and that' but it was nothing because I know about cars from my dad, he has really given me support and it was only through him that I went back to join the team. Otherwise the boys had forced me to leave, making it seem that I wanted to, but I didn't, it was their behaviour which made me go.
>
> (Blackman and Brown 1993: 47)

Good teacher management and control should eliminate most of this negative behaviour, but to avoid a repressive atmosphere teachers and pupils need to become more gender-sensitive in order to establish more equitable experiences for girls in formerly male-dominated areas of the curriculum. A more difficult situation arises when retired male engineers, unused to working with young women in a technical framework, are recruited to help with work in schools.

The nature of the technology curriculum

The most recent version of Design and Technology in the National Curriculum (1999) allows more presentation flexibility for the teacher and curriculum developer. The evaluation of products now makes reference to aesthetic, social or environmental aspects as well as technical performance, which may help the operation of girls' reflective skills. All materials can now be used by pupils at Key Stage 3, although the position of food as an option only in Key Stage 3 may reduce its importance in the eyes of pupils and ensure that an opportunity for sex differentiation occurs. There is an increased emphasis on the industrial context, but also greater reference to the community and the effects of technology on society.

Different perspectives can cause aspects of technology to become devalued, and can create teaching and learning environments more comfortable for some pupils than others. For example, allowing food to be available only as an option in Key Stage 3 devalues technology based and developed in the home and, by association, the traditional skills of women. This can create a more comfortable *milieu* for boys than for girls. Unless teachers are aware of these subtle gender interactions and take steps to counter them, girls may be at a disadvantage.

Society's expectations

The expectations of society continue to be strongly sex-stereotyped with little recognition that its gendered nature constrains the potential development of both males and females. Boys may reject activities with a female or feminine association and girls feel less than comfortable when a masculine bias, often unrecognised by teachers, is present. Where choice of participation is offered, stereotyping operates to reinforce the gendered nature of society.

Girls are entering GCSE Design and Technology examinations in numbers comparable to boys and are out-performing boys, but many of them choose to work within food and textiles. This then sustains gender differentiation in the range of skills developed, and in career choices.

Within this context those working in technology education assume a certain responsibility, for technology and technical activities are some of the most affected by stereotyping. Their assumptions, attitudes, actions and the materials they produce may either contribute to this reinforcement or challenge it.

Conclusion

Although technology education and its antecedents have been strongly sex differentiated and gender-stereotyped, the current place of technology in the National Curriculum provides both an imperative and an opportunity, albeit limited by the chosen framework, to change this *status quo*. Research has provided insight into the obstacles to participation, and to ways in which their participation may be supported. This requires the recognition of different ways of working and generating knowledge and the valuing of the special skills girls may have developed.

The frameworks adopted within curricular materials and the suggestions made for presentation for pupils may facilitate gender-inclusive experiences. However, much will depend on the mediation of classroom teachers, in their projection of assumptions and their management of classrooms including the behaviour of boys. This points to the need for substantial in-service programmes in gender-awareness for teachers of Design and Technology.

References

Blackman, S. and Brown, A. (1993) *Evaluation of Young Engineers: a case study linked to Technology and the National Curriculum*, Guildford: Department of Educational Studies, University of Surrey.

Culley, L. (1986) *Gender Differences in Computing in Secondary School*, Loughborough: Loughborough University of Technology.

Galton, M. (1981) 'Differential treatment of boy and girl pupils during science lessons', in Kelly, A. (ed.) *The Missing Half*, Manchester: Manchester University Press, pp.180–91.

Grant, M. and Harding, J. (1987) 'Changing the polarity', *International Journal of Science Education* 9(3): 335–42.

Harding, J. (1989) 'Making technology education a reality for girls', in J. Head, (ed.) *Girls and Technology*, London: Centre for Educational Studies, Kings College.

Head, J. (1989) 'Gender and education', in *Girls and Technology*, London: Centre for Educational Studies, Kings College.

Hildebrand, G. (1995) 'Assessment interacts with gender: the case of girls and physics in Victoria, Australia', paper presented at the UNESCO/Institute of Education Colloquium 'Is there a Pedagogy for Girls?' London, January 1995.

HMI (1989) 'Girls learning mathematics', *Education Observed* 14, London: Department of Education and Science.

HMSO (1994) *The Rising Tide, Women in Science, Engineering and Technology*, London: HMSO.

McCulloch, G., Jenkins, E. and Layton, D. (1985) *Technological Revolution? The Politics of School Science and Technology in England and Wales Since 1945*, Philadelphia, PA: Taylor and Francis Inc., and Falmer Press.

Murphy, P. (1990) 'Gender differences: implications for assessment and curriculum planning', paper presented at the BERA Symposium on Social Justice and National Curriculum, Roehampton, London, August 1990.

SEAC (1991) *The Assessment of Performance in Design and Technology*, London: SEAC.

Spear, M. (1984) 'Sex bias in teachers' ratings of work and pupils' characteristics', *European Journal of Science Education* 6: 369–77.

Walden, R. and Walkerdine, V. (1985) 'Girls and mathematics, from primary to secondary schooling', *Bedford Way Papers 24*, London: Institute of Education, University of London.

Whyte, J. (1986) *Girls into Science and Technology*, London, Boston and Henley: Routledge & Kegan Paul.

Acknowledgements

This paper is one of a set of papers from the Royal College of Art Schools Technology Project which holds the copyright. It was written for teachers writing for the project to inform their underlying philosophy. The full set of papers is available at nominal cost from the Project on 020 7590 424.

17 Raising the attainment of boys in Design and Technology

David Spendlove

Following on from the previous chapter, where the performance of girls was considered, this chapter examines boys' performance. It reflects on the success of initiatives designed to improve girls' participation and achievement, and points out that this success has led to the performance of boys being labelled as 'under achievement'. It asks what should now be done about this, something you may wish to consider, and presents questions at the end of the chapter to guide you in this.

Introduction

The short history of design and technology has been closely linked with gender issues in response to differential participation of girls and the changing examination success of girls and boys. Harding, in the previous chapter, identified that 'all three antecedents of Technology have been sex differentiated in the past. They have been the most strongly gendered of all curriculum areas'. The subject of design and technology has, however, continued to evolve from what were predominantly male dominated activities to its current position; it continues to exist uncomfortably alongside the 1944 Educational Act philosophy of 'equality of opportunity'.

Many initiatives were introduced during the 1980s which have some connection with the continuing gendered evolution of design and technology. These included the Technical Vocational Educational Initiative (TVEI), Women into Science and Engineering (WISE), Girls and Technology Education (GATE) and Girls into Science and Technology (GIST). Each maintained a gender and equal opportunities philosophy. These projects were primarily designed to encourage access and participation of girls into the traditionally male-dominated subjects of Science and Technology, with the object of increasing female participation in the secondary phase, undergraduate level courses and subsequently career choices in these areas.

The success of these interventionist programmes was variable. However, the outcomes of government legislation (Education Reform Act 1988) in establishing the General Certificate of School Education (GCSE), Ofsted and National Curriculum technology have all had a much more profound effect on increasing female participation and success in the subject.

With the establishment of compulsory Design and Technology for all Key Stages in 1994 and 1996, the outcomes have manifested girls' participation in design and technology into complete dominance of the subject, as measured by end of Key Stage teacher assessments and GCSE examinations. This pattern of success in design and technology is now replicated in virtually all GCSE subjects and has led to serious concerns within schools, with boys being labelled as 'underachievers' (Ofsted 1997, p. 9).

Politically, educationally and through the publication of 'league tables', the subject of boys' perceived underachievement has become a major concern, and many equal opportunity and gender issues that were on the agenda for the 'girl intervention programmes' are now paradoxically being re-examined from a boys' perspective. Biological, psychological, and sociological factors need to be examined. In addition, the changing nature of the subject matter, out-of-school experience, expectations, the changing role of the male in society and the nature of teaching, learning and assessment have to be re-examined.

The context of the design and technology gender gap

One conventional method of measuring school and pupil performance at GCSE level has been to count the number of students achieving five or more A* to C grades at GCSE in public examinations. This measure is used to inform the public, schools and politicians, via 'league tables', of the relative success of schools. Since this system was adopted in the late 1980s (which coincided with the introduction of GCSE), there has always been a gap in performance outcome in favour of girls over boys. However, what is now noticeable is that the gap is widening. Furthermore in Design and Technology, with schools legally obliged to offer the subject to all pupils in England at Key Stages 3 and 4, the gap is increasing significantly in favour of girls.

Prior to the Education Reform Act (1988), there was a completely different pattern of assessment. Examination was in two tiers – Certificate of Secondary Education (CSE) and General Certificate of Education (GCE) O Level. What is now recognised as design and technology was made up of a diverse range of individual subjects. Participation was clearly divided by the sexes and comparison of attainment was difficult.

The extent of the gender subject division at the start of the 1980s can be seen by examining Figure 17.1 (source: Girls And Technology Education (GATE) project at Chelsea College 1981), which illustrates the clear sex divide in subject participation at CSE level.

From Figure 17.1, it can be seen that those subjects which were to contribute to the new Design and Technology (metalwork, woodwork, technical drawing, needlework, and domestic subjects) occupy the extremes of the table. The CSE examination was specifically for lower ability pupils and the higher number of entries for these subjects at this level reflects the low academic status that these subjects had.

The GCE table for the same year (see Figure 17.2) indicates a lower number of entries for the more demanding examination. In addition, the difference in academic expectations of teachers does not appear to transcend the gender issue.

(%) Boys	(%) Girls		Total entries
0	100	Needlework	38,594
9	91	Domestic subjects	128,299
18	82	Commercial subjects	94,539
30	70	Biology	193,027
36	64	French	147,446
English 50	50	English	588,381
Art 51	49		163,597
Technical Drawing 96	4		95,983
Woodwork 98	2		61,213
Metalwork 99	1		59,702

Figure 17.1 The GATE project CSE subject breakdown

(%) Boys	(%) Girls		Total entries
0	100	Needlework	18,594
3	97	Domestic subjects	52,696
27	73	Sociology	46,210
42	56	Eng. Literature	250,493
46	54	Art	121,200
46	54	Eng. Language	500,564
49	51	History	134,977
Technical Drawing 96	4		95,983
Design and Technology 97	3		9,208
Woodwork 99	1		15,182
Metalwork 99	1		13,015

Figure 17.2 The GATE project GCE subject breakdown

There remained a clear sex division at the higher GCE O level, as Harding points out. […]

Through the establishment of a common system of examining GCSE and the introduction of National Curriculum Technology (later followed by Design and Technology), the formal legislation for addressing equal participation was put in place. Participation of girls increased significantly at all Key Stages.

The GCSE course (1988) was designed to tap a wider range of skills and attainment whilst employing a wider range of teaching styles, skills and assessment techniques. There was an increasing emphasis to be placed upon the application of knowledge through the enhanced role of coursework, and a movement away from memorising facts in response to concerns about the validity of the context of terminal examination assessment' (Gipps 1994, p. 217).

> Cresswell (1990) analysed the results from the 1989 AEB GCSE examinations in English, mathematics and science ... A clear pattern emerged from the data: girls' average coursework marks were higher than boys' in every case. In mathematics and combined science boys' marks on the other (non-coursework) components were, on average, higher than girls' marks; in English the girls' average written paper marks remained higher than the boys' average marks, although the difference was less for the coursework.
>
> (Arnot 1998, p. 37)

A consistent pattern of success for girls began to emerge during the early 1990s, although initially through the tiered examination approach (ironically a reason for moving away from the previous system). Girls were generally being entered for the middle (safer ground) tier and were consequently restricted by an attainment ceiling. 'The researchers were particularly concerned about the potential underestimation of girls' ability evidenced by their overrepresentation in the intermediate tier' (Gipps 1994, p. 224). It could therefore be argued that girls' increased success at GCSE is due to teachers gaining confidence in the placing of pupils in the correct tiers and that girls' progress in the past has merely been restricted by the lack of equal opportunities in schools. If this is true, then perhaps we are now seeing a more accurately reflective pattern of performance by both sexes.

The establishment of Ofsted and the legislative requirements of a four-year 'quality assurance' inspection cycle have monitored equal opportunities and further increased accountability. Schools and departments are expected to have equal opportunities policies in action.

> There is an increasing consciousness of differences in the educational performance of boys and girls, but in one third of schools the monitoring of progress of boys and girls is weak. Where differences of performance are identified, this information is not adequately used to review practice and inform such planning.
>
> (Ofsted 1996, p. 8)

The inspection service, although recognising the higher standards of achievement of girls, does little to advise on how to respond to this changing performance, and merely uses it as another indicator to quantify a department's achievements or weaknesses.

> In both key stages, more girls than boys achieve higher standards when working with resistant materials, textiles and food although the boys tend to do better with systems and control activities.
>
> (Ofsted 1996, p. 10)

Table 17.1 Teacher assessment for National Curriculum Design and Technology, 1997

Subject	Assessment	% achieving level 5 and above	Girls	Boys
Design and Technology	Teacher assessment	56%	64%	49%

The 1996 report was compounded by the 1997 Ofsted report, which reviewed inspections from 1993 onwards.

> Girls have increasingly made better progress and achieved higher levels of attainment than boys in all areas of D&T except systems and control. In general, girls manage their work more effectively, meet deadlines and take greater care over the quality of presentation. They frequently write at greater length, but not necessarily more analytically or creatively than boys. Few D&T departments analyse the reasons for such differences in performance, and so they have no strategies for raising standards overall.
>
> (Ofsted 1997, p. 138)

Ofsted Chief Inspector Chris Woodhead further commented on the overall issue of boys' performance: '… the failure of boys and in particular white working class boys is one of the most disturbing problems we face within the whole education system' (1994). It is interesting that Woodhead clearly saw the issue as 'the failure of boys' and not the success of girls or as a consequence of the interventionist programmes of the 1980s.

The Ofsted role in quality assessment can be considered as deriving information from subjective observations, as the criteria for examining standards in education are not sufficiently articulated or quantifiable. National Curriculum and GCSE assessments do, however, provide a quantifiable and measured outcome through testing and assessment at the end of Key Stage 3 and Key Stage 4. The National Curriculum arrangements for Design and Technology at Key Stage 3 in 1997 and 1998 were based upon teacher assessment. Table 17.1 highlights the gap in performance based upon National Curriculum criteria over Key Stage 3.

As the teacher assessments are based upon assessments over a three-year period focused on projects created by teachers, questions arise as to whether teacher assessments are biased, or whether the make-up of teachers' tasks and assignments for pupils is gender biased. In addition, is the National Curriculum gender biased/balanced?

The Consortium for Assessment and Testing in Schools suggested that 'boys appear to be slightly under-predicted in TA (teacher assessment)' (CATS 1991, p. 57). This has a significant impact on boys' attainment, as there has been a movement away from Standard Attainment Tests (SATS) which tended to appeal more to boys' abilities: '… it was acknowledged that some of the SAT's key features

Table 17.2 1999 % A–C results for Design and Technology

Boys	Girls	Difference
43%	58%	+/–15%

Table 17.3 1999 (1997 National Curriculum cohort) Design and Technology by gender entry and subject residuals

Design and Technology subject	Entry	Overall residual	Boys entry (%)	Boys residual	Girls entry (%)	Girls residual
Electronic products	17,051	–0.32	91	–0.31	9	–0.36
Engineering	3,885	–0.29	90	–0.25	10	–0.67
Systems and control	14,768	–0.41	88	–0.41	12	–0.42
Resistant materials	105,540	0.04	76	0.05	24	–0.01
Graphic products	88,582	–0.22	58	–0.31	42	–0.11
Design and technology	3,265	0.11	51	0.02	49	0.22
Food technology	101,115	0.14	26	–0.16	74	0.24
Textiles technology	41,112	0.10	5	–0.28	95	0.12

rendered the assessment tasks more accessible, and therefore more fair' (Gipps 1994, p. 208).

The implication is that the National Curriculum assessment evolved from a system based upon teacher assessment and formal SATS. Unfortunately, due to the difficulties in administering the testing, the SATs were dropped (with the exception of mathematics, English and science). Subsequently teacher assessments remained, which generally favour girls. Although this is not sufficient to explain the considerable gap in performance at Key Stage 3, it must be considered as an important factor and must be examined before further groups of boys are labelled as failures and underachievers.

If the 1997 cohort's progress is monitored through to the 1999 GCSE results (see Table 17.2), it can be seen that the gap in attainment remains consistent.

In addition, the issue of a stereotypical gender division by entry (as in 1980) is still prevalent as shown in the 1999 entries (see Table 17.3).

Table 17.3 illustrates that the subject may not have been successful in addressing gendered perceptions. Within the subject, pupils can choose which material area they wish to work in for their examination course, and there is clearly still a subject division by gender.

Conclusion

Literally millions of pounds have been spent on Design and Technology within the last decade, updating and resourcing workshops and laboratories. This has been part of the essential growth of the subject. However, comparatively little has been spent on researching the teaching and assessment processes within the subject.

This lack of research has meant that the debate about boys underachieving, assessment issues and legislative effects irrespective of gender has operated at a low level.

This chapter raises essential questions which those involved in the subject must be prepared to tackle if the subject is to continue to evolve in order to establish a subject which has equality at its core.

- Is the current gender gap in design and technology a function of an approach that is not well founded, and how desirable is it to have such a gap?
- Do National Curriculum teacher assessments need to be standardised to ensure greater accuracy of the data produced and, if so, how can this be achieved?
- Are more flexible approaches in the assessment of Design and Technology needed to avoid gender bias? If so, what form would these be in?
- Is design and technological capability currently assessed by the National Curriculum and GCSE?
- How should schools analyse the data collected from National Curriculum assessments, and how should this information be reported? In addition, how should the information be used to inform teaching methods?
- How do new educational reforms (for example Literacy Hour, National Curriculum) impact upon the progress of particular groups of pupils?
- Is the use of extended projects in Design and Technology the most effective way of gathering evidence for assessing ability, and does this method favour particular groups of pupils?
- Do self-fulfilling prophecies established through the labelling process at Key Stage 3 impact upon and transcend GCSE achievement?
- Is the existing gender entry pattern within design and technology focus areas desirable?

References

Arnot, M. and Weiner, G. (1998) *Recent Research on Gender and Educational Performance*, London: Open University.

Department of Education and Science (1989) *Task Group on Assessment and Testing – A Report*, London: DES.

Department of Education, Victoria (1998) *Gender Perspectives in Assessment and Recording*, Melbourne: Community Information Services.

Equal Opportunities Commission (1996) *The Gender Divide*, London: HMSO.

Girls And Technology Education (1981) *Objectives of Design and Technology Courses: As Expressed in Public Examination Syllabuses and Assessment*, London: CSME.

Gipps, C. and Murphy, P. (1994) *A Fair Test: Assessment, Achievement and Equity*, Buckinghamshire: Open University Press.

Grant, M. (1983) *The What, Why and How of GATE (Girls And Technology Education)*, Chelsea College: Centre for Science and Mathematics Education.

Hutchinson, D. and Schagen, I. (1994) *How Reliable is National Curriculum Assessment?*, Berkshire: NFER.

Ofsted (1996) *Subject and Standards. Issues for School Development Arising from Ofsted Inspections 1994–1995*, London: HMSO.

Ofsted (1997) *Secondary Education 1993–1997: A Review of Secondary Schools in England*, London: HMSO.

18 Learning in and for community

Values in Design and Technology

Ruth Conway

There is now a recognition that the designing and making of products and systems has an impact on society, sometimes in positive ways and sometimes in negative ways. What is valued in technology can be thought to reflect dominant values. This chapter argues for a more explicit and open discussion of these values in Design and Technology education, and should help you to think about how you can introduce values into your own teaching, and make explicit the ones already there. It should be noted, however, that the role of education is to encourage pupils to develop values for themselves, not just taking on uncritically those of others.

The aims of technology education

At the start of her Massey Lectures, Ursula Franklin spoke of technology as having 'built the house in which we all live' and of the house 'continually being extended and remodelled' (Franklin 1992: 11). The quality of life of the many and diverse human communities within its walls, even the very survival of life itself, depends on the priorities shaping the design of this technological home. 'To improve the quality of life now without damaging the planet for the future' requires priorities rooted in such values and attitudes as an 'appreciation of all living things, their needs and interrelationships'; 'concern for social justice globally' and recognition 'of the need to develop lifestyles which respect resource and carrying capacity limits' (Panel for Education for Sustainable Development 1998: 3, 5, 6).

> Technology based on the simplistic change-equals-growth-equals-progress paradigm constituted 'a reckless incursion into the future.' ... It must be a spur to a different way of using knowledge as wisdom and to seeing our sojourn here as a trusteeship – a cooperative and constructive endeavour rather than a competitive struggle. It goes to the heart of how we see ourselves and, therefore, of how we should educate our children.
>
> (Tomlinson 1990: 16)

Or, as Bryan Chapman has expressed it: 'Do we really want to educate young people so that they can deploy their technological skills on the trivia of affluence? ... Or do we want to educate them for a world in which, if they do become technologists, their science and technology will be directed to attempting to ensure the survival of Planet Earth?' (1991: 58). Granted these are broad-brush, even rhetorical, questions, but the answers shape the type of technology curriculum that will be developed. For instance, in adult life, 'cooperative and constructive endeavour' aimed at ensuring 'the survival of Planet Earth' must involve dialogue between experts and users. This requires respect for different experiences, a readiness to debate conflicting perspectives and values, and an acceptance of responsibility for the community as a whole and its wider interactive relationships. People are totally unprepared for such participation in decision-making if their education gave them no experience of probing the social, environmental, moral and spiritual issues associated with technological products and processes, and of making carefully considered value judgments.

In recent years, technology education has become an important part of general education in many countries. 'Well beyond what might be achieved through traditional technical courses ... [there is] wide recognition that enabling pupils to make sense of technology should be one of the major priorities of the curriculum of the future' (Barnett 1994: 52). The World Council of Associations for Technology Education (WOCATE) includes in its mission statement the intention to focus international efforts toward 'recognition of the diverse and lifelong nature of Technology Education and the importance of the complex interactions between technological, social, and natural environments' (1993: 10). Its founding conference also declared:

> The quality of life afforded by a society is directly related to the extent to which its peoples understand, effectively use, and develop technologies.
> Technology education develops critical survival skills for citizens in a society dominated by change.
>
> (1993: 14)

How such declarations translate into a technology curriculum is itself the result of complex interactions between economic, political, social, and environmental concerns, and ultimately the worldwide views of curriculum developers. 'Traditionally, technology courses have concentrated on technique, on questions of *how*, but goals of technological literacy require serious consideration of purposes and outcomes – questions of *why*, and *with what result*' (Barnett 1994: 53). As a follow-up to the World Conference on Education for All in 1990, UNESCO organized a large-scale project, '2000+: Scientific and Technological Literacy for All,' which addressed the question, 'What kinds of educational provisions and teaching are needed to ensure scientific and technological literacy for all, which in one extreme set of circumstances may be a requirement for survival, and in another for national economic development which does not jeopardise environmental quality?' (Layton 1993b: 16). One of the emerging issues was the social shaping of school technology. Taking the case of the technology curriculum in England, David Layton identified a number of stakeholders:

- *Economic functionalists* who insist that school technology should lay the foundations of knowledge and skills for future training, especially in relation to intermediate vocational qualifications;

  voc

- *Professional technologists* who think that school technology should be char- acterized by rigour, working to industrial standards of quality, and the acquisition of knowledge in mainstream engineering areas;

  Engineer

- *Sustainable developers* who emphasize that school technology should empower people with the knowledge, skills, and values to undertake and control technological developments which achieve an acceptable quality of life not only for us, but for succeeding generations, North and South;

  sustain.
  tech.

- *Women* who urge that school technology should enable girls to define tech- nological challenges, and respond to them, on their own terms, so counter- ing gender biases incorporated in present-day representations of technology;

  gender

- *Liberal educators* who are concerned that school technology should initiate children into the unique cognitive mode of technology and help them to construct and control this symbolic world.

  broad –
  & symbolic

(Layton 1993b: 18)

The outcome of the debate among these value positions affects the skills, knowl- edge, perceptions, and attitudes that are actually taught and encouraged in schools. It affects, for example, the breadth of understanding of what constitutes 'technological capability', the messages about technology conveyed in the attitudes of the teachers, the choice of products made or evaluated, the constraints that are taken into account, the criteria that are used for evaluation, the extent to which fitness *of* purpose is considered as well as fitness *for* purpose. ...

Educating for responsibility

One focus of the debate is the responsibilities that are to be taught and learned, bearing in mind that 'technology curricula need to be realistic in reflecting the real world of technological activity, and feasible in terms of pupil characteristics and the nature of the school context' (Medway 1993: 29). Barnett gives an example:

> If the responsibility of the designer is to be taught, what degree of 'realism' should be striven for? In the real world of technology, to whom and for what is the designer responsible? – to mankind in general for the future of the planet, or to a line manager for the efficiency of a sub-system meeting the specific technical requirements of a tightly-drawn design brief? As a rule, the autonomy and discretion of designers is strictly limited ... Should the tech- nology curriculum mirror the circumscribed reality of designer-as-technician or attempt to pre-figure alternative, value-sensitive practices in which wider responsibilities are acknowledged?
>
> (Barnett 1994: 56)

Is realism to be equated with 'industrial design activity that is not driven by necessity as much as commercial opportunity' (Bozeat 1996) or with an assessment of the pressing needs of people and the natural environment? A group of eight Quaker schools in England felt that they were faced with a foregone conclusion in favour of the former by draft proposals for assessment criteria for public examinations in technology:

> The proposals would not encourage any pupil to take the needs of the poor seriously, let alone recognize the impressive technical achievements of the third world. There would be no incentive to consider such issues as the supply of fresh water or the unnecessary promotion of baby food mixes in developing countries. Intermediate or appropriate technology was not mentioned. Nor were alternative modes of production. The document seemed to take for granted a whole bundle of assumptions concerning the nature and purpose of design and technological activity ... that it should be high tech, profit orientated, capitalist in inspiration.
>
> (Pitt 1991: 34)

One of those schools, the Mount School in York, then developed, and put into practice through the projects undertaken by the pupils, a design and technology curriculum aimed at 'equipping pupils to become active collaborators in the creation of a more peaceful, just, and sustainable society' (Pitt 1991: 34). Their stated aims list widely recognized facets of technological capability – identifying areas of human need, generating design proposals, making artefacts or systems, and appraising processes and outcomes of technological activity – but add the explicit intention of enabling and encouraging the pupils:

- to deepen their concern for the poor and those at the margins of society (both locally and internationally);
- to deepen their awareness of the need to look after the earth's resources and ecosystem;
- to challenge racial and gender stereotyping;
- to develop respect for others, and the skills necessary to work in groups (including the ability to be self-critical and to accept criticism from others).

(Pitt 1991: 35)

There is an underlying assumption here that education for responsible participation in a rapidly changing technological world depends not so much on the 'realism' of exact replication of industrial techniques and constraints, but on developing the skills needed to explore the full human and environmental context of any project and to reflect critically on its purpose and outcome. The need is not for training in order to be a compliant operator in production for a consumer market, but for education that gives a person confidence to pay careful and compassionate attention to those who might be implicated, to weigh responsibly any conflict of interests, and to make explicit the basis on which they are making the necessary value judgments. The priority is not learning a fixed body of knowledge and skills, but learning how to use that knowledge and those skills to respond to the needs of the community with sensitivity, imagination and courage.

Designing for quality

The current National Curriculum in England states:

> Teaching should ensure that knowledge and understanding are applied when developing ideas, planning, producing products and evaluating them.
>
> (DfEE/QCA 1999: 137)

At Key Stage 3 this includes the ability to identify and use criteria that help pupils judge the quality of products, including

(a) the extent to which they meet a clear need;
(b) their fitness for purpose;
(c) whether resources have been used appropriately;
(d) their impact beyond the purpose for which they were designed.

Examples are given for this final point; they include 'the global environmental impact of products and assessment for sustainability'.

This invites an understanding of quality that includes far more than appearance and function. Espousing technical and aesthetic values is not enough; judgment of quality requires exploration of a product's implications and impact. Such a definition opens up the possibility of encouraging pupils to use criteria such as those drawn up by the Mount School:

1   How does it (both process and product) serve to satisfy the real needs of those at the bottom of society, immediately and in the long term, locally and globally?
2   What is the ecological impact?
3   Is it enabling in its process as well as its product? Or are people alienated, bored, stupefied?
4   Does it (both process and product) serve to hide or highlight relationships of domination and oppression within society? In particular, does it challenge sexist and consumerist assumptions?
5   How does it allow for or encourage participation among consumers and others affected?
6   Is it durable and easily reparable?
7   Is it comprehensible to the nonspecialist?
8   Is it reversible or modifiable if seen to be in need of improvement?
9   Is it necessary at all?

(Pitt 1991: 35)

The last criterion forces consideration not just of fitness *for* purpose, but of fitness *of* the purpose. This in turn requires a technology education that allows reflection on fundamental beliefs and values:

> Antipersonnel mines score highly on fitness for purpose and affordability, but their effect on environment and quality of life is (intentionally) disastrous. Should they therefore be classed as good or poor quality products?
> It is only within a framework which highlights questions of value that the complex and potentially contradictory nature of the notion of a 'quality product' can be explored. An approach which is value-purblind will seek to ignore these contradictions, but once words such as 'quality' are deployed with the intention that they should mean something more than 'well-crafted,' then it is difficult to force the genie of values back into the bottle of 'fitness for purpose'.
>
> (Barnett 1994: 57)

Taking military technology as an acute case of dissociating quality of design from fitness of the purpose, Barnett faces the question as to whether technology education should realistically prepare young people for 'the unacknowledged contract of employment that involves the sale of conscience along with labour':

> A truthful reflection of the real world of technology would acknowledge that many people, whether or not by unfettered choice, get their livings in the process of devising and fashioning engines of death, and that much money, material, and ingenuity is thereby expended. An idealistic, forward-looking curriculum, *critically* aware of what is, and concerned with what *ought* to be, might wish to promote the view that it should neither be, nor seem, 'normal' for this to be the case.
>
> (Barnett 1994: 59)

Technology is the context

'Social purposes are lived out *through* technology – technology embodies the purposes and constitutes our lives' (Olson 1993: 2). It is therefore not enough to ensure that a technological activity or product is examined in its context, exposing the human and environmental implications and even asking questions about its purpose: it has to be acknowledged that technologies are the context. Technology is itself shaping the value judgments we are making about it. This is the power technology exercises over us. Living *in* and acting *on* the world cannot be separated. If by default or lack of more fundamental sources of inspiration and commitment we let the technological environment dominate our experience, then technology will itself become the guiding force for action.

It is for this reason above all that 'there is a need to bring values up into the light of day in the teaching and learning of design and technology; to categorize them and make them the subject of deliberation and critical reflection between pupils and between pupils and teachers' (Layton 1992: 53). It is also the reason why

Layton includes in his list of functional competencies to be taught through the technology curriculum that of 'technological evaluation or *critic competence*':

> The ability to judge the worth of a technological development in the light of personal values and to step outside the 'mental set' to evaluate what it is doing to us (e.g., it might be encouraging a view of social problems in terms of a succession of 'technological fixes' rather than more fundamental considerations).
>
> (Layton 1993a: 61)

Critic competence is the kingpin of technology education. Without it, there is a slide into trivialization, giving young people skills but no confidence in putting those skills to worthwhile and responsible use, and no awareness of the enticing but shallow foundations that technology itself is building into 'the house in which we all live'.

Educating the educators

If technology education is indeed to help young people develop skills of critical reflection on 'what is' and on 'what ought to be', and if it is to prepare them for effective participation in and for communities that are heavily influenced by technology, it will depend above all on the attitude and approach of teachers who have themselves first reflected on the '*why, and with what result*'. If critic competence is to be taught, it must first be learned.

This is not to deny the importance of dealing with the technical questions of *how*. A major focus in the training of technology teachers must be specialist knowledge and skills, both those generic to all technological activity (e.g., problem-solving procedures, feedback mechanisms) and those that are specific to a particular branch of technology such as mechanical engineering, textiles, electronics, food technology, graphics, biotechnology. There must also be a focus on the pedagogy, on how teachers can convey their skills, knowledge, understanding and enthusiasm in a way that releases and develops their pupils' capability, creativity, and ability to work constructively with others. But technology teachers have to be weaned away from the easy route of isolating products from the complexities of their context, relying on specialist expertise and teaching as if technology is value-free. They 'need encouragement to include reflection on moral values, and social relations reified in technical objects' (Hansen and Olson 1993: 7). They also have to acknowledge that 'technical ways of knowing and acting do not provide the tools for analysing the moral value of technical systems' (Olson 1993: 2). Along with all other teachers, they will need to ground their teaching in an honest reflection on their own beliefs and convictions and be ready to learn how 'to live on the edge and to deal with uncertainties' (Riggs 1996: 8):

> 'Good' teacher education necessarily implies enabling future teachers to think about and justify what they will be doing as teachers in terms of fundamental beliefs about humans, society, nature, knowledge, and ethics. This is essential

if they are to be autonomous in the sense of being able to take responsibility for their actions as teachers.

(Bearlin 1987: 2)

In the United Kingdom there have been a number of initiatives to 'ensure that adequate consideration is given to value judgments in design and technology and the beliefs that underpin the value judgments; and to promote appropriate classroom strategies for this' (DATA 1997: 2). These initiatives share Barnett's conclusion:

> If we accept the 'must do better (or else)' verdict on the human technological record, then technology education needs a significant focus on what might be. The role of *critique*, i.e., critical analysis with a view to informing better practice, must be acknowledged … The key question, however, in view of all the possibilities which [new technologies] may open up, is 'what is worth doing?' Many things are *possible*, but what is *worthwhile*? Who shall decide what is worthwhile, and on what criteria?
>
> (Barnett 1994: 62)

Glenda Prime, of the faculty of education of the University of the West Indies, offered an approach to this key question at the time of the founding of WOCATE:

> It is probably true that the Caribbean and other 'developing' countries have a unique contribution to make to world thinking about technology education. For in the majority world, where unemployment and underemployment are rife, where large numbers of people exist on subsistence farming, and where capital for large scale investment is scarce, we will be forced to see technology education from an entirely different perspective from the one which is seen in industrialized nations. We will have to strip it bare of its 'high-tech' trappings and see its true role as the empowerment of all our people to improve their own lives, through self-reliance and interdependence and through the enhancement of social and international relationships – a role that is perhaps equally applicable to all nations but is often under-emphasized where survival needs are not so glaring. The Caribbean contribution can be the placing of this aspect of technology education in center stage.
>
> (WOCATE 1993: supplement)

Prime here judges 'worthwhile' by the criteria of social justice, empowerment, interdependence, and the enhancement of relationships. One cannot overestimate, however, the changes of heart that are needed if these are to become the dominant emphases! Much more prevalent is the 'impulse to go on inventing, developing, and producing regardless of society's needs' (Picey 1983: 171). Furthermore, as already noted, technology teachers often find it difficult to acknowledge that they are handling more than a purely technical subject, one in which 'the most fundamental choices are between attitudes in mind' (1983: 169); nor do they find it easy to open up issues that might have life-changing consequences. But if sights are to be set on 'justice, peace, and the integrity of creation' (to use the motto launched in 1983 by the Sixth Assembly of the World Council of Churches), a technology education is needed that will stimulate, rather than stifle, thoughtful debates on priorities, on what ought to be developed and for what purpose – an education that opens hearts and minds to expectations and commitments that are ultimately of far greater significance than those generated from within technology itself.

References

Barnett, M. (1994) 'Designing the future? Technology, values, and choice', *International Journal of Technology and Design Education* 4(1): 51–63.

Bearlin, M. L. (1987) 'Feminist critiques of science: implications for teacher education', paper presented at GASAT 4 Conference. Gender and Science and Technology Association, c/o Dr J. Harding, 6, Ullswater Grove, Alresford, Hants SO24 9NP, UK.

Bozeat, R. (1996) 'Developing an appreciation of our technological heritage through education and interactive multimedia', paper presented at JISTEC '96. Jerusalem International Science and Technology Conference 1996.

Chapman, B. (1991) 'The overselling of science education in the eighties', *School Science Review* 72(260): 47–63.

DATA Guidance Notes (1997) *Exploring Value Judgements in Design and Technology*, Wellesbourne: The Design and Technology Association.

DfEE/QCA (1999) *The National Curriculum Handbook for Secondary Teachers in England*, London: DfEE/QCA.

Franklin, U. (1985) *Will Women Change Technology or Will Technology Change Women?*, Toronto, Ontario: ICREF/CRIAWI.

Franklin, U. (1992) *The Real World of Technology*, Toronto, Ontario: Anansi Press.

Hansen, K-H. and Olson, J. (1993) Rethinking Technology in Education: An Action Research Approach. Unpublished project proposal, Ontario: Mathematics, Science, and Technology Education Group, Queens University.

Layton, D. (1992) 'Values in Design and Technology', in C. Budgett-Meakin (ed.) *Make the Future Work. Appropriate Technology: A Teachers' Guide*, Harlow: Longman Group UK for Intermediate Technology.

Layton, D. (1993a) *Technology's Challenge to Science Education*, Buckingham, UK, Bristol, PA: Open University Press.

Layton, D. (1993b) 'Design and Technology in schools: a comparative view', *Design & Technology Teaching* 25(2): 16–20.

Medway, P. (1993) 'Issues in the theory and practice of technology education', in E. W. Jenkins (ed.) *School Science and Technology: Some Issues and Perspectives*, Leeds, UK: Centre for Studies in Science and Mathematics Education.

Olson, J. (1993) 'Technology as social context', unpublished paper for workshop, 'Exploring the Relationship of Science, Technology, and Society in Education', IPN, Kiel.

Pacey, A. (1983) *The Culture of Technology*, Cambridge: Massachusetts Institute of Technology Press.

Panel for Education for Sustainable Development (1998) 'Education for Sustainable Development in the Schools Sector. A Report to DfEE/QCA 14 September 1998', Reading: Council for Environment Education, Development Education Association, RSPB and WWF-UK.

Pitt, J. (1991) 'Design and Technology and social responsibility', *Design and Technology Teaching* 24(1): 34–36.

Riggs, A. (1996). 'Beliefs, values, science, and technology education', paper given at Morals for the Millennium Conference, University College of St. Martin, Lancaster, UK.

Tomlinson, J. (1990) 'New visions for old', *Times Educational Supplement*, 5 January 1990.

WOCATE (World Council of Associations for Technology Education) (1993) *Newsletter* 1: 1.

19 Citizenship and Design and Technology

Gwyneth Owen-Jackson

This chapter explores what is meant by 'citizenship' and how this might be implemented in schools. It then considers how Design and Technology, which is intended to prepare pupils for 'tomorrow's society', can contribute to citizenship education. Examples are given from different areas of Design and Technology to show how elements of citizenship can be incorporated into the teaching of the subject. It is hoped that these will encourage you to see how your own practice can be expanded and enhanced by embracing these new ideas.

Introduction

You will now be aware, having read other chapters in this book, that Design and Technology is relatively new to the school curriculum in Britain and is just beginning to establish its identity and become known and understood.

Citizenship is an even more recent newcomer. It was first introduced into the curriculum in England with the 2000 National Curriculum, becoming compulsory in secondary schools in September 2002. In Wales, citizenship education is taught through Education for Community Understanding, and in Northern Ireland through two cross-curricular themes, Education for Mutual Understanding and Education for Cultural Heritage. Elsewhere, citizenship may be taught through cross-curricular themes with alternative names, or there may a subject called 'Civics' on the curriculum, which will contain elements of citizenship.

What is citizenship?

Citizenship is a concept that is not easy to define and is described by Maiteny and Wade (1999) as 'problematic', and by Kerr (1999) as 'a contested concept'. Kerr writes that 'citizenship education is concerned with young people's understanding of society and, in particular, with influencing what pupils learn and understand about the social world' (1999: 1). The reason he describes it as a contested concept is because there are 'differing views about the function and organisation of society' (1999: 3). Also, the views of society will vary over time and will be dependent on those with political and social dominance. For Maiteny and Wade it is problematic because they believe that pupils can be taught about the structures and processes within an organized society, but that it is more difficult to teach them 'to understand what it means to be a citizen and to develop the skills needed for active citizenship and to exert pressure for change' (1999: 37).

In many ways citizenship has a similar history to that of Design and Technology. It has never existed in its present form in the English school curriculum, but it does have antecedents rooted in other subjects. Fogelman (1997) offers some evidence of history in quoting Batho (1990), who described 'the teaching of civics and citizenship since Victorian times', and others (see Edwards and Fogelman 1991), but I think we can take it that citizenship in its present form is quite new.

So why do we have citizenship education on the agenda now? Kerr identifies the concerns of many when he says that 'there are still concerns about issues of national identity; social cohesion and diversity; national culture' (1999: 21). He goes on to say that there has been a particular concern about 'growing apathy toward the formal political process' (1999: 22) and cites other research (Crewe *et al.* 1996; Phillips 1997; Arnot *et al.* 1996) which has 'concluded that there is a perceptible decline in civic culture in English society and a marked absence of a political and moral discourse in public life'.

If citizenship is taken to refer to educating pupils about 'society' and preparing them to participate in that society, then aspects of this would previously have been found in various areas of the curriculum: in history, through its teaching of social and political history; in geography, in teaching about how societies develop; in extra-curricular activities such as charity projects and community projects. Pupils would also learn something about society from how the school is structured and organized, for example, whether or not there are school councils, how school rules are devised, how miscreants are dealt with. Fogelman (1997) agrees with this broader picture, and states that 'any discussion of citizenship education rapidly identifies that it is not solely a question of curriculum content and organisation', but that it also includes the ethos of the school, values and teaching styles.

In the current National Curriculum in England, however, there is a specific subject called 'Citizenship', which is defined through the learning outcomes described in the document.

Citizenship in the National Curriculum

The idea of this new subject was first broadcast in 1997 when the Secretary of State for Education and Employment stated the aim 'to strengthen education for citizenship and the teaching of democracy in schools' (DfEE/QCA 1998: 4). He then set up an Advisory Group to produce a framework for citizenship education in schools. The final report of the Advisory Group was published in 1998 and became part of the proposals for the 2000 National Curriculum. In order to give schools time to plan and prepare, the proposals were not made a compulsory part of the curriculum until 2002.

Citizenship education is described as having three strands – social and moral responsibility; community involvement and political literacy – and is said to involve not only knowledge and understanding but also values and skills.

The aims and purposes of citizenship education were described in the Final Report as:

> To make secure and to increase the knowledge, skills and values relevant to the nature of practices of participative democracy; also to enhance the awareness of rights and duties, and the sense of responsibilities needed for the development of pupils into active citizens; and in so doing to establish the value to individuals, schools and society of involvement in the local and wider community.
>
> Democratic institutions, practices and purposes must be understood, both local and national, including the work of parliaments, councils, parties, pressure groups and voluntary bodies; to show how formal political activity relates to civil society in the context of the United Kingdom and Europe, and to cultivate awareness and concern for world affairs and global issues. Some understanding of the realities of economic life is needed including how taxation and public expenditure work together.
>
> (DfEE/QCA 1998: 40)

The report goes on to describe the 'essential elements' of the subject, which are: concepts; (appropriate) values and dispositions; (appropriate) skills and aptitudes; and knowledge and understanding. Learning outcomes are then listed in relation to the elements of skills and aptitudes and knowledge and understanding.

Teaching citizenship

The National Curriculum does not dictate to schools how citizenship is to be taught. Some schools will make a 'slot' for it on the timetable and will have teachers teaching schemes of work for a dedicated syllabus. In some schools the role of pastoral staff will be vital in teaching, or coordinating, the teaching of citizenship. The form tutor may be involved in teaching sessions, or pastoral staff may be involved in teaching personal and social education which will cover elements of citizenship. The Final Report (DfEE/QCA 1998) does suggest, however, that schools may choose to combine elements of citizenship within other subjects, and some will choose to adopt this approach. The initial guidance offered to schools (QCA 2000) is more explicit in suggesting how links may be made with other subjects, including Design and Technology.

This guidance also suggests that some citizenship education might occur through the teaching strategies adopted, as well as through the actual content. Strategies suggested as suitable include the use of research activities, group work and discussion, simulation and action.

Citizenship and Design and Technology

The National Curriculum for England includes a statement on the importance of Design and Technology which includes the following elements:

[pupils] learn to think and intervene creatively to improve quality of life
pupils ... become autonomous and creative problem solvers, as individuals
and members of a team
they combine practical skills with understanding
they reflect on and evaluate ...

(DfEE/QCA 1999: 134)

The National Curriculum in Wales includes common requirements which
teachers should cover through the teaching of their subject. One of the common
requirements is 'Curriculum Cymreig' which states that:

Pupils should be given opportunities, where appropriate, in their study of design and technology to develop and apply knowledge and understanding of the
cultural, economic, environmental, historical and linguistic characteristics of
Wales.

(ACCAC 2000: 5)

In Northern Ireland, the National Curriculum gives examples of how technology and design can contribute to the cross-curricular theme of Education for
Mutual Understanding/Cultural Heritage (EMU) through:

- co-operative working
- evaluating the impact of technology in modern times
- considering the influence of technology upon modern culture and in other
  cultures, and the positive and negative implications ... on society, the
  economy and the environment.

(DENI 2000: 4)

Technology and design can also contribute to the cross-curricular theme of Economic Awareness in Northern Ireland through considering the economics of
production.
   All of these tie in well with the essential elements described in citizenship, in
which pupils should:

recognise, reflect and act upon ... values and dispositions ... in particular
those which underlie their attitudes and actions as individuals and as members
of groups or communities
[pupils should have] positive attitudes to themselves, as individuals, and in
their relationships with others
[pupils should] think critically, develop their own ideas, ... recognise the contribution of others
[develop knowledge in relation to] environmental and sustainable
development

(DfEE/QCA 1998: 41–2)

In citizenship, pupils should discuss social and cultural issues, problems and events and identify the role that various institutions have in influencing their lives and communities. They should be 'actively involved in the life of their school, neighbourhood and wider communities' (DfEE/QCA 1999: 184). The programme of study states that they should be taught 'the need for mutual respect and understanding' of different groups in society, and 'the work of community-based, national and international voluntary groups'. They should develop skills of enquiry and communication, analyse information about social and cultural issues, and contribute to group and class discussions. They should also be taught to 'use their imagination to consider other people's experiences'. In addition, at Key Stage 4, there is a requirement for pupils to be taught 'how the economy functions, including the role of business and financial services' and the 'rights and responsibilities of consumers'.

Surprisingly, although the English National Curriculum indicates where citizenship may have links with other subjects, such as English, Science, Mathematics, Art and Design, Music and Geography, it does not suggest links with Design and Technology. Yet, looking at the Programmes of Study, it is easy to see how elements of citizenship may occur naturally within Design and Technology lessons, where pupils are often required to engage with social and cultural issues and problems.

QCA guidance on the teaching of citizenship does, however, suggest that Design and Technology can contribute in the areas of: 'appropriate use of resources; the global, environmental impact of products; assessment for sustainability' (QCA 2000: 14). The Programmes of Study for Design and Technology illustrate further possibilities for links, in that they require pupils to undertake research, consider a range of issues including the needs of users, generate ideas, prioritize actions, reconcile decisions, evaluate and take account of environmental impact, sustainability and economic factors. Pupils should also work both individually and in groups. Maiteny and Wade (1999: 41) describe citizenship education as 'developing awareness of our social, economic and ecological impacts'. There are many ways in which the requirements of the Programmes of Study for Design and Technology and Citizenship can be met through pupils analysing, designing and making products.

Much work in Design and Technology is based on pupils analysing products to identify their strengths and weaknesses in many aspects, including their costs and benefits in broad terms such as how their production and use might impact on the environment. When researching, prior to design, pupils could be asked to research materials that they might use; for example, in textiles they could research new fabrics made from recycled materials. When considering users of products, projects could be developed which take account of those with special needs, for example physical disabilities, in resistant materials or systems and control projects, or special dietary requirements in food technology. Pupils could be asked to consider the environmental impact of products, their materials, manufacturing processes or packaging. All of these could take place within the natural teaching of the subject,

Implementation of Citizenship in D&T Research

and are not specially devised extras, although they may require careful thinking through of tasks and assignments.

The QCA guidance suggests that pupils participate in local communities, whilst the Key Stage 4 Programme of Study for Design and Technology in England requires pupils to take part in design-and-make projects of their own interest and linked to the community (pupils in Wales are not required to study Design and Technology at Key Stage 4, but may elect to do so). As Maiteny and Wade point out, young people may not participate in formal structures but they may do so in others, for example environmental protest groups, and citizenship education 'must allow for more pupil involvement in the institutions of greatest relevance to them (1999: 41). Cogan and Derricott (2000: 176) also state that 'one of the major stated reasons by youth for their lack of interest in civic and public issues is that in their school learning the relevance of in-school work is never brought to bear upon the real issues of the day in their own communities'. In Design and Technology, this interest could be harnessed into a purposeful and meaningful project for the pupil, which may also have benefit to the local community, so meeting the needs of citizenship education within good Design and Technology teaching.

Citizenship is concerned not only with the local and national communities in which pupils live, but also with the global community. Again, it is not difficult to see how Design and Technology can contribute to this. Any material area can discuss the source of raw materials – wood from South American rainforests, food products transported across the globe – and the effect of this on distant communities. They can discuss the positive and negative effects of changes to sources of raw materials, inventions of new materials, changes to production processes or the location of these, and changes in consumer preferences and purchases. Examples of this include the change Marks and Spencer's made in sourcing their textiles products from British companies to foreign ones; the effect of Sony moving to South Wales; the impact of Fairtrade products becoming more readily available.

The previous chapter might provide other ideas for linking Design and Technology teaching with social and cultural issues and there are resource materials available which offer further examples and ideas. One such resource is 'Looking at values through products and applications' (DfEE 1995), which lists values that might be considered, questions that might be asked and gives case studies of products that could be evaluated. Nuffield materials include the idea of considering 'winners and losers' when developing products, who benefits from the idea and who loses. The Intermediate Technology Development Group has a range of materials which provide information about developing countries, and suggestions for how these could be incorporated into teaching. The idea behind all of these is not necessarily to impart particular values or attitudes to pupils, but to encourage pupils to think about these issues, become informed, make their own decisions and develop their own values.

In addition, it was mentioned earlier that teaching strategies can be used to demonstrate elements of citizenship. The strategies given as examples, such as research, group work and discussion, simulation activities and practical activities are regularly used in Design and Technology; in fact they are an intrinsic part of the subject.

These links between Citizenship and Design and Technology will not occur without some careful planning by design and technology teachers. Thought will have to be given to how tasks and assignments can be presented to cover these areas, for example, planning projects which include local social issues such as the needs of the elderly, or young children. This will be particularly important in Wales, where teachers are required to provide opportunities for pupils to meet the common requirements of Curriculum Cymreig, and in Northern Ireland where they should have opportunities to cover the requirements of EMU. Pupils themselves could be asked to identify needs within their local community. Local groups and voluntary groups could be invited in to talk to pupils; in fact the Final Report on citizenship suggests that there should be 'active contributions' from the local community (DfEE/QCA 1998: 26). Pupils could explore the local community from the perspective of a disabled person and identify areas where improvements could be made. When products are designed and made it could be an essential part of the assignment that the marketing of the product is considered, so teaching about the business side of industrial practice. This will not be an easy task for teachers but one that may be worthwhile in the long run. (Teachers will also need to be mindful of the statutory responsibility in the 1986 Education Reform Act to be even-handed when dealing with controversial issues. They will need to be confident in handling difficult discussions and sensitive to pupils' needs.)

Conclusion

Citizenship is an important subject on the curriculum, serving both personal and social goals for pupils, but it will not have the required effect if pupils perceive it as something separate from their own lives and interests. Design and Technology can help to bridge that gap. Design and Technology has a body of knowledge and skills which pupils can learn, but these too need to be put into a meaningful context if they are to have any relevance for learners. Design and Technology, by its very nature, should be contemporary, aware of current interests and issues and responding to them. It is an active subject: pupils have to *do* as well as know; they have to be actively involved in their learning.

An advantage to Design and Technology of emphasizing its links to citizenship is that it can show itself to be a part of pupils' general education, rather than be valued for its instrumental or vocational benefits. It can show the value of educating pupils to think about where products come from, what they are made from, how they are made, and the impact of their decisions as consumers.

I am not suggesting that Citizenship and Design and Technology are one and the same thing; they clearly are not and there are areas within each of them which are not relevant to the other. What I am suggesting, though, is that there are valid areas of overlap, in which Design and Technology can make a worthwhile contribution to citizenship education, for the benefit of all concerned.

References

ACCAC (2000) *National Curriculum for Design and Technology*, Cardiff: ACCAC.

Arnot, M., Araujo, H., Deliyanni-Kouimtzi, K., Rowe, G. and Tome, A. (1996) 'Teachers, gender and discourses of citizenship', *International Studies in the Sociology of Education* 6(1): 3-35.

Batho, G. (1990) 'The history of the teaching of civics and citizenship in English schools', *Curriculum Journal* 1(1): 91-100.

Cogan, J. J. and Derricott, R. (2000) *Citizenship for the 21st Century: An International Perspective on Education*, London: Kogan Page.

Crewe, I., Searing, D. and Conover, P. (1996) 'Aspects of citizenship in Britain and the United States: a comparative study', Brentwood: University of Essex.

DENI (1999) *Programmes of Study for Technology and Design*, DENI.

DfEE (1995) *Looking at values through products and applications*, London: DfEE.

DfEE/QCA (1998) *Education for Citizenship and the Teaching of Democracy in Schools: Final Report of the Advisory Group on Citizenship 22 September 1998*, London: QCA.

Edwards, J. and Fogelman, K. (1991) 'Active citizenship and young people', in K. Fogelman (ed.) *Citizenship in Schools*, London: David Fulton.

Fogelman, K. (1997) 'Citizenship education' in J. Bynner, L. Chisholm and A. Furlong, (eds) *Youth, Citizenship and Social Change in a European Context*, Aldershot: Ashgate.

Kerr, D. (1999) *Re-examining Citizenship Education: The Case of England*, Slough: NFER.

Maiteny, P. and Wade, R. (1999) 'Citizenship education', in S. Bigger and E. Brown (eds) *Spiritual, Moral, Social and Cultural Education: Exploring Values in the Curriculum*, London: David Fulton.

Phillips, P. (1997) 'Citizenship and civic education: colloquium on education and citizenship', Citizenship Foundation: London.

QCA (2000) *Citizenship at Key Stages 3 and 4: Initial Guidance for Schools*, London: QCA.

20 'Employability skills'

The contribution made by making activities

Richard Tufnell, John Cave and John Neale

Mainly because of its history, Design and Technology is often perceived as being a vocationally-based subject. Whether you support that view or not, Design and Technology – like all other subjects – must take responsibility for preparing pupils for life after school. For most pupils this means employment, and so some thought needs to be given as to how to best prepare pupils for the world of work. This chapter considers the contribution that Design and Technology makes to this.

The chapter is an edited version of a paper presented at IDATER 98 and develops earlier work carried out by the authors. The work reported here was presented in a final report, Learning through making – executive summary *(The Crafts Council 1998).*

This chapter draws on the findings of a research project, funded by the Crafts Council 'Learning through Making' project and the Technology Enhancement Programme, into the competencies and capabilities which young people develop by being involved in making activities.

Employers' views were elicited via a structured interview using a variety of techniques. Forty employers took part in the process with 21 per cent coming from the manufacturing sector, 47 per cent from the service sector and 17 per cent from the public sector. Interviews were undertaken with senior staff with responsibility for staff recruitment, who at the time of the interviews were unaware of the focus of the research.

Central to the research was the exploration of the extent to which young people develop generic 'employability skills' by involvement in making activities. The first phase of this research established that teachers of making believe this to be the case and this conclusion was echoed by the Chief Executive of SCAA, Dr Nicholas Tate, who commented on:

> ... the skills for employability it (design and technology) promotes.

> (Tate 1996)

In recognising the value of practical activity in developing these skills he also made the following observation:

> At the moment it may be that design and technology is bearing too great a

burden of responsibility for developing skills that need to be curriculum-wide and not the preserve of a single subject.

A clear indication that the development of 'employability skills' is now seen as an essential aspect of statutory education. This view supports the importance of this research in assisting those involved in making activities by demonstrating its value and how their contribution can be enhanced.

The concept of 'employability skills' is a relatively novel one which has emerged because of the increasing importance placed on vocational education, which is certainly not novel. As detailed by Wellington (1993), there are many instances since the late-nineteenth century of governments taking specific actions to encourage education to meet better the needs of industry and commerce. However, since 1976 Government policy has been far more explicit in this regard, possibly because the needs of industry and commerce are changing ever more rapidly and global markets have heightened levels of competitiveness. Consequently, a number of government departments, in addition to the Department for Education and Science (DES) and the Department for Education and Employment (DfEE), have become increasingly interested in educational issues. In particular, the Department of Employment (DoE) and the Department of Trade and Industry (DTI) broke the monopoly which the DES had formerly enjoyed. Their involvement enabled government policy to be enacted outside the constraints within which the DES was obliged to operate. For example, during the early 1980s the Manpower Services Commission (MSC), funded by the DoE, introduced the Technical and Vocational Education Initiative (TVEI) creating a major impact on education provision. Introduced without consultation and managed by a national steering group, TVEI could target funding in a partial manner, unlike the DES. By the end of the 1980s, employment and education had emerged as two key, yet intimately entwined, political issues. This was recognised by the amalgamation of the DES and the DoE, forming the Department for Education and Employment (DfEE) – a practical attempt to rationalise and coordinate government policy in this field.

The concepts of 'core skills' or 'key skills' are ones for which most organisations concerned with post-16 education, such as the Confederation for British Industry (CBI) and the National Council for Vocational Qualifications (NCVQ), produced different inventories. Common to all are competency in relation to numeracy, communication, IT, teamwork and problem-solving. The introduction of these core skills into the curriculum is seen as a means of introducing breadth and balance into over-academic curriculum, such as many traditional A level courses. They provide a means of meshing the vocational with the academic and assist in furthering skill transfer and flexibility of qualification. The CBI report *Towards a Skill Revolution* (CBI 1989) strongly supported the notion of common learning outcomes and advocated that they should be a core element of all training and vocational courses. The report defined them as:

- values and integrity
- effective communication

- applications of numeracy
- applications of technology
- understanding of work and the world
- problem-solving
- positive attitudes to change
- personal and interpersonal skills.

The Dearing Report (Dearing 1996) in discussing core skills stated that:

> Employers want entrants with a good command of language, both oral and written, and also a good grasp of basic arithmetic without the help of a calculator.

The report also acknowledged that employers wish to see:

> ... entrants to employment, possessing or developing a range of skills that are valued highly in all forms of work. These include:

- Personal and inter-personal skills, in particular, effectiveness in working as a member of a team.
- The ability to manage one's own learning, as a skill needed for life-long learning.
- A positive problem-solving approach.

However, later in the report (page 50 onwards) the term 'key skills' is used, to make a distinction between them and the mandatory 'core skills' in GNVQ (communication, the application of number and IT). In recognising the need to develop these key skills four reasons are given for their development:

> There is a gap between the skills required in the workplace and those commonly offered by the new entrants to work. There is a need to continue developing these skills in post-16 education; unless used, the skills deteriorate. Students benefit from experience of applying the skills in context. Information technology is fast developing, and students need opportunities to maintain, develop, and update their skills.

Dearing also advocated the desirability of developing personal and interpersonal skills, quoting the CBI survey of employers (1995) as evidence of the need. This survey rated the importance of the six most important core skills as:

Communication	90%
Working with others	85%
Numeracy	84%

Personal skills	79%
Problem-solving	76%
Use of IT	75%

However, no clear definition is given beyond the reference to the six skills identified in the CBI survey and detailed in appendix A4 of the report.

There is no reference to the term 'employability skills' in the Dearing Report. The term has come into usage without a clear definition of what exactly these skills are. The term was used in the title of a consultative document published by the DfEE (1996):

> A consultative document on improving employability through the 14–16 curriculum.

This document was concerned with:

> … how we can bring the worlds of education and employment closer together to enable young people to develop as citizens and to acquire the skills and attitudes to help secure their future employability.

Tate (1966) also noted:

> … the contribution of design and technology to one of the areas to which SCAA is giving particular attention at the moment – skills for employability.

The report of the SCAA/Design Council Conference: Models of the Future: the contribution of Design and Technology to the Curriculum, at which Tate gave the keynote address, concluded that the key attributes employers are seeking consist of:

- Problem-solving
- Teamworking
- Technical skills
- Flexibility
- Planning skills
- Multi-tasking
- Visual literacy
- Communication skills
- Creative thinking
- Interpersonal skills
- Commercial awareness
- Project and time management skills
- Practical experience.

Although this list of 13 skills is not exclusive to design and technology, Archer is quoted in the report as observing:

> These skills are common to a number of subject areas, but only in design and technology are all of them applied at once.
>
> (Design Council 1997)

The chief executive of the Design Council supported this view:

> We believe that design thinking is transferable thinking and that it could be transferred to the advantage of the learning programme.

His belief supports the view that involvement in designing and making provides a realistic context in which 'employability skills' can be experienced and developed. Our research examined employers' priorities in relation to a broad definition of 'employability skills'.

The research

The following table shows the percentage of those involved in the research from each of the employment sectors.

Employment sector	% participating
Primary	0
Supply	0
Manufacturing	26
Construction	3
Service	44
Transport	5
Financial	5
Public Sector	18

The high percentage from the service sector is perhaps indicative of the economy of north London where the majority of participants were located. However, it should be noted that organisations such as design consultancies are classified in this category. ...

For the purpose of the survey 'employability skills' were defined as follows:

> Those general skills which are not necessarily subject/job specific but which enable an individual to operate effectively within an organisation.

[...]

	Frequency as %
Ability to communicate when doing things	59
Ability to cooperate and work with others	46
Ability to organise things and people	23
Motivation in the accomplishment of tasks	18
Job specific skills	18
Initiative, energy, persistence and self-discipline in tasks	15
Ability to comprehend through listening, reading and doing	15
Adaptability in changing circumstances	17
Conscientiousness, honesty, reliability	15
Application of knowledge in the solution of practical problems	10
Ability to analyse, synthesise and plan	10
Sense of social responsibility	10

The table above shows the 'employability skills' listed most frequently by the employers we surveyed.

When all the coded 'employability skills' are placed in three generalised categories, they divide in the following way:

Cognitive abilities	17%
Personal qualities and attitudes	24%
Practical competencies	59%

[…] This is good evidence that employers correlate 'employability skills' with practical skills. Other skills, mentioned less frequently, are shown below.

Cognitive abilities	Personal qualities and attitudes	Practical competencies
intelligence	personality	relevant experience
decision-making	enthusiasm	attendance/punctuality
business understanding	attitude	common sense
awareness of good customer service	maturity	computer skills
intellectual/academic	dedication	work under pressure
	open to criticism	attention to detail
	willingness to learn	
	commitment/professionalism	

The employers were then asked to class the skills they had identified as: less important; important; very important; essential.

One statement, 'ability to cooperate', was ranked more highly than all the others – 86 per cent of respondents rating it as essential and the remaining 14 per cent as very important. The next highest rated statements were 'conscientiousness, honesty, reliability' and 'ability to communicate when doing things'. Sixty-one per cent rated both as essential. At the other extreme, three statements received a very low importance rating:

	% less important
Awareness of historic, technological and cultural heritage	82
Appreciation of artistic style and development of taste	69
A personal set of moral principles, capacity to make moral decisions	64

The full list of rankings is shown below:

Statement
Ability to cooperate
Conscientiousness, honesty, reliability
Initiative, energy, persistence and self-discipline in tasks
Ability to communicate when doing things
Motivation in the accomplishment of task
Ability to comprehend through listening, reading and doing
Acceptance of responsibility
Ability to think logically
Ability to handle factual information
Problem-solving
The capacity to view problems from different angles and perspectives
Ability in changing circumstances
Perseverance, application
Application of knowledge in the solution of practical problems
Ability to organise things and people
Job specific skills
Ability to reflect and think independently
Open-mindedness
Ability to think creatively and formulate new hypotheses and ideas
Ability to analyse, synthesise and plan
Skills in handling and using equipment
Self-confidence, spontaneity

(continued overleaf)

Intellectual curiosity, the ability to question established values

Self-knowledge of talents and weaknesses

Sense of social responsibility

Willingness to experiment

Ability to undertake self-directed learning

A personal set of moral principles, capacity to make moral decisions

Appreciation of artistic style and development of taste

Awareness of historic, technological and cultural heritage

If these statements are analysed in relation to the three categories of cognitive abilities, personal qualities and attitudes and practical competencies, then practical competencies as a general category are rated as being the most important by employers. [...]

The data was also analysed by the employment sector. As the number of responses in some sectors was relatively low, sectors were combined in a meaningful way to create three groups: Manufacturing and construction; Service, transport and finance; Public sector. The mean ratings are given below.

Category	Manufacturing and construction	Service, finance and transport	Public sector
Number of respondents	11	21	7
Cognitive abilities	2.42	2.46	2.41
Personal qualities and attitudes	2.46	2.50	2.59
Practical competencies	2.96	3.00	2.77

All three sectors conform to the overall response pattern. Even the public sector, which includes the 'caring professions' and frequently requires a high level of interpersonal skills, surprisingly places practical competencies higher than personal qualities and attitudes. [...]

Conclusion

The data reveal that employers are extremely pragmatic and highly focused when making decisions about potential employees. Practical capability, or as one person commented, 'the common sense to get on and do the job with the minimum of fuss', seems to be the main factor. [...]

The focused view also emerged strongly in respondents' requirements in relation to an understanding of the key sectors of the economy. Employers indicated that the key skills required for employment are delivered by Information Technology, English and Mathematics. This fully supports the Government's emphasis on these key aspects of the school curriculum. In the light of the Dearing Report on Higher Education, which placed a strong emphasis on learner-managed/independent/ autonomous/lifelong learning, the low importance placed on 'ability to undertake self-directed learning' perhaps indicates employers' lack of familiarity with the changes which are beginning to take place in the education system as it attempts to become more cost-effective and less labour-intensive.

An individual's productivity seems key to all employers. This is confirmed by the low rating given to statements such as 'a personal set of moral principles, capacity to make moral decisions', and subjects such as Personal Health and Social Education and Religious Education. However, there appeared to be a difference of view depending on the size and nature of the organisation. For example, one respondent commented: 'We can't afford the luxury of issues such as these, all our decisions are taken on the basis of our survival. That is our priority.' This was further confirmed by another person who observed: 'We do not employ new graduates or people who have not proved that they can do the job. We want people who can do the job from day one.' Both comments were made by individuals running companies of less than 25 employees. The same views were not expressed by the larger organisations involved. Many of these indicated that it was the organisation that had a moral responsibility for issues such as training. One commented on his organisation's commitment to staff training on a weekly basis and the opportunity this provided for individuals continually to extend their capabilities. Of most significance is the evidence that employers correlate 'employability skills' with practical skills. This is important evidence to support the place of practical activity in the statutory curriculum, if via this experience young people have the opportunity to develop capabilities so highly regarded in the workplace.

The National Curriculum for England (DfEE/QCA 1999) explicitly identifies key skills which are considered to be 'embedded' in the national curriculum. These are: communication; application of number; information technology; working with others; improving own learning and performance; problem-solving. The document goes on to identify 'thinking skills' which complement the key skills and are also embedded in the National Curriculum. The thinking skills are: information-processing; reasoning; enquiry; creative thinking; and evaluation.

Although no explicit reference is made to Design and Technology the processes and content of the subject mean that it is clearly able to contribute to the development of the key skills and thinking skills identified.

In Northern Ireland, the introduction to the National Curriculum for Technology and Design states that, at Key Stage 3 and 4, education should, *inter alia*, provide 'rich and varied contexts for the development of thinking and reasoning skills …' (DENI 1999: 1).

References

CBI (1989) *Towards a Skill Revolution*, Report of the Education and Training Task Force, London: CBI.
CBI (1995) *The Needs of Employers*, Employers' Survey, London: CBI.

Dearing, Sir Ron. (1996) *Review of Qualifications for 16–19 year olds*, London: SCAA.

Design Council (1997) *Models of the Future: the Contribution of Design and Technology to the Curriculum*, A Design Council discussion paper.

DfEE (1996) A *Consultative Document on improving employability through the 14–16 Curriculum*, London: Department for Education and Employment.

Tate, N. (1996). *The Contribution of Design and Technology to the Curriculum*, Keynote address, SCAA/Design Council Conference – Models of the Future. London: Cafe Royal.

Wellington, J. (1993) *The Work Related Curriculum*, London: Kogan Page.

TVEI

The Technical and Vocational Education Initiative (TVEI) announced by the Manpower Services Commission in 1982 was a major initiative aimed at rectifying the situation. This initiative enabled consortiums of schools and colleges to develop curriculums from 14 to 18 that would meet certain general criteria, for example, greater technical and vocational emphasis; links between schools and colleges and the world of work; and the introduction of regular assessment based on previously established criteria. TVEI was indicative of Government adopting new strategies as it represented the first major development in schools which was not funded by or wholly responsible to the normal education authorities. These funds were significant and enabled schools, especially those involved in the piloting phase, to update and introduce equipment previously beyond the reach of schools in the state sector.

Section 5
Teacher learning

21 International trends in Design and Technology

Marc J. de Vries

Design and Technology is now becoming embedded into the national curriculums of England, Wales and Northern Ireland. But this has not been achieved easily: there have been years of debate, and several changes to national curriculums, before it began to be accepted and understood. In this chapter the experiences of countries, including the UK, in developing technology as a part of the general education of secondary pupils are considered.

Introduction

Probably there is currently no school subject around which there is so much debate as there is around technology education. To a large extent this is because technology education is a relatively new subject in the school curriculum, when we mean technology as a contribution to general education for all pupils (of course, there is also vocational, technical education, which does have a long tradition; in this article we shall focus on technology education as general education). Although technology education in all countries has a sort of historical background – usually in craft education – the changes towards technology education are so fundamental that one could easily be justified in calling it a new subject. Of course, other school subjects go through major changes also. Science education, for example, has become increasingly linked to everyday life phenomena that pupils directly experience for themselves. Furthermore, there has been a growing sense of awareness of the role played by pupils' preconceptions which they bring to science, and how these can be transformed into more scientifically valid concepts by creating effective educational situations. But even with these sorts of changes, science education remains science education in a recognisable way. And maybe more importantly, the changes are made by teachers who have been specifically educated to teach science. In that respect the situation is different for technology education, where in most countries teachers of other subjects have been retrained, or moved without retraining, to become technology teachers (often in addition to their other teaching roles). These teachers often do not have much more than a basic knowledge of technology as a subject, which is sufficient to teach it adequately, but does not enable them to create a new school subject. An additional problem for technology education is that, contrary to most other school subjects, it has no directly equivalent discipline in the academic world. Science educators can draw from the academic disciplines of physics, chemistry and biology to get a conceptual basis for their teaching. For technology education, one could of course think of the various engineering disciplines in the academic world, but it is generally felt that following those would create too narrow a scope for teaching technology. And other than those disciplines, there are no others that combine all the different aspects that one would like to bring together in technology education.

In such a situation – a relatively new school subject without a direct academic equivalent – it is hardly surprising that the emergence of technology education causes a lot of fundamental discussions with respect to curriculum content, teaching strategies and ways of assessment, just to mention a few aspects.

Aims of technology education

The motivation for creating a school subject that focuses on technology as a discipline and as a phenomenon in our culture has been for most countries that (future) citizens ought to have a good concept of what technology is and the skills to deal with it effectively. The importance of this is, in the first place, that it will enable them to live in a modern society in which technology has come to play such a vital role. 'Living' in this respect means more than surviving. They ought to have control over technology rather than vice versa. That means that they should not only have the skills to use technology in a safe and proper way, but also know how technology is developed, what decisions are made in that process, and what roles they can play in influencing those decisions … Second, it enables them to make a well-based choice to opt either for a technological or a non-technological career. Several countries have implemented technology education because of the concern for an adequate national technological workforce. Even though the social debates of the 1970s, which often had a negative image of technology as a background, have faded away, for many people it is still not an attractive option to work in the field of technology. Enrolment in engineering training programmes, both in the academic and in the vocational sectors, in several countries is too low to guarantee the technological workforce these countries need. Attitude research has shown that there is a relationship between a narrow concept of technology, which envisions technology mainly in terms of the *outcomes* of technology, i.e. products, and a negative attitude towards technology. In particular, this results in gender differences: boys more often seem to feel comfortable in dealing with machines and equipment while girls show more interest in the human and social aspects of technology, which in their concept of technology plays only a minor role. This tends to result in a general lack of interest in technology on the girls' part (Raat and De Vries 1986). If both boys and girls would acquire a better, more balanced concept, that encompasses technology as knowledge, as artefacts, as skills and as volition (Mitcham 1994), rather than as artefacts only, this would result in a more sophisticated attitude towards technology and more sophisticated career choices. This implies that in technology both products and processes need to be given sufficient attention. In the third place, specific areas of technical knowledge and skills can be seen as aims for technology education, but then we are already making a transition to vocational education, which aims to prepare pupils for specific technological careers, and as stated before, here we shall focus on technology education as general education.

These considerations in many countries have resulted in adequate political support for the introduction of technology education, often as a compulsory school subject.

Issues in the development of technology education

In different countries with their different economic and social situations, different approaches to technology have emerged. It would be impossible to describe them all, but one way to gain an impression of the variety is to describe the extremes in which specific aspects of technology have been given a strong emphasis. They can be seen as specific wavelengths in the whole spectrum of possible approaches: one will hardly ever find them as such, but all existing approaches can be seen as either close to one of these wavelengths or as a combination of wavelengths (a similar strategy has been used in an OECD project on Science, Maths and Technology education; see Black and Atkin 1996). Thus the following approaches can be identified (De Vries 1993):

- a craft-oriented approach
- an industry-oriented approach
- a science-oriented approach
- a 'high-tech' approach
- an engineering concepts approach
- a key competencies approach
- a design-oriented approach
- a social issues approach.

Through increasing international contacts, the differences among the approaches we find in various countries gradually become less prominent than the categorisation above suggests. But each of these extremes causes a discussion about the proper role of the aspect that it has overemphasised. We shall now consider each of these aspects in more detail.

The role of craft skills

As stated earlier, in most countries technology education has its roots in craft education: often this is still noticeable in current practice. Technology education to a large extent means making workpieces. Whatever else may be involved around those workpieces, the skills for making simple technical devices is still present in most programmes. In general it is felt that making products remains an essential element in technology and that pupils should experience this aspect. There are, however, situations in which this idea is abandoned. In the United States so-called modular curriculum programmes can be found in which production tools and equipment have been replaced by computers and – often automated – equipment for experimenting with sophisticated technological devices. There is a debate ongoing about the pros and cons of these modular programmes. One of the objections against them is that vendors rather than educationalists seem to determine the content of technology education. But primarily the fact that pupils no longer get any feeling or *Fingerspitzengefühl* for technical materials and tools is seen as a serious disadvantage of these modular programmes.

The role of industry

In particular, in the former Eastern bloc in Europe, one could see a technology education approach that was strongly biased towards industrial production. Pupils in 'polytechnic education' had to learn the various industrial production processes, including work preparation. This was motivated by the strong ideological role of industry in those countries at that time. The political changes at the end of the 1980s have resulted in a substantial decrease in the importance of technology education (for example, in Hungary), mainly because of their ideological flavour. But in the USA too the direct precursor of what is nowadays called 'technology education' was called 'industrial arts' and thus in its very name showed a certain bias towards industrial aspects of technology (Hayles and Snyder 1982). As curriculum organisers, the social systems of construction, production, transportation and communication were used in this approach and the same headings were used under the new name of 'technology education'. In Germany, one of the options for technology education is called *Arbeitslehre/Technic*. The term *Arbeitslehre* relates to the world of work and the *Arbeitslehre* stream claims to be able to combine technology, economy and home economics into one school subject (Brauer-Schröder and Sellin 1996). In France textbooks for the subject *Technologie* showed similar interests: often they started by making pupils consider what is needed to start a technological business company. In the UK traditionally there is a good relationship between technology and industry. Industries and educationalists work together to produce learning materials and mutual visits take place between companies and schools. Although industrial aspects should not be overemphasised, as if business interests should be prominent in technological developments, it is yet necessary that pupils gain a good insight into how technology is practised in industry. Therefore technology education programmes should be kept up to date in terms of developments in industry. In that respect there is a current need to pay more attention to quality aspects in technology education. Quality has become a key issue in industry, not only in the sense that finished products need to be checked for possible failures, but even more that quality encompasses every aspect of customer satisfaction. That starts with the identification of the requirements for the product (the so-called 'design-inbuilt' quality) and stretches out to the service that is offered to the customer in the user phase of the product life-cycle and even to the final phase when the product is discarded by the user and may be recycled or re-used. This life-cycle perspective on quality is mirrored in the life-cycle approach to environmental awareness in industry: here too the whole life-cycle needs to be taken into account.

This development in modern industries too needs to be implemented in technology education programmes.

The role of science and mathematics

The role of science and mathematics is a most complex matter in technology education (Layton 1993). In the first place most countries have technology teachers with a non-scientific background (they often came from craft and/or arts education). For those teachers it is difficult to deal with science concepts effectively in their technology lessons. Alternatively science teachers in their science teaching often claim to deal with technology, but then appear to take technology as 'applied science' and pay insufficient attention to the complicated process that leads from scientific knowledge to a technical device or system (apart from the fact that in principle this process does not even start with scientific knowledge). Thus there seems to be a dichotomy here which is not easy to overcome. Finland is an example of a country where this split has led to struggles between science educators and craft educators. Yet, as science plays an important role in many current technological developments, there is a need to make pupils aware of this relationship. Knowledge from science about the properties of materials, energy and information as the basic 'stuff' with which technologists work is crucial to a good understanding of the development of new devices and systems. In this respect there is a pressing need for in-service training of both science and technology teachers to ensure a more effective relationship between science education and technology education to reflect the real-world relationship between science and technology. But there is a more fundamental problem here: philosophical and historical studies into the development of new products have shown that scientific concepts often need some sort of transformation in order to be usable for the engineers. This complicates the relationship between science and technology substantially (De Vries 1994b). Similar problems can be expected when technology teachers in their lessons try to use the abstract scientific concepts that have been learnt in science education. Here too a certain transformation is needed that requires input from both science educators (and mathematics teachers) and technology educators.

The role of information technologies

As with the previous aspects of technology, the aspect of the information technologies can be and has been overemphasised in the practice of technology education. The so-called modular curriculum programmes in the USA have been mentioned already. In particular, in countries with strong electronics industries, like France and Israel, we see the danger of making pupils use information technologies in such a way that they are amazed by them rather than gaining a good understanding of the nature of technology. In such cases pupils build constructions that are controlled by a computer, learn which button to push at which point, but do not acquire an understanding of the basic system concepts behind those constructions. At the same time, experiences in these countries have shown the enormous potential of information technology as a learning tool. Computers can do simulations and calculations, and can yield access to worldwide data (e.g. through the Internet) which pupils can use when doing their (design) project work. And besides that, the use of information technologies in technology education contributes to a realistic concept of technologies, because they play an increasingly important role in all phases of technological developments.

The role of engineering concepts

The quest for a conceptual basis for technology is an ongoing concern (De Vries and Tamir 1997). This debate is often coupled to the issue of whether or not technology education should be taught as a separate school subject. Those who favour a separate subject rather than integration into science or other subjects often use the argument of technology having its own body of knowledge and methodologies. This debate is particularly concerned with technology education at the level of secondary education. In primary education there is a different culture in the curriculum and there is more or less general agreement that here technology education should not be taught as a separate subject. Several individuals in various countries have suggested conceptual bases for technology education, people like DeVore (1980) and Todd (Todd *et al.* 1985) in the USA, and Blandow (1993), Lutherdt (1995) and Wolfgramm (1994/95) in Germany, just to mention a few. In the project Technology for All Americans, an effort is made to base new national technology education standards on such a conceptual basis (Dugger 1997). But the generality of the concepts they come up with, according to others, conflicts with the specificity of the concepts that engineers seem to use most in practice. One of the concepts that generally comes out as basic is the systems concept. Systems process materials, energy and information by basic functions like transforming, connecting, separating, transporting, storing and retrieving. Even though the concept of systems may not always play a dominant role in the work of engineers, from a didactical point of view it can be useful, because it helps pupils to gain a more fundamental insight into the technologies they see around them rather than detailed knowledge about specifics. Moreover it frees technology educators from the need of constantly trying to keep up to date in terms of introducing the newest technologies. Especially in countries that cannot afford high-tech equipment (such as African countries), this would be an approach to teach technology effectively without necessarily spending a lot of money on resources. In The Netherlands this and other basic concepts have become the basis for technology education textbooks.

The role of key competencies

The idea of competencies that have a general and transferable character has come from industry, in particular in Germany (there the term *Schlüsselqualifikationen* is used and sometimes we find this inadequately translated as 'key qualifications'). Industry has stated the need for a workforce that has skills like cooperating, problem-solving, innovative thinking, communicating: technology education would be a subject *par excellence* where such competencies could be acquired. Teaching those competencies in the eyes of industrialists would be much more useful than teaching specific skills with school equipment that, compared to industry standards, mostly is outdated anyway. There is, however, serious doubt about the claim that doing specific technology project work would 'automatically' yield transferable skills, and even the mere existence of such skills is sometimes questioned. Research by McCormick and others has shown that teaching and learning 'general' skills can never be separated from specific content areas. This is reflected in design methodological research, which has shown that designing a corkscrew is really something different from designing a television camera. Hence it can be questioned whether there exists such a thing as 'general design skills'. On the other hand, various design processes do show common features that could be related to linked skills. Further research is needed to reveal the nature of such commodities.

The role of design

The example of design skills and general competencies brings us to our next aspect: the role of design as such in technology education. Here the UK is the most prominent example of a country in which we find an approach that is evidently biased towards this aspect. In the past this has even resulted in a criticism by professional engineering associations in the UK that design in 'Design and Technology' education could be about anything and totally lacked content focus. On the other hand, the history of technology education in several countries shows a resistance against design activities in technology education that was fed by the false assumptions that designing would not be possible with pupils of primary and secondary school ages. Here practice in the UK has been very valuable in proving the feasibility of real design work in schools. Through international contacts we can now see other countries importing this aspect from the UK. A major drawback here has been discussed already in the previous section: schoolbooks often use very general flowcharts for design processes that suggest that any design can be made by following such a general scheme. Here we should be careful not to use these schemes too rigidly, but rather as a checklist of activities that somewhere in the process need to be given attention.

The role of social issues

By including the design phase of a product in technology education programmes, almost automatically social issues come into our scope. Design requirements are directly related to human and social needs. On the other hand we find human and social norms and values in the using phase of technology. Technology Assessment has been developed as a policy tool for decision-making with respect to technological developments. In general one can say that in some Scandinavian countries, in particular Sweden, this has played a visible role in technology education programmes. In countries such as the USA and Canada, we have seen the emergence of so-called STS (Science, Technology and Society; see Solomon and Aikenhead 1994) programmes that usually focused on specific 'trendy' social issues (nuclear power, environmental pollution and genetic engineering can be mentioned as examples of such issues which, in the past, have attracted the interest of science educators in STS programmes). Often the decrease in interest in such specific and time-dependent social issues caused the disappearance of STS programmes. Another problem with the STS programmes in the past was that, as in the 'applied science' approach, the technology component had not been developed strongly in terms of the process of creating new technological devices and systems. It was only the existing technology as such that was the target of social debate; the way decision-making in those development processes could be influenced by social concerns was hardly dealt with. Enhancing this aspect (i.e. combining social issues with design activities) could repair this weakness.

Conditions for technology education

From the previous sections it has become evident that various aspects of technology need to be combined in technology education programmes. This makes them multi-dimensional which places high demands on teachers and resources. Many conditions need to be met in order to allow adequate teaching and learning about technology. In this section we shall discuss the following conditions:

- the availability of well-trained teachers;
- the availability of sufficient and adequate facilities (including teaching and learning materials);
- educational research to support the further development of technology education;
- international cooperation to enable countries to gain from each other's experiences.

Teacher education

Whatever wonderful programmes can be developed for technology education, in the end it all depends on the willingness, knowledge and skills of teachers to implement them. The fact that associations for technology educators flourish is an indication that, in general, technology educators have a positive attitude towards renewing their programmes. However, they often lack the expertise to design the renovations themselves. In this area there is evidently a role for universities and (other) teacher training institutes; indeed, some of these have produced useful collections of articles for technology teachers (e.g. Banks 1994; McCormick *et al.* 1994; Williams and Williams 1997). Some countries (e.g. the UK and The Netherlands) in addition have an elaborate system of support centres to help teachers to implement changes in their teaching practice. In addition, the technology teacher associations often are a valuable source of support for teachers.

Training programmes for teachers usually have the following components:

courses on technological content, courses on educational issues, school apprenticeships and industrial visits (De Vries 1994a). The difference between technology teacher training programmes and those for other subjects is that for the former the student teacher often has to build up the school subject almost from scratch (e.g. writing their own teaching and learning materials and designing and equipping a technology lab.).

Learning materials and facilities

As technology education activities almost constantly require materials and tools, it is a challenge for technology educators to work with a limited budget and yet keep pupils working on practical design-and-make activities. As technology education in many cases still has to fight for its position in the school, the teacher has to get rid of the misconception, often held by school boards and parents, that technology is just about tinkering and handicraft. This can be done by developing a technology education programme that reflects the true nature of technology and then communicating about this with the school management and with parents.

Educational research

In terms of supporting educational research, the situation is still inadequate in a number of countries. Probably the best situation can be found in Germany, in France and in the UK, where several universities have good educational research programmes for technology education. In the USA we also find several universities with such a research programme, but recent surveys of the content of those programmes have shown that there is a strong tendency to focus on curriculum content and that there is hardly any research focused on pupils (Zuga 1997). Furthermore, universities seem to compete rather than cooperate, which often causes inefficient use of means from a nationwide perspective. In general, education research for technology education can relate to three fields:

- the aims and content of curriculums (*what to teach*);
- the characteristics of pupils, like preconceptions and attitudes (*whom to teach*);
- the creation of adequate educational situations in which the right content is conveyed to the learner (*how to teach*). This field also includes assessment strategies and tools.

This last-mentioned topic is one of particular importance, given both the complexity of assessing the various activities (like project work in which all sorts of aspects need to be evaluated) and the relevance of proving that the aims of technology are somehow realised in practice (Mottier and De Vries 1997). It is desirable that an international agenda for educational research in technology education be established (Jenkins 1992).

International cooperation

As the development of technology is a constant struggle that is complicated by the relative newness of the school subject, international cooperation is an almost indispensable condition for a successful development. Although each country has a specific background and situation, much can be learnt from experiences abroad, both in terms of successes and pitfalls. In the past decades this feeling has resulted in the emergence of some international organisations that enable contacts between experts from various countries. In some cases existing international bodies, like OECD, NATO and UNESCO, have extended their scope of interests to include technology education; in other cases new dedicated organisations were initiated, like WOCATE (the World Council of Associations for Technology Education), EGTB (the European Association for Technology Education; EGBT is the German abbreviation; see Kussmann and Tyrehan 1994) and PATT (Pupils' Attitudes Towards Technology, a small foundation that biennially organises international conferences on various aspects of technology education). In some cases national technology education organisations, such as the ITEA (International Technology Education Association) and the EPT fraternity (Epsilon Pi Tau) in the USA and DATA (Design and Technology Association) in the UK, have included international aspects in their activities. Not only conferences but also scholarly journals provide a platform to exchange experiences. The *International Journal of Technology and Design Education*, the *Journal of Technology Studies*, and the *Journal of Technology Education* are examples of journals with international authorship and readership.

Technology education in the twenty-first century

It can be expected that most trends in technology education of the late twentieth century will be continued in the twenty-first century. Partly thanks to increasing international contacts, technology education will become more mature (i.e. richer combinations of the various issues dealt with above will emerge) and as a result, technology education will be able to establish a sound position in schools. The low-level image of technology education will gradually disappear and technology education will be taken more seriously as a contribution to the general education of all future citizens by policy-makers, industries, school boards and parents. It is to be hoped that this will also result in the allocation of more resources for educational research to support technology education developments, in particular in those countries that at the moment hardly have any. The still ongoing fundamental debates on curriculum content, teaching and learning strategies (including assessment) call out for such resources and thus justify this allocation of means. Given the dynamic character of technology itself, it can be expected that technology education will always remain a dynamic field of teaching and learning. This presents a challenge to all parties involved.

References

Banks, F. (ed). (1994) *Teaching Technology*, London: Routledge.

Black, P. and Atkin, M. (1996) *Changing the Subject: Innovations in Science, Mathematics and Technology Education*, London: Routledge.

Blandow, D. (1993) 'Innovation and design for developing technological capabilities in general education', in M.J. de Vries, N. Cross and D.P. Grant (eds), *Design Methodology and Relationships with Science*, Dordrecht: Kluwer Academic Publishers.

Brauer-Schröder, M. and Sellin, H. (eds) (1996) *Technik, Ökonomie and Haushalt in Unterricht. Arbeitsorientierte Allgemeinbildung in Europa*, Baltmannsweiler: Schneider Verlag Hohengehren GmbH.

DeVore, P. W. (1980) *Technology: An Introduction*, Worcester: Davis Publications.

Dugger, W. E. (1997) 'Technology for all', in T. Kananoja (ed.), *Seminars on Technology Education*, Oulu: University of Oulu.

Hayles, J.A. and Snyder, J.F. (1982) 'Jackson's Mill industrial arts curriculum theory: a base for curriculum derivation', *Man Society Technology* 41(5), 6–10.

Jenkins, E.W. (1992) 'Towards an agenda for research in technology education', in D. Blandow and M. J. Dyrenfurth (eds), *Technological Literacy, Competence and Innovation in Human Resource Development*, Erfurt/Columbia: WOCATE/AEA.

Kussmann, M. and Tyrehan, G. (eds) (1994) *Technology Education: On the Way to a Eurocurriculum School Technology*, EGTB Report 2. Düsseldorf: Europäische Gesellschaft für Technische Bildung.

Layton, D. (1993) *Technology's Challenge to Science Education*, Buckingham/Philadelphia: Open University Press.

Lutherdt, M. (1995) 'Key qualifications – content of general and vocational education', in L. Mottier, J.H. Raat and M.J. de Vries (eds), *Teaching Technology for Entrepreneurship and Employment*, Proceedings PATT-7 Conference, Eindhoven: PATT-Foundation.

McCormick, R., Murphy, P. and Harrison, M. (eds) (1992) *Teaching and Learning Technology*, Wokingham: Addison-Wesley and the Open University.

McCormick, R., Murphy, P. and Hennessy, S. (eds) (1994) 'Problem solving processes in technology education: a pilot study', *International Journal of Technology and Design Education* 4(1): 5–34.

Mitcham, C. (1994) *Thinking through Technology: The Path between Engineering and Philosophy*, Chicago: University of Chicago Press.

Mottier, I. and Vries, M.J. de (eds) (1997) *Assessing Technology Education*, Proceeds PATT-8 Conference, Eindhoven: PATT Foundation.

Raat, J.H. and Vries, M.H. de (eds) (1986) *What Do Girls and Boys Think of Technology?*, Eindhoven University of Education.

Solomon, J. and Aikenhead, G. (eds) (1994) *STS Education: International Perspectives on Reform*, New York: Teachers College Press, Columbia University.

Todd, R.D., McCrory, D.L. and Todd, K. (1985) *Understanding and Using Technology*, Worcester: Davis Publications.

Vries, M.J. de (1993) 'Approaches to technology education and the role of advanced technologies: an international orientation', in A. Gordon, M. Hacker and M.J. de Vries (eds), *Advanced Educational Technology in Technology Education*, Heidelberg: Springer Verlag.

Vries, M.J. de (1994a) 'Teacher education for technology education', in M. Galton and B. Moon (eds) *Handbook of Teacher Training in Europe*, London: David Fulton and Council of Europe.

Vries, M.J. de (1994b) *Science and Technology Teacher Training: What Training for What Type of Teaching?*, Paris: Council of Europe.

Vries, M.J. de and Tamir, A. (eds) (1997) *Shaping Concepts of Technology: From Philosophical Perspectives in Mental Images*, Dordrecht: Kluwer Academic Publishers.

Williams, J. and Williams, A. (eds) (1997) *Technology Education for Teachers*, Melbourne: Macmillan.

Wolfgramm, H. (1994/95) *Allgemeine Techniklehre*, Hildesheim: Verlag Franzbecker.

Zuga, K.F. (1997) 'An analysis of technology education in the United States based upon an historical overview and review of contemporary curriculum research', *International Journal of Technology and Design Education* 7(3): 203–7.

22 Research in Design and Technology education

Frank Banks

This is an important chapter with which to finish as it outlines the role that you can play in continuing to develop Design and Technology. In looking at research in Design and Technology it covers several of the areas you have already read about, but this time in terms of the research carried out in that area and the implications for classroom practice. It finishes by looking at how you, as a teacher, might develop your own classroom-based research and contribute to the development of Design and Technology education.

This chapter is based on a document produced for the Open University PGCE course.

Introduction

How do pupils learn, and what is effective teaching, in the relatively new curriculum area of Design and Technology? In 1990, England and Wales took the lead in making technology a compulsory subject, part of all pupils' general education from 5 to 16 years. Northern Ireland quickly followed with 'Technology and Design' which in content is similar to that being introduced in The Netherlands, Colombia, New Zealand and many other countries (Van der Velde 1992; Pena 1992; Ferguson 1992; NICC 1992). Across the world, the introduction of this subject is drawing on the curriculum traditionally associated with craft, design and science (particularly physics), along with the social implications of science and technology (often called 'science, technology and society' or STS) in different ways in different countries. However, although there have been many years of research investigating how pupils learn in the traditional academic subjects, the same attention has still not been given to pupils' acquisition of practical capability or the way they design and make, and solve problems, in a technological context.

In England in particular, there has been ongoing work throughout the last decade of the twentieth century to adjust the National Curriculum (NCC 1993; SCAA 1994; QCA 1999). This has led to a considerable debate about the aims of design and technology for all and its educational benefits. Due to the comparatively early introduction of the subject in Britain, and its study by pupils from the age of five, teachers here are well placed not only to exploit the research that has been done into learning in Design and Technology, but also to contribute to that work themselves.

A major goal of educational research is to improve our understanding of teaching and learning in order to enhance the experience of our pupils. The Teacher Training Agency (TTA) in England is keen to enable teacher-practitioner research to flourish and make teaching more evidence-based. Increasingly teachers are taking an important role in looking critically at their own practice.

This chapter will consider:

- recent research in Design and Technology teaching and learning
- research in other fields of particular value to Design and Technology teachers
- how Design and Technology teachers might themselves become researchers in their own workplace.

Research in Design and Technology teaching and learning

By doing research in Design and Technology education, researchers attempt to understand the learning that goes on among pupils and teachers together in workshops and classrooms. These settings are within schools which, in turn, are part of a larger social, economic and political framework. Educational research, therefore, is a form of social research and is different from that undertaken in science and engineering laboratories, although it sometimes adapts their research methods. There is a range of purposes for educational research and even some disagreement as to what should count as research (see Hammersley 1994). In this chapter I will focus on those studies which directly inform classroom practice, particularly teaching and learning strategies. The particular areas of research in Design and Technology education we will consider are:

- technological capability
- problem-solving
- modelling.

These areas have been covered in earlier chapters so you will be familiar with the ideas discussed, but here I am looking at them from the research perspective.

Technological capability

As indicated in the introduction to this chapter, and in the previous chapter, technology is becoming a component of general education around the world and the basic question that needs to be asked is 'What contribution does Design and Technology make to the pupil's learning?' Black and Harrison (1985) were among the first to attempt an answer to this by analysing the interplay between design-and-make tasks in technology and the resources of knowledge and processes needed to carry them out. They described this interaction as 'technological capability'. In particular, they were keen to resolve the differences between technology and science in schools. This split has continued to be a source of confusion for many years (see Smithers and Robinson 1992) and the formation of National Curriculum technology in 1990 from a number of contributory subjects which excluded science has exacerbated the problem. The most extensive empirical work to investigate the nature of technological capability was mounted by the Assessment of Performance Unit (APU) Design and Technology project which ran from 1985 to 1991, and still has importance today.

This period saw rapid changes in classroom practice due to the introduction of both GCSE and the National Curriculum. As APU researchers worked with pupils in developing ways in which they could test attainment in Design and Technology, they were forced to reconsider the nature of the intellectual processes they were attempting to assess. This work attempted to get to grips with what actually goes on in Design and Technology lessons as pupils work on their projects. The researchers found the real-life contexts in which the pupils operated difficult to analyse.

> One of the most intractable difficulties with which we were grappling was that processes (as opposed to products) are difficult to assess because you can't see them ... One can of course observe pupil behaviour – and hope that our interpretation of that behaviour is the same as the pupil's. For example, if we observe a pupil measuring the length of a shadow cast by a stick in the ground, we might assume that the pupil was investigating the angle of the sun. But then it turns out that he was actually doing some consumer testing on tape measures – to see which of his three was the easiest to use reliably, and while we weren't watching – he had also been measuring all sorts of other things.
>
> (APU 1991: 23)

However, the APU came to a view of the nature of technological capability which mirrored Black's and Harrison's original conception that the processes of technology are informed by other 'resources' of knowledge, to which the APU added communication.

The APU was keen to assess the totality of learning in the Design and Technology workroom. There was a need, the unit team realized, to look at much more than the final product and associated design folder to understand the ways in which pupils worked. Too often the project folder became a product in its own right as teachers used it as an instrument of assessment in GCSE schemes. In this way the folder ran the risk of becoming invested with more importance than was warranted within the totality of the design-and-make activity.

During the six-year project the APU team worked towards a means to categorize technological capability. Their suggestion was the following:

Procedural qualities:
  – recognizing issues in the task;
  – developing proposals for a solution;
  – appraising the proposals through the issues;
  – growing ideas;
  – planning the work.

Communication qualities:
- – the clarity of communication;
- – the complexity of the communication;
- – the confidence of communication;
- – the skill in communication.

Conceptual qualities:
- – understanding and using materials;
- – understanding and using energy systems;
- – understanding and using aesthetics;
- – understanding people.

(APU 1991: 152)

The team analysed and categorized technological capability in order to develop a means of assessing the extent to which pupils possess that capability. The preliminary nature of this research work in describing technological capability is conveyed in the APU's final report.

> In the process of refining these categories, we recognized the dilemma of developing the marking scheme as a research exercise at the same time as needing it for a monitoring exercise. The former purpose demanded a degree of flexibility as qualities became clearer in the minds of the team, but the latter demanded precision for markers to be reliable.
>
> (APU 1991: 152)

Design and Technology is about tackling tasks in the made world of products, systems and environments which lead to a resolution that results in an improvement for someone. As such it involves the solution of a number of problems and it is to the research work on pupil problem-solving that we next turn.

Problem-solving

The 'design process'

Some researchers, such as Eggleston (1996), see the 'design process' as the unifying element between the different material areas of Design and Technology. Moreover, this process is seen as a general problem-solving technique which can be applied in many different contexts. Discussions about Design and Technology as a vehicle for the teaching of problem-solving quickly become emotionally charged, as those who have argued for 'technology for all' have seen problem-solving as central to technological activity and quite different from the craft tradition, with its emphasis on just making. Indeed, proponents of the subject have used this argument as a principal way of advocating that Design and Technology should have an enhanced status in the school curriculum because a general ability to solve problems is central to satisfying human needs. However, it is important to consider dispassionately the evidence for such a general problem-solving ability engendered by Design and Technology.

The learning context

Glaser (1984), Layton (1993), and Hennessy and McCormick (Chapter 8, this volume) all suggest that learning is heavily influenced by the context in which it occurs. Pupils do not easily transfer their ability in a particular activity from one learning 'domain' to another. Teachers have long bemoaned the fact that, for example, pupils can do graphs in Maths lessons but not in Science; or can investigate materials fairly in Science but not in Design and Technology. Similarly, design and technology teachers have assumed that if pupils are taught to investigate the factors influencing the design decisions for making a product, for example a moisture sensor, then they will be able to transfer those techniques to consider the different design decisions for, say, batch food production. The evidence is that pupils do not easily transfer their understanding across these different contexts and require considerable support from their teacher to help them do so. One strategy to help with this issue may be to build up a 'repertoire of solutions' or 'rules of thumb' to various problems in specific areas. As well as working in different materials, pupils can be exposed to various skills and processes such as: fabric printing; knowledge of mechanisms; hedonistic ranking related to food testing; use of a 'potential divider' in electronic control systems. This issue is not confined to learning in Design and Technology; many people are able to add up effectively when shopping in a supermarket but find a similar sum set in a Maths lesson very difficult. Neither is it restricted to pupils.

An example of this was illustrated at an Open University summer school. We involved teachers in designing a device to help open jars (e.g. for those with arthritis). A group of science teachers was designing a conical grip, but did not have sufficient knowledge of possible ways of screwing the cone down onto the jar. The tutor sent them to look at a pillar drill to see how the vertical movement was achieved from a rotational movement. Because they were not CDT or technical teachers, they lacked the 'knowledge of solutions' that would have enabled them to think of a solution (Open University 1993: 68).

There is, therefore, a need for 'focused tasks' to help pupils learn specific procedures.

Situated-cognition

Some researchers, investigating how people tackle problem-solving, see such a close association in a particular context between the knowledge needed to solve a problem (conceptual knowledge) and an understanding of what action needs to be done to tackle that problem (procedural knowledge) that they would deny that it is possible to separate the two. These researchers claim that such a separation is invalid as people think within the context in which they find themselves. Such learning in context is known as 'situated-cognition' (discussed in Chapter 8). It is an extreme position of that described above, but it does reinforce the suggestion that teachers should help pupils by developing a knowledge of possible 'solutions'.

An appreciation of the importance of situated-cognition also implies that care needs to be exercised in designing schemes of work, to ensure that they help pupils progress in the way that they are required to tackle problems. Glaser (1984) and Murphy (1991) suggest that when pupils are presented with problems in unfamiliar contexts they tend to use everyday knowledge to tackle them. For example, a group of Year 9 pupils was set the problem of investigating the thermal insulation properties of various textiles in a Science lesson. The investigation suggested by many pupils (particularly the boys) was that they should lag identical beakers with the different materials and plot comparative cooling curves. When the same problem was set within the context of choosing the best material for a mountaineer's jacket, however, the problem became more difficult, with girls in particular focusing on the context. Bringing everyday knowledge to bear, they rejected materials unsuitable for manufacture (such as cotton wool) and modelled the situation by making the material into a small jacket. This research has important implications for how we teach both procedural and conceptual knowledge in Design and Technology.

Explicit teaching of design procedures

Many teachers emphasize the usefulness of Design and Technology by choosing everyday problems as contexts for pupil projects. However, pupils will not progress in their approach to solving different problems if they simply re-use everyday knowledge to tackle them. The Understanding Technological Approaches (UTA) study at Goldsmith's College, London, looked at issues of progression (particularly across Key Stages) in some detail (see Kimbell *et al.* 1996). Murphy and McCormick (1997) discovered that there needs to be an explicit teaching of design procedures such as investigating, specifying and evaluating if pupils are to become more sophisticated in the techniques which they employ. Similarly, if a task requires a specific concept such as an understanding of mechanisms, that needs to be built explicitly into the sequence of lessons. Many curriculum packages take this line; the Nuffield design and technology course has 'resource tasks', the RCA project is structured around whole tasks often set in an industrial or commercial context, and the technology enhancement programme (TEP) has technology files.

We need to be careful, however, in ensuring that the knowledge supplied is in an appropriate form. An abstract understanding of, say, a series circuit and Ohm's law will not enable a pupil to exploit easily the idea of a potential divider. In constructing schemes of work, McCormick and Banks (1994) suggest that the teaching of conceptual knowledge (such as science ideas) be analysed carefully by addressing the following questions:

- What are the science ideas which may be needed for this 'design-and-make' task?
- Which of these do we need to teach? What do the pupils already know from elsewhere?

- What is appropriate not to teach? Some concepts (just like devices) might be better left as a 'blackbox' idea – one which can be used even though it is not fully understood.

(McCormick and Banks 1994: 65)

Modelling

There are many forms of modelling in Design and Technology lessons; two-dimensional, three-dimensional, mathematical and computer modelling are all seen as ways in which pupils can communicate their ideas to others and also generate and develop those ideas for themselves. Such 'thinking on paper' has been investigated by a number of researchers. Liddament (1993: 92) suggests that models are commonly used to:

- obtain ideas about the finished appearance of a design;
- see how the design might be improved;
- develop or refine the design;
- show possible faults in the design;
- study possible prototypes;
- test mechanisms, circuits, or other parts;
- represent features such as scale, proportion, etc.;
- check features such as weight, feel, etc.

(Liddament 1993: 92)

He counsels against assuming that the information carried by two-dimensional drawings is unambiguous. Often, the details of a design are not conveyed to a novice by the drawing alone, and sometimes the graphic convention (such as orthographic projection) is more difficult for a pupil to understand than the device it is illustrating.

Anning (1992) illustrates the way preliminary drawing on paper can become divorced from the eventual activity of creating in three dimensions. Young children in particular find the translation between two and three dimensions difficult. The research indicates that they appear to think in different ways in the two modelling contexts: the aspects of the problem they consider when using modelling kits, for example, are different from those they bring into play when drawing out their ideas.

Using the examples of 20 case studies of professional designers, such as architects, engineers and theatre designers, Garner (1994) showed how drawing helped these people when thinking about their designs. A practice that appeared to have been common among the different designers was the use of sketches to stimulate their own ideas and to clarify more carefully the problem they were trying to solve: 'This "homing in" extends the contribution of drawing from a problem-solving to a problem-finding strategy' (Garner 1994: 68).

Teachers are able to exploit some of this research by offering a variety of media, including construction kits and reclaimed materials, to help pupils develop their ideas while modelling. They can also engage with the pupils by asking questions and making comments such as:

- 'how does this work?'
- 'tell me about this part ...'
- 'what if this were ...?'
- 'I like the way that this shape ...'
- 'how do you think you can make this?'
- 'have you looked at ...?'
- 'we cannot make this because we haven't the special equipment, but if we changed this ...'
- 'have you seen the way the clips work on a ...?'
- 'I'd like to see some notes for each part on your drawing to help explain ...'
- 'let's ask some of the class if they've got some ideas how this part could be improved ...'
- 'instead of making this part we could use one from ...'

(CCW 1993: 13)

Computer modelling is becoming increasingly sophisticated and available in the school classroom and workshop. CAD (computer-aided design) and CAM (computer-aided manufacturing) are very important activities in the Design and Technology curriculum for England (QCA 1999). These techniques enable technologists to concentrate on testing out their ideas qualitatively, removing many of the problems of sophisticated mathematics which would be beyond the capabilities of pupils (and many professional engineers too!) and which have traditionally been necessary in simulating the behaviour of dynamic systems. For example, the movement of a car piston can easily be drawn and modelled on school software. Simple spreadsheets are available and widely used by pupils to manipulate things such as the factors which affect the conflicting demands of cost and insulation for the specification of an energy-efficient house. Software is available to show a visual representation of the design of the building, including the ability to 'walk through' the house using 'virtual reality'. Research into the ways pupils learn and develop their modelling skills using this technology is still at a relatively primitive stage.

Research in other fields of particular value to Design and Technology teachers

Educational research which has a bearing on the way pupils and teachers interact in schools will be of value to teachers, but any subset of that research selected for particular consideration is bound to be partial and only give a glimpse of the wealth of evidence available. However, the following three research areas have been chosen for special consideration:

- children's learning in science
- gender issues in the curriculum
- assessment issues.

The rationale for this selection is that pupils are often encouraged to use science knowledge in Design and Technology lessons and there has been a considerable amount of work on pupils' understandings in this area. Some aspects of Design and Technology – such as electronics, pneumatics and the use of resistant materials, and the physical sciences – have been particularly attractive to boys rather than girls and, as Harding and Spendlove indicate (see Chapters 16 and 17), this creates imbalance in pupils' experiences. Finally, the particular problems for assessment in Design and Technology highlighted by the APU work described above, and discussed by Kimbell in Chapter 15, are embedded within wider issues concerning assessment in schools.

Children's learning in science

In the past, school science contained a lot of information which teachers had to 'transmit' to pupils. Science curriculum projects in the 1960s (such as Nuffield Physics) emphasized the importance of practical work, and a maxim of the time was:

> I hear and I forget,
> I see and I remember,
> I do and I understand.

So the purpose of the practical work was largely to reinforce the understanding in a 'seeing is believing' sort of way.

Since the early 1980s, this view of the learner as an empty vessel into which we can pour knowledge, and the view of good teachers as 'careful pourers', has been questioned (see Driver 1983). It was discovered that practical work sometimes reinforced incorrect concepts because the learner already had some prior ideas about the concept which had been built up from a very young age; pupils are not 'empty vessels'. For example, many children (and some adults!) think heavy objects fall faster than light objects – after all, a cannon ball falls faster than a feather! A pupil already has certain ideas about gravity and the teacher's idea that all objects fall together (provided we ignore air resistance) just seems to contradict common sense.

We cannot afford to ignore the ideas which pupils already hold. The research suggests that pupils construct their own meaning of the world around them by incorporating new ideas into their current understandings. In Science, therefore, pupils are often required to modify or abandon their current understanding and, perhaps not surprisingly, they do so reluctantly. Practical work is important but should be used to challenge the pupils' view of the world rather than simply attempt to illustrate the theory put forward by the teacher. Scott has summarized the following points about a constructivist view of learning for pupils:

1   Learning outcomes depend not only on the learning environment but also on the prior knowledge, attitudes and goals of the learner. What is already in the learner's mind matters.

2   Learning involves the construction of knowledge through experience with the physical environment and through social interaction. Individuals construct their own meaning.

3   Constructing links with prior knowledge is an active process involving the generation, checking and restructuring of ideas or hypotheses. The construction of meaning is a continuous and active process.

4   Learning science is not simply a matter of adding to and extending existing concepts, but may involve their radical re-organisation. Learning may involve conceptual change.

5   Meanings, once constructed, can be accepted or rejected. The construction of meaning does not always lead to belief.

6   Learning is not passive. Individuals are purposive beings who set their own goals and control their own learning. Learners have the final responsibility for their learning.

7   Students frequently bring similar ideas about natural phenomena to the classroom. This is hardly surprising when one considers the extent of their shared experiences – school life, hobbies, clubs, television, magazines, music, etc. Some constructed meanings are shared.

(Scott 1987: 7–8)

Science concepts, such as energy, are often used in Design and Technology and it is important to realize that the pupils will already have an idea of this concept which they have built up from their everyday lives, as well as attending lessons in school. The research findings suggest that we should find out what the children already understand about a concept and adapt our teaching accordingly. Such a teaching sequence is shown in Figure 22.1.

As discussed above, it is important for design and technology teachers to be clear about why pupils need to learn a scientific concept for use in Design and Technology work. In order to use a particular idea for practical action, it is sometimes the case that a full scientific explanation is unnecessary and the teacher may decide not to teach it, or that the scientific explanation is too abstract to be useful.

[Reconstruction of knowledge] involves creating or inventing new 'concepts' which are more appropriate than the scientific ones to the practical task being worked upon … Science frequently advances by the simplification of complex real-life situations; its beams in elementary physics are perfectly rigid; its levers rarely bend; balls rolling down inclined planes are truly spherical and unhampered by air resistance and friction. Decontextualisation, the separation of general knowledge from particular experience, is one of its most successful strategies. Solving technological problems necessitates building back into the situation all the complications of 'real life', reversing the process of reductionism by recontextualising knowledge. What results may be applicable in a particular context or set of circumstances only.

(Layton 1993: 59)

The message for teachers from this research is to think carefully about the purpose of teaching a particular scientific concept for use in Design and Technology. Will a robust scientific explanation help the work in hand? If an explanation is needed to

PHASE	PURPOSE	METHODS
I Orientation	Arouse interest and set the scene	Practical activities, real problems to solve, teacher demonstrations, film clips, videos, newspaper cuttings
II Elicitation of ideas	To enable pupils and teachers to become aware of prior ideas	Practical activities or small group discussion followed by reporting back
III Restructuring of ideas (a) clarification and exchange (b) exposure to conflict situations (c) construction of new ideas (d) evolution	To create an awareness of an alternative viewpoint – the scientific one – to (a) modify (b) extend or (c) replace with a more scientific view Recognise alternative ideas and critically examine own Test validity of existing ideas Modify, extend or replace existing ideas Test validity of newly constructed ideas	Small group discussions and reporting back Teacher demonstration, performing personal experiments, worksheets Discussion, reading, teacher input Practical work, project work, experimentation, teacher demonstration
IV Application of ideas	Reinforcement of constructed ideas in familiar and novel situations	Personal writing, practical activity, problem-solving, project work
V Review change in ideas	Awareness of change of ideas and familiarisation with learning process to allow the pupils to reflect upon the extent to which their ideas have changed	Personal writing, group discussion, personal diaries, reviewing work, posters etc.

Figure 22.1 Constructivist teaching sequence

Source: Adapted from Needham, R. (1987) *Teaching Strategies for Developing Understanding in Science*, Centre for Studies in Science and Mathematics Education, University of Leeds, p. 7.

improve the design-and-make assignment, teachers should be aware that pupils may have already constructed their own understanding of the relevant concept from science lessons and elsewhere, and should try to discover the pupils' preliminary ideas in order to challenge them and help them adopt the accepted scientific view. Close liaison with the Science department will clearly help teachers to predict the likely 'misconceptions' of pupils (see Engineering Council 2000).

Gender issues in the curriculum

> Women have never lived without technology. Yet we have barely a toehold in the discourse and direction of it.
>
> (Hynes 1989: 9)

Although written some years ago, and there have been some advances since, Hynes's comment identifies the concern that has been expressed about the lack of women in engineering and the physical sciences for many years. Throughout the 1980s a number of initiatives were funded to investigate the reasons why girls were under-represented in science and technology:

GIST   Girls in Science and Technology

WISE   Women in Science and Engineering

GATE   Girls and Technology Education

SOS   Skills and Opportunities in Science for Girls

GASAT   Girls and Science and Technology

Before the introduction of Design and Technology as a subject for all pupils, the upper years of courses were predominantly single-sex. Entrants for GCSE wood and metal craft subjects were almost exclusively male and for home economics subjects almost exclusively female. Even now the optional elements within the subject reflect the traditional gender-specific subjects (see Harding, Chapter 16). As the century turned, the gender issues had shifted to concern about boys' general underachievement in relation to that of girls (see Spendlove, Chapter 17).

Research has focused on a number of issues which have been considered to be the cause of the gender imbalance and result in women being under-represented in the designing and making area. Although women are out-numbered by men in the work of product design, they are the principal consumers of technological products. Researchers have looked at:

- the attractiveness of Design and Technology as a subject for women and strategies for improving their participation
- gender bias in the classroom or workshop
- the potential impact of women's views on the nature of technology.

The final point is extremely important.

More significantly, many technological objects are inappropriate for the needs and preferences of most female consumers and users. Male designers and ergonomists take account of women through anthropometric studies and market research, but do not necessarily translate this knowledge into products commensurate with women's requirements and needs (Bruce 1986: 172).

However, increasing the number of female designers necessitates encouraging the involvement and retention of more girls across all aspects of the subject at school. The first two points above are therefore of crucial importance to teachers.

Research into gender issues has a relevance across the curriculum and particularly to the way we set tasks in Design and Technology. The APU for Design and Technology found that girls appear to be better at identifying tasks, investigating and appraising ideas, whilst boys seem to be better at generating and developing ideas (APU 1991: 205).

The study also noticed that the girls generally did better in the tasks focused on 'people', but the boys generally did better in the tasks involving 'industry'.

Work around the world looking at science shows that in many countries girls do worse than boys in physics. In open-ended tasks the difference is less marked, with girls doing better in observational tasks. Some work done by the APU for Science is shown in Figure 22.2. The reasons for these differences may be complicated and deeply rooted in the roles we expect women to adopt in our society. Some clues are indicated in the results from Thailand which buck the international trend. Here girls do as well as boys in physics and out-perform them in chemistry. The researchers suggest that this may be because in Thailand science is compulsory and is taught practically with many of the tasks presented in a female context. They also point out that women participate fully in all areas of employment.

The work done in Britain illustrates gender differences in a number of areas. Girls have less experience with certain tools and measuring instruments than boys. Their hobbies are less likely to include using construction sets and they tend not to tinker with items around the home. Randall (1987) also noticed that the school experience of practical work is different for girls and boys. Contrary to what is thought about boys monopolizing classroom time, in the workshop girls had more frequent, and longer, teacher contacts than boys. Randall found, however, that the requests were for help and encouragement, and the teachers rather accepted this position, reinforcing the girls' sense of inadequacy.

The results of work conducted by the Secondary Science Curriculum Review gave a number of suggestions for making science more 'girl friendly' and many of the recommendations are applicable to Design and Technology:

1   Organise practical work in mixed groups from the first day. If pupils have already chosen to work in single-sex groups, or pupils object, and the result is less work achieved, ensure that each bench has some boys' groups and some girls' groups.

2   Avoid placing girls and boys in competitive roles.

3   Address questions to specific pupils by name rather than choosing the first hand up.

4   Choose girls by name to come out to help with demonstrations.
5   Praise girls for good ideas as well as neat work; praise boys for neat work as well as good ideas.
6   Never ask a boy who understands something to help a girl who does not.
7   Encourage girls to be self-reliant and think things out for themselves.
     [...]
13   Ensure fair distribution of good apparatus.

(Hackett 1989: 21–2)

At the time of writing, there is growing concern about the performance of boys in Design and Technology (see Spendlove, Chapter 17) but as yet there is little research to report on. Another area where research is lacking is the low take-up of food technology and textiles technology by boys. As shown earlier, there have been many projects promoting resistant materials and systems and controls to girls, but little, as yet, in the opposite direction.

APU test	Results from APU
Use of graphs, tables and charts	$B_{15} > G_{15}$
Use of apparatus and measuring instruments	$B_{15} > G_{15}$
Observation	$G > B$
Interpretation	$B_{13,15} > G_{13,15}$
Application of:	
biology concepts	$B = G$
physics concepts	$B > G$
chemistry concepts	$B_{15} > G_{15}$
planning investigations	$B = G$
performing investigations	$B = G$

B boys' performance

G girls' performance

B_x performance of boys aged x

G_x performance of girls aged x

$>$ better than

Figure 22.2 Some international survey results

Source: Adapted from Murphy 1991: 114.

Assessment issues

Assessment, generally, is an aspect surrounded by many questions and much discussion and is a topic of continuing debate.

The work of the APU discussed above focused on the specific problems associated with describing and assessing technological capability. The researchers had to come to an agreement about what it was they were attempting to assess before they could devise any tests. However, there are wider issues surrounding assessment which all curriculum areas need to be aware of, and the following questions provide a focus for them. These questions are posed in Section 7 of the Open University course E819: Curriculum, Learning and Assessment, and adapted here:

How to set the scene and how to ask the right question?

The point has been made that pupils bring with them to the classroom prior experiences which they draw on when constructing their understanding of a problem posed to them. The extent to which they are able to access their prior knowledge will depend on the way a particular task is set. The science APU researchers found that the success of an individual at a task was greatly influenced by the inclusion of an explanatory diagram or cartoon (DES 1989).

Similarly, the provision of a set of equipment will constrain the response in a particular way. For example, a problem-solving activity with a range of possible solutions, such as devising a way of bridging a certain gap, can be turned into a restricted one-solution 'puzzle' by withholding tools and materials. Sometimes the task becomes harder rather than easier, as the answer can only be done one way and the pupil is left to guess what the teacher expects as a solution. This can affect pupils' learning in Design and Technology as well as the outcomes of their assessment.

The language of a question will often convey different meanings to the range of pupils being tested: 'Large scale monitoring of school children's performance shows that many (around 40%) fail not because they provide the wrong answers but because they answer different questions' (Open University 1990: 102). There is no easy way around the problem of different interpretations by the pupils of the task set. Teachers can only take account of the different ways in which pupils might tackle it and make allowances for valid alternatives.

What mode of response to choose?

Many curriculum areas (such as Design and Technology) assess both content and process. It is often much more difficult for pupils to describe a procedure in writing, such as how to use a particular tool than it is to actually carry out the procedure. In many examiners' reports, prior to GCSE, comment was often made about the poor understanding of practical techniques when described in a written exam. This evidence was used to suggest that pupils did not do enough practical work in lessons. While this may indeed be true, it may also have been the result of asking for a written response to a practical task.

What mode of expression to use?

Pupils are asked to respond to questions in different ways in different subject areas, and the way the response is framed will affect the mark awarded. A Science write-up, for example, might be expected to focus on specific details and be presented in a particular literary style whilst a History or Geography account may be more open. If one style of pupil response is valued more by the teacher than another, and so credited more highly, it could be erroneously interpreted as a difference in achievement. Design and Technology project portfolios usually contain a variety of graphic and written material and pupils are usually able to express themselves in a variety of ways. However, these need to be considered for their appropriateness and quality, and credited accordingly.

These general points relate to work carried out by researchers into aspects of assessment practice throughout the 1980s, mainly by the APU teams in different curriculum areas. Assessment is related to the intended learning and the ways in which pupils learn. There are many questions which need to be asked in relation to assessment in the development of Design and Technology education. So little is known about how pupils think and learn to do practical design-and-make assignments, and much valuable work can be done by classroom teachers in this area.

Researching in your own workplace

> Teachers are too often the servants of heads, advisers, researchers, text books, curriculum developers, examination boards, or the [government] among others. By adopting a research stance, teachers are liberating themselves from the control position they so often find themselves in.
>
> (Hopkins 1985: 3)

As suggested in the introduction to this chapter, teachers are well placed to become involved in investigations in their classrooms. Such an idea may, at first sight, appear daunting. However, since the 1980s many teachers have applied systematic techniques to the evaluation of their work so that it merits the title 're-search'. In Britain, the 'teacher as researcher' movement developed from the work done by Lawrence Stenhouse in developing the humanities curriculum project, which involved teachers in research in their own classrooms.

Curriculum projects are intended to improve the quality of teaching and learning in classrooms, but their impact often falls short of the developers' intentions as the teachers implementing such schemes are not fully aware of the improvement (or otherwise) which may be taking place. By becoming more aware of the effects of alteration in their practice, teachers become not only active in improving the learning experiences of their pupils but also critical of educational policies, materials or syllabuses which affect their work.

Research methods

This is not the place to engage in long discussion about different research strategies. However, in order to evaluate critically what is happening in the classroom, there are four key stages to follow:

1   Identify the focus of the investigation
2   Decide what evidence needs to be collected
3   Analyse and interpret the collected evidence
4   Report on what is discovered.

This does not imply a linear process with a perfectly formed final 'answer'. What is discovered is often ill-formed and speculative, becoming the starting point of another 'cycle of reflection' as a further issue is identified.

Naturally, you will want to focus on issues which are of particular concern to you, perhaps the way pupils use 'brainstorming' techniques, work together in groups or use sketches or models for initial ideas. Maybe a new examination syllabus has been adopted, or new textbooks, which need to be the target of an investigation. After observing the effects of the change, you are in a position to analyse what has been discovered and suggest a way forward. The reporting phase may, in fact, be simply a personal note to do something about what has been discovered in order to improve personal action in an individual lesson or during the next round of project work. Alternatively, it could be a report to a departmental meeting, or even an article for wider circulation in a professional journal. By engaging in a conscious evaluation of a specific part of their work, teachers can themselves become key players in their own professional development:

> ... the outstanding characteristic of the extended professional (teacher) is a capacity for autonomous professional self development through systematic self study, through the study of the work of other teachers and through the testing of ideas by classroom research procedures.
>
> (Stenhouse, cited in Hopkins 1985: iv)

What is being suggested here is a systematic appraisal and extension to the evaluation which naturally occurs when a new project, scheme of work or programme is introduced into a department. By taking a 'research' position you can ensure that the data collected is more reliable and any decisions made will be more valid.

Conclusion

Although Design and Technology is still a relatively new area of the curriculum and there is not the same quantity of research evidence on which to draw as there is in, say, Mathematics and Science, there are a number of key areas where important developments are taking place. Many of these important areas have been highlighted in this chapter and other chapters in the book, but the choice is naturally limited by space and for that reason may appear somewhat idiosyncratic.

All researchers publish their findings in publications that are available in local academic libraries but classroom teachers are also in a position to add to the accumulating evidence about teaching and learning in technology education. By sharing that information in professional journals such as that of the Design and Technology Association, the *Journal of Design and Technology Education*, teachers can work together to improve the quality of learning for pupils.

References

Anning, A. (1992) 'Learning design and technology in primary schools', in R. McCormick, P. Murphy and M. Harrison, (eds) *Teaching and Learning Technology*, Wokingham: Addison-Wesley.

APU (Assessment of Performance Unit) (1991) *The Assessment of Performance in Design and Technology*, London: School Examinations and Assessment Council.

Black, P. and Harrison, G. (1985) *In Place of Confusion: Technology and Science in the School Curriculum*, London: Nuffield-Chelsea Curriculum Trust.

Bruce, M. (1986) 'A missing link: women and industrial design', in A. Cross and B. McCormick (eds) *Technology in Schools*, Milton Keynes: Open University Press.

CCW (1993) *Generating Developing and Communicating Ideas in Design and Technology*, Cardiff: Curriculum Council for Wales.

DES (1989) *Science In Schools Age 13: Review Report*, London: HMSO.

Driver, R. (1983) *The Pupil as Scientist?*, Milton Keynes: Open University Press.

Eggleston, J. (1996) *Teaching Design and Technology*, (2nd edn), Buckingham: Open University Press.

Ferguson, D. (1992) 'Technology: A challenge for education in New Zealand', in D. Blandow and M. Dyrenfurth (eds) *Technology, Literacy, Competence and Innovation in Human Resource Development*, Proceedings of the First International Conference on Technology Education, Weimar, Germany.

Garner, S. (1994) 'The importance of graphic modelling in design activity', in F. Banks (ed.) *Teaching Technology*, London: Routledge.

Glaser, R. (1984) 'Education and thinking: the role of knowledge', *American Psychologist* 39(2): 93–104.

Hackett, G. (1989) 'Equal opportunities project – starting at the top' in *Change in Focus: Towards Better Science 2*, Winter 88/89, London: SSCR/ SCDC.

Hammersley, M. (1994) 'MA Study Guide Section 2' in E824: *Educational Research Methods*, Milton Keynes: Open University Press.

Hopkins, D. (1985) *A Teacher's Guide to Classroom Research*, Milton Keynes: Open University Press.

Hynes, H. P. (1989) *Reconstructing Babylon: Women and Technology*, London: Earthscan Publications.

Layton, D. (1993) 'Science education and praxis: the relationship of school science to practical action (II)', *Studies in Science Education* 19: 63–75.

Liddament, T. (1993) 'Using models in design and technology education: some conceptual and pedagogic issues', in IDATER '93, Loughborough University of Technology.

McCormick, R. and Banks, F. (1994) *Study Guide E650: Design and Technology in the Secondary Curriculum*, Milton Keynes: The Open University.

Murphy, P. (1991) 'Gender differences in pupils' reaction to practical work' in Woolnough, B. (ed.) *Practical Science*, Milton Keynes: Open University Press.

Needham, R. (1987) *Teaching Strategies for Developing Understanding in Science*, Leeds: Children's Learning in Science Project.

Open University (1990) *E819: Curriculum, Learning and Assessment*, Milton Keynes: The Open University.

Open University (1993) *E823: Technology Education*, Milton Keynes: Open University Press.

Pena, M. (1992) 'Technology in the general curriculum: A Latin American perspective' in D. Blandow and M. Dyrenfurth (eds) *Technology, Literacy, Competence and Innovation in Human Resource Development*, Proceedings of the First International Conference on Technology Education, Weimar, Germany.

QCA (Qualifications and Assessment Authority) (1999) *National Curriculum Design and Technology*, London: HMSO.

Randall, G. J. (1987) 'Gender differences in pupil-teacher interactions in workshops and laboratories' in G. Weiner and M. Arnot (eds) *Gender under Scrutiny*, Milton Keynes: Open University Press.

Scott, P. (1987) *A Constructivist View of Learning and Teaching Science*, Leeds: University of Leeds.

Smithers, A. and Robinson, P. (1992) *Teaching in the National Curriculum: Getting it Right*, London: The Engineering Council.

van der Velde, J. (1992) 'Technology in basic education' in D. Blandow and M. Dyrenfurth (eds) *Technology, Literacy, Competence and Innovation in Human Resource Development*, Proceedings of the First International Conference on Technology Education, Weimar, Germany.

Index

Shuard, H. 111
Simon, H.A. 130
Simonton, D.K. 162
Sinclair, Clive 21
situated cognition 110–11, 303–4
sloyd movement 31
Smail, B. 64
Smith, R. 136
Smith, S. 111, 114
Smithers, A. 40, 164, 300
Snow, C.P. 16
Snyder, J.F. 290
social context 242–3
social issues: citizenship 34, 267–73;
    environmental concerns 7, 12, 22–3,
    257–8; international trends 293–4;
    learning in and for community 257–65,
    see also gender
Society of Art Masters (SAM) 32
Solomon, J. 34, 294
Spear, M. 245
Sperry, R.W. 132
split-brain studies 132–3
Stables, K. 84, 96, 163
Steers, J. 32, 33, 144
Stenhouse, Lawrence 315
Sternberg, R. 55, 99, 161, 162
Stevens, Richard 126
students *see* pupils/students
summative assessment 84
Sussex University: Science Policy Research
    Unit (SPRU) 21
Sutherland, S. 230
Sutton, R. 162
Swansea research 65–73; attitudes to
    design and technology 66–7;
    perceptions of design and technology
    67–9; what makes a good technology
    pupil 70–3
Sweden 31, 81, 293
Swift, J. 144
systems and control 60–1

Tamir, A. 292
Tate, Nicholas 275–6, 278
Taton, 178
Taylor, D.W. 162
Taylor, R. 144–5, 147–8
teachers and teaching: education of 263–5,
    294–5; explicit teaching of design
    procedures 304–5; gender and teaching
    styles 244, 245; modelling and 157–8;
    perceptions of design and technology
    81–2; problem-solving and 51, 118–20;

research on 300–2; researching in own
    workplace 314–16; standards 61–2;
    teaching of thinking skills 54;
    technology 31–44
teamwork 113–14
Technical and Vocational Education
    Initiative (TVEI) 276, 284
technology: attitudes to 64–5, 66–7, 73–4,
    80–2, 245; capability and 28; change
    and 21, 22, 25–6; checks and balances
    11–13; citizenship and 34, 269–73;
    clients and 20–1; as context 262–3;
    control of 16–17; craft tradition 31–2,
    289–90; ensuring balance in 9–11;
    excesses of 4–6; expression and
    development of ideas 26–8; future 17;
    industry and 290–1; learning concepts
    and processes 79–89; in national
    curriculum 34–44, 49, 181, 182, 185–6,
    246–7, 261; nature of 19–20, 179–80;
    positive and negative effects 6, 7–8,
    22–3; reshaping society 3–4; science
    and 23–5, 33, 34, 177, 180–90, 291;
    'siren call' 6–7; stages of 13–15; today's
    8–9; understandings of technological
    knowledge 82, *see also* education in
    design and technology
telecommunication 5
television 6
Thailand 311
thinking 113, 162; lateral thinking and
    creativity 57–8; teaching of thinking
    skills 54; what designers do 125–6, *see
    also* problem-solving
Thistlewood, D. 32, 144, 165
Thomas, J.C. 130
Thomas, R. 117
Tiberghien, A. 97
Tipler, F.J. 17
Todd, R.D. 292
Toffler, A. 16
Tomlinson, J. 257
Torrence, E.P. 55, 56, 161, 165
tradecraft tradition 31–2, 289–90
Tyrehan, G. 296

UNESCO 258
Union of Concerned Scientists 12
United States of America 289–90, 291,
    293
user issues: progression and 206–7, 218–19

values 58–9
van der Velde, J. 299